DUALISM

The Original Sin of Cognitivism

Books by William R. Uttal

Real Time Computers: Techniques and Applications in the Psychological Sciences

Generative Computer Assisted Instruction (with Miriam Rogers, Ramelle Hieronymus, and Timothy Pasich)

Sensory Coding: Selected Readings (Editor)

The Psychobiology of Sensory Coding

Cellular Neurophysiology and Integration: An Interpretive Introduction

An Autocorrelation Theory of Form Detection

The Psychobiology of Mind

A Taxonomy of Visual Processes

Visual Form Detection in 3-Dimensional Space

Foundations of Psychobiology (with Daniel N. Robinson)

The Detection of Nonplanar Surfaces in Visual Space

The Perception of Dotted Forms

On Seeing Forms

The Swimmer: An Integrated Computational Model of a Perceptual-Motor System (with Gary Bradshaw, Sriram Dayanand, Robb Lovell, Thomas Shepherd, Ramakrishna Kakarala, Kurt Skifsted, and Greg Tupper)

Toward a New Behaviorism: The Case Against Perceptual Reductionism

Computational Modeling of Vision: The Role of Combination (with Ramakrishna Kakarala, Sriram Dayanand, Thomas Shepherd, Jaggi Nalki, Charles Lunskis Jr., and Ning Liu)

The War Between Mentalism and Behaviorism: On the Assessibility of Mental Processes

The New Phrenology: On the Localization of Cognitive Processes in the Brain

A Behaviorist Looks at Form Recognition

Psychomyths: Sources of Artifacts and Misrepresentations in Scientific Psychology

Dualism: The Original Sin of Cognitivism

DUALISM

The Original Sin of Cognitivism

William R. Uttal

Arizona State University

 LEA LAWRENCE ERLBAUM ASSOCIATES, PUBLISHERS

2004 Mahwah, New Jersey   London

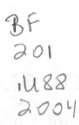

Lawrence Erlbaum Associates, Inc., Publishers
10 Industrial Avenue
Mahwah, New Jersey 07430

Cover design by Kathryn Houghtaling Lacey

Library of Congress Cataloging-in-Publication Data

Dualism : the original sin of cognitivism / William R. Uttal.
    p. cm.
    Includes bibliographical references (p.) and indexes.
    ISBN 0-8058-5129-1 (alk. paper)
1. Cognitive psychology—Philosophy. 2. Dualism—History. I. Title.
BF201.U88 2004
153—dc22   2004053197
                                                        CIP

Books published by Lawrence Erlbaum Associates are printed on acid-free paper,
and their bindings are chosen for strength and durability.

Printed in the United States of America
10 9 8 7 6 5 4 3 2 1

For Mit-chan

Contents

Preface

For the last 5 years, I have been navigating a new and relatively unfamiliar river of psychological thought. After nearly a lifetime of empirical reductionist neurophysiological and perceptual psychology research, I became concerned that our data and theories were presenting an incomplete picture of the nature of current scientific psychology. There appeared to be a number of unspoken assumptions lying beneath the huge amount of laboratory activity that are largely ignored. For reasons that are still unclear to me, I reverted to a role that has long been anathema in modern psychology—that of a constructive critic and gadfly of the deep-seated roots of our science. My goal in recent years has been to study the conceptual assumptions that lie beneath the methods, the data, and most of all, the theories of modern scientific psychology. This redirection of my energies has resulted in a series of books that in turn have dealt with some of the most fundamental of issues in psychology. These issues are:

- Reductionism—*Toward a New Behaviorism: The Case Against Perceptual Reductionism* (1998)
- Accessibility—*The War Between Mentalism and Behaviorism: On the Accessibility of Mental Processes* (2000)
- Localization—*The New Phrenology: The Limits of Localizing Cognitive Processes in the Brain* (2001)
- Perception—*A Behaviorist Looks at Form Recognition* (2002)
- Sources of Erroneous Thinking—*Psychomythics* (2003)
- Dualism—*Dualism: The Original Sin of Cognitivism* (the present work) (2004)

As the titles of these books indicate, I have undergone a major conversion in my philosophical orientation. From my reductionist background and training as a physiological psychologist, I now find myself re-embodied as a rather radical proponent of a nonreductive behaviorism. My version of a "new" or "revitalized" behaviorism is not identifiable with any particular one of the older behaviorisms, but it does share with most of them the conviction that psychology's search for the internal working of mind or, in its newest incarnation—"consciousness"—is an unfulfillable quest.

In this book, I examine one of the main assumptions, a pervasive dualism, that guides not only modern cognitive mentalism, but also most of the theologies, philosophies, and psychologies that have preceded it. My argument is that human intellectual history has left traces in our thoughts and culture that are still playing a significant role in influencing the study of the mind sciences—including cognitive psychology. Although the influence may be cryptic or indirect, it is still there and helps to explain the incorrect insistence on the accessibility of mental processes that is the hallmark of past and present mentalisms.

To make this argument, however, it is necessary to understand more of the intellectual history of this particular worldview—dualism. Thus, I have found it necessary to go far back into human prehistory to explore what modern science knows or infers about human thought processes and how they have evolved with regard to the relation between the natural and supernatural. This book, to a much greater extent than I had originally planned, has evolved into a review of dualism throughout the ages. In it, I review several periods of human existence, each of which is heavily involved with the problem of the persistence of mind and the nature of its relationship to the body. This is hardly a topic that can be ignored by psychologists if for no other reason than we are at the end of an intellectual evolutionary process that has enormous implications for our current ideas about our science. It seems highly unlikely that this evolution is at an end. Therefore, there also remains the usual historical hope, that there will be some insight about the present obtainable from looking at the past.

Dualism—the idea that there are two levels of reality—certainly arose very early in the human past. However, its influence and persistence have been one of the main themes of the history of human thought. Indeed, as I show in this book, it was a very natural outcome of life experiences and the presumed nature of human cognition. The questions asked and more or less explicitly answered affirmatively in this book are: Does dualism influence our scientific theories of psychology? If so, should dualism be put aside in the search for a more objective analysis (i.e., behaviorism) of human mentation?

No one who studies these problems and answers them as I have here is likely to avoid substantial negative reactions from colleagues with a different view of scientific psychology's foundation assumptions. I am sure that, as other materialist behaviorists have discovered, this is a sensitive area. Some critics will simply reject the validity of the questions being asked; some will challenge details but agree that the topics are worth discussing; and some will challenge these ideas on a more personal basis. However, after writing on topics like the present one for some years, I am convinced that because there is a substantial underground of opinion that psychology needs a review of its conceptual foundations even more than further enhancement of its empirical findings. If these books provide some stimulus for increased attention to these fundamentals, then, just perhaps, psychology can avoid going down some of the same old erroneous paths that have blemished its past.

Of one thing, I feel absolutely confident: The science of psychology deals with the foremost problems of human existence. It is important just because it overlaps in terms of its subject matter with those of theology and philosophy. However, a close corollary of this commitment to a common subject matter is the fact that an objective, scientific approach free of extraneous influences is critical to progress in this field.

ACKNOWLEDGMENTS

Writing a book like this is inherently a solitary endeavor. Nevertheless, I have been helped by the wisdom of a number of colleagues during the period in which I wrote it. Continuing his intellectual stimulation and my education is my colleague Peter Killeen of Arizona State University. Ed Morris of the University of Kansas read and commented on the draft of my section on J. R. Kantor. Bryan Midgley of McPherson College helped me find a particularly obscure biography of J. R. Kantor and also made useful comments on a chapter. Jay Moore of the University of Wisconsin-Milwaukee also provided me with some key references, as did Mark Reilly of Arizona State University. Warren Egmond made penetrating comments on one chapter. My ASU colleague Jay Klein also continues to introduce me to new and relevant ideas from his vast knowledge of psychological history. Harry Bahrick reviewed the entire manuscript and his suggestions and comments were extremely helpful. Our local, miniature version of the metaphysical society also played an important role in keeping me connected to the thoughts of others. I owe a debt to David Hestenes, Peter Killeen, Warren Egmond, Richard Schuster, and Rob McDuff that is larger than any of them could appreciate. The indirect influence of many others, whom I hope I have always adequately cited, can be discerned throughout this book.

I was also privileged, once again, to enjoy a visiting appointment at the University of Hawaii during the summer of 2003. My thanks to Karl Minke for making this visit possible.

For what is for me an unbelievable number of years, I have received the support of a wonderful woman—my wife Michiye. May, as she is known to most; Mit-chan, as she is known to fewer; Mom as she is known to three, has made it possible for me to pursue my work while at the same time becoming a wonderfully talented artist herself. Both she and her paintings grace our home now in a way that I could never have anticipated when we were married a half century ago. Whatever I have accomplished is due to her wisdom, partnership, and love. This book is dedicated to her alone on the occasion of our 50th wedding anniversary—December 20, 2004.

—*William R. Uttal*

1

Introduction

1.1 THE THESIS

Scientific psychology has long sought to achieve a level of objectivity comparable to the other sciences. Indeed, in an effort to separate its methodology and contributions from its philosophical forebears, it has sometimes been accused of an extreme form of "method envy" resulting in what Koch (1992), presumably tongue in cheek, described as *physicophilia*, to wit:

> Experimental psychologists have traditionally suffered from a syndrome known as hypermanic physicophilia (with quantificophrenic delusions and methodico-echolalic complications ... (p. 264)

As modern instrumentation and mathematical–statistical tools evolved in their sophistication, it has seemed to many observers that psychology cum physics has been approached, if not achieved. However, embedded deep within the implicit structure and assumptions of modern scientific psychology lay conceptual entanglements with the theological and philosophical past that are not so easily unraveled. I believe these vestigial entanglements, although largely unappreciated, still play an important role in the conduct of a huge amount of psychological research, specifically in any mentalist approach. This book is about the profound and significant relationship between the primitive fear of death and the resulting dualisms on the one hand and modern mentalist theories on the other.

There are several reasons why psychology is still struggling after centuries to be acknowledged as a natural science of the same power as physics or chemistry. Some of the reasons are epistemological; it is still a matter of debate just how far we can go in explaining cognitive processes as opposed to just describing behavior (see Uttal, 1998). Even more fundamentally, it is still uncertain just how accessible mental activity may or may not be (see Uttal, 2000). There is ample, although not overwhelming, evidence that the enormous complexity, nonlinearity, and complex interaction of both the neural and cognitive domains pose what may be intractable problems of analysis and explanation for anyone with the temerity to study human mentation. Thus, there may be fundamental barriers of explanation for a science of the mind (if not of behavior) preventing broad acceptance of psychology as a valid scientific undertaking. Indeed, it does not take any substantial exposure to the councils of engineers, attorneys, politicians, and both biological and physical scientists to appreciate a deep reluctance on the part of many to include psychology within the rubric of the natural sciences or to accept its findings as compelling guides to policy decisions.

Another reason that scientific psychology confronts resistance to general acceptance within the scientific community is its persisting confusion with the work of its predecessors—namely, philosophy and theology. The problem arises from the simple fact that the subject matters of each of these fields of inquiry overlap to a substantial and perhaps irretrievable degree. Psychology, philosophy, and theology[1] all seek to deal with and make sense of mental activity. In particular, with a few exceptions (one notable exception, of course, is a more or less extreme behaviorism) all three types of scholarship are in part concerned with the study of intrapersonal sentient awareness—our consciousness of our own being—however broader their domains may be. The approaches taken by each field, however, are not identical nor are their methods, no matter how common the subject matter—the mind/soul/spirit/ego—may be for all.

The joint problem faced by all three fields of study, is that this common subject matter is of such enormous importance and general relevance to so many aspects of human existence that its study and consideration could hardly be constrained to any one alone. There is no rational, logical, or intellectually compelling way to dissuade philosophers, theologians, and psychologists from considering such questions as: How do we think? What are the future evolutionary prospects of our consciousness? Does some aspect of mind persist after bodily death? Is mind purely a brain process? The search for understanding of the fundamental nature of the human mind is of supreme importance to scholars and lay persons alike from many different callings and for many different reasons.

---

[1] I distinguish here and elsewhere in this book between philosophy and theology in spite of the fact that for millennia the former was solely concerned with the latter's problems. For several centuries, technical philosophy has, however, charted its own course and the two fields no longer are synonymous no matter how much their respective subject matters overlap.

Each approach, of course, has its limitations; philosophy typically struggles from a lack of appreciation of what the more objective and less speculative scientific schools have discovered. Likewise, the methods of scientific psychology are constrained and limited in their ability to answer all of the questions that inquisitive humans ponder. Theology, on its part, suffers from any semblance of objective analysis and must, in the final analysis, fall back on intuitions, beliefs, and faiths that cannot be substantiated by anything considered acceptable evidence or compelling logic by either science or philosophy. Thus, regardless of their own particular individual limits and constraints, it is easy for one approach or the other to make the case that the others are incapable of solving problems of such enormous magnitude. Philosophy suffers from a paucity of facts; psychology from inadequate methodology; theology from a pervasive and ultimately destructive strategy of creating unfounded and unsubstantial hypothetical entities; and all three are convinced of the pervasive illogic or incompleteness of the other two. The very answerability of some of the most fundamental (or most easily asked) questions is itself rarely questioned.

The historical range of approaches to the study and consideration of mental activities is, therefore, enormous and justifiably so. It is hard to imagine any aspect of human existence that would not be touched in one way or another by a deeper understanding of human mentation. The primeval urge of humans to understand and preserve their essential selves and their world cries out for the most speculative theological answers even in the presence of solid contradictory scientific evidence. It is hard for conscious and curious humans to ignore this cry. The ubiquitous presence of theological ideas among what most certainly is the vast majority of human beings living today attests to the compelling power of that urge. It is equally hard to imagine how any of the many different aspects of human mentation could avoid influencing psychological science or philosophy, or for that matter almost any other aspect of human life.

The converse is also true—the prevailing concept of the mind is always heavily influenced by developments in other human activities. As history has repeatedly demonstrated, the concept of the mind continuously evolves under the influence of developments in many other fields of endeavor including, the economic, social, technological, scientific, religious, political, military, and educational. Obviously even the most objective and esoteric scientific interpretations of the nature of mental activity persistently and deeply interact with many other aspects of our society. In doing so, they both reflect their central importance in any explanation of human existence just as the subject of mind subjects itself to influences and pressures to which few other topics in the natural sciences are subject.

This book explores the history and impact that one central and persisting idea—dualism—is having on scientific psychology in the 21st century. In particular, it is concerned with the specialized and restricted question of the influence of nonscientific attitudes and beliefs (particularly those forth-coming from current theological and philosophical thinking) on our theo-ries concerning the nature of the mind. The argument, in a nutshell, is that a primeval "fear of death" created an age-old search for antidotes to the unac-ceptable horror of the cessation of one's personal mental existence. This search led inexorably to deeply embedded supernatural ideas that often do not rise to the level of consciousness of modern psychological scientists yet still may have profound effects on both theory and experimentation.

More specifically, this book is concerned with the nearly universal theo-logical and frequently (though not universal) philosophical solution—dual-ism—to what has come to be called, in modern terminology, the mind–body problem. Dualism proposes a second kind of extraphysical or supernatural kind of reality beyond raw physicalism. Such a dualism, it is argued here, pervades a surprising amount of modern, quasi-scientific thinking about the nature of cognitive processes albeit very often in a cryptic and unacknowl-edged form. The core of the argument is that modern dualisms, emerging from age old awarenesses of the brevity of life, tend to force our thinking about mind in such a way that mental processes become confused with tan-gible and analyzable objects.

Supernatural dualisms, it is further suggested, create a universe in which the rules of a naturalistic physical science are supplanted by supernatural processes. Wherever such a dualism is embedded in the logic of a science, however cryptically, mythical entities and factual distortion of the science become not only possible but also likely. The issue is thus raised: What damage has been done to a scientific study of the mind by deeply embed-ded dualisms operating below the ken of modern psychologists?[2]

To answer this rhetorical question I trace the history of the paleoan-thropological, biological, historical, religious, and philosophical concepts of life and death and show how each has had profound effects on what are be-lieved to be even the most pristine and objective theories of the mind. The historical chain starts with fear of death and ends with a crypto-dualism that seems to permeate much of mentalist psychology. I argue that there is a chain of intellectual evolutionary development that passes through this prim-itive fear to animisms, then polytheisms, then monotheisms, then a kind of de-theologized modern philosophy, and finally to a superficially sanitized cognitive psychology.

At the outset of this discussion, the fact must be acknowledged that this topic may be anathema to many "hard nosed" psychologists. Despite a long history of conferences on the relation between psychology and religion,

---

[2]The word "psychologist" is used here as a shorthand for all scientists who are attempting in one way or another to understand mental activity. It includes cognitive neuroscientists as well as others who approach the problem from such diverse directions as biochemistry or computer simulation.

many of my colleagues argue that we should keep our science free of the intrusion of such "philosophical" contaminants in order to produce a truly
objective science of mentation. I argue, on the contrary, that deep within
our most fundamental assumptions can be discerned the substantial impact of primitive attitudes toward death and, specifically, the difficulty that
is embodied in dealing with the cessation of our own personal consciousness. The balm that is applied to this problem is the generation of a conceptual model of dual realities—physical and mental—that profoundly impacts
on the nature of even some of our proudest "objective" theories.

I.2 ORGANIZATION OF THIS BOOK

In this book, it is argued that there is a virtually irresistible chain of logic
(as well as illogic) from the most primitive awareness of death through the
history of sophisticated theological beliefs through current philosophy to
some serious misemphases in the modern science of psychology. In particular, I argue that the residual traces of dualist escape hatches from the terror of the termination of personal existence have erroneously led to the
cognitive mentalisms that dominate scientific psychology today. The result
is that all mentalisms including current "cognitive" psychologies as well
as their introspective predecessors commit the same error—assuming, a
priori, that intrapersonal mental activity can be accessed, analyzed, and reduced as if it were a tangible object composed of more or less fixed component modules. This model—mind as interpersonally accessible and analyzable *object*—exists in contradiction to mind as intrapersonally inaccessible
unified *process*. The price paid for such a fundamental misconception is
that the usually cryptic axiom of dualism inhibits the development of a
truly scientific psychology based on a purer kind of objective and public
observation of interpersonal behavior. Following this introductory chapter,
the problem is dealt with in a number of different ways.

Chapter 2 considers the distant, prehistoric past of the Paleolithic period
during which the first signs of a cognitive awareness of death appears. Archeology and paleontology now have begun to provide some, although
highly equivocal, evidence about primitive behavior that can be interpreted
as reflecting early awareness of the great discontinuity between living and
dead organisms. This chapter makes the case that the main root of historical theologies and, ultimately, of erroneous psychological theories, is to be
found in the emerging self-awareness of one's individual physical mortality.

Chapter 3 carries the review forward into the Neolithic period where the
evidence is much more compelling. The artifacts are more numerous, the
transparency of their meaning in terms of the supernatural more clear-cut,
and the interpretive leaps less drastic. The sheer abundance of human Neo-

lithic remains is so much greater than the relatively rare Paleolithic finds that a much clearer picture of early cognitive activity can be discerned.

Chapter 4 is a review of recorded (i.e., historic) theological views of death, mortality, and the potential of an afterlife. Writing, the technique of recording ideas in a tangible form, plays the key role in carrying us beyond raw inferences to more explicit records of what people were thinking. It is in this context that we can see how the root—the awareness and, perhaps, fear of death—gave rise to the ubiquitous religious beliefs of the duality and separability of the mind from the body. If there is any single idea that is common to all religions, it is the universal idea that some kind of persistence of the essence of our personal mental life follows death. This idea is not only explicit in virtually all religions but, I argue, also implicit in some modern psychological theories.

Chapter 5 examines modern religions to determine their views on life, death, and the afterlife. The concept of an afterlife, based on a dualist premise of an extraphysical form of reality, is the central and universal core of all modern religions, a diverse body of beliefs that is followed by the majority of the world's populations. This chapter also continues a consideration of the evolution of religion from the animisms that dominated Paleolithic times to the polytheisms of the Neolithic and early historic periods to the near universal monotheisms of modern religions.

In chapter 6, two approaches to the consideration of death that were and are closely interwoven—the religious and the philosophical are teased apart. In this chapter, the emphasis is on the modern nontheological philosophical, considerations of potential ideas about reality, consciousness, and the vestiges of dualism that still play a significant role in philosophical discourse. Of course, it is not always easy to separate religion and philosophy. Until quite recently in the course of recorded history, philosophy was dominated by theological questions. It was not until the last few hundred years of the intellectual enlightenment that alternative explanations based on nontheological premises even began to be considered. It was in this context that the very answerability of some of the questions raised earlier began to be considered as legitimate topics for debate.

Chapter 7 goes on to discuss the role of dualism in the terms of the psychology of the last century or two, the period during which a psychological protoscience began to emerge that declared itself separate from the strictures of both theology and philosophy. As noted, it is not always possible to slice these closely interwoven topics apart, but, certainly, Freud's view of the role of death in our lives represented a different kind of thinking than did that of the theologians or theologically based philosophers. In his writing, death was more often dealt with explicitly, unlike its cryptic role in the study of cognition that is the hallmark of today's "scientific" psychology.

Chapter 8 summarizes the thesis presented in this book. Here I summarize the argument that even the most modern widely accepted scientific psychologies and psychological theories are influenced by the deeply and pervasively embedded ideas about death and its putative antidote—dualism. In particular, the emphasis on mentalist cognitivisms, so prevalent in today's psychologies, is presented as a case study of this kind of compelling influence toward theoretical misconstrual. In this chapter, I also consider the difficulties that have hindered the development of a truly objective scientific psychology—behaviorism—as a result of these theological and quasi-theological pressures toward mentalisms. No book that dealt with topics such as these could end without expressing the fact that many of the issues raised are at least unresolved and perhaps irresolvable.

1.3 A GLOSSARY OF CRITICAL TERMS

In each of my previous books, I provided a list of definitions of the relevant terms and critical words. The purpose of these mini-lexicons was to reduce to a minimum the typical misunderstandings that arise in any discussion of mental constructs. A significant portion of psychological controversy, I am convinced, is a result of the differing connotations of the essential vocabulary. Nevertheless, precise denotations are extraordinarily difficult to construct in spite of a millennia-old effort to define the mind or any of its near synonyms. In general, definitions of mental terms connote more than they denote and those connotations differ widely among different participants in the great debates. Of late, therefore, it has become increasingly clear that there may be insurmountable difficulty in providing consensual, useful, and operational definitions of items from what is essentially the domain of a private set of experiences and phenomena.

Furthermore, it is apparent that, all too often, attempted definitions of mental terms turn out to be circular; "a" is defined in terms of "b" and, then, "b" in terms of "a." Nothing is added to the precision of our language and nothing to the rigor of the controversies by such circularity. Perusal of even the most comprehensive dictionaries typically displays this kind of circularity and imprecision. It may be of some interest, on the other hand, to consider the sources of this lexicographic difficulty by trying to anchor them to specific referents. However futile the task, at least a modicum of discussion of the intended meaning of key terms may help to ameliorate some of the confusions certain to appear as we proceed through this discussion. We start with the most recalcitrant word of all—"mind."

1.3.1 Mind

One of the most surprising facts encountered in the critical examination of any putatively mentalist psychology is how uncertain and vague is the definition of the central entity with which it is concerned—*mind*. In Uttal (1978), I devoted 10 pages to a search for a definition of this key concept. With some retrospect, it is becoming increasingly obvious to me that the effort was not, and perhaps could not be, fulfilled. I am now convinced there are several good reasons for this continuing failure to arrive at satisfactory definitions of what we mean by something of which we all have first-hand knowledge. These reasons include (a) the inaccessibility of mental processes; (b) the lack of concrete anchors in the physical world to which our measurements can refer unambiguously; (c) the ill-conceived effort to equate mind with un-measurable "inner experiences" or "consciousness"; (d) the dualist separa-tion of the mind (whatever it is) from the body; and (e) the confusion of ob-jects with processes. Although some of these reasons may seem to be more argumentative than the others (e.g., c, d, and e) in fact, all may be synonymous responses to the inescapable epistemological limits on what can be known about something that can only be indirectly inferred from observations of ex-ternal behavior. In earlier works (Uttal, 1998, 2000), I discussed some of the technical and theoretical barriers that made any such bridge building from be-havior to inner awarenesses questionable, if not downright futile.

What did emerge from the 1978 exercise was the conviction that, at best, our efforts could only result in a list of attributes rather than a precise de-notation of what is meant by the term *mind*. Even if this is as far as our sci-ence can go, it is not without its value. Therefore, I now summarize the fea-tures of the meaning of *mind* that are common to almost all of the definitions provide by a number of the authors discussed there.

1. Mind is an individual and not a community process. A meeting of the minds is a literary metaphor, not a scientific one.

2. Direct, unequivocal interpersonal communication of primary mental states, processes, or actions is not possible. All such communication is medi-ated by behavioral responses, be they verbal, endocrine, or postural. An in-direct inference about the nature of mind from interpersonally observable behavior is, at best, a treacherous and noisy path to knowledge.

3. Any insights we have of what is going on in a "mind" are, therefore, indi-rect and, for all purposes, unverifiable. The two main reasons for this opacity are: (a) The fact that many quite different mechanisms can produce the same overt behavior, and (b) As a result of (a), extraordinarily complex and non-linear systems like the brain–mind are particularly recalcitrant to analysis into meaningful sets of cognitive components.

4. Even though mind is fundamentally inaccessible, it is not a supernatu-ral phenomenon. It is a real process of the brain reflecting real physical (i.e., neural) actions, albeit highly complex ones.[3]

---

[3]In recent years I have also become convinced that, however correct this statement may be as an ontological axiom, it is unlikely, because of the inherent complexity of the salient neural nets, that we will ever be able to identify the details of neural interconnectiveness that account for even the simplest cognitive process. Thus is our ontology separated from our epistemology.

5. Mind is best considered to be a function or a process rather than as an organ, object, or thing.

6. The word *mind* is very closely related in purported definition to other terms from other domains of study including "consciousness," "awareness," "soul," and the "true ego."[4] Therefore, natural and supernatural explanations sometimes become erroneously intertwined. (Herein lies the core of the problem for scientific psychology that is the concern of this present book.)

7. Mind is alternatively considered to be either an aggregate of individual functional modules or a unitary process. This is the one of the most fundamental debates in modern psychology. It is possible, however, that this debate is irresolvable and results from the conceptual error of considering mind as an object rather than a process.

(Abstracted and extended from Uttal, 1978, pp. 207–208)

Even if this is a reasonably acceptable set of properties that can partially fill the need for a plausible definition of the elusive concept of mind, it should be emphasized that it represents a far different model of mind than either the dualist notion of an immortal soul or the current theory of a modular and accessible mind that is the central tenet of contemporary cognitive psychology.

Finally, it is important to appreciate the near synonymity of the various words used to denote mental processes over the ages. Whether the **S** word or the **M** word was used by theologians, philosophers, or psychologists, respectively, all made reference to what was essentially the same set of activities and events. Of course, how each school or approach interpreted and explained the same process differed substantially. Should readers of this book wish to pursue this matter further, an excellent source is a collection of reprinted discussions of the nature of the "mind–soul" (Robinson, 1998). There he tabulates a variety of definitions including:[5]

1. . . . our soul, . . . , is composed of the Tetrad; for this is intelligence, understanding, opinion, and sense . . . (Pythagoras, p. 17)

2. It must necessarily be allowed that the principle of intellectual operation, which we call the soul of man, is a principle both incorporeal and subsistent. [That is, to be able to exist on its own without material support.] (Thomas Aquinas, p. 33)

3. Characteristics of the mind: (a) . . . inasmuch as the body is by its very nature always divisible, while the mind is utterly indivisible. (b) . . . the

---

[4] It is highly likely that it is impossible to distinguish any of these terms in an operational manner. They all denote the same thing, concept, or process, however much they may differ in their respective interpreter's emphasis and connotations.

[5] Page numbers are from Robinson (1998) from which original sources may be obtained.

mind is not immediately affected by all parts of the body, but only by the brain, ... (Rene Descartes, p. 41)

4. ... the mind is a nobler work, and of a higher order than the body, even more of the wisdom and skill of the Divine Architect hath been employed in its structure. (Thomas Reid, p. 101)

5. I believe that 'consciousness' when once it has evaporated to this estate of pure diaphaneity, is on the point of disappearing altogether. It is the name of a nonentity, and has no right to a place among first principles. (William James, p. 115)

6. Nevertheless, the difference in mind between man and the higher animals, great as it is, certainly is one of degree and not of kind. (Charles Darwin, p. 243)

7. One of the defining features of mind is that its contents are uniquely owned in that every idea, feeling, or desire is someone's. (Robinson, p. 287)

(Abstracted from Robinson, 1998)

One can only conclude from a perusal of Robinson's collection of great thoughts about the nature of mind that the difficulty of defining this elusive term is not a new problem but is one that has been with us throughout a very long history. Articulate and thoughtful as all of the scholars he reviewed in his book (as well as others I have not quoted) each of them confronts the same difficulty in defining mind that bedevils modern scientific psychology.

1.3.2 Life

How primeval concerns with death led to the persistent mentalisms of antique theologies as well as modern cognitive psychologies is a major theme of this book. It comes as something of a surprise, given how easy it is know when the process has occurred, that the word *death* is almost as difficult to define as is the word *mind*. Here, too, there is a reason for lexicographic intractability: Death is usually defined in terms of the cessation of life[6] and life itself is also remarkably recalcitrant to precise and rigorous definition. Therefore, let's start at the beginning and seek some agreement on how we should use the term "*life*."

Perhaps the best known of those who posed the query—"What is life?"—was Schrödinger (1944). He was one of the first to explicitly state in modern terms the concept that life was a result of and bound by the same physical

---

[6]The *cessation* of life is to be distinguished from the *absence* of life. Inanimate materials that have never exhibited living process are usually not considered to be "dead." I speak more about this later in this chapter.

and chemical laws that controlled our material universe. Indeed, his ideas about the need for complex structures and statistical processes to protect against "haphazard, 'single-atomic' events" (p. 18) and for thought to be the result of "well ordered organization . . . [that] must obey strict physical laws" (p. 8) imply a highly materialist answer to the posed question.[7] Indeed, his discussion of "negative entropy" as a property of living material was prescient in the field. Schrödinger's contribution was to nail down the idea that life is but a physical process and to express the interdisciplinary view that many different kinds of science would have to contribute to understanding it.

Other authors who have asked the question "What is life?" have, to the contrary, often wandered off into poetry and nebulousness that, while making good reading, leaves little into which scientists can sink their empirical teeth. In a beautifully illuminated book with the same title as Schrödinger's—*What is Life?*—Margulis and Sagan (1995), although supportive of Schrödinger-like physical-chemical materialism throughout, attempt to answer the query with such aphorisms as:

> [Life] is a material process sifting and surfing over matter like a strange, slow wave. It is a controlled, artistic chaos, a set of chemical reactions so staggering complex that more than 80 million years ago it produced the mammalian brain that now, in human form, composes love letters and uses silicon computers . . . (p. 33)

And

> Life is planetary exuberance, a solar phenomenon. It is the astronomically local transmutation of Earth's air, water, and sun, into cells. (p. 49)

And

> Life is the strange new fruit of individuals evolved by symbiosis. Swimming conjugating, bargaining, and dominating, . . . Life is an extension of being into the next generation, the next species. (p. 117)

---

[7]Schrödinger's statement that "living matter . . . is likely to involve 'other laws of physics' hitherto unknown . . ." (p. 69) has been designated by Rorty (2001) in a review of Ceccarelli's book (2001) as an example of "studied ambiguity" that "left everybody, reductionists and anti-reductionists alike, free to read whatever stirring suggestions they pleased into Schrödinger's text" (p. 2399). I don't agree. Schrödinger was simply asserting the limits of scientific explanation that were known at that time, not providing an escape hatch of "studied ambiguity." His lectures were given in 1943, long before the seminal discoveries of Watson and Crick—discoveries that certainly constituted "just as integral a part of this science as the former [known laws of physics]" (Schrödinger, 1944, p. 69). Even though Schrödinger raises the dilemma posed by the possible effect of mental processes on the body he was, in the final analysis, clearly a materialist when he asserted that "My body functions as a pure mechanism according to the laws of nature" (p. 87).

Whether such elegant rhetoric helps us to precisely define life for the purposes of scientifically defining death is not problematical; obviously, it doesn't. However, what Margulis and Sagan (1995) indisputably do contribute is one of the best semipopular discussions of the history and science of life on Earth yet to be published. However good it is as an update of Schrödinger's long out-of-date physicalist definition, they did not provide the definitively inclusive and exclusive definition we seek of the elusive word *life* so avidly desired by so many for so long.

A good modern dictionary (*American Heritage*) defines life as:

> The property or quality that distinguishes living organisms from dead organisms and inanimate matter, manifested in functions such as metabolism, growth, reproduction, and response to stimuli or adaptation to the environment originating from within the organism.

There is an obvious problem with all such proposed scientific definitions of life: They are aimed at a moving target. As science progresses and as we learn more and more about the properties and mechanisms of living and nonliving entities, we discover that the dividing line between the animate and the inanimate is constantly shifting. Computer programs can be written that arguably display some lifelike properties and viruses exist at the border between life and nonlife in a way that may make any precise definition equivocal for the foreseeable future.

What is clear is that life as we know it is a complex chemical process[8] made possible by the same physical principles of molecular combination and atomic bonding underlying all chemical reactions. Even more specifically, it has been suggested that protein chemistry may be the distinguishing characteristic of life. Again, it is uncertain that this particular kind of chemistry is necessary for life of some kind even if it is sufficient; other quite plausible structural components might be equally capable of producing entities that we could hardly distinguish functionally from earthly life.

Thus, any attempt to define life in terms of the specific components of which it is constructed will always be subject to potential modification or rejection. Nevertheless, life does have certain attributes that distinguish it from what are generally agreed to be nonliving processes such as crystallization or elaborate computer programs.[9] The difference is that these attri-

---

[8]Although life seems to be bound up in the chemistry of carbon on Earth, it is by no means certain that there is anything special about this kind of "organic" chemistry. There is no chemical reason to assume that living entities that are based on other chemicals in the periodic series may not inhabit other worlds. Orderly complexity, rather than a specific carbon chemistry, seems to be all that is necessary.

[9]The idea that some computer programs comprise a kind of "artificial life" stretches credulity. Although their behavior may be analogous to that of simple organisms, there is little beyond the enthusiasm of a few computer specialists to support the idea that a program might evolve into something we would consider to be alive.

butes are functional ones rather than structural ones. Even so, it is clear that none of these is individually adequate to precisely define life; collectively, however, they do help to be more specific in our search for a well enough constrained definition of this elusive property. For example, a simple list of the functions that are definitive of life might include the ability to carry out such processes as responding to stimuli, consuming energy, growing, and reproducing as well as the ability to move about. Of course, a steam engine carries out some of these processes and more advanced "self-organizing" systems may even have the ability to reproduce parts of themselves. On the other hand, not all indisputably living beings move on their own: Some sponges, corals, and even some bivalves remain fixed in their location throughout all or most of their lives.

Many other authors and scientists have attempted to define life in other terms. Another set of criteria or attributes of a system that may help to define it as a living form has been provided by Pidwirny (2000). His list includes:

1. Organisms are complex and highly organized.
2. Organisms metabolize energy from the environment and change it from one form to another.
3. Organisms are homeostatic; they regulate their bodies to maintain stable parameters.
4. Organisms respond to stimuli.
5. Organisms make copies of themselves by either sexual or asexual methods.
6. Organisms grow and develop from simple initial states.
7. Organisms adapt and evolve by mutation and natural selection.

A more extensive, necessarily overlapping, tabulation of the set of processes that collectively are carried out by systems that we would consider to be living was proposed by Miller (1978).[10] It is reproduced here not only for its own worth but to illustrate just how difficult it is to produce precise and concise definitions of this illusive word—*life*. Miller's emphasis is on life as a system of coordinated processes or subsystems. For him, life is adequately defined as a system that exhibits a sufficient number of a set of subsystem functions or attributes. It is important to note that although his taxonomy is defined in terms of systems and pseudo-components, it is, in fact, a collection of actions or activities carried out by subsystems rather than a collection of objects. It is the process, rather than the specific mechanics or

---

[10]Jim Miller died in 2002. His stimulating directorship of the Mental Health Research Institute at the University of Michigan was appreciated in later years by those of us who worked with him there.

chemistry of the subsystem that characterizes the living entity. Miller's (1978) outline of the characteristic subsystems includes:

SUBSYSTEMS THAT PROCESS BOTH MATTER-ENERGY AND INFORMATION

1. Reproducer, the subsystem that is capable of giving rise to other systems similar to the one it is in.

2. Boundary, the subsystem at the perimeter of a system that holds together the components that make up the system, protects them from environmental stresses, and excludes or permits entry to various sorts of matter-energy and information.

SUBSYSTEMS THAT PROCESS MATTER-ENERGY

3. Ingestor, the subsystem that brings matter-energy across the system boundary from the environment.

4. Distributor, the subsystem that carries inputs from outside the system or outputs from its subsystems around the system to each component.

5. Converter, the subsystem that changes certain inputs to the system into forms more useful for the special processes of that particular system.

6. Producer, the subsystem which forms stable associations that endure for significant periods among matter-energy inputs to the system or outputs from its converter, the materials synthesized being for growth, damage repair, or replacement of components of the system, or for providing energy for moving or constituting the system's outputs of products or information markers to its suprasystem.

7. Matter-energy storage, the subsystem that retains in the system, for different periods of time, deposits of various sorts of matter-energy.

8. Extruder, the subsystem that transmits matter-energy out of the system in the forms of products or wastes.

9. Motor, the subsystem which moves the system or parts of it in relation to part or all of its environment or moves components of its environment in relation to each other.

10. Supporter, the subsystem which maintains the proper spatial relationships among components of the system, so that they can interact without weighting each other down or crowding each other.

SUBSYSTEMS THAT PROCESS INFORMATION

11. Input transducer, the sensory subsystem, which brings markers bearing information into the system, changing them to other matter-energy, forms suitable for transmission within it.

12. Internal transducer, the sensory subsystem that receives, from subsystems or components within the system, markers bearing information about significant alterations in those subsystems or components, changing them to other matter-energy forms of a sort, which can be transmitted within it.

13. Channel and net, the subsystem composed of a single route in physical space, or multiple interconnected routes, by which markers bearing information are transmitted to all parts of the system.

14. Decoder, the subsystem that alters the code of information input to it through the input transducer or internal transducer into a "private" code that can be used internally by the system.

15. Associator, the subsystem that carries out the first stage of the learning process, forming enduring associations among items of information in the system.

16. Memory, the subsystem that carries out the second stage of the learning process, storing various sorts of information in the system for different periods of time.

17. Decider, the executive subsystem that receives information inputs from all other subsystems and transmits to them information outputs that control the entire system.

18. Encoder, the subsystem that alters the code of information input to it from other information processing subsystems, from a "private" code used internally by the system into a "public" code that can be interpreted by other systems in its environment.

19. Output transducer, the subsystem which puts out markers bearing information from the system, changing markers within the system into other matter-energy forms which can be transmitted over channels in the system's environment.

(Reproduced in its entirety from Miller, 1978, p. 3)

Miller's list is probably the most formidably complete of the functional criteria of life yet presented. It has the advantage of specifying functions rather than specific structures capable of carrying out those functions. Our knowledge of analogy now makes it clear, however, that many different mechanisms, some of which would be difficult to characterize as being "alive," would be capable of carrying out at least the preponderance of these same functions.

Miller's extensive list, however, has an important advantage—it is free of any specific chemical or physical details of the possible mechanisms or chemistries that could carry out these functions. At the very least, therefore, it defines life independently of carbon-based chemistry of which we are constructed. There is nothing to preclude quite different chemistries or physical mechanisms than those instantiating organic processes on earth from producing the functions on this list and to meeting this set of criteria for life. Similarly, many modern machines also can be designed in such a way that they also carry out or, at least, simulate the same functional attributes. Indeed, with the exception of the reproductive process (and the self-organizing and self-replicating systems being discussed these days) many machines already exist that would be hard to distinguish from living entities on the basis of the attributes of Miller's list. At the very least, what should be appreciated is that tabulations such as this one may serve as heuristics for the *properties* of artificial devices that may eventually exhibit at least some of the functional attributes of life.

An important aspect of Miller's list (or any other that may be or has been proposed in its place[11]) is that it does not require that *all* of the processes listed be instantiated to define a living organism, only a preponderance is required to define an entity as being alive. It is possible to contemplate the existence of an unbounded entity or one with many internal boundaries that still might exhibit enough other properties of this list so that it could be designated as a putative living form.

A recent effort to define life has been presented in a short essay by Koshland (2002). First, he proposed a nutshell definition like the ones presented earlier in this section. He suggested

> . . . a living organism is an organized unit, which can carry out metabolic reactions, defend itself against injury, respond to stimuli, and has the capacity to be at least a partner in reproduction. (p. 2215)

However, he then expressed discontent with this brief definition and turned to a much longer multicriterion definition similar to those discussed by Pidwirny (2000) and Miller (1978). Koshland suggests that the seven pillars of activity that define life are:

1. A *Program* that acts as an "organized plan" to guide life processes. Life as we know it on earth uses DNA to instantiate this program.

2. The capacity to *Improvise* or change that program. That is, the ability to mutate or alter the program and then to evolve by a process of natural selection to meet new challenges.

3. *Compartmentalization* is also a required characteristic of living organisms because of the need to maintain its own chemical kinetics in isolation from interfering activity from the outside.

---

[11]Another effort to define life in terms of its properties can be found in Crick (1981). His familiar list of properties, however, is encumbered by an all-too-serious, however critical, consideration of "directed panspermia" (the intentional seeding of life from some distant origin)—a theory for which not a shred of evidence exists.

4. Next, Koshland suggests that a living entity must be an open system. That means that its use of *Energy* must be thermodynamically balanced to recycle products and to maintain an internal equilibrium. Here he is suggesting that there must be a system of biochemical cycles operating within the compartmented organism.

5. Closely related to the idea of *Energy* utilization is *Regeneration*. By this characteristic of a living entity, Koshland is referring to the need for both ingesting metabolic supplies from the outside world as well as the need to be able to repair tissues that are damaged by overuse. An extension of this regeneration criterion is the process of reproduction. Reproduction, from Koshland's point of view, permits the organism to essentially "start over" when it is no longer able to repair itself.

6. *Adaptability* is an essential criterion for living organisms, but not on the slow pace of genetic improvisation. Rather it is necessary for the living entity to be able to respond very quickly to stimuli to prevent damage to itself or to meet immediate environmental situations. This is the germ of behavior and all mental processes, a germ that has grown into the magnificent properties of the thinking organism of which humans are the most highly developed example.

7. Koshland presents *Seclusion* as his final characteristic of life. By this property, he is referring to the necessity for biochemical reactions to go on in relative isolation from each other. With all of the chemical activity in a living creature, it is imperative that one reaction does not interfere with another. Thus, they must be "secluded" from each other. He also alludes to the ability of portions of the DNA molecule to be selectively activated or deactivated as another example of the necessity for this kind of exclusion.

(Paraphrased from Koshland, 2002, pp. 2215–2216)

In the final analysis, lists of the kind just discussed provide a limited kind of definition by tabulating functional properties. However, such lists do not provide the tight, simple "nutshell" definition of life one would like. It is interesting to note that these three long lists are not exclusive or contradictory; in large part, processes that are used as criteria in one are either explicitly or implicitly present in all of them. Miller's "ingestor" is certainly a homologue of Koshland's idea of the need for regeneration.

To sum up this discussion, answering the question "What is Life?" is not as easy as it may have initially seemed. Rosen (1991) asserted that it could only be answered in a formal language as follows:

Life is a manifestation of a certain kind of (relational) model [instantiated in the form of a graph]. A particular material system is living if it realizes this model. (p. 254)

He went on to argue that the model cannot be a "machine" in the usual sense—"syntax" alone is not sufficient to describe life because it does not adequately involve the high levels of complexity exhibited by even the simplest organism. The key criterion of the model of an organism, according to Rosen is that it is "closed to efficient causation" (p. 244), by which I believe he means that the defining properties of a living organism are internal rather than external. In so doing he rejects the Cartesian notion of life as a machine and adopts the idea of life as a particular kind of complex organization.

If Rosen's cryptic model is not satisfying, neither is any other nutshell definition of life. Perhaps, all we can do is describe its properties and await some "Darwinian stroke of genius" that will help us achieve a deeper understanding of the question "What is life?" Whatever life is, its antithesis—death—is much easier to define, simply by asserting its negative relation to life.

1.3.3   Death

Given the various definitions and tabulations of the functional attributes of life, the absence of any need for a unique definition in terms of the special chemistry of earthly life, as well as the uncertainty of the medical criteria of death, what can now be said to define death? An initial suggestion is that it is simply the negation of the functional attributes that were used to define life. A non-reproducing, non-information processing, non-energy consuming antithesis of the living form is, ipso facto, "dead." There is, however, one important caveat—the dead entity must have previously met the criteria of life. This kind of definition, achieved only by negating another one, however, is not a satisfactory way to define death or anything else for that matter. Stating what something is not is not the same as stating what it is. Such definitions by exclusion are typically inadequate because they leave open what may be infinitely large domains into which the referent might fall and still not come close to meeting the needs of a consensus definition. Logicians have characterized this kind of definition as being "too broad" (i.e., it includes entities that are not part of the intended definition).

Thus, death, although usually defined in different words, typically involves the dual criteria of (1) the absence of a set of properties that had putatively defined life and (2) the requirement that, whatever it is, it is a state that follows a state of preexisting life. Although the word has become a metaphor for other issues (e.g., "the *death* of imperialism"), in the intended sense used here it virtually always refers to the successor state of an entity that once lived as opposed to the functionally indistinguishable state of an object that never lived. This is no panacea definition, of course, for as we see later, the criteria for determining that some of the living functions have actually ceased may be themselves ambiguous.

None of this is new, of course; there is a long-standing tradition that defines life in terms of death. For example, Bichat (1771–1802), an early physiologist, suggested, "life consists in the sum of the functions, by which death is resisted" (Bichat, 1827, p. 10). Although modern in choosing functions as the criteria of life and death, this antique definition typifies the confusion by making the meaning of the two words circularly intertwined.

In summary, bodily death is relatively easily observed, is ubiquitous among living forms, yet it is defined with only the greatest difficulty and then only in negative or exclusory terms. At best, it is defined as the inverse of the positive attributes of something else—life. Unfortunately, as discussed earlier, the search for a definition of life is encumbered with its own problems if anything approximating precision of meaning is sought. Like so many other words that are intended to define complex processes or events, such definitions often turn out to be circular and inadequate.

In most instances, this vagueness of the denotation of life and death is inconsequential. The boundary between the living and the dead is sufficiently sharp to serve most practical needs. However, there are some situations in which it does matter. The classic ambiguity of definitions of life and death erupt into popular concern when they suggest the possibility of a premature burial (as so eloquently described by Poe, 1850). Another is the much more recent combined practical–ethical issue concerning when it is proper to "harvest" donor organs. Greenberg's (2001) discussion of the problems faced by physicians in determining that a patient is sufficiently "dead" is necessary reading for anyone interested in the problem of medical death.

1.3.4 Dualism

Since this term is key to the central thesis of this book, it is necessary to define it as completely as possible. By a dualism, I refer to a worldview that incorporates the idea that there can be two kinds of reality, one natural, material, or physical, and the other immaterial, supernatural or, in a popular misuse of the word, metaphysical. Dualisms are the antitheses of monisms, the philosophies that assert that all aspects of our existence are explicable in the language of one kind of reality and that reality is of the physical world. To monists, the mental is but a property or product of the physical. Dualist thinking, on the other hand, provides the conceptual foundation for a host of superstitions and theological beliefs by excusing them from necessary compatibility with the laws of physics, chemistry, mathematics, and biology. Thus, dualisms can and do invoke entities that are observable only in "miraculous" situations during which no evidence can be obtained or event replicated. This is a clear denial of the most fundamental axioms of modern science!

Not all dualisms are theologies; philosophers, as well, have proposed various ideas that are essentially dualist yet do not involve theological hypothesis. The remainder of this book elaborates on this all too sparse definition by describing the many forms that dualisms have taken over the millennia. Suffice it to say for the moment, dualism is ubiquitous throughout the history of human thought.

1.3.5 Mentalism

Throughout this book, I refer to the approach to psychology known as mentalism. Mentalism and dualism are closely related causally as well as in their essential meanings. To the dualist, as just discussed, there are two kinds of reality. This ontological concept permeates much of scientific psychology, particular those versions that can be classified within the rubric of mentalism. The following concise, but inclusive, definition of mentalism was provided to us by Moore (1981):

> ... mentalism may be considered as a particular orientation to the explanation of behavior, involving the following implicit or explicit features: (a) the bifurcation of human experience into a behavioral dimension and a pre-behavioral dimension, (b) the use of psychological terms to refer to organocentric entities from the pre-behavioral dimension, and (c) the use of the organocentric entities as causally effective antecedents in explaining the behavior. (p. 62)

Perhaps, the key and most controversial aspect of mentalism is that it is a psychology in which subjective experiences are part of the applicable database. Mentalists argue that these private internal states are either inferable (by the experimenter) or reportable (introspectively by the individual observer). Behaviorists deny this argument. It is important to appreciate, however, that at least some versions of behaviorism are crypto-mentalisms. Thus, any effort to limit scientific psychology to purely behaviorist tenets has proven in the past to be extremely difficult to achieve. Behaviorism represents a major challenge to cognitive psychology for cultural, historical, and religious reasons that become apparent as we proceed through this book.

1.4 QUESTIONS ANSWERABLE AND UNANSWERABLE

Much of human existence has been dedicated to the search for answers to profound questions that have repeatedly, if not universally, arisen as people have pondered the significance of the events of their lives. As a curious species, we have sought to provide meaning and explanation for both the things that happen regularly each day as well as to those extraordinary and unlikely events that happen only occasionally. Indeed, it can be argued that one of the main activities of humans has been their never-ending search for understanding of the nature of their minds.

In this section, I propose there are three great categories of such questions; three categories defined, not in terms of their frequency of occurrence or universal importance, but rather in terms of the degree of certainty with which they are likely to be answered by the tools and methods of an objective science. The first of these—the unanswerable ones—includes deep matters of faith or philosophical speculation for which there is a total absence of any scientifically acceptable evidence that could lead to their resolution. A second category of questions includes those that exist in an intermediate state in which the very question of their intractability or answerability is itself an issue. The third category includes those that are not only ponderable but, in all likelihood, answerable, in terms of reliable and valid scientific measurements. This third category of questions includes those that can be answered by robust logical chains as well as by empirical evidence. In the following sections, the three types are considered in turn.

1.4.1 Scientifically Unanswerable Questions

At the outset of this discussion, one point must be made absolutely clear. Questions that deal solely with the supernatural (i.e., questions for which no germane empirical evidence can possibly be obtained) are always going to be impossible to answer in scientific (i.e., naturalist) terms. Those who pose such questions remove them from the domain of the natural sciences by invoking entities and laws of interaction that operate outside of the realm of those known in the natural world. In fact, the critical clue that something above and beyond the natural is being proposed is a postulated law that is, itself, in contradiction to the otherwise developed and accepted body of scientific laws. When a question includes axioms or assumptions that are in contradiction to natural laws or invokes immeasurable processes and entities, without question it means that any effort to definitively answer it would be futile. A prime characteristic of such a question is that one or more of its premises invoked levels of ontological reality that go far beyond the physical one. Any question framed in a dualist context, for example, is, a priori, unanswerable. It should, therefore, be beyond the pale of psychological or any other kind of scientific inquiry.

Although not all would agree with this assertion, it seems that the ubiquitous belief in supernatural entities is really the only evidence that they exist. However ubiquitous, the robustness of this "argument by consensus or poll" is a particularly fragile kind of evidence on which to base explanations of our experiences and our world. This is particularly evident when we are also bombarded with strong pressures (i.e., the fear of death) propelling us toward positive answers to what are actually unanswerable theological questions. Efforts to justify extraphysical states are further mitigated by the enormous variety of religious and supernatural beliefs with their wide divergence on matters such as the nature of a God or Gods, their ideas about the nature of the human mind–soul, and their respective teachings concerning its continuation in many kinds of afterlives. On a more immediate behavioral and social level, the sources justifying a moral life and the ways in which "evil" must be explained also vary enormously among religions and nations.

Questions that are not possible to answer in a rigorous scientific manner include such age-old conundrums as:

- Is there a God or is there a pantheon of Gods?
- Whose God is the correct one?
- Is there life or consciousness of any kind after death?
- If so, what is the nature of the afterlife?
- Is there a heaven, a hell, or a more complex hierarchy of such afterlives?
- Do good and evil exist?[12]
- What is good and what is evil?

Unanswerable though they may be, almost every human has been confronted with such questions by the social milieu in which they are embedded as well as by their own intellectual curiosity.[13] Many of the devout reject even the act of asking the questions. Most turn to their local teachings to provide the wide array of different affirmative answers provided by popular religious doctrines. The questions and answers so accepted lie in the domain of faith and belief. Anyone who searches for a naturalistic justification of these beliefs or absolute answers (in the sense of scientific certi-

---

[12]I refer here to theological views of good and evil. Purely sociobiological, social, or logical arguments for codes of conduct can lead to utilitarian, self-centered, or altruistic interpretations of good and evil without invoking any supernatural forces.

[13]Although it is not certain given the sensitivity of the question, it seems likely that as many as 95% of the general American population believe in God according to an ABC poll reported by Morin (2000). Quite to the contrary, when the members of the National Academy of Sciences were polled, it was reported that 93% "disbelieve or are agnostic on the existence of God" (Larson & Witham, 1998). They also reported that, generally, these academy level scientists had progressively reduced their belief in God. Surveys carried out in 1914 had shown 70% of these "greater" scientists disbelieved and in 1934 had shown disbelief at the 85% level. (Both of these earlier studies were originally carried out by James Leuba.)

tude) to such questions will probably be disappointed. However, proof is rarely a part of such searches; rather, certain foundation axioms (e.g., my soul is immortal; God exists) are accepted and complex cultural, ceremonial, and theological structures built on those presumptions.

The essential problem faced when seeking answers to such questions is the total absence of any relevant empirical evidence. As Francis Bacon (1620) said long ago in his classic *Novum Organum*:

> For what a man had rather true were he more readily believes.

As our contemporary Carl Sagan (source unknown) rephrased this idea,

> ... as much as I want to believe ... and despite the ancient and world wide cultural traditions that assert an afterlife, I know of nothing to suggest that it is more than wishful thinking.

Given this void of evidence, if one is willing to accept a natural, rational, logical, and enlightened view of a world that exhibits the properties and obeys the laws of a single kind of natural reality, it is more consistent to reject the additional immeasurable and supernatural reality that is required for the much-desired perpetuation of our individual consciousness.

The many positive, absolute, and, if I may, dogmatic answers to this first type of question abound in rich variety specifically because there is no scientific strategy to directly answer such questions and no logical strategy can prove a negative (i.e., there is no ghost in the belfry!).[14] The only way to show that something is not there is go and look! Unfortunately, science is incapable of "looking" at the invisible and the unmeasurable.

For all practical purposes, we are still in the same position on these matters as was Plato when he wrote of the trial and death of Socrates. The words Plato places in Socrates' speech are as salient, and the implied question is as unanswerable today as it was 2,400 years ago:

> For the state of death is one of two things: either the dead man wholly ceases to be and loses all consciousness or, as we are told, it is a change and a migration of the soul to another place. And if death is the absence of all consciousness and like the sleep of one whose slumbers are unbroken by any dreams, it would be a wonderful gain. . . . If that is the nature of death, I for one count it as a gain. (From Plato's *The Apology* as reprinted in Gould, 1971, p. 25)

---

[14]The "impossibility of proving a negative" is formalized in statistical analysis and experimental design. A "good" experiment is formulated in terms of a null hypothesis—the conjecture that no difference exists between two conditions. One can only "reject" the null hypothesis indicating a measurable and significant difference between the test and control differences. One cannot "accept" the null hypothesis because of a reported insignificant difference to prove that there was no difference or that something does not exist.

24 CHAPTER 1

Hall (1999) commenting on a published discussion of the possibility of rapprochements between science and religion speaks directly to the answerability issue when he asserts that:

> Science has no killer demonstration proving that religion and the supernatural are untrue. But it has amassed mountains of negative evidence, from every avenue of scientific research, demonstrating that supernatural assumptions are not required to explain the world as it is. Such negative evidence is not meaningless ... (p. 2)

The point Hall was making is that, in principle, even in not in practice, natural science can provide a complete explanation of life and mind without invoking any supernatural axioms, assumptions, or concepts. The unanswerable questions of theology, however, will always be clouded with doubt. If science's answer is not yet complete, at least it has the possibility of providing answers to all questions of the natural (i.e., observable) world. One beautiful aspect of such a "complete" science would be its simplicity; it would not have to invoke multiple kinds of reality—some observable and some not; some following natural laws and some not. Even more important, it would not create inconsistencies between those two kinds of reality, a continuing difficulty for any theory that invokes extraphysical or supernatural explanations of cognitive phenomena.

The fact that this first class of questions appears to be scientifically unanswerable does not mean, however, that questions about the influence of these beliefs and ideas cannot be sociologically and historically examined and possibly answered. No matter how "unreal," religious and other supernatural ideas have played an enormous role in intellectual development throughout history. Indeed, it is a major goal of this book to ask a question about the interaction between supernatural beliefs and studies of natural phenomena. Specifically, the issue—How does a particular view (i.e., dualism) of the nature of the mind–soul influence what are supposed to be objective theories of cognitive functioning?—is confronted here.

1.4.2 Questions of Uncertain Scientific Answerability

There are, as noted earlier, some questions whose very answerability is still contentiously debated among philosophers and psychologists. Some would consider these metascientific questions about the goals of psychology and their attainability to be more challenging than the specific technical issues themselves. For example, is it really possible to objectively access the underlying activity or mechanisms of the human mind through introspection or experimental assay methods? Behaviorists, in general, think not.

Mentalists, quite to the contrary believe that, in general, it is possible. Should we ever be able to resolve this question in favor of the mentalists, then modern cognitive psychology would have justification for their analytic and reductive "explanations" of mental activity. Similarly, the question of animal awareness, especially concerning any limits on their degree of awareness, would become answerable if it was agreed that mental processes were, in fact, accessible.

If, on the other hand, we are actually constrained to pursue a science limited to measurements of the parameters of overt (and, thus observable) behavior, then many of the questions of animal and human consciousness would have to be considered essentially unanswerable. The problem one faces when confronting this category of questions is that they are of uncertain answerability. Debates concerning answerability of questions like these rage on; unfortunately, the answers provided to them seem often to be based on assumptions more akin to religious "faith" than on robust empirical proof.

Two other questions, on which I have written extensively, are those dealing with the analyzability and reducibility of cognitive processes. The first issue concerns whether mental activity can be broken up into modules or subunits. The amount of discussion on this issue has been extensive (e.g., Fodor, 1983; Uttal, 2001) and the very intensity of the ongoing debate suggests that it has not yet been adjudicated. Similarly, discussion of the second issue—reducibility—revolves around our ability to identify the neural equivalents of mental activity; my recent book (Uttal, 1998) is only one of the many discussions of this topic. The other side of the debate is carried to an extreme in which it is suggested that psychology will disappear entirely and be replaced by an "eliminative reductionism" (e.g., Churchland, 1986).

There are other questions that have perplexed scholars for centuries whose answerability also remain matters of current contention. For example—Can people imagine their own death? Nevertheless, it is clear that an answer to the answerability of this question depends on terminology and assumptions that themselves are so nebulous that one is free to take either side depending on even more vague assumptions, axioms, and what can only be described as horrendously inconsistent clashes of personal philosophy and scientific knowledge.

Thus, there are deeply profound questions that permeate classic as well as modern thought for which it is not yet possible to generate a final answer with regard to their answerability. If there is anything that can be said with assurance as one looks over the wide range of opinions on such matters, it is that a popularity poll is a terribly inadequate way to resolve them. Proofs that are more convincing must eventually come from logical analyses or from the implications of other sciences.

1.4.3   Scientifically Answerable Questions

The third category of questions includes those for which there seems to be a high likelihood of closure particularly if we are able to agree on the meaning of some of the words and terms used therein. For example, potentially answerable questions would include:

- What is life?
- What is death?
- What are the criteria of biological death?
- Is cerebral death the same as brain death?
- What are brain death, cardiac death, and pulmonary death respectively?
- How can we ease the pain and suffering of the dying?
- How does the contemporary view of death (and its byproduct—dualism) affect contemporary scientific inquiry? (This, of course, is the target question of the present book.)
- What are the transforming relations relating stimuli to responses? (This, of course, is the generic form of the question whose answer is sought in specific detail by modern behaviorists.)

Obviously, the answers to questions of this class of what I believe are fundamentally answerable questions can still be contentious; a final answer in terms of the laws of physics and chemistry may not be available for many years. Barring some yet to be discovered epistemological barrier, it seems likely that complete answers to such questions may eventually be obtainable.

It must be acknowledged, however, that some questions that seem amenable to scientific analysis in principle may not be answerable because of some other practical constraint or limitation such as simple combinatorics or nonlinear complexity. For example, a monistic, naturalist, realist, explanatory, and neuroreductive model of the mind might accept the principle of a complete, tight, identity, relationship between the neural network of the brain and cognition. Yet, for other reasons, proving and explaining the details of this relationship may represent an intractable problem. For example, brain–mind identity may be impossible to establish, not because they are not ontologically identical, but because the critical level at which that identity becomes manifest is so combinatorially complex that it can be unequivocally demonstrated (e.g., by irrefutable mathematical proof) that it cannot be analyzed.

1.5   THE RELATION OF SCIENCE AND RELIGION

As noted earlier, the primary goal of this book is to demonstrate the impact of residual dualist attitudes on the course of theory development in scientific psychology. The task at hand is to trace the logic of the connection from the first primitive awareness of the transition from life to death to many of the modern mentalist theories of cognitive processing. To do so, it must be established that there is a reasonable assurance that there is a historical connection between the fundamental assumptions of religion and scientific psychology. Once having made the connection, the series of links in the chain of logic from the earliest concepts of death to modern mentalism can then be traced.

The relation between religion and scientific psychology has been both explicit and implicit throughout the history of the science of experimental psychology and its even more modern version—cognitive neurosciences (see chap. 7). Even if there is little argument about the common philosophical and historical roots from which the two approaches to the study of the mind–soul emerged, it has to be agreed that the new "physicophilic" empirical psychologies intrude, however subtly, onto a domain that has long been staked out by theologians. Analogous discussions of the nature of mind–soul permeate both fields in spite of the substantial and irreconcilable differences between them with regard to conclusions. Scientific psychology has always been threatening to theologies simply because the topics which each field is concerned overlap to such a substantial degree. For example, many of the criticisms raised against behaviorism have been aimed at its supposed rejection of the ethical and moral aspects of human life. Although this kind of criticism is usually overstated (e.g., "behaviorism is antireligious"),[15] it cannot be denied that in looking over the work of the early behaviorists, one finds repeated evidence of their personal antagonism toward religious ideas. For example, Watson (1924) denigrated the "religious background of current introspective psychology" (p. 3) and argued, "If the fear element were dropped out of any religion, that religion could not long survive" (p. 4).

Tolman (1932), another distinguished behaviorist, also was forthcoming about the implications of his theory of purposive behaviorism when he said, "I have, I believe, a strong anti-theological and anti-introspectionistic bias" (p. xviii). The most outspoken of modern behaviorists, B. F. Skinner, repeatedly argued that religious tenets constantly intruded into the science of psychology. (See chap. 7 for a more complete discussion of his views on

---

[15]See Uttal (2000, p. 136) for a summary of the main arguments made against behaviorism and the typical scientific irrelevance of these arguments. There is in psychology no better example of the confusion of humanistic and scientific goals and the intrusion of the former into the latter.

religion.) Other psychologists have also spoken out on the issue. Beit-Hallahmi (2001, p. 214) reminds us of comments by Allport (1950) who asserted that "Modern psychology is rather proud of being a psychology without a soul" and by Kantor (1963) who commented on the "naturalization and secularization of the soul, and finally its disappearance" as a result of the development of a scientific psychology.

More than 70 years ago, an entire book was dedicated to the conflict between behaviorism and religion (King, 1930). In that book theologians such as Mark (1930) argued that "The issue between behaviorism and religion is clear cut and definite" (p. 273). Rawl (1930) was equally emphatic when he said, "Point by point, the central convictions of [such] a religion are negatived [sic] by radical behaviorism" (p. 298).

The point made by Mark and Rawl was that religion was, in fact, being challenged by behaviorism and that there was an intrinsic conflict between the two. The point being made by the behaviorists was that religion was contaminating a scientific study of the mind. Regardless of which defensive position one chooses to take, both points of view express a common concern about the antagonistic relationship that has long existed between the two fields. This point itself establishes their commonality; only conceptual or geographic neighbors really have reasons to fight. Behaviorism, because of its essentially natural science orientation, has always been the particular target of theological attacks on scientific psychology.

Today, there is a considerable, and considerably surprising, effort to accommodate religion and science. Three strategies are evident here:

1. The first involves the separation of the exclusive content of religion and science into two separate domains. "You tend to your field, and we shall to ours." This strategy has been very explicit from time to time. One interesting example was the following note delivered to the participants at the beginning of a meeting of the Vatican Academy of Sciences (Pontifica Academia Scientiarum) in 1966.

> As to the meaning of the term "consciousness," the Study Week intends that it strictly designates the psychophysiological concept of perceptual capacity, of awareness of perception, and the ability to act and react accordingly.
>
> Consequently, the subject which the invited scientists are requested to discuss, has to be duly delimited by this semantic acceptation, which is of a strictly scientific character.
>
> It is obvious, that every extrapolation of the meaning of the term "consciousness" leading the subject into an extrascientific field, would be contrary to the spirit of the Study Week. (As quoted in an article by H. Schaefer in Eccles, 1966, p. 522)

In this context, no effort at accommodation is made; lines of demarcation are drawn to avoid conflicts and the two contenders in the battle over the ultimate nature of reality never leave their own corners.

2. The second means of resolving conflicts between science and religion has come from efforts to show how the two approaches to understanding the mind–soul are complementary and not inconsistent. Many distinguished scientists have chosen this strategy and seek to ameliorate the differences and to argue that one does not exclude the other. Even the paragon of modern science, Albert Einstein, sought to find a place for both in his worldview when he said:

> If one conceives of religion and science according to these definitions then a conflict between them appears impossible. For science can only ascertain what is, but not what should be, and outside of its domain value judgments of all kinds remain necessary. Religion, on the other hand, deals only with evaluations of human thought and action: it cannot justifiably speak of facts and relationships between facts. (Einstein, 1941)

Beit-Hallahmi (2001) summarizes this strategy by pointing out that:

> . . . many individuals in the modern world, including scholars, are engaged in the following two behaviors:
>
> • They still support religious naturalist assertions in the absence of evidence.
> • They are ready to support supernatural affirmations by calling them poetry or expressive language and by disregarding their status as affirmations for those who make them. (p. 226)

3. The third strategy of dealing with any conflict or inconsistency between science and religion is simply to ignore the issue entirely and live with the inconsistency by so ignoring it. I recall a deeply religious colleague who was also a diligent and productive laboratory scientist—in particular, a psychobiologist. If that person dealt at all with the contradictions that existed between his professional activities and his personal religious views, it was clear that he simply ignored them until a confrontation was unavoidable. To this fellow, even a discussion of the philosophical issues that pertained directly to his work was anathema. His reaction to a proposed discussion of the history of the mind–body problem was an emotional explosion in place of contemplative discussion.

Although many expressions of the interrelationship of psychology and theology may seem to be coming from the distant past, the current situation is also indicative of a continuation of the interaction, if not the antagonism, between the two domains of discourse. Even if one ignores the considerable scholarly activity revolving around such topics as the *psychology of religion* (a topic of enormous general interest, but one quite different than the one—*religious influences on psychology*—toward which this book is aimed) there is still a substantial literature on the conflict between or accommodation of psychological science and religious doctrine. The argument is not always over the specifics but rather is centered on the general issue: Is there an innate conflict or is an accommodation possible between science and religion?

In a special 1999 issue of the popular journal *Skeptical Inquirer*, the editors asked a number of well-known scholars, scientists, and lay persons, all of whom had been previously identified as skeptics of one persuasion or another, to consider such issues as whether or not the supernatural claims of religions could be studied with scientific methods. The results are tabulated in Table 1.1. In spite of the fact that this group was selected from a pool of identified "skeptics," half supported the idea that religion and science could not only coexist but could provide "complementary" paths to understanding our world. It was surprising, or in Hall's (1999) words, "plainly dismal," to read that half of the distinguished skeptical commentators who had contributed to this special issue felt that supernatural claims could be evaluated scientifically or, at least, could be dealt with separately. Apparently, there is a great deal of contention about the possibility of a détente between the two schools of thought.

TABLE 1.1
Hall's (1999) "Dismal" Summary of the Special Issue
of the *Skeptical Inquirer* on Science and Religion

	Supernatural claims can be subject to scientific testing	*The supernatural has been tested and found wanting*	*Ethics is not exclusively or preferentially a domain for religion and the supernatural*	*Science is not silent on the subject of ethics, but is itself an ethical system*
Kendrick Frazier	No	No	Yes	No
Chet Raymo	Yes?	Yes?	Yes?	No
Paul Kurtz	Yes	Yes	Yes	No
Eugenie C. Scott	No	No	Yes?	No
Barry Palevitz	No	No	No	No
Zoran Pazameta	No	No	?	?
Victor J. Stenger	Yes	Yes?	?	?
Steven Novella, M.D., and David Bloomberg	No	No	No	No
Steve Allen	Yes	Yes	?	?
Mike Reiss	Yes?	?	Yes	?
Steven Pinker	Yes?	Yes?	?	?
Steven Jay Gould	No	No	No	No
Richard Dawkins	Yes	Yes	Yes	No
Ernst Mayr	No	No	?	?
Totals	Yes = 7 No = 7	Yes = 6 No = 7	Yes = 6 No = 3	Yes = 0 No = 8

Note. Reprinted with permission of Norman Hall (Hall, 1999).

Others have argued in somewhat different terms by alluding to the potential completeness of science. Do we really need anything beyond science, as it will eventually develop, for a complete description of our world? In other words, are both natural science and supernatural theologies necessary to complete our understanding of ourselves and the universe in which we live or can science do it all on its own? Clearly, these are issues of monumental importance for which closure has not yet been achieved.

Some of the participants in the *Skeptical Inquirer* special issue, I am happy to report, did argue from a naturalist point of view. Their suggestion was that science, in general, said all that could be said about all kinds of reality. Any of the tales that are told in "holy" scriptures or by prophetic word of mouth, according to them, should be subject to the same standards required of any other scientifically researchable topic. If they conflict and cannot meet these standards, such supernatural ideas must be rejected. The current adherence to the point of view that the scientific model must take priority is itself another very modern expression of the overlap of the subject matter of the two domains, and the fact that controversy still reigns in this important field of human thought.

Clearly, even among scientists and scholars, there are still open questions. Such uncertainty leaves the door open to the question of the relation between science and religion. Equally clearly, of all the sciences, psychology is the most likely to be impacted simply because its domain of inquiry is so similar to the one dealt with by theology. Some of that impact is in the form of antagonistic criticism; some is in the form of cryptic accommodations of the standards and values of scientific psychology to the tenets of theological systems; much more of it should be in the form of an explicit rejection of supernatural, extraphysical ideas.

In summary, it is important to realize that regardless of the reality of the supernatural, beliefs in it are as real as any other thoughts and can have a direct impact on subsequent scientific inquiry. It is the question of how one set of those beliefs, those associated with the fear of death and the eventual emergence of a dualist concept of the mind, that we explore in this work. Spelling out the bare bones framework of the logical chain from a primeval awareness of death to modern mentalist cognitivisms is the topic of the next section.

1.6   A CHAIN OF LOGIC

The main purpose of this book is to follow the chain of logic and illogic that leads from the most primitive awareness of the distinction between the living and the nonliving to certain predilections on the part of contemporary mentalist psychologies. To reiterate the main point, it is the thesis presented here that there is a compelling, albeit cryptic, influence of dualist ideas on contemporary cognitive psychology. To understand that influence it is necessary to trace the history of dualist thinking from its most distant known past in the upper Paleolithic period up the chain of prehistory and then history through modern philosophy and scientific psychology. This section presents a brief précis of that logical chain, a précis that will be fleshed out in subsequent chapters.

1. The initial step in this logical chain is an undocumented, and perhaps unknowable, one that occurred an unknown number of years ago in human cognitive prehistory—the emergence of a primeval awareness of death. The ubiquity of death could not have been ignored from the dawn of self-consciousness. Whatever it was that was different between the living and the all-too-often suddenly nonliving was terribly obvious. Not only were one's dead companions immobile and unproductive, but after a while the dead began to smell rather badly. Something was dreadfully different! They had changed! Even the most primitive level of thinking led to questions about the differences and how one should respond to them. Whether there are traces of these behaviors and thought processes in the paleoanthropological remains controversial.

2. Contrasting sharply with the unresponsiveness of one's dead companion was presumably the first murky realization of one's own mental existence. "*Cogito ergo sum*" being only a much more modern manifestation of what was painfully obvious to early humans—"I am aware that I am aware and this awareness is a precious thing, indeed." Therefore, when "my" companion was no longer cogitating (as best as could be inferred from the absence of behavior) something obviously had changed. The body was still there; perhaps the difference was that *something was gone*. It was not a long conceptual leap to the fearful realization that "I," too, am very likely to cease to be aware and, thus, to be sentient in the manner that I now enjoy. We have to assume that even at a primitive level of self-awareness, this was a dreadful prospect.[16]

3. Once an awareness of the inevitability of others' deaths and, therefore, of the likely termination of one's own cognitive existence became a part of these early worldviews, the fundamental curiosity of primitive humans was kindled. At that stage of primitive intellectual development, a quest presumably was begun that has persisted to this time—the search for an understanding and explanation of death and for an escape hatch from the awfulness of

---

[16]Of course, I am phrasing these thoughts in a modern language. The specific terminology and thought processes in which these ideas were originally framed will never be known.

one's own mortality. There was a compelling intellectual pressure to answer the most fundamental questions such as: What is death? How can I avoid such a terrible fate as the termination of my own consciousness—my essential being—at the end of my physical existence?

4. Early humans, therefore, out of fear and wonder, were forced into seeking an escape hatch from a particularly horrendous fate—the cessation of their own being. Adaptive intellects that they were and are, it should not have been too great an invention to assume some kind of personal survival depended on the fact that the body and the sentient mind need not be irretrievably interconnected. Indeed, the experiences of dreaming and other kinds of disembodied hallucinations were also powerful stimuli for the invention of the concept of a dual nature of mind and body. Thus, the rhetorical question—What was that something that was gone from my dead companion?—was answered in the terms of a separate kind of entity existing in a separate kind of reality! There was, hopefully, something that survived the body's disintegration that had its own separate kind of existence. Such a primitive dualist explanation would be a balm to the terror of the loss of personhood posed by one's knowledge and fear of inevitable death; it would assuage the fear to a considerable degree by proposing a means for continuation of the most essential aspect of one's being—the conscious mind. Thus, the seed of the supernatural, of dualisms, and of all subsequent religions was sown.

Surprisingly, the invention of a dualism may not have been such an "unnatural" thing to do for any kind of "thinking" entity. Minsky (1963) suggested (in a comment that I have quoted several times in the past) that even a thoughtful computer would "naturally" evolve a dualist concept of a separate mind and brain in much the same way that humans had done over the millennia. He said:

> The argument is this: our own self-models have a substantially "dual" character; there is a part concerned with the physical or mechanical environment—with the behavior of inanimate objects—and there is a part concerned with social and psychological matters. It is precisely because we have not yet developed a satisfactory mechanical theory of mental activity that we have to keep these areas apart. We could not give up this division even if we wished to—until we find a unified model to replace it. . . . Now, when we ask such a creature [an autonomous computer] what sort of being it is, it cannot simply answer "directly"; it must inspect its model(s). And it must answer by saying that it seems to be a dual thing—which appears to have two parts—a "mind" and a "body." Thus, even the robot, unless equipped with a satisfactory theory of artificial intelligence, would have to maintain a dualist opinion on this matter. (p. 449)

Thus, there is a compelling pressure, initiated by the very human passionate desire for self continuation, by the hope that mind could go off on its own, and by a kind of logical imperative, to develop or invent some kind of a dual or separate form of personal immortality.

5. The next few steps are less certain in terms of the exact historical sequence. Most likely, however, the unarticulated hypothesis that "my self-awareness" (soon to be called the *soul* and later the *mind*) can be separated from "my body" raised the possibility of other kinds of mind/souls. Since "things" did things to people, perhaps things, as well as other animals, also had minds of some kind. Thus, arose the foundation belief for what humans were later to call animisms—the ascription of consciousness to what otherwise appear to be inanimate objects or subhuman organisms.

6. The primeval self-awareness and its offspring—fear of death—were also fertile breeding grounds for several other related ideas. Contemporaneous, in all likelihood, with the projection of mental processes to inanimate objects and animals was the emergence of corollary questions such as—What happened to "my consciousness" when "my body" decayed? Where did "my mind" then reside? From such questions came what were probably some of the earliest ideas of an afterlife, eventually a perpetual one, where minds could continue to enjoy the exquisite pleasure of conscious experience. Some of the earliest of the afterlife domains were likely to have been simple reflections of the natural environment—the sky, the earth, a tree, or some other totem object in which not only "my mind" but also the "spirits" of my ancestors might reside. Equally plausible was the next evolutionary step— these tangible loci evolved into much more ephemeral locations eventually to culminate in complex ideas of a variety of kinds of heavens and hells.

7. The awareness of one's own personal consciousness also was the seed-bed from which other kinds of supernatural minds were to grow. If, a simple logic went, "I" can maintain consciousness without a receptacle (i.e., my body) perhaps there are other supernatural consciousnesses that exist without bodies or receptacles of any kinds. Since there are obviously both benevolent and malevolent forces at work in my simple world, perhaps some of these disembodied entities are bad and some are good. Thus was the idea of disembodied, supernatural Gods and Goddesses invented in the normal course of this logical evolutionary chain. It is then but a short step to a multiplicity—a pantheon—of Gods, Goddesses, angels, jinns, devils, goblins, demons, and a host of other supernatural, humanlike, behaving, and decision-making minds that will affect and, perhaps even control the individual's life.

8. The invention of powerful Gods and other supernatural entities that could directly influence our lives led inexorably to the creation of a number of other new ideas and functions. Priests, shamans, and other interlocutors who were able to efficiently communicate with the Gods had to be designated, structures in which to house God's tangible symbols had to be constructed, and perhaps, most of all, rituals that standardized the intercourse

between Gods and human, had to be designed and implemented. After the invention of writing, the rituals once communicated by song and story were written down in Holy Scriptures to further organize the emerging tenets of "acceptable" religions.

9. Somewhere in this chronology, the evolution of religious concepts became more complex and sophisticated than simple death cults. As the human mind evolved so, too, did the complexity of the questions asked. It is a considerable step beyond a primitive fear of death to asking such hugely important teleological questions as: Why are things as they are? Are we evolving toward some kind of a predetermined goal? Is our development the ultimate outcome of a series of random processes? Other issues were appended to the basic fear of death as humans pondered the nature of the world and of themselves. Nevertheless, this trend toward theological complexity was a mere veneer on the universal foundation, the one omnipresent motivating question all religions seek to answer: How can I avoid the cessation of my own conscious existence?

10. Another aspect of the evolution of religious principles and ideas was the utility of such ideas for the amelioration of social problems. Religion not only assuaged the fear of death but it provided codes of conduct and commandments that helped to alleviate the clashes of pure self-interest that seems to characterize human society. It may be argued that there is no essential need for religion to play this role, but it certainly was an easy way to instruct people to "do unto others as you would have others do unto you" *in peril of danger to the immortal part of your existence*!

11. Thus, even as religions became more and more formal and sophisticated organizations, the primeval concept of a separable mind and body became more and more specifically defined, albeit in many different ways by many different religions. However diverse each theology might be, many authors including Achté (1980) have noted that "Immortality of the soul [i.e., as distinct from the transient nature of the body] is the most essential concept of all religions" (p. 3). The highly developed dualisms of all major religions may vary in detail but they all reflect the ubiquitous human need to find an alternative for the ultimate horror—the total cessation of one's conscious existence.

12. The scope and impact of the primitive self-awareness and the fear of death that emerged at some unknown point in our evolutionary prehistory was, therefore, enormous for almost all aspects of our later history. The amount of human effort expended over the last four or five millennia to provide satisfying explanations of the mysteries of our existence has been enormous. So far, in the presentation of this logical chain, I have traced only the evolution as it was evidenced in theology, but there are parallel chains of causal influence on philosophy, economics, ethics, warfare, and eventually

science. These nontheological, pragmatic fields of endeavor have also had their effect on psychology. With the enormous pressure toward dualist thinking (i.e., mind as a distinctly different kind of reality subject to totally different and even contradictory sets of rules than those governing the physical world) the contrary theory that mind was a natural process of a material structure became eminently unfashionable until quite recently. Monistic materialisms are still relatively unfashionable and accepted by, at best, a very small portion of the human population. (See Uttal, 1978, chap. 2, pp. 36–86, as well as chap. 6 in this book, for more complete discussions of the various philosophical theories of the relationship between mind and body.)

13. Nevertheless, there is among scientists an increasing reluctance to accept theological explanations for natural phenomena. There has, therefore, been a substantial effort in the past century to detheologize studies of the mind. This effort has taken two main directions. On the one hand, behavioral psychologists have simply rejected the accessibility of an intrapersonally accessible mind and have concentrated on the observable and tangible behavior of organisms. In this way, the problem has simply been finessed. On the other hand, mentalist psychologists have tended to accept the accessibility of the mind, but to consider it in highly concrete terms in much the same way that an object might be studied. Herein lies the root of the fallacy with which I contend in this book. To consider mind as an analyzable *object* as opposed to an integrated *process* opens the door to considering it as something distinct from the mechanism that generates it. Therein lies the basis of the implicitly dualist and cryptic supernaturalism of current mentalist psychologies.

14. This then brings us to the final step in the logical chain from fear of death to the influence of sophisticated dualist thinking on modern scientific psychology. This book proposes that the primitive dualist solution of a mind as a separable entity of a different kind of underlying reality, coupled with the widespread general acceptance of some of the more modern derivatives of the theological resolution of the fear of death (see chap. 5), has left a residue of dualist thinking that affects many currently popular mentalist psychologies. This residue permits a kind of neo-dualism to creep into the theories and even the experimental designs of research in cognitive and other mentalist psychologies. This neo-dualism is unspoken; it is implicit; it is cryptic; it is likely to be denied by cognitivists if specifically challenged about its role in their science. However, the approach to the study of mind as a separable, modular, analyzable, accessible object, rather than a unified, irreducible, and intangible process with multiple properties, has within it the fossilized remnants of a dualist concept of mind clearly distinguishable from a single natural reality. Mentalists, it is argued, treat mind as if it were an organ or group of organs rather than as the observable process of an incredibly complex material substrate—the brain. It is this approach

to mind as a substantial object—rather than as process—that lies at the heart of some of the most egregious myths[17] of modern psychology.

In summary, I propose that this implicit dualism, so influential as a causal factor in modern psychology, is a direct result of the primitive fear of death. The reification of the mind as a kind of quasi-object has reoccurred over the many years since human consciousness appeared. It continues both to be a major contributor to human thought including what is supposed to be scientifically pristine psychological theory. It is, however, the foundation of an erroneous way to conceptualize mind that should be replaced with an emphasis on mind as process.

The chain of explanation from primitive self-awareness and fear of death through more or less sophisticated dualisms to the cryptic neo-dualism of modern cognitive psychologies is, of course, a disputable and contentious one. There is no "killer argument," in this instance as in so many other debates about the nature of the human mind, that can provide unequivocal support for such a hypothetical–logical chain. Like any other tale reciting the implications of ancient events, its truth or falsity is clouded by the assumptions and vested interests of those who interpret that history. Nevertheless, there is at least a trail of circumstantial evidence that behaviorists like Skinner (1987) were correct when they said that the reason that non-mentalist psychologies such as behaviorism were unsatisfying to many scientists and laypersons alike lay in the fact they seemed (incorrectly from his point of view) to challenge the role of religion in human life. In short, Skinner argued there were forces at work that led science away from objective behaviorisms to mentalisms not because of any scientific criteria or evidence, but rather because of a pervasive influence of ancient fear-of-death, medieval dualist, and modern crypto-dualist thinking.

The focus of this book is on the proposition that basic religious beliefs typified by a vestigial dualism are still contaminating scientific psychology. This thesis is demonstrated by exploring the history of mind in the archeological, theological, philosophical, and historical domains over many thousands of years. There is no better place to start such a discussion than at the beginning and the beginning is to be found in the science of paleoanthropology.

---

[17]This is not the only source of erroneous psychomyths. See Uttal (2003) for a discussion of many other sources of misconceptualizations in this important but terribly challenged science.

2

The Paleoanthropology of Dualism

2.1 THE TASK

The thesis of this book is that an implicit and cryptic modern day dualism has evolved from a primeval awareness of death. It is proposed that the emerging and persisting fear of the loss of one's personal identity still pollutes current mentalist theories of psychological function—particularly as they are evidenced in current cognitive psychologies. To completely understand how such a thing could have happened it is useful to look back over the ages to determine the context in which the awareness and fear of death first emerged. The history of the concept of death is intimately related to the evolution of the cognitive processes that characterize the modern human—*Homo sapiens sapiens*.[1] In such a context, profound questions must be answered. These questions include:

- When did people begin to think?
- When did they begin to appreciate death?
- Was death conceived as a negative thing?
- When did they begin to think of the soul (mind) as a separable aspect of existence?
- When did they begin to invent the supernatural?
- What did symbolic art mean to them?

---

[1]See pages 51–52 for a discussion of the distinction between *Homo sapiens* and *Homo sapiens sapiens*.

- When did modern cognitive processes evolve?
- Did our hominid predecessors exhibit the same cognitive capability as modern humans?
- If so, what explains the uniqueness of our modern subspecies?
- Can material remains tell us about the intangible aspects of behavior?
- If so, can we infer anything about cognition from the behavioral evidence?
- What evidence is available that could possibly answer such questions?

And, of course:

- Is it possible to answer such questions?

Whatever answers to such questions that may be forthcoming must come from the sciences called *Paleontology* (the study of fossils from distant geological times) and *Archeology* (the study of the ancient remains of human life and culture). *Paleoanthropology*, however, the specialized study of human fossils, and archeology suffer from a common handicap when it comes to estimating the nature of the thought processes of our distant ancestors. That handicap is the total absence of any kind of fossils or remains of cognitive processes! Whatever we believe we know about the mental activity of earlier humans and their predecessors are, at best, tenuous and remote inferences from the material objects that do, themselves, leave physical traces of one kind or another. For that matter, there are also no direct remains of behavior, although the leap from an object to an inference about its use may be relatively more direct than the one from the behavior to the underlying thought process. Therefore, although there are cases that seem to have left a more or less obvious suggestion of behavior (e.g., an implement that apparently would have been useful in performing some mundane task) there is always some residual doubt and uncertainty about the use to which an isolated or unusual device may have been put by people whose cognitive processes were likely to have been very different from our own.

The inferential leap from behavior to thought, therefore, is the most problematic part of the multistage task of going from material remains to thought. Even if the behavioral utilization of an object is inferred correctly, the unanswered conundrum of the accessibility of the associated mental process from the behavioral act always remains. The problem is not unique to Paleoanthropology; it is of the same genre as the one confronted by modern psychologists when they attempt to access the thought processes of an observer by measuring behavior in either an experimental or natural setting. The difficulty of such a task is drastically exacerbated when a paleoanthropologist seeks to determine from limited fossil remains and artifacts what early humans or human-like creatures were thinking tens and even hundreds of thousands of years ago.

The most basic epistemological root of the problem is that it is entirely possible for many completely different cognitive processes to give rise to identical behavioral responses just as it is for a wide variety of different machines to produce the same action. Therefore, given the additional problem that validity of the inferred behavior may have been uncertain, determining what was in the "mind" of a prehistoric being from paleontological or archeological evidence will always be encrusted with enormous uncertainty and doubt. The result is that paleoanthropology is a field filled with such a high level of unavoidable controversy that even a psychologist, a practitioner of a field of science that is itself prone to extensive and contentious debate, is startled.

It is interesting, therefore, to note that many of the conceptual battles fought among archeologists revolve around the same issue of the accessibility of the mind as the analogous one faced by psychologists. In the former case, the question is: What can be inferred through the conceptual window provided by artifactual clues? Arguably, for psychologists, the portal to accessing cognitive processes is interpersonally observable behavior. In other words, the critical question in both sciences is: Just how far can one leap from the observable evidence, be it artifact or behavior, to the underlying cognitive activity? It seems possible that some traditional psychologists (with the possible exception of behaviorists) and paleoanthropologists have overestimated what can be seen through such a clouded window. Salmon (2001), for example, in agreement with the suggestion that it is far more difficult than usually appreciated to infer mind from object, suggested that some of the older "prescientific" archeological interpretations might have represented "some sort of dubious Paleopsychology" (p. 237).

Dennett (2001) also drew the analogy between the traditional inferential approach to archeology and behaviorism. He pointed out that much of what is called cognitive archeology is, in fact:

> . . . just good old fashioned mentalist reasoning—in particular the exercise of reverse engineering about the likely or almost certain uses to which things have been put in the past, and why. (p. 2)

In the early 1970s, some skeptical archeologists began to challenge even the possibility of a deep penetration into ancient cognitive processes based on material remains. They did so for the same reasons that behaviorism has traditionally challenged cognitive accessibility in human psychological experimentation. This new point of view came to be known as *processual archeology;* it was argued by this group of archeologists that it was dangerous to go too far from the observed measurements and the artifacts to infer in-

tent or thought to the original artisans. "Processualists" contended that the
field should be severely limited to barebones descriptions and to the same
high standards of proof that characterized all of the rest of science. A de-
ductive, as opposed to an inductive, approach to science was emphasized
in such pioneering works as those by Binford and Binford (1968) and by
Watson, LeBlanc, and Redman (1971).

Of course, constraining unfounded speculative leaps from artifact (or behavior) to thought is not a new idea, even for archeology, but one that has
been percolating around in all of the humanities and social sciences for
many years. The essence of Francis Bacon and Rene Descartes' appeal for
an organized scientific method was to protect it from armchair speculation.
Specifically, in the modern context of anthropology, Franz Boas (1938)
stated:

> ... it is not possible to predict the behavior resulting from the historical
> events that made people what they are. This problem is essentially a psycho-
> logical one and beset with all of the difficulties inherent in the investigation of
> complex mental phenomena of the lives of individuals. (Cited in Binford, 1987,
> pp. 5–6)

As I have argued elsewhere (Uttal, 1998, 2000) the debate between behaviorism (contending that only observations of interpersonally observable
and repeatable responses are acceptable as scientific data) and cognitive
mentalism (contending that hypothetical constructs inferred from behavior
can be a rich source of knowledge of human mentation) remains one of the
key issues in current psychological science. Obviously, it has no more been
resolved for archeology than it has been for psychology. Any conclusions
drawn by archeologists, as well as those by psychologists, will always be
handicapped by a lack of resolution of this fundamental debate. For a lucid
account of the current and controversial state of "processual" archeology
(particularly the revisionist response to it), readers are referred to Salmon
(2001).

It is clear that some mental and behavioral processes will always be especially intransigent to inference from material remains. For example, consider the problem of speech. Obviously, speech, both in terms of the vocal-
izations themselves and the thoughts behind the vocal articulations, leaves
no fossils or remains. Speech is, at best, indirectly indicated by the social
coordination physically evidenced in shards, garbage middens, village
fence posts, and the like. Such behavior, it is not too unreasonable to argue,
might as well have occurred in a community without vocal speech or even a
manual sign language available to it. It can be argued, on the contrary, that
such signs of coordinated activity could have occurred without intentional
communication among the members of a group that had very little means

of speech or sign communication. This is not an empty class of possibilities. It is likely that the societies of insect colonies and the highly organized schooling behavior of fishes operate in very much this manner. This mode of organized behavior is characterized by a system in which each individual reacts more as a participant in a self-organizing system dependent more on the behavior of others of its kind than on linguistic communication.[2] Such prelinguistic behavior has been designated as a *mimetic skill*, not in the sense of imitation, its conventional definition, but rather as Donald (1991) uses the term:

> Mimetic skill or mimesis rests on the ability to produce conscious, self-initiated, representational acts that are intentional but not linguistic.... reflexive, instinctual, and routine motor acts are excluded from this definition, as are simple imitative and conditioned responses, ... (p. 168)

 Conclusions concerning language based on material remains obtained from the distant past will, therefore, always be equivocal. There is perhaps no more vigorous debate in all of Paleoanthropology than the one over whether Neanderthals had language or the degree to which their language may have shared common features with our own, if they did. Arguments based on the anatomy of the vocal system or the presence or absence of brain regions known to be involved in our highly linguistic species are indirect at best and irrelevant at worst. (See Uttal, 2001, for a discussion of the frailties of any argument based on the precise localization of such high-level cognitive functions in the brain.)

It will, therefore, never be certain just how many of our own criteria, assumptions, and introspections are influencing our inferences and interpretations of situations from worlds in which the most basic psychological processes may differ drastically from our own. The possibility of totally misinterpreting the meaning of some artifact is omnipresent especially since time has separated the object from the intent of its makers. This uncertainty was well expressed by Bell (1994) when he noted:

> Interpretations can yield understanding; that is, they explain phenomena. Since interpretations are not testable, however, there are no reliable criteria for deciding between them, or for moving beyond them. Only testable theories can deliver insight and further understanding.... In brief, if theories of

---

[2]Of course, given the level of human evolution extant even at relatively early times, such a hypothetical situation is of a lesser probability than the current point of view emphasizing rich information flow through speech or signs among early *Homo sapiens sapiens*. But, this is not the point. Rather, the point is that it is not possible, however low the *probability* of a process, to totally discount its *possibility*. Other social situations may reflect their own very different reasons for doing what they do. Conclusions concerning the nature of the thought processes of our predecessors based on our own cognitive styles may be severely biased.

the prehistoric mind are to be rooted in the artefactual [*sic*] data, and if they are to exploit artefactual data to yield even better theories, then they must be testable. (p. 15)

This refrain echoes the long standing, although mirror image, admonition of Popper (1959) that it is not the general verifiability, but rather the specific falsifiability of a theory that determines its value and helps to distinguish the scientific from the superstitious and supernatural. Unfortunately, herein lies the rub, so to speak. Neither the verifiability nor falsifiability of a theory that leaps from artifact to behavior to mentation is any more testable than is any psychological approach that purports to extract the nature of mental activity from behavioral observations.

The general problem posed by the current inaccessibility of cognitive processes, therefore, is further compounded by the eons that stand between our cognitive strategies and those of ancient individuals and societies, all of whom faced considerably different survival challenges. If there are any doubts about the impenetrability of this persistent barrier, one has only to compare the logic underlying the contemporaneous behavior of western Europeans from that of contemporary indigenous peoples such as those of the central New Guinea river valleys. Indeed, one does not have to go that far—a comparison of the logic of an American neo-Nazi with that of a member of the American Civil Liberties Union suggests that vast differences in the basic assumptions and intellectual logic of even closely related members of contemporary cultures may exist.

The point is that it is all too easy to project "our" thought processes onto those of another group (thus committing what William James referred to as the psychologist's fallacy—see page 270) and, in so doing, to reify mythical cognitive hypotheses. Every effort must, therefore, be made to avoid this kind of scientific error particularly when we look back across the millennia to examine the thought processes of beings who may not even be of our own species. The possibility of equally adaptive but totally alien modes of logic, thought, and behavior among our predecessors cannot be overlooked. The intrinsic difficulty in validating any paleoanthropological theory of cognitive processes is profound. In Binford's (1987) words:

> The fact nevertheless remains: archeologists have no informants [anyone or any way to validate their inferential interpretations]. We cannot see the past from the ancients' cultural perspective because they cannot tell us what that might have been. We have no truth by authority emanating from the past. (p. 398)

In such a situation, Binford (1987) goes on to argue that there are only two remaining strategies for archeology to pursue. The first is to adopt a "universalistic interpretive approach," that is, to simply accept and concentrate on the attributes of human existence that seem so common to all humans. The second strategy is to avoid any deep cognitive interpretations of the past, but rather to "exploit" the archeological evidence for our own current purposes. As we shall see, both of these alternative strategies are popular today as well as that of those who choose to ignore the accessibility and absent informant constraints altogether.

2.2   THE PALEOANTHROPOLOGY OF DEATH[3]

2.2.1   The Ancient Past: The Middle Paleolithic

Graves, to the degree they can be authenticated as intentional and ritual, have deep significance for any analysis asserting that cognitive attitudes toward death led to burial practices carried out, not just to dispose of the body, but also to soothe, honor, or perpetuate the dead individual's life or spirit. If one is to attempt the difficult task of inferring the cognitive processes concerning death of our distant predecessors from the material remains found in graves, it is necessary to acquire unequivocal and convincing evidence of active, intentional, and ritualistic intervention by ancient humans or proto-humans in the manner in which they dealt with their dead. For all practical purposes, it is generally agreed that the archeological record concerning intentional burials is silent prior to 100,000 BP (years **B**efore the **P**resent). Sometime after that milestone date, proto-human and human artifacts and extraneous materials have been discovered associated with burials in a way that many paleoanthropologists believe reflect primitive death rituals, and thus an appreciation of its meaning. At the outset of this discussion, it is important to appreciate that there remains an enormous amount of controversy concerning this point. It was not until much later in the prehistoric record that unequivocal evidence of funereal practices first appears.

To provide a meaningful time line for the following discussion, it is necessary to be familiar with the standard classification scheme used by paleoanthropologists to order the prehistoric and historic epochs. The epochs that are relevant to a discussion of the evolution of attitudes toward death are the latter two stages of the *Paleolithic* or "Old Stone Age." It was in the million year long Paleolithic period, roughly speaking, that hominids de-

---

[3]In the highly incomplete review that follows, I have only sampled some of the most prominent of the archeological sites that pertain to human bodily and artifactual remains. Paleoanthropology is a gigantic field and one that is beset with enormous controversy concerning the meaning of many of its findings. I am sure that one or another professional in the field would find exceptions to virtually any point I make. What I have tried to do is to represent the consensus but make clear where controversy exists.

veloped increasingly refined techniques for chipping stone—the main material for their tools and weapons.[4] The Paleolithic archeological period is typically broken down by anthropologists into three separate epochs:

- The Lower Paleolithic—from 1 million to 100,000 BP
- The Middle Paleolithic—from 100,000 to 40,000 BP
- The Upper Paleolithic—from 40,000 to 10,000 BP

The Paleolithic period was followed by what paleontologists have called the Mesolithic period; it is assumed to have lasted for a millennium or two from about 9000 or 10,000 BP to about 8000 BP. About 8000 BP, a dramatic revolution occurred in manufacturing stone implements; this period, designated the Neolithic epoch, lasted until about 5000 BP. In this New Stone Age, polishing and grinding stones, as opposed to just chipping them, led to extraordinary cultural developments.

The Neolithic period was relatively brief, however; sometime around 5000 BP, metals were discovered and metallurgy further changed the world. This new technology rapidly supplanted stone as the cultural material of choice during two sequential periods designated the Chalcolithic (from approximately 5000 BP to 4000 BP) and the Bronze ages (from about 4000 BP to about 3000 BP), respectively. About 3000 BP, the culturally influential extraordinary invention of iron working techniques occurred. Polished stone, bronze, and iron were among the most important cultural discoveries that led inevitably to the rich fabric of our modern technological society as well as to increasingly sophisticated religious systems.[5]

The task of anyone interested in putative grave rituals and drawing inferences about the concept of death from them has to be broken up into several steps. First, it is necessary to locate sites that contain human remains; surprisingly, this is the easiest and least controversial step compared to the later stages of the process; it is generally not a matter of debate that the usually serendipitously discovered materials are or are not humanoid bones. There is, surprisingly, what may be considered to be a substantial number of middle Paleolithic graves, perhaps numbered in the hundreds. The older ones are rare, but after about 100,000 BP, both early and modern human remains and entombments are found scattered across major portions of the world, first in Africa, then in the rest of Europe and Asia and,

---

[4]Of course, other materials such as wood and bone were almost certainly used throughout the several "lithic" periods. However, these materials are ephemeral and stone artifacts are thus the defining cultural items for the various stone ages.

[5]However, they were not the only developments. See chapter 3 for a discussion of the many other technological and social developments of the Neolithic period that contributed to modern society.

finally, in the Americas. The number of modern human graves begins to proliferate after 40,000 BP and the list grows longer each year as new discoveries are made.

The second and more difficult step in the overall task is to establish beyond a doubt that candidate graves are truly the result of intentional burials and not the result of accidental entombments. Some of the later ones are unambiguously intentional, but earlier graves are often clouded with serious doubt about their intentionality and the significance of the included nonskeletal materials. The problem, once again, is that the physical remains do not speak directly to motive or thought and inferences must be drawn from what are sometimes very vague and ambiguous clues.

The third and most difficult step, therefore, is to go beyond intentionality to make the huge inferential leap from the material evidence to what those ancient beings may have been "thinking" when they carried out this newly evolved proto-ritualistic behavior. When intentionality and ritual have been proven, it becomes reasonable to speculate that death had become a cognitive reality.

It was during the middle Paleolithic that the possibility of intentional graves and tombs arose for the first time. It is only in the upper Paleolithic, however, that all dispute and doubt can reasonably be cast aside. It is in the latter epoch that we find the first unequivocal evidence of human attitudes toward death, the supernatural, and the roots of modern religious practices. In this section, I review a few of the earliest material indications that cognitive processes concerning an awareness of death may have surfaced in primitive humans.

To begin, as noted earlier, it is, for all scientific purposes, certain that there is no evidence of any intentional burials in the lower Paleolithic (i.e., prior to 100,000 BP). The first, although highly controversial, bits of evidence for intentional burials, are to be found in the inferred funeral activities in the middle Paleolithic of members of another species than our own— *Homo neanderthalensis*—who first appear in the archeological record several hundred thousand years ago. The Neanderthals were predecessors (in time if not in heritage) and, almost certainly, contemporaries for at least a short period with modern man; they disappeared somewhere between 40,000 BP and 20,000 BP[6] from the archeological record.

Although the evidence for intentional burials during the upper Paleolithic is quite clear and not generally disputed by paleoanthropologists, the

---

[6]The uncertainty implied by this range of dates for the extinction of Neanderthals is the source of some of the greatest of paleoanthropological debates and controversies. When, exactly, did they disappear? Why did they disappear? Did they coexist with modern man at the same time and at the same place? Did they become extinct or did they interbreed and merge with modern man? These questions are certainly among the greatest mysteries of human prehistory.

middle Paleolithic evidence is fraught with uncertainty and controversy, not only for Neanderthals but also for both archaic and modern forms of humans. The specific issue now faced is whether or not the mainly Neanderthal burials of the middle Paleolithic were intentional. The antithetical view held by a deeply committed minority of paleoanthropologists is that most of what appeared to be intentional burials by Neanderthals could be better and more simply explained by natural causes. Unfortunately, the evidence is so fragmentary and ambiguous that it has led to an enormous amount of controversy reflecting the uncertainty of the meaning of materials that may be as much as 100,000 years old.

It was in the early part of the 20th century that the first reports of middle Paleolithic, specifically Neanderthal, intentional burials were published by Bouyssonie, Bouyssonie, and Bardon (1908, 1913). In this famous site, La Chapelle-aux-Saints in France, the inference of intention and ritual was based on the findings of a few stone tools and some red ochre. Although many paleoanthropologists now accept the idea that Bouyssonie and his colleagues were correct in their conjecture that these burials were intentional, dedicated critics, most notably Gargett (1989, 1999), have argued that the presumption of intent was unfounded and that *all* middle Paleolithic burials could better be explained by natural causes, sources, events, and processes. This point of view is not unexpected. The evidence from the early Neanderthal burials is almost always flimsy and equivocal. For example the Teshik-Tash juvenile, one of the first Neanderthal burials found in central Asia (Uzbekistan) was declared to be not only intentional but also a ritual burial only because of the presence of a small contemporaneous fire near the grave as well as a few ibex horns found in the grave (Gremyatsky & Nestourkh, 1949).

Notwithstanding the criticisms of Gargett and the fragility of the data, other paleoanthropologists have come to the conclusion that Neanderthal humans of the middle Paleolithic not only intentionally buried their dead but also decorated the graves with flowers, stones, bones, and other objects. These inclusions suggested some kind of human manipulation that seemed to have symbolic or ritual significance.

One of the earliest and perhaps most famous of these putative intentional ritualistic burials of a Neanderthal was that of a male skeleton discovered in the Shanidar caves of Iraq in a grave that appeared also to contain pollen grains and other vegetable matter. Solecki (1975) interpreted this 60,000-year-old material as representing the residue of flowers that had been used in a burial ceremony. Even though this burial has become one of the icons of current theories of intentional middle Paleolithic burials, the inference that this burial was both "ritual" as well as intentional has recently been criticized by Sommer (1999). Sommer suggested that the pollen evidence of a flower-draped corpse was not convincing because of the presence of rodent burrows surrounding and intruding into the grave area. He argued that these burrows could have provided a portal through which animals might have brought vegetable material. Although this material might have appeared to be a funeral offering, it was, in fact, the result of food storage activities carried out by quite a different species than *Homo neanderthalensis*. Another important piece of evidence challenging the "intentional" nature of this particular burial was the fact there were several other "burials" within the Shanidar cave itself that had clearly been the result of accidental entombments.

In spite of the arguments raised by scholars like Gargett and Sommer, many other pieces of material evidence from this time period have led other paleoanthropologists to conclude that at least some of the Neanderthal burials were both intentional and ritual. A fascinating discussion presenting both sides of the controversy can be found in a comprehensive article by Riel-Salvatore and Clark (2001). The discussion is particularly well balanced by appended commentaries written by scholars on both sides of the debate.

The southwest of France has been particularly rich in providing suggestive evidence of the intentionality of these middle Paleolithic burials. Caves in La Ferrassie (Capitan & Peyrony, 1909), Regourdou (Bonifay, 1962), and Le Moustier[7] (Peyrony, 1930) have all provided suggestive evidence that many paleoanthropologists have interpreted as ritual burials. In recent years, additional attention has been directed at other Neanderthal sites such as the Qafzeh cave (Vandermeersch, 1969, 1996) and the Kebara cave (Arensburg et al., 1985) in Israel. However, according to Gargett (1999), all of these are equivocal with regard to their intentionality.

Among the most convincing, although still questionable, evidence of Neanderthal ritual burials was found in a collection of recently discovered graves at St. Cesaire in France (Leveque & Vandermeersch, 1981). Here, Neanderthals had been buried with what were surprisingly modern tool kits. However, these graves were quite recent, dating only from 36,000 BP, possibly about the time the last Neanderthals lived. The modern interpretation of these graves is further confused by the fact that they were found quite close in space and nearly at the same time attributed to Cro-Magnon remains. It is, therefore, arguable that artifacts from the two cultures could have been intermixed. If so, this evidence would be the source of misleading interpretations of Neanderthal "intentional" burials.

In spite of the criticisms of Gargett and Sommers and continuing debate about the issue, most evidence suggests that at least some of the last Neanderthals did intentionally bury their dead—albeit for reasons that are

---

[7]The Le Moustier site became the prototype of European Neanderthal culture, now referred to as "Mousterian."

not always easy to determine. This brings us to the problem of inferred motivation and, thence, to the target of this chapter, the cognitive processes that may have motivated intentional burials.

Even if we presume that it was not until the last 35,000 or 40,000 years or so that evidence of intentional burials becomes unequivocal, there remains a further problem: What does this evidence mean in terms of the human attitudes toward death at that time? Not all burials, even if they are intentional, must necessarily be associated with either a ritualistic response to or even to a sense of the significance of death. It is quite within the realm of possibility that even a flower-cluttered burial was a simple practical response to an unpleasant problem: Corpses do not smell very good and flowers ameliorate that smell a little! Some paleoanthropologists have suggested that an untended corpse also poses a dangerous attraction to other creatures that may wish to do harm to your kind. We must not forget that in the middle Paleolithic humans were not just predators but were also prey. Furthermore, it has been suggested that the animal or plant remains found in these supposedly ritual "burials" may not actually represent symbols of an appreciation of the meaning of or a reverence for death, but, rather, the detritus found in any convenient garbage dump! Even the oft-cited fetal positioning of skeletons as evidence of ritual burial may have had a simple, practical reason—a folded body can be put in a smaller and easier to dig hole. Such uncertainties clearly demonstrate how difficult it is to go from even clear-cut behavior (intentional burials) to the cognitive motivation behind that behavior.

Even if it were possible to unequivocally determine that the burials were both intentional and ritual, there is even a greater logical leap to be made than the one from burial to intent to be accounted for. That is the leap from the symbolic meaning of an intentional grave to the cognitive processes of those burying their dead. It is arguable whether the act of burial itself says anything about such primitive cognitive capabilities. Practical hygienic concerns may have anticipated and even stimulated subsequent ritual processes. A case still has to be made for the cultural and psychological significance of even an intentional grave and it is here that speculation often takes the place of hard evidence.

This is a topic of enormous current interest, contentiousness, and sometime ad hominem controversy in current archeological studies as can be seen in the review by Hayden (1993). In this article, he sets out the counterarguments offered by those who accept a high level of cognitive powers on the part of Neanderthals. He asserted that many of those who seek to minimize their cognitive and cultural capabilities do so in a prejudiced effort to "dehumanize" this type of early human (p. 120). The implication here is that other current humanistic criteria (e.g., an implicit effort to maintain the uniqueness of the spirit of modern man) are supplanting purely scientific standards. Clearly, this is another example of how pure science can be polluted by extrascientific considerations.

Regardless of which side is correct in this debate, it is clear that the argument revolving around the meaning of intentional and ritual burials by Neanderthals, if such burials did in fact exist, is still unresolved. Indeed, it may remain so in the future because of exactly the same antagonisms faced when cognitivists and behaviorists become locked in virtually the identical debate: that is, the uncertain status of the conceptual bridges from behavior (or from material remains) to the specifics of consciousness or mental states.

It is not until the temporal boundary between the upper and middle Paleolithic that unequivocal evidence of intentional and symbolic burials became available. By this time, Neanderthals had been all but completely replaced by modern *Homo sapiens sapiens*. It is here that we have much more convincing evidence of specific cognitive processes being involved in funeral rites.[8] I now turn to this time period.

2.2.2   The Less Ancient Past: The Upper Paleolithic

As we move into the upper Paleolithic period, the cloud of uncertainty begins to disperse and a culture of burials and grave rituals becomes much more distinct. Mithen (1994) pointed out that it was at the boundary between the middle and the upper Paleolithic that the world changed enormously. He suggested that the difference in the nature of the artifacts reflected a quantum leap in human cognitive abilities. He says (wisely noting that it is still debated whether this was a real change in culture or a change in paleoanthropological methodology) that:

> Changes in the archeological record that may reflect the first appearance of fully modern cognition appear after c. 50,000 BP with the start of the Upper Paleolithic. Most notably, we see the introduction of bone, antler and ivory technologies, the creation of personal ornaments and art, a greater degree of form imposed on stone tools, a more rapid turnover, of artefact [sic] types, greater degrees of hunting specialization and colonization of arid regions. (p. 32)

Specifically, the implications that such matters have for inferring attitudes about death not only become more explicit, but also more complex. One of

---

[8]Nothing here that I have said about the paucity or controversial nature of a Neanderthal or middle Paleolithic appreciation of death per se should be interpreted as an argument that such cognitive processes were absent in the "minds" of those subspecies of Homo. Rather, the point is that the evidence is not conclusive that an abstract concept of death was a part of their consciousness. In spite of the widespread acceptance by paleoanthropologists of the idea these middle Paleolithic burials were both intentional and ritual, a considerable amount of controversy concerning their meaning still exists among scholars of this period.

the most striking things about this period is that the Neanderthal population had become (or was becoming) extinct and the discovered remains were increasingly those left by modern humans—*Homo sapiens sapiens*. It was around 50,000 to 40,000 BP that these modern humans moving north from Africa began to occupy the European continent and, for reasons that are still controversial, take the place of the Neanderthals who had lived there for perhaps as long as 200,000 years.[9] At the very least, we do know that archeological evidence suggests that both subspecies overlapped to a considerable degree; indeed, both were present at roughly the same time in what may actually have even been the same caves in modern day Israel. If, how, or when they may have interacted, however, is still not known.

Whatever the cause of the eventual decline and disappearance of the Neanderthals, it is clear that sometime after 30,000 BP and before 20,000 BP they were completely gone from the paleoanthropological record. During this time, modern humans—*Homo sapiens sapiens*—had replaced them virtually around the world. This upper Paleolithic record in which the archeological traces of this, our, people extends across much of Europe and Russia to China, as well as in Africa, the locus of what is now generally agreed to be the original home of not only modern but all previous human forms. Furthermore, modern humans by this time had already populated much of the world including Australia and the northeastern regions of Asia. Clearly, the spread of *sapiens sapiens* was very rapid once they started to migrate out of Africa along a route that seems initially to have passed through the Middle East.

The human migration that emerged from Africa around 50,000 or 40,000 BP occurred during what is now considered to be the final stages of the last great ice age. The Neanderthals, who had been so well adapted for 2,000 centuries to the colder conditions, came under pressure from the more adaptable human subspecies as well as the changing environment. This time, better than any other, marks the beginning of the supremacy of *Homo sapiens sapiens* on our planet.

One fascinating question concerns the origins of modern humans. *Homo sapiens sapiens* did not spring fully evolved out of nothing; there are indications of modern forms of *Homo sapiens* that go back 100,000 years or more.

---

[9]Plausible answers to the question of what happened to the Neanderthals have mainly been forthcoming from two competing theories. On the one side are those who suggest they interbred with the modern sapiens human strain and thus "disappeared" only in the sense of becoming a part of modern humanity. On the other side are those who suggest modern humans were simply more successful at adapting to the changes that occurred in the postglacial world about 50,000 BP with their newer weapon technologies and cognitive skills. From this point of view, Neanderthals were simply less successful at the inevitable competition that must have occurred when two communities were trying to occupy the same ecological niche. Such a situation inevitably leads to extinction—the presumed fate of *Homo neanderthalensis* according to this theory.

(Even this antiquity ignores the previous 5 or 6 million years during which the various forms of hominids increasingly diverged from their common ancestral roots.) Some of the most exciting paleoanthropological discoveries of recent times were the unearthings of what appear to be essentially modern human fossils in the Klasies River mouth cave (Singer & Wymer, 1982), the Boomplaas cave (Deacon, 1979), and the Wonderwerk cave (Malan & Wells, 1943) in modern South Africa. These middle Paleolithic excavations were exceptional in that they produced fragments of bones that differed only slightly from the equivalent ones of both upper Paleolithic modern humans and, indeed, of us. All three of these cave sites, therefore, produced suggestive evidence of the existence of modern humans from as far back as 100,000 BP and possibly much further. None of these ancient *Homo sapiens sapiens* sites, however, showed any evidence of intentional burials or any other kind of artifacts.

The picture of the antiquity of modern humans is not simple, however. Remains of apparently modern humans have also been found further north in South Africa that may be from an even earlier time. The Border cave in the Zululand region has also provided some human remains of great antiquity. Butzer, Beaumont, and Vogel (1978) suggested that the modern humans found there may have been present as long ago as 195,000 BP. Recently, Vogel (2001) dated the previously mentioned Klasies River cave and Border cave remains over a time range that extends from 160,000 BP to 70,000 BP. This dating is not without its controversy, however, as other paleoanthropologists have suggested that they were, at the oldest, only (!) 100,000 years or so in age.

Some paleoanthropologists distinguish between archaic humans (*Homo sapiens*) and modern humans (*Homo sapiens sapiens*) as representing two distinguishable species or, at least, subspecies. The archaic form is often reputed to have emerged as long ago as 400,000 BP. Perhaps, like Neanderthals, it probably was an evolutionary descendent of their common ancestor—Homo erectus. The Klasies River people, however, were apparently fully modern and, thus, a member of the *sapiens sapiens* subgroup. It is not clear exactly when sapiens became *sapiens sapiens*, but it certainly must have been before the Klasies and Border cave people, perhaps as long ago as 200,000 BP but possibly as far back as 300,000 BP. A full review of the most ancient evidence for the existence of the even older archaic ancestors of modern humans can be found in Brauer (2001).

On the other hand, it should not be too surprising the emigration of essential modern humans from Africa at the beginning of the upper Paleolithic had to be based on an existing creature; as noted earlier, modern *Homo sapiens sapiens* must have evolved from some preexisting creature. Unfortunately none of these South African caves gave any indication of anything that could be used as a clue to the general cognitive capabilities of these early humans and specifically with regard to their attitudes—if any—toward death. In these ancient sites, only a few bone fragments were found and no evidence of artifacts, much less of intentional burials.

What we can be confident of is that modern humans very similar to the Klasies River people started to migrate north into Eurasia, most probably through the near east.[10] This migration may have begun as early as 100,000 BP. Such an early date is suggested by fragmentary remains of archaic forms of modern humans in the Skhul caves near modern Haifa in Israel (McCown & Keith, 1939) that have now been dated to 90,000 BP. Whenever it started, the modern human migration was certainly in full swing into Europe no later than 40,000 BP as evidenced by the massive dispersion of archeological sites found throughout all of the Eurasian continent that date later than that time.

One possibility is that there may have been multiple dispersal events. There may have been an earlier wave of migration than the one into Europe about 40,000 BP. There is disputed evidence that a modern skull obtained from Lake Mungo in Australia dated to a period that may be ancient as 71,000 BP (Thorne et al., 1999).

This early date for the Lake Mungo finds opens up another area of controversy. It may have been that the migration into Europe did not come directly through the eastern shores of the Mediterranean (the Levant) as usually suggested. Rather, the population of Europe may have occurred as a side shoot of an earlier migration that mainly went along the coastal areas of Arabia, India, and Malaysia. This would account for the very early dates of some of the remains in Eastern Europe as well as the extremely ancient dates of the Lake Mungo finds. Indeed, some Malayan modern human tools have been found and arguably dated to 74,000 BP in the debris from a volcanic eruption. If these dates are correct, then modern humans did not dis-

---

[10]The "out of Africa" interpretation, which I consider here as the most plausible scenario, is not, however, without its critics. The antithetical theory is that modern humans evolved independently several times in several different locations around the world. It is certain that hominids of one kind or another were widely spread throughout the world long before this final dispersion of modern humans. The Javanese and Peking varieties of Homo erectus (an archaic form of hominid) date from as far back as a half a million years BP. An earlier find of Homo erectus in Dmansi in the Republic of Georgia has recently been reported (Vekua et al., 2002); it dates from 1.7 million years BP. Clearly, some forms of early humans had already left Africa and had populated almost all of the world with the exception of the Americas by the time Homo sapiens sapiens migrated.

A finer level of disagreement concerns the route by which this African migration of Homo sapiens sapiens took place. The conventional assumption is that it took place through modern Sinai, Israel, and Lebanon. However, the obstacles provided by the Sahara Desert suggest it may have been through modern Eritrea across the Red Sea and up along the coast of Arabia. This scenario suggests that Europe was actually populated through the Tigris–Euphrates valley. See also the discussion on the Malayan and Australian finds that are dated to times more than 70,000 years ago that further complicate the analysis.

perse first to Europe but initially went through south Asia to Australia. Other findings (Lahr & Foley, 1994) suggest that the coastal migration occurred possibly as early as 100,000 BP. The possibility of an early (i.e., older than 40,000 BP) direct migration from some part of Africa to Australia, therefore, cannot be rejected out of hand.

A relatively precise date for the most significant migration of *Homo sapiens sapiens* into Europe, however, is not disputed. Among the earliest European evidence of *Homo sapiens sapiens* occupation that have been reliably dated are the fragmentary human remains found in the Bacho Kiro site in what is now modern day Bulgaria. Kozlowski (1996) concluded that these were modern humans dated from as long ago as 43,000 BP. Other less certain dates of 46,000 BP have been attributed to other nearby Bulgarian sites, for example, those at Temnata Dupka. Given the proximity of Eastern Europe to the likely path through the Near East,[11] this early date for these sites makes sense.

By 40,000 BP, it is certain that the migration had spread modern humans over most of the rest of Europe. Caves in Spain (El Castillo) and in the Don River and Ural Mountain areas of modern Russia have also been attributed to shortly after or contemporaneous with the Bacho Kiro site. This was clear evidence of the rapid dispersion of African *sapiens sapiens* people over all of Europe and, subsequently to Asia, ultimately coming to the Americas around 12,000 BP across a land bridge that joined Siberia and Alaska at that time.

Throughout the 30 millennia following 40,000 BP, the archeological grave remains became more and more complex, artistic, and expressive of ever more intricate ritual. The implications, although still strained, about the cognitive process of early humans became more direct. This 30,000-year-long period corresponds to the latter 10,000 years of the middle Paleolithic and 20,000 years of the upper Paleolithic period in Europe and is usually divided up into the following periods, each of which is characterized by its own cultural artifacts (mainly based on a stone tool typology) rather than by a distinctive anatomy or geological stratigraphy:

- The Aurignacian—40,000 BP to 30,000 BP
- The Gravettian—30,000 BP to 22,000 BP
- The Solutrean—22,000 BP to 18,000 BP
- The Magdalenian—18,000 BP to 11,000 BP[12]

---

[11]Stringer (2000) also supports the theory that the population of Europe actually was a side shoot of the coastal migration through south Asia.

[12]Paleoanthropologists sometimes allude to two additional periods. The first was Chatelperronian defined as the period from about 32,000 BP to 27,000 BP. However, any remains associated with this culture are now thought to be the product of a late Neanderthal group. Quite pos-

It is in this 30,000-year period that we first find compelling evidence of a cognitive awareness of the significance of death. It is here also that the first glimmerings of a nascent dualism appear in the traces of modern human culture and presumably in the thoughts of people who, for all practical purposes, were certainly anatomically and arguably cognitively modern. However uncertain we may be of the intentionality of Neanderthal burials, all doubts must be cast aside after the onset of the "Out of Africa" migration. In addition to single burials, cemeteries (groups of graves) have been discovered that add credence to the idea that the people of that time had highly refined theories about the meaning of death and how it should be confronted. Less direct, but also suggestive of a high level of cognitive ability are the vast assemblage of objects that probably had some symbolic roles. Sometimes these are associated with death rituals, but, at the very least, they suggest the existence of increasingly diverse kinds of abstract thought.

The story is obviously complex and gets increasingly intricate as more and more discoveries are made, many of which are still inadequately dated. Nevertheless, there is an emerging sequence that does make sense. So let's begin with what is considered the archetype of modern humans—the Cro-Magnon people. The term Cro-Magnon has come to be virtually synonymous with all prehistoric *Homo sapiens sapiens* living throughout the Euro-Asian region. The original Cro-Magnon excavations, however, specifically refer to the remains found near the village of St. Eyzies in modern day France at a site being excavated for a new railway station. The Cro-Magnon human remains, which were originally reported by Lartet (1868) long before the Bacho Kiro discovery, have been reliably dated to 37,000 BP. The skeletons were found in several arguably decorated graves. However, to this day, it is not certain if the seashells, flint tools, and other grave goods were actually ceremonial offerings or were simply items that had been scattered about in the neighborhood of the actual burial site.

The discovery of the Cro-Magnon people of Saint Eyzies in 1868 was an immediate scientific sensation coming as it did only a decade after the publication of Darwin's (1859) bombshell *On the Origin of Species by Means of Natural Selection* and virtually contemporaneously with the even more shocking *The Descent of Man and Selection in Relation to Sex* (Darwin, 1871). These were heady times for paleoanthropology, indeed! In the very same year that Lartet published his discovery, other scientists were already discussing the implications of this extraordinary find. Broca (1868), the great

---

sibly, as noted earlier, the relatively advanced objects found associated with this period may have been borrowed from contemporary Cro-Magnons. The second supplementary period is defined as the Azilian era and is presumed by some to have lasted from about 9000 BP to 8000 BP. It is now lumped with the Mesolithic period that followed the upper Paleolithic with which we are concerned here.

neuroanatomist of speech, and Pruner-Bey (1868), an eminent although reputedly racist, anthropologist of the time, immediately published articles interpreting the Cro-Magnon burials based on Lartet's descriptions. Indeed, the find was so important that the cultural style and remains observed in the Cro-Magnon graves at St. Eyzies defined both what came to be known as the Aurignacian culture type and the modern Eurasian human anatomical type. They were also among the first, if not the earliest, signs of ritual burials by European *Homo sapiens sapiens*.[13]

Perhaps 7,000 to 10,000 years more recent than the original Cro-Magnon finds were the Grimaldi caves found near the modern border of France and Italy (Riviere, 1887). One grave was especially interesting. The skeletons of two children had been extensively decorated with tooled seashells and animal teeth. There was ample evidence that these graves had been intentional given the number of shells and teeth that had been pierced to construct these complicated and probably very valuable necklaces.

In addition, the graves had been liberally sprinkled with ochre. The use of burial ochre, itself, is an interesting story. This mineral has a long history of being associated with burials from early Neanderthal times through the middle and upper Paleolithic as well as in modern human burials in the Neolithic period. Sprinklings of ochre have been found in the burials of many different cultures, including those in the Americas and Australia. Why it is so ubiquitous in burials can only be guessed at. However, one speculation is that the red color of the material reminded people of blood and this might have been a presumed means of providing replenishment of this "vital juice" following a traumatic or fatal injury.

An even more extraordinary Aurignacian Cro-Magnon gravesite from a slightly later time was found in 1956 at Sungir northeast of Moscow in modern Russia (Bader, 1978). It has been dated to a period variously estimated from about 30,000 BP to about 25,000 BP. The most amazing aspect of this group of five buried individuals was the extraordinary amount of grave "jewelry" attached to the skeletal remains. Necklaces, pendants, other bone and tusk artifacts, as well as huge numbers of pierced beads had been placed on or around the skeletons. One adolescent boy was buried with 4,900 ivory beads and a young preadolescent girl with 5,200 beads. Obviously, an enormous amount of time and effort went into the decoration of these children's corpses at the time of their death. Equally obvious, was the special significance of this effort filled ritual; that significance can best be

---

[13]Whether the St. Eyzies people were the originators of the Aurignacian culture is also still an open question. It has been suggested that the flint tools of the type found there actually represented a culture that had been imported from further east in Europe.

interpreted as an appreciation or, at least, a hope for a continuing life for which they should be suitably attired.[14]

The Gravettian period saw continued development of grave rituals as evidence in many east European sites. In 1986, three *Homo sapiens sapiens* skeletons dating from about 27,000 BP were discovered near the village of Dolni Vestonice in modern Czechoslovakia (Klima, 1995). Here again, there was an extraordinary abundance of grave objects. Necklaces of dog's teeth and ivory and even what may have been a painted mask decorated one of the three skeletons. The bodies of the three had also been extensively sprinkled with red ochre, a ritual that was becoming usual rather than rare. Gravettian sites such as these provided some of the earliest evidence of ceramics including small figurines and shards that had impressions of woven material. Other Gravettian sites were particularly interesting because early forms of what appear to be religious art began to appear here in large numbers. Female figurines called "Venus figures" dating from this time have been excavated in huge numbers across all of Europe.[15] These figures have regularly been described as fertility symbols because of their exaggerated bosoms and buttocks.

During the next two epochs, the Solutrean and the Magdalenian, archeological sites become ever more numerous and the evidence for burial rituals ever more clear. Beyond the artifacts of the graves, these periods saw the beginning and eventual development to extraordinarily high levels of two- and three-dimensional art.

This brief sampling provides what is at best an incomplete list of a few of the major middle and upper Paleolithic sites in which grave decorations indicating some kind of intentional ritual and a well developed appreciation of the brevity of life have been unearthed. However uncertain the intentionality of some of the older burials may have been, there is no question that about 40,000 BP there was a major behavioral and, quite possibly, an associated cognitive revolution. At the very least, there was a quantum leap of complexity of burials and associated rituals at the very most, death indisputatively became a cognitive reality. As such, questions were raised

---

[14]An interesting speculation has recently been attributed to M. Stiner of the University of Arizona concerning bead adornments, particularly of perforated shells. She suggests that beads were not just decorations but were a means of communicating status as a result of the increasing human population.

[15]Among the oldest of the Venus Goddess figurines was the now famous Venus of Willendorf discovered in 1908 (Szombathy, 1909). It is currently dated as having been carved between 26,000 BP and 24,000 BP. Interestingly, an almost identical "Venus" was found in Gagrino on the Don in Russia dating from about this same period. A question is, therefore, raised about the interactions between these widely separated peoples.

and answers proposed, the latter including the roots of supernatural dualisms that are the foundations of modern religions.

2.3 CONCLUSION

In this chapter, I am concerned about the significance of prehistoric burials of the middle and upper Paleolithic epochs as they pertain to the evolving concept of death. The awareness that life cannot be indefinitely prolonged coupled with the preciousness of an individual's own consciousness led to a fear of death according to the logic spelled out in chapter 1. This ubiquitous dread and the emerging hope that there was some kind of an escape hatch from the inevitability of the termination of one's corporeal existence was, I argue, the key instigating factor in the invention of the supernatural and the subsequent development of modern religions. Death fears gave rise to a dualist approach to the nature of reality including the fundamental idea of the immortality of the mind/soul. There was no denying the obvious fact that the body did not survive long after the cessation of the life processes, so a huge proportion of human ingenuity was directed at providing an explanation that preserved the invisible, but intrapersonally universal, evidence of one's own mental life. These were extraordinary developments in cognitive evolution—the awareness of, followed by a fear of death, and the subsequent invention of an immortal mind existing in a separate and distinct kind of reality to assuage that fear.

Why should such a cognitive development have occurred at this time, whether it is as early as 100,000 BP (unlikely) or around 40,000 BP when there was much stronger evidence of intentional and ritual burials? The answer to this question can reasonably be interpreted in terms of an evolutionary leap in the cognitive powers of this particular branch of the tree of Homo evolution. Notwithstanding the long history of tool making, something occurred at about this time that allowed humans to think not only in terms of material artifacts and objects, but also in terms of abstract, intangible, and transcendent entities such as mind, death, pictures, and symbolic representations of many different kinds.

There is, therefore, in all of these paleoanthropological findings ample additional evidence that transcendental cognitive processes took an enormous evolutionary leap sometime after 50,000 BP. For example, the development of artistic expression[16] began to appear at about 30,000 BP in the

---

[16]It is important to appreciate here that not all art represents a step into the supernatural. Pictures of animals and maps can both serve useful practical functions without invoking anything other than a kind of symbolic representation. Decoration of practical objects also can appeal to an incipient aesthetic sense without supernatural overtones. This is not to say that such symbolisms may not eventually become associated with supernatural concepts, but rather that they need not.

transition time from the middle to the upper Paleolithic period. Indeed, many authorities (e.g., Chase & Dibble, 1987; Lindly & Clark, 1990) in the field have concluded that there is virtually no evidence of any kind of symbolic behavior prior to the boundary to the middle and upper Paleolithic periods. This is so despite the fact, as we see in this chapter, that anatomically modern *Homo sapiens sapiens* may have been present 100,000 years earlier. Of course, the older sites are much less numerous than the newer ones and new discoveries may eventually suggest otherwise. For example, a new report by Henshilwood et al. (2002) described an extraordinary new find of some middle Paleolithic abstract art consisting of regular patterns of scratches on pieces of red ochre that date to 70,000 BP. If the date is confirmed and if this was not just an atypical and isolated event, we would have to reconsider the dating of early symbolic representation and, thus, of the probable date that the great leap of cognitive evolution took place.

Not even the upper Paleolithic cave art[17] dating from the Magdalenian period, as abundant and sometimes magnificently creative as it was, must necessarily be interpreted to be an indication that this enormous growth of cognitive and intellectual powers dealt directly with death. Some of this art, quite to the contrary, may have had a very different orientation, toward life or fertility, or with the need to develop some supernatural or, for that matter, natural assistance with hunting. Graves, however, speak specifically to death, the fear of death, and what happens after death.

Tattersall (1997) described the significance of the Cro-Magnon, Sungir, and the other intentional burials of the upper Paleolithic as follows.

> First, in all human societies known to practice it, burial of the dead with grave goods (and the ritual invariably associated with placing such objects in the grave) indicates a belief in an afterlife: the goods are there because they will be useful to the deceased in the future. Grave goods need not necessarily be everyday items, although everything found at Sungir might have been, since personal adornment seems to be a basic human urge expressed by the Cro-Magnons to the fullest. Nevertheless, whether or not some of the Sungir artifacts were made specifically to be used in burial rituals, what is certain is that the knowledge of inevitable death and spiritual awareness are closely linked. In Cro-Magnon burials there is ample evidence for both. It is here that we have the most ancient incontrovertible evidence for the existence of religious experience. (pp. 10–11)

This is the point of this chapter; within the time period discussed, we have the first evidence that a primeval cognitive awareness of death

---

[17]The spectacular paintings at Chauvet, and Lascaux in France and Altamira in Spain, have usually been dated to the Magdalenian period (18,000–11,000 BP). However, some new evidence suggests that the Chauvet paintings may come from a period 10,000 years earlier—about 31,000 BP.

emerged and a proto-dualism evolved. These cognitive processes, there-fore, have an enormous antiquity in human existence. From these roots grew advanced philosophical dualisms as well as the ubiquitous religions that are accepted by the vast majority of modern humans. Later it will be shown how a pervasive and cryptic dualist assumption in our scientific thinking muddies the theoretical statements of mentalist psychologies.

The mere antiquity of these death fears does not by itself, it may be ar-gued, uniquely justify acceptance of the more sophisticated dualisms that were to follow. Nevertheless, it can be argued that these ancient and com-pelling attitudes produce a nearly universal pressure toward inventing a so-lution that solves the very human problem posed by the day-to-day obser-vations of a finite bodily existence. As we see in the next chapter, the Paleolithic proto-dualism led inexorably to the more sophisticated dual-isms, rituals, and full-blown religions of later times. Indeed, an argument can be and is being made that a primeval fear of death still controls a huge amount of human activity and thought, not only including all religions—all of which are characterized by some concept of the immortality of the mind–soul—but also in more secular aspects of human existence.

Finally, in concluding this chapter, a comment about the uncertainty at-tached to any inferences about the mind or behavior drawn from archeo-logical evidence must be reiterated. The story presented here is replete with controversies, contradictory interpretations, ambiguous findings, inap-propriate logical leaps, and debates based on what are sometimes terribly inadequate data and flawed assumptions. Some of the most fundamental questions have not yet been incontrovertibly answered. Answers for even some of the most concrete of these questions simply are not yet at hand, much less for some of the intangible ones listed at the beginning of this chapter. For example, paleoanthropologists still debate one class of ques-tion for which answers should ultimately be possible. This class includes those of such gigantic import for our understanding of human history as:

- Did modern humans evolve in Africa and then spread from there or did they evolve several times in several different places?
- When and where did *Homo sapiens sapiens* first appear?
- Did Neanderthals coexist with modern humans?
- Did Neanderthals go extinct because of competition with modern hu-mans or did they simply disappear into the modern gene pool by inter-breeding?
- When did symbolic representation first appear?

How much more difficult it is to answer questions of a different class that deal, not directly with material traces, but with inferences that grandly leap from material remains to assumed behavior to thought processes such as:

- • When did humans first become aware of death?
- • When did humans invent the concept of the supernatural?
- • Did the fear of death lead to the concept of the supernatural?
- • What does a particular behavior mean in terms of the associated thought processes?

The first of these two classes of question can, in principle, be answered with certainty as more and more data is accumulated. The second class, however, requires conceptual, logical, and inferential leaps that are quite different in kind and are likely to be contentious for a much longer period. In the next chapter, however, the conceptual and inferential leaps from physical evidence to what people are thinking are much shorter. The artifacts of the Neolithic period and metal ages are both much more numerous and explicit. The archeology of these subsequent times provides clear evidence of the continuing development of complex religions from the primitive fear of death and proto-dualisms that probably first emerged in middle Paleolithic times and that was clearly evidenced in the archeology of the upper Paleolithic. We now take this next step in the prehistory of the mind.

3

The Neolithic Archeology of Dualism

3.1 THE ROOTS OF CIVILIZATION

Chapter 2 shows how a critical boundary in time, culture, and presumably cognitive skills, demarcated the middle and the upper Paleolithic periods, respectively. Somewhere around 40,000 years ago several important events occurred. One was the migration out of Africa of *Homo sapiens sapiens* to most of the rest of the Eurasian continents. Although this subspecies had apparently been present in Africa for many tens of thousands of years prior to this great migration, it was not until this time that massive cultural changes occurred that clearly distinguished what we have referred to as the middle Paleolithic from the subsequent upper Paleolithic. This was a critical time in human prehistory, not just because of the great migration but also in terms of our concern with the evolution of human thought concerning death.

The upper Paleolithic was an important part of our story because likely it was at that time that humans first became aware of the nature of death. It is during this period evidence is indisputable that humans buried their dead and, more important for present purposes, ritualized their burials. An intentional burial with grave goods is the primary piece of evidence of Paleolithic cognitive awareness of what bodily death signified. Such an interpretation, of course, is also premised on the existence of a sense of self or of consciousness, for which no direct evidence can be forthcoming.[1] Nev-

---

[1]This statement may be disputed by pointing out that tools and weapons of various kinds had long been made by Homo sapiens sapiens and their predecessors. However, it is possible to imagine how such utilitarian devices may have been made without an explicit conceptual awareness of one's own self and the eventuality of death. Whatever the implications and uncertainties of such theories, the one indisputable fact is that there is no indisputable evidence of self-consciousness and a fear of death until the upper Paleolithic period.

ertheless, if we give these early humans the same credit we give to our-selves, then it is but a short step to the suggestion that not only were they aware of death, but they were also afraid of it. The argument presented here is, quite simply, that this awareness and fear of death led to the postu-lation of specific remedies to what must have been a totally unsatisfactory concept of an all-too-limited mortality. Almost universally, that remedy was formulated in terms of a separate bodily and mental existence—a proto-typical dualism.

The exact story of the emergence of the supernatural, in general, and dual-ism, in particular, is still clouded by many uncertainties. Not the least of these uncertainties is the leap that must be made from material remains to the then extant cognitive processes. Whatever the limitations of the strategy of inferring cognitive processes from material remains, there is no question that a considerable amount of additional evidence of human thought proc-esses appeared in the next, but still prehistoric, period of human existence—the Neolithic era. Indeed, sometime near the end of the upper Paleolithic a series of extraordinary cultural developments occurred that were so influen-tial they revolutionized human society. This transition probably occurred over several thousand years. Collectively, however, they defined a boundary at about 9,000 or 10,000 years BP between the last stages of the Old Stone Age—the upper Paleolithic period we discussed in the previous chapter—and the Neolithic period that is the topic of this chapter.

An intermediate period between the Paleolithic and Neolithic eras is sometimes invoked as the Mesolithic epoch. This middle period repre-sented cultures that were a mixture of the traits of both the predecessor and successor eras. The main criterion for invoking the Mesolithic interval was the fact that, as far as we know, there was no fired pottery used during this time. Other characteristics of the Neolithic stage of human develop-ment, however, were becoming widespread.

As usual, in a field in which inferences must be drawn from sometimes incomplete or barely suggestive remains, there is considerable controversy and uncertainty about the timing of any of the particular cultural inventions that are now to be discussed. However uncertain some of the dates men-tioned may be, even if they were spread over a period of 2,000 or 3,000 years, these enormous changes in life style were the key factors in provid-ing a technological and social foundation for what later scholars would re-fer to as *civilization*. Indeed, it is quite probable that the "invention" of each of these major cultural activities or objects was not a singular event that could be attributable to a single person or even a single place. For example, "amber waves of grain" did not suddenly blossom across the countryside. Rather, agriculture was an innovation that, like most others, was an accu-mulation of small discoveries and insights, that occurred in many places si-multaneously, that took advantage of particular local wild crops, and that may have taken millennia to become institutionalized in the form of exclusively agricultural life styles.

Let us now consider these cultural and technological inventions that were to define the Neolithic period. The most significant of them include:

1. The archetypical invention of the Neolithic period, of course, was the development of techniques to grind and polish stone tools rather than simply to chip them out of a larger rock by pressure flaking—the method that had previously characterized all of the Paleolithic subperiods. Grave objects and other remains from the Gravettian period on began to be characterized by stunning renderings of the human figure and other artifacts that reflected a whole new way of working with stone. By the Paleolithic–Neolithic boundary period stone working had gone through a complete revolution, so much so that it led to the designation of the Neolithic by modern archeologists and paleoanthropologists as an entirely new period of human prehistory.

2. Closely associated with new stone working techniques was the revolution in food acquisition. Prior to the Paleolithic–Neolithic boundary, humans were primarily hunter–gatherers. Somewhere around 10,000 BP,[2] however, humans began to domesticate crops at culturally significant levels. That is, Neolithic humans began about this time to intentionally plant and harvest plants rather than to just gather what had been fortuitously grown. The impact of such a cultural invention cannot be underestimated. It meant that food would be available on a much more dependable basis and that some members of the community could be committed to other activities than hunting and gathering. It also meant that the nomadic existence of the Paleolithic hunter–gatherers would have to be at least partially replaced by a more sedentary life style so that crops in a particular location could be attended to for at least part of the year. Thus, the planting of seeds for food also planted the seeds of modern urban civilization. Both plant roots and residential roots could now be put down. What was the first domesticated crop?

---

[2]As is usual in the study of prehistory, this figure has now been disputed. There is some modern evidence that rye may have been cultivated as early as 13,000 BP even though full-blown agriculture did not commence until millennia later. Rice, also, may have a much longer history than the 6500 BP date usually suggested. The evidence for any specific date is scant and, in principle, negative. That is, the "discovery date" depends on the absence of earlier findings. Even more profoundly, there may be no specific evidence available simply because most crop "remains" would be ephemeral. Agriculture may have developed slowly and continuously from what may be trivial and untraceable beginnings. Perhaps it would be better to look for a marker such as the beginning of "settled agriculture" rather than the first planned plantings. Certainly, the evidence for an agricultural revolution in the Mesolithic or Neolithic eras is much greater during those periods than in earlier ones. What is also certain is that climatic and other changes occurring around 10,000 BP were concomitant with an enormous number of significant changes in human life style. One of the most important of these was the transition to settled agricultural communities.

Given the perishability of plant materials, it is difficult to definitively answer this question but millet, wheat, barley, and rye have all been suggested as the pioneering crop.

3. Occurring in the archeological records at about this same time was the first evidence of animal husbandry—the domestication of other creatures to do the bidding of the Neolithic humans. Wild pigs and wolves (ultimately to become dogs) seem to have been the pioneering companions for humans and dogs, in particular, may have predated this period. Reindeer also seemed to have been domesticated as early as the Paleolithic–Neolithic boundary.

4. The technology of weapons and tools also took a gigantic leap about 10,000 BP. The first evidence for the bow and arrow and the spear thrower appear in the archeological record at this time suggesting that they were probably invented near the end of the upper Paleolithic. These weapons gave the Neolithic hunters enormous additional power. It has been proposed that these new tools ultimately permitted small numbers of hunters to do so well in their hunting that additional opportunities developed for some of the population to be diverted to other skills and trades. Agricultural tools, such as stone sickle blades that could be set in wooden handles, also begin to appear in the archeological record at the Paleolithic–Neolithic boundary greatly adding to the productivity of a smaller band of agriculturalists than had previously been required to sustain life.

5. As agricultural and hunting efficiency increased, Neolithic humans did not have to move about as had been required by the depletion of naturally occurring local resources. There was, therefore, a growing tendency to stay put in favored locations. This semipermanent, albeit quasi-nomadic, existence provided the necessary stability for the beginning of social organizations and settled village life. Clans and families as well as leaders and chiefs became almost inevitable, as did more elaborate, albeit semipermanent, residences.

6. Woven woolen cloth (suggesting an early domestication of sheep or goats) also appears in the archeological record about 10,000 BP. The invention of cloth was a significant milestone in dress. Heavy, inflexible animal skins could then be replaced by much lighter and more flexible, but still warm, man-made materials.

7. The Neolithic era was also the period at which baked pottery made its earliest appearance in the archeological record. The invention of pottery is sometimes attributed to the early Japanese, but given its widespread dispersion during the middle and later Neolithic period, it is likely that baked clay containers represented another example of simultaneous invention. Many Neolithic sites, however, did not contain pottery remains until as late as 7000 BP. Indeed the earliest millennia of the Neolithic period are typically designated by paleoarcheologists as PPN—*Pre Pottery Neolithic*.

8. The use of sun-dried bricks in the construction of semipermanent houses was another important early Neolithic development. Residences could then become more permanent structures rather than the temporary huts and tents that were constructed during the nomadic Paleolithic era. The casual use of fortuitously available, preexisting caves was largely replaced during this time by concern for the design and construction of dwellings, an incipient form of architecture.

9. Throughout the Neolithic period, there is a progression in the size and complexity of houses and the number that was gathered together into more permanent communities. These semipermanent "villages" evolved later into the great cities of the world. There is dispute about what is the oldest community that could be called a city but the usual contenders are Jericho in modern Israel, Jarmo in modern Kurdistan, and Catal Hulyuk in modern Turkey. The proposed settlement dates for these communities are approximately 9000 BP, 8800 BP, and 8500 BP, respectively. Whichever was first is almost incidental. What is important is that about this time the agricultural and technical developments made it possible for the first time for stable communities of significant numbers of people to be established. It is important to appreciate that the dynamic of village and then city growth depended on a large number of factors including the technological one we have been discussing, but also climatic changes, and the accident of living in a clement region.

10. Considerable evidence of commerce and trade appears in the Neolithic archeological record. Sometimes this was merely in the form of a stone or a shell that had to come from a distant location. In other instances, the vestigial traces of the trade of other items, such as particular kinds of pottery not locally available, were uncovered in the archeological remains.

11. A major aspect of Neolithic life was its enormous dispersion. Archeological sites with traces of human habitation are found over virtually the entire earth. The Neolithic period was a time of enormous dispersion of humans including the previously uninhabited Americas.[3]

12. During the Neolithic period, compelling evidence of a vast increase in the complexity of burials, proto-religions, and views of the supernatural ap-

---

[3]The time at which the earliest Americans appeared is another area deeply enmeshed in controversy. The usual assumption has been that around 12,000 BP Asian people came across the Bering straits. The first undisputed traces (e.g., weapon points) of Native Americans are from the Clovis (New Mexico) culture and are dated to about this time. However, a few disputed sites suggest a much earlier arrival or perhaps several different waves of migration into the Americas. One of the best known of these pre-Clovis sites is the Meadowcroft rock shelter in Pennsylvania (Adovasio, Gunn, Donahue, & Stuckenrath, 1978). Radiocarbon dates there have suggested an antiquity that may be as old as 19,000 BP. However, this antiquity has been challenged by Haynes (1980) among others and then re-refuted by Adovasio, Gunn, Donahue, Stuckenrath, Guilday, and Volman (1980). Other even older (25,000 BP) settlement by seafarers from southeastern Asia or Polynesia is even more speculative. The question of pre-Clovis Native Americans is still a matter of debate.

pear. Along with the continuing evolution of cities from agricultural villages came a progressive increase in the complexity of tombs and graves. For the first time, graves were not simply hollows dug out wherever they could be, perhaps enhanced with a few stones, and perhaps including simple decorations or offerings. Rather, they became formidable structures themselves sometimes accompanied by or constructed of great stones now referred to as Megaliths. The size of some of these monster rocks still defies adequate explanation of how they may have been shaped and moved by people who had no cranes, wheels, or any of the other familiar devices that provide mechanical advantage. Rituals of death were no longer simple matters of interring bodies, but of complex ancestor worship and other elaborate rites. What had been, at best, a few Paleolithic fertility or death cults evolved into much more sophisticated versions of the relationship between humans and the unseen world of the supernatural including much more elaborate views of the afterlife. During this period, there was an ever-increasing use of symbols and representations of entities that were obviously thought of as being supernatural (i.e., of Gods and Goddesses who had to be dealt with in terms of icons and effigies). Religion at this time, according to some scholars, may have been transitioning from a purely cult-like utilitarian stage to one in which elaborate myths of the kind Cauvin (2000) referred to as a "general theory of a self-regulating world" (p. 209). Accompanying this increasing conceptual complexity was an increase in the commitment of physical space to the supernatural. Shrines, temples, other buildings, and even single specialized rooms in one's domicile totally dedicated to the religious beliefs become commonplace in Neolithic times.

Clearly not all of these developments occurred at exactly the same time. It was a complex process in which some early steps were taken prior to the full flowering of Neolithic culture. For example, there is new evidence that villages or communities of hunter–gatherers occurred 2,000 years before plants and animals were domesticated. Perrot (1966), for example, has excavated and described such a village in early Neolithic Israel. This intermediate culture of semisedentary hunter–gatherers has sometimes been referred to as the Natufian culture (circa 10,000 BP) (as well as the Mesolithic) and represents either the last vestiges of the Paleolithic, the first instantiation of the Neolithic, or much more likely, a period of continuous transformation between both.[4]

These observations of the physical changes that occurred during the transition from the Paleolithic to the Neolithic were accompanied by what can only be interpreted as coincident cognitive changes. Chief among those

---

[4]It must not be forgotten that all periods of human life are arbitrary designations and demarcate not sharp boundaries but gradual periods of progressive change.

for which we have evidence were the substantial developments in religious thinking. It is to the topic of Neolithic religious ideas, particularly with regard to the existence of an afterlife and the increasingly formal dualistic ideas, to which we now turn. By examining the evolution of such ideas during this period, we see how the Paleolithic proto-dualism grew into the widespread and increasingly elaborate religions of Neolithic times. All of the problems of interpretation and inference concerning what people were thinking, of course, still remain. The examination of this phase of prehistory must still be carried out on the basis of material remains without the aid of historic records: Writing was yet to be invented. However, the archeological evidence is so extensive that a much clearer picture now begins to emerge from the gloom of prehistory of what people were thinking about the supernatural. What is clear is that much of this thinking was aimed at the idea of a kind of supernatural afterlife. Again, the best evidence for this conclusion comes from the increasingly sophisticated burial cultures that were in the process of evolving during the Neolithic period.

3.2 NEOLITHIC BURIALS

Neolithic burials, like those from the Paleolithic, are still among the most important pieces of evidence and the most compellingly suggestive indications of the cognitive processing of information concerning death. Dualism, the basic concept of the continuation of some kind of mental existence after death, was becoming much easier to accept as the dominant philosophy of human life in the "New Stone Age" epoch. In this period, the simple, sparse, and infrequent internment goods of the upper Paleolithic period were succeeded by much more complex and abundant materials. This reflects an increasing commitment to the idea of some kind of afterlife by the Neolithic successors to the Old Stone Age people. Foods, weapons, household tools, containers, jewelry, and ceremonial objects such as animal skulls are now to be found in abundance in addition to human skeletal remains. Although the earliest entombments, as already noted, usually did not contain ceramics, by the middle of the Neolithic period fired pottery became a common part of burial material.

This brings us to another important aspect of Neolithic burials—their remarkable ubiquity. By Neolithic times, people had populated virtually all areas of the planet and, as a result, their remains, both skeletal and artifactual, are found worldwide nowadays. Virtually every area of the world, including the Americas and Siberia, is now found to contain graves of varying degrees of complexity ranging from simple pit burials to complex tombs. Table 3.1 provides some sense of the number of sites that have been discovered and excavated just in the Middle East. Obviously, modern hu-

TABLE 3.1

Cauvin's (2000) Tabulation of the Locations and Dates of Only a Small Sample
(From the Near East) of the Neolithic Burial Sites That Have Been Discovered to Date

Calibrated dates BC	Radiocarbon dates BP	Maison de l'Orient periods	Western Anatolia	Central Anatolia	Phoenician (coast) and Cyprus	Arid zone of the Southern Levant Transjordan Negev–Sinai	Jordan valley Damascus basin	Middle Euphrates	Eastern Taurus	Syrian Desert	Sinjar	Zagros
	7000 BP	6	Ilıpınar	Hacılar	Larnou pottery cultures	YARMUKIAN	NOMADS ?	Sabi Abyad	?	ACERAMIC Neolithic nomads	HASSUNA CULTURE	ACERAMIC of the ZAGROS
6000					Amoq A–B Ras Shamra VB–A Byblos Early Neolithic	Shaar Ha Golan 'Ain Ghazal		Abu Hureyra 2C Damishliya		El Kowm 2 "PNA"	Kúltepe (nomads) Sotto Umm Dabaghiyah	Jarmo
	7600 BP	5		Çatalhöyük	KHIROKITIA CULTURE	Final PPNB of the Black Desert 'Ain Ghazal 'PPNC'				Final PPNB sedentary: El Kowm 2 nomads: Qdeir 1		
7000					Late PPNB Shillourokambos Labwe Ras Shamra VC Tell aux Scies	Late PPNB 'Ain Ghazal	Late PPNB Abu Gosh Ramad I–II Beisamoun	Late PPNB Tell Assouad? Abu Hureyra 2B Halula		Late PPNB Bouqras	Late PPNB of the Sinjar Magzalia	Aceramic Jarmo Ali Kosh Gani Dareh
	8000 BP	4		ASIKLI CULTURE			Middle PPNB of Palestine Jericho PPNB Munhata	Middle PPNB Abu Hureyra 2A Halula Mureybet IV B	PPNB of the Taurus Cafer Höyük Nevali Çori Çayönü			
8000				?				Early PPNB Mureybet IV A	Basal Çayönü		NEMRIKIAN Nemrik	? Zawi Chemi Shanidar
	8600 BP	3					SULTANIAN Jericho PPNA Netiv Hagdud	Late MUREYBETIAN Mureybet III B Cheikh Hassan, Jerf el Ahmar	?			
9000					KHIAMIAN of Lebanon Sables de Beyrouth	Khiamian Abu Madi I (Levels 5–12)	Jericho 'protoneolithic'	Early MUREYBETIAN Mureybet III A			QERMEZIAN Qermez Dere	
	9600 BP	2					KHIAMIAN El Khiam, Salibiyeh IX Hatoula	KHIAMIAN Mureybet II Mureybet I B	Hallam Cemi Tepesi			
10,000						Recent NATUFIAN of the Negev	Final NATUFIAN Tor Abou Sif	Final NATUFIAN Mureybet I A Abu Hureyra I C				
	10,300 BP	1			Late NATUFIAN of Lebanon Sables de Beyrouth Saayideh	Rosh Zin Rosh Horesha	Late NATUFIAN Eynam, upper levels	Late NATUFIAN Abu Hureyra I A–B	?			Zawi Chemi Shanidar
11,000							Early NATUFIAN Eynan El Wad Hayonim	Early MUREYBETIAN Early NATUFIAN		Early NATUFIAN of El Kowm	?	
	12,000 BP	0		?	GEOMETRIC KEBARAN Abri Bergy	?	GEOMETRIC KEBARAN	GEOMETRIC KEBARAN	GEOMETRIC KEBARAN	GEOMETRIC KEBARAN	GEOMETRIC KEBARAN	ZARZIAN
12,000												

Note. From Cauvin (2000, p. xviii). Reprinted with permission from Cambridge University Press.

mans had nearly universally dispersed in the Neolithic and were living a life style that was much further developed than that of their upper Paleolithic predecessors. In the following paragraphs, a few of the better known sites are discussed with an emphasis on their death rituals and tombs.

One of the most interesting paleoanthropological sites from the Neolithic period was found in the Franchthi caves in Greece in the late 1960s (Jacobsen, 1981). This cave was quite unique in being occupied from as long ago as 22,000 BP to as recently as 5000 BP. Thus, it contains a nearly complete record of developments that occurred in a particular part of the world as it was continuously evolving culturally. The group of Franchthi graves that have been dated to around 10,000 BP typically contained no grave goods. However, by 6000 BP the graves contained marble and clay implements, even in those of infants. The Franchthi graves also contained an unusual number of human and animal figurines. Personal tool kits were found buried with adults at about this time suggesting that survivors believed that dead community members might need these tools in their afterlife.

One of the oldest natural mummies discovered to this time was found, quite surprisingly, in the desert of Nevada. The "Spirit Cave Man" had been buried with few artifacts but the burial had obviously been very carefully done. In addition to fibrous mats, the body had been wrapped in a fur robe indicating a ritual concern for the body and, presumably, an even deeper concern with what was going to happen to his "spirit" following his physical death. The Spirit Cave Man has been reliably dated to a very specific, as well as very startling, time—9415 BP—for the new world.

The Spirit Cave Man is of interest because it was mummified and because it was so richly endowed with grave goods. However, it was by no means the oldest new world human remains to be found. In late 2002, an older human skull (originally discovered in 1957 near Mexico City) was reevaluated and dated to 13,000 BP. Now known as the Penon Woman III, this skull was of particular interest because it was not Mongoloid, as are most Native Americans, but rather appeared to be from Caucasoid stock, perhaps of Ainu heritage. Needless to say, this is a controversial suggestion, and much more will probably be heard of this discovery before too long.

The rich Neolithic culture of the new world would be the basis of a complete book in itself; however, such a discussion must be left to others. The point here is that many of the cultural revolutions of the Neolithic period were occurring in many places simultaneously around the world. A problem yet to be solved is whether this was the result of independent invention or of an extraordinary and surprising amount of communication among early people.

An early Neolithic community on the other side of the world that showed a remarkable collection of unusual grave objects was the famous biblical site of Jericho (9000 BP) in modern Israel. A clear indication of the importance of the dead, something that may well be interpreted as evidence or a vestige of some kind of an ancestor cult, was the discovery of painted and plastered human skulls with cowry shells or plaster replacing the eyes (Garstang & Garstang, 1940; Kenyon, 1957). Reconstruction of the face may have been an attempt to provide a pictorial memorial of the departed or, perhaps, to preserve some vestige of his physical identity. These and other later burials were often made within the foundations of homes, again suggestive of special respect for ancestors. Other locations, for example, Hebron, in the same region produced stone masks of human faces; objects that also presumably carried the same ritual significance as the plastered skulls from Jericho.

Among other ritual processes, many sites throughout the world, including those at Jericho and others in such faraway places as what would become the British islands, removed the flesh from skeletal remains. The suggestion is that the relative permanence of the skeleton provided a link between this world and the following one—again supporting the idea of an afterlife for which preparations had to be made.

The site at Catal Huyuk, settled within a few hundred years of Jericho, also has been shown to have a rich burial culture (Mellaart, 1967). Like the Jericho remains, skulls were often found without the rest of the skeleton. Surprisingly, inasmuch as the two settlements were not geographically close, some Catal Huyuk skulls also had cowry shells substituted for the eyes. The most interesting aspect of the human remains found in both of these sites, however, was the indication of the substantial amount of energy that went into the burial ceremonies. Obviously, religion, death cults, and burial rituals were developing far beyond the problematic, at best simple, Paleolithic burials discussed in the previous chapter.

Another interesting feature of the Catal Huyuk graves was the very large number of female figurines. These were very similar to the Venus figures from upper Paleolithic graves exemplified by the classic prototype found at Willendorf. The similarity in shape belied the great difference in age: The Willendorf "Venus" had been entombed 15,000 years earlier than those found at Catal Huyuk! We can only guess at the links that may have existed between these two cultures so separated in time and space.

The rotund Venus figurines were not only found in Catal Huyuk graves but also in specially dedicated "religious" rooms in the houses of the residents themselves. These rooms are now considered to have been exclusively chapels or sanctuaries, often accompanied by effigies or representations of bulls (Cauvin, 2000).[5] One interpretation is that these "mother

---

[5]It is interesting to speculate that these primitive "bull" religions left cultural traces that continue on to this day. Bulls play an important role in the mythology of Knossos on Crete, later historic Greek culture, and, of course, in the Spanish and Portuguese traditions of our time. Another question that might be asked is: What symbolic relation is there between these ladies and

Goddesses" were interlocutors who helped make the transition between life and death just as mothers played such a central role in bridging the transition between nothingness and life.

The Middle East and Europe were not the only places that the Neolithic revolution was taking place. The Neolithic people of China had also undergone significant cultural changes by this time. They were widely diverse in their simple cultures and presumably their languages by the middle and late Neolithic. Around 7000 to 5000 BP, the predecessors of today's Chinese migrated into the Yellow and Yangtze River valleys and laid the groundwork for what was to be the longest lasting civilization in human history—China. It was at this time and this place that a single language and culture seems to have congealed and the concept of a specifically Chinese Neolithic civilization can be defined.

Two groups of early Chinese settlers are better known than any others—the Yangshao and the Lungshan. The Yangshao Neolithic villages were probably settled in the period 7000 to 5000 BP, whereas the Lungshan culture dates from about 5000 to 4000 BP. It may have been that the Lungshan people displaced the Yangshao who had arrived at an earlier time, but there is always the possibility that the earlier culture simply evolved into the later one and that they did not represent distinctly different people ethnically or culturally. The Yangshao and Lungshan cultures are distinguished mainly on the basis of their distinctive pottery styles. Of the Lungshan people, we know very little. There is a suggestion they were likely to have been the ancestors of the Xia and Shang civilizations that followed and, therefore, there is a continuous sequence of Chinese civilizations and its prehistoric predecessors from 7000 BP to the present. Other less well-known cultures include the one defined by the burials at Dawenkou. These people apparently lived at the same time as the Yangshao and, according to some scholars, may have been antecedents of the Lungshan.

The religious practices of these Neolithic Chinese peoples are not well known. At the famous[6] Banpo location there is an extensive cemetery from which 250 graves have been identified. Discovered with the skeletal remains were bone and stone beads, and a few red clay pots. Only much later did the Chinese begin to bury large amounts of jade with the dead. We do know from Banpo and other similar sites that there was a substantial effort

---

the bulls? The obvious one is that each represented something about the male and female aspects of life. Cauvin (2000) goes much more deeply into this aspect of the Neolithic religious cults and my readers are directed there for an up to date statement of what has been conjectured in this regard.

[6]Banpo is on the outskirts of Xian. Xian is now most famous for the terracotta soldiers that were buried by the first emperor of China 6,500 years later. Having seen both Banpo and the soldiers, I think Banpo deserves much more attention than it usually receives.

to bury their dead in group cemeteries. Children were usually buried in jars close to their own homes. Both of these facts attest to the strong sense of community at this Neolithic site. The early tombs reflect a strong conviction of the existence of some kind of an afterlife and imply belief in a world of spirits, particularly of one's ancestors.

The best known of the late Neolithic period are those from a major cemetery at Dawenkou (Anonymous, 1974) and reflect the fact that ritual burials were including an ever-richer variety of grave goods. The best described of the Dawenkou graves is Tomb 10, the grave of a middle-aged woman. The important thing about this grave was the rich variety of materials entombed with her. Her grave goods contained 94 pieces of pottery with geometric designs, many bones of a variety of animals and, most significant in the historical sense, three jade objects. One of these latter objects was a well-polished jade ax. Obviously this was a valuable object and its placement in the grave indicated a very high degree of respect for the dead. Ritual respect for the dead was becoming a very expensive enterprise, indeed, for the Chinese as well as other Neolithic cultures.

Other notable Neolithic sites include those found in the Greek islands; many of those discoveries had the additional advantage that they could be placed in a precise chronological order by the specific sequence of increasingly sophisticated pottery that developed in the period following 8000 BP. The pre-ceramic (PPN) tombs of the early Neolithic Greek period were followed by graves filled with pottery of different, but well ordered, types. This regular sequence of ceramic transitions also occurred in many other places including China, Korea, India, East and West Europe, as well as other parts of the Mediterranean basin and the Americas. For archeologists, ceramic shards became the best measuring sticks of ancient time until the development of the recent chemical and physical measures for dating objects.

The early Greek Neolithic settlements were startling in their complexity and implications for the emerging religiosity of the residents. However, they were not unique and ever more numerous finds dating from the next two millennia of the Neolithic period have been discovered from all parts of the world. It is not necessary for the purposes of this book to review them all. It is important to appreciate, however, that the increasingly elaborate tombs and shrines for the dead continued to be created during this period in all parts of the inhabited world.

It is important to reemphasize that the major point of this discussion of Neolithic burials is that the increasing abundance of grave goods attests to the increasingly important role that the idea of immortality played in the life of so many people in so many places around the world. The inference, untestable and improvable but highly probable, to be drawn from this abundant evidence is that people from all over the world had developed deeply held concepts of an afterlife that, however inexplicit at their time, involved two forms of reality, a material one and a spiritual one. However robust or frail such an inference may be, what is indisputable is that people were able and willing to spend an enormous amount of time and energy ritualistically dealing with the dead and perhaps, more fundamentally, with their expectations for the future of the dead.

Just how extensive this commitment to death rituals was can be discerned in another aspect of Neolithic burial phenomenon—the Megaliths. In addition to the creation of extensive mounds of earth, Neolithic death cults in many parts of the world were able to harness enough human energy in terms of raw numbers, either at a single moment or spread over sufficiently long periods of time, to move huge stones or megaliths. Although the exact purpose of all of the megalithic monuments will always be in dispute, the prevailing opinion among archeologists is that these stones were intended to serve as permanent repositories for the spirits of the dead. The word "permanent" is the salient one in this context; these stone monuments were probably intended to provide continuity for the spiritual vestiges of a person in the next life forever simply by virtue of their enormous size. These monumental accomplishments were among the most compelling evidence of human attitudes toward death and immortality prior to the invention of writing and the beginning of the historic period. Not only were huge amounts of energy and resources dedicated to building the structures themselves, but also elaborate grave goods were increasingly common in megalithic tombs of the Neolithic period.

Another impressive fact about the Megalithic tombs and monuments is that they have been found in so many different locales in the world. The propensity for humans to build tombs or monuments from massive rocks dispersed worldwide during late Neolithic times. There are a few instances of such finds in North America, and there is virtually no place in Europe or Western Asia where they were not found. A tabulation of the many locations in which they have been discovered can be found in Witcombe (2002), a fascinating and exhaustive Internet site on prehistoric art.

Perhaps the oldest megalithic monuments were discovered in 1974 (Wendorf, Schild, & Zedeno, 1996; McKim, Wendorf, Mazhar, & Schild, 1998; Wendorf, Schild, & Associates, 2001) at Nabta Playa in the desert of southern Egypt. It has been dated to about 7000 BP (Malville, Wendorf, Mazar, & Schild, 1998). Although it was apparently not a human tomb, this site contained a number of cattle remains that had presumably been intentionally buried there, perhaps as some kind of a religious offering. The significance of this ancient megalith may be evaluated in terms of the respect they indicated for dead animals as well as for human dead. On the other hand, these animals may have been sacrifices that accompanied some now lost human burial. Another role that the Nabta Playa megaliths may have played was as an astronomical calculator in the same way as did the much later megaliths of Stonehenge in modern England—the first phase of which has now been dated to be no earlier than about 5000 BP (Atkinson, 1956).

We can only speculate why the Neolithic peoples were so caught up by these huge stone monuments and the structures they built from them. Levy (1946) suggested the following:

> . . . in the Neolithic attitude to stones, man's will has entered to make a cove-nant with an unseen power, for whom he has taken the first step to provide a habitation, and indeed the pillar of rough-worked stone remained as an indis-pensable adjunct in a place dedicated to worship, even after the building of shrines had become a custom. (p. 125)

Thus, the Megalith might have served several purposes; first as a domicile for the invisible Gods; second, as a residence for the spiritual remains of their very visible dead; and, third, possibly as astronomical observatories. Of course, these three functions may not have been as neatly demarcated as the previous sentence suggests.

As I have already noted, the megalithic culture, whatever its motivation, spread widely throughout Europe and Asia. Examples have been found in locations ranging from present day Spain to Germany to Denmark and into Ireland as well as Mediterranean islands such as Malta. Malta, in particular, became a "holy island thronged with temples . . ." (Levy, 1946, p. 131) some of which were above ground and others dug from subsurface rock. Many of these structures apparently were designed to serve the combined functions of tomb and temple and, in addition, they possibly may have served as heal-ing centers. Perhaps the largest in sheer numbers of stones are to be found in Carnac in French Brittany. This enormous field of megaliths (over a mile long and composed of as many as 11,000 individual stones) was arranged by its builders into a series of parallel lines. The Carnac megaliths are dated to a period around 5000 BP.

Among the most numerous are the monumental tombs found in the Mecklenburg–Vorpommern region of Germany. A comprehensive study of this area by Schuldt (1972) listed 1,145 megalithic burial tombs of one size or another. Holtorf (2002) estimated that originally there may have been as many as 5,000 and, furthermore, that as many as 25,000 may have been con-structed in Denmark in a short 500-year period (from 3900 BP to 3400 BP). The reason these tombs were built was, in Holtorf's words, that they were "indicators for a concern of their builders with a prospective future." Here, therefore, it is not just the fact that any ritual grave goods were found in the graves, but the magnitude of the graves themselves serve as evidence of a deep seated conviction on the part of Neolithic peoples that there existed an afterlife—the key imprint of a dualistic point of view about the nature of reality.

Megalithic tombs were also found widely scattered in the British Islands including England, Ireland, Scotland, and Wales. More than 1,500 tombs of various types and sizes were found in Ireland alone. Although many were simple "portal" dolmens consisting of one horizontal stone laid across two vertical ones and slanting toward the rear, others such as the famous Newgrange or Knowth passage tombs were enormous structures above the ground with subterranean chambers at the end of long tunnels. Others were assemblages of large stones arranged in simple patterns below earthen mounds.

Megaliths were also found in one form or another in East Asia, Oceania, and even in the new world. Another interesting collection of huge Neolithic stone monuments was discovered in the early 19th century in the Vidarbha region of India. These were clearly burial markers and are fully described in Mohanty and Walimbe (2002).

Another ubiquitous aspect of Neolithic megalithic structures was the extensive use of abstract engravings or drawings. These symbols were quite unlike the very realistic Magdalenian cave paintings of animals, art that seemed to be more concerned with the practicalities of the hunt than with the afterlife. Megaliths, either as god-homes or as repositories for the spirits of departed humans, were indisputably associated with the supernatural and, in particular, the perpetuation of the nonmaterial aspects of the human. In other words, megaliths are especially interesting in terms of the evidence they provide for dualist ideas.

There are other ideas of the specific intent behind the construction of these enormous monuments. One line of thought (Thomas, 1991) suggests that these tombs were designed to serve as a "pathway from the world that we know to the supernatural spirit world that we do not know." An implication of this line of thought is that it was a conscious effort on the part of the Neolithic people to continue the natural life of an individual with a perpetual spiritual existence, perpetuity being guaranteed by sheer massiveness. Although we will probably never know exactly what thoughts were in the minds of the Megalithic builders, it seems a logical extrapolation from the very existence of these tombs to the idea that some expectation existed about an afterlife beyond the death of the body. This brings us to the next issue to be discussed. What do we now know about the emerging religions of the Neolithic period and, in particular their dualistic attitudes toward an afterlife?

3.3 NEOLITHIC RELIGIONS

However uncertain may be the meaning of the various, but always cryptic, archeological remains that have been discovered in the last century or so, there is no question that by the beginning of the Neolithic period religious ideas had evolved to a very high level of complexity and sophistication. It was not just a few burials or cave paintings that stood as evidence but an entire cultural edifice that was paid for by a substantial commitment of resources and human energy. The sedentary life that blossomed in the Neolithic made it possible for elaborate cults, rituals, and proto-religions to flourish. For the first time, rooms, whole buildings, and eventually monumental structures were dedicated to the spiritual and the supernatural. For the first time, there was a surplus of human energy such that not only individuals but entire social classes could become shamans and priests and spend all of their time serving the supposed needs of their Gods and Goddesses, free of earlier personal responsibilities to hunt or gather. Material goods were also in sufficient abundance so that grave goods could be much more elaborate than in earlier times. Furthermore, material wealth was increasing greatly enough so that a society could afford the cost (or, if you prefer, waste) of interring items of great value with the dead.

For these reasons, the evidence of a deepening human concern with death and the rituals that surrounded it grow both more abundant and clearer. Bodies were not just put in simple shallow Paleolithic-type graves with a few questionable grave decorations. Rather, during the Neolithic, bodily remains were interred in unusual manners, sometime painted, sometimes plastered, sometimes stripped of their flesh, dismembered, or displaying some other kind of ritualistic processing. The nature of grave offerings also began to be much more elaborate. Something that had not been encountered previously, to the best of current paleoanthropological knowledge, was the practice of sacrificing humans to be entombed in the graves of high-ranking individuals. These human offerings, it is assumed, were made in an effort to provide service personnel for high-ranking individuals in their afterlives.

All of these rituals imply that the dead (at least the high-ranking dead) were treated with a reverence and respect suggesting that the primeval fear of death had evolved into a profound commitment to the idea that the death of the body does not mean the death of the mind/soul/spirit. This new view implied that the residents of an afterlife had material requirements that had to be satisfied with far richer grave goods (and supporting staff) than in previous times.

The fact that entire communities could become centers of religious activity also attests both to this new way of life and the importance of emerging religious ideas. For example, Tel Halaf, a very large Neolithic village (or, depending upon one's criteria, a very small city) seems to modern archeologists to have been mainly dedicated to religious activities. Major excavations documenting this predominant religious role of Tel Halaf were carried out and reported by von Oppenheim (1932). Once again, for reasons that are still not well understood and about which we can only speculate, it was a Goddess, rather than a male God to which this village/city was dedicated. Figurines of this female deity were found in many of the graves at this site.

Archeologists still quibble over whether the main building at Tel Halaf was a temple or a palace; in either case, this location in ancient Mesopotamia (currently a part of modern Syria) clearly played a special role in near eastern religious culture during its heyday 7500 BP to 6500 BP. Indeed, the period has occasionally been referred to as the Halafian period.

In conclusion and summary, the abundance of archeological evidence for the importance of religion, with its heavy emphasis on how one should cope with death, makes it clear that by middle Neolithic times—around 6000 BP—an enormous amount of human energy, both physical and mental, was directed toward supernatural things and the afterlife. There was, therefore, considerable evidence of a widespread and deep conviction that the world consisted of two kinds of reality—one, temporary, tangible, and natural and the other, permanent, invisible, and supernatural. Dualism and the religious rituals that attended it were ubiquitous and, perhaps, even dominated all world cultures during the Neolithic era. Certainly, a substantial portion of the archeological evidence is associated with religious practices during this time.

This chapter has been only the briefest survey of some of the most important of the Neolithic archeological sites. For those interested in more detailed discussions of the artifacts and their relation to early religions, I recommend Levy's (1946) now classic book, Eliade's (1978) scholarly study, and Loftin's (2000) recent discussion of ancient prehistoric practices in his history of religion.

The argument made so far in this book is that this dualism evolved from a primitive fear of death. The evidence for this interpretation up to this time is necessarily indirect. In pursuing the thesis, all of my sources and I have had to go from material archeological remains to implied cognitive processes (often intervened by behavioral assumptions) by processes of inference and induction that, admittedly, sometimes strain logic and credulity. We are extrapolating back from modern to ancient thoughts in ways that are not immune to challenge. There were, as noted earlier, no witnesses or respondents to either refute or confirm some of these inferences. However, around 6000 BP, just as communities such as Tel Halaf were disappearing, an extraordinary cultural development occurred—the invention of writing. From that point on, the leaps of logic and inferences could be corroborated by witnesses who, however alien they may have been in their thinking, for the first time left much more direct evidence of their thoughts in the form of written documents.

The next chapter deals with what the epochal invention of writing tells us about the attitudes toward death of our fellow humans in what subsequently came to be characterized as the Historic era.

4

The Early Written History
of Religious Dualism

4.1   THE BIRTH OF HISTORY

So far in this book, the tale being told is one based on reasonable inference
and plausible interpretation. Human remains and artifacts, sometimes in
the sparsest of amounts and most cryptic of form, are used to build theories of what or what was not being "thought" by Paleolithic and Neolithic
humans. It has never been (and presumably never will be) possible to verify or refute theories of the actual state of the prehistoric mind for the simple reason that direct communication with those thoughts is not possible. A
few grains of pollen or a small, plump figurine, therefore, produced wildly
contentious debates about the cognitive processes of people who were, at
the very least, vastly different culturally from us and, possibly very different cognitively. Indeed, our knowledge of the minds of even anatomically
modern humans is so limited that there can be no assurance that the behavior of our predecessors, much less their cognitive processes, could be
inferred from either the fragmentary remains or the grand architectural
monuments they left behind. The problem, as noted earlier, is not unique to
studies of cognitive antiquity; there is an enormous parallel difficulty faced
by even the most modern psychological science to access mental processes on the basis of behavior. That problem is that identical behavior can
be caused by a vast number of different motivations and underlying
thought processes. Behaviors and artifacts, therefore, share common neu-
trality with regard to these underlying cognitive processes.

Around 4000 BCE,[1] however, another earthshaking cultural invention changed this picture completely and irreversibly. Writing, the direct representation of ideas in the forms of symbols pressed into clay, carved into rock, or dribbled onto sheets formed from plant residues or animal skins began to appear. This embodiment of a supremely important idea—the direct recording of intangible human thoughts in the form of tangible markings—removed at least some of the obstacles to the interpretation of the thoughts of people who lived in ancient times and with whom we could not have direct idea-to-idea contact. Even though it is likely that there had been oral histories passed from generation to generation prior to the written ones, such ephemeral communications ultimately left no tangible traces as various peoples and cultures came and went from the world scene. With the advent of writing, however, for the first time, thoughts expressed in oral form could be recorded in a way that permitted them to persist for longer than the duration of a brief sound wave.

Writing is a totally different means of communication than speech. It permitted the thoughts of some of our predecessors to be perpetuated, especially when the writing was done on some kind of permanent medium such as stone. The written record made it possible for people in distant locations to communicate as well as for people living in different times to appreciate the thoughts of others who had preceded them.[2]

To fully understand the impact of writing on our understanding of the history of dualist and religious ideas about death, we have to know something about what it is as well as how, when, and where it originated. By way of definition, writing can be considered to be a rule-based system of symbols or scripts recorded in some permanent or semipermanent medium to convey information from one time or place to another. There is enormous variety in the kinds of information communicated in the written form. In-

---

[1]Somewhat arbitrarily at this point in this book, I change the system used to date events, peoples, and objects from a fluctuating "BP" to a more constant "BCE." The reason for this is simple, with the advent of writing, history, in its truest sense, begins. Dates become much more precise and better documented and it is even possible to cross-reference them to other contemporary events. The sliding scale BP is always changing; P—the present is not a stable temporal reference. It is desirable, therefore, to anchor it to a specific date in human history. For western historians, this reference is the traditional year in which the birth of Christ is celebrated. Dates prior to this event are referred to as BCE (Before the Common Era) and those after are referred to as CE (During the Common Era) in accord with contemporary historical and archeological practice. The phrase "Common Era" is, of course, synonymous with the phrase "Christian Era" reflecting the dominant religion of western civilization during the last 2,000 years.

[2]Of course, the written record can also lie. There is no question that distortions and propaganda can be set down on stone or papyrus as well as uttered. However, writing represents such a giant leap in communication possibilities with those distant in time or space, beyond the vagaries of speech or of inferences from behavior, that any such hesitation pales into insignificance compared to the magnitude of the advance it represented.

deed, one of the most distinguishing properties of writing is its intrinsic universality; writing can convey virtually any idea or thought, sometimes, even concepts that cannot be expressed in words. It may deal with uttered sounds, with material objects, or with abstract concepts equally well. If special mathematical notations are considered to be writing as well, the domain of ideas that writing can represent is functionally infinite. On the other hand, the particular medium, language, or symbol set that is used for writing is irrelevant; it is the meaning attached to the symbols and their rule-based organization, not the symbols themselves, that makes it possible to efficiently convey such a broad range of information between the writer and the reader.

Although one may quibble over the most efficient code, both pictorial hieroglyphics and alphabetic letters can equally well tell the most intricate stories. There are no written languages that cannot, in principle, be intertranslated once the symbols and the rules are understood. (This holds true for the simplest of languages including the binary Turing machine that is also, in principle, capable of representing any idea or concept.) All languages are subject to decoding once one knows the rules and symbols.[3] Each may have its own syntax and even its own symbols, but all are in principle capable, like the binary code, of universally representing any and all ideas. Sometimes it may be necessary to invent a new word to increase the efficiency of a language, but it is almost always possible to use whatever vocabulary is available to represent, however inefficiently, some abstract or complex concrete idea.

Nevertheless, one has to be very careful about how to approach a coding problem of this sort. The particular font or inscription method and the material by which and on which they may be inscribed are among the irrelevancies to a study of the informational significance of a language. One is reminded of the wisdom of Kety (1960) when he described the discovery of a mythical intelligent and civilized, but illiterate, society that suddenly encountered a book for the first time. He described how various laboratories were set up by this illiterate society to examine this new entity including laboratories of anatomy, chemistry, biochemistry, physiology, and psychology. Kety's point was that none of those laboratories make any progress until the information scientist begins to poke about among the tiny stains that are arranged in such neat order on the pages. Nothing about the cellulose from which the book was made, the chemistry of the ink, the anatomy of

---

[3]This statement should not be misconstrued to mean that all languages would ultimately be translated. Practical considerations may prevent us from knowing the symbols and rules. Evidence of this, as we see later in this chapter, is to be found in the writing systems that are yet to be deciphered or those translations that are still subject to debate. Of course, it is possible, if not probable, that modern cryptographic techniques may solve even the most recalcitrant translation problem in the future.

the pages, or the binding material mattered in understanding the true nature of a "book." Rather, it was only the symbols, the pattern into which
they were arranged, and the rules by which these tiny stains were organized that really mattered.

Two main themes repeatedly occur when scholars speculate about the
origins of writing. First, some suggest it is an outgrowth of primitive counting markers. For many millennia prior to the invention of writing, it was
likely to have been a common practice of traders to use a simple token or
marker to represent each item being bought or sold. A bag of a certain number of stones or markers could, for example, represent an equivalent number of bags of grain. Perhaps the system was later elaborated into one in
which a distinctive mark might have been placed on each marker to indicate it represented measures of grain and a totally different mark used to
indicate a tool of some sort, a sheep, or even a person working in a mine, respectively. Harris (1986), for example, suggested that the next step in writing evolved from this kind of token system as a convenient and efficient
way of counting when large numbers were involved. He said:

> A token-iterative sign-system is in effect equivalent to a verbal sublanguage
> which is restricted to messages of the form: "sheep, sheep, sheep, sheep . . ."
> or "sheep, another, another, another . . ."; whereas an emblem slotting system
> is equivalent to a sublanguage which can handle messages of the form
> "sheep, sixty." (p. 145)

The "emblem slotting" system permitted records to be maintained in a
much more efficient manner than the "token-iterative" one. Efficiency aside,
the point of Harris' comment is that primitive counting systems such as
these may well have been the immediate antecedents of elaborate systems
of writing that were eventually able to represent much more complex ideas
than simple numerousness. Once the idea of inscribing different kinds of
marks to represent different things occurred, it was only a short step, according to Harris, to inscribing symbols that represented observable processes (such as commercial exchanges). The step from symbols that dealt
with numbers or commerce to intangibles, such as Gods and death, was obvious, if not immediate, once the idea of symbolic representation had
dawned on these protoliterate people.

This is a very pragmatic view of the origin of writing closely associated
with the beginning of trade and commerce and the need for counting. A not
entirely antithetical interpretation of the origin of writing was that it emerged
from pictorial, rather than numerical, roots. Writing, on this theory, evolved
through several stages. The earliest form would have been simple pictograms that were isomorphic reproductions of the shape of an object; a pot
could be easily represented by a small drawing, as could a sheep, a moun-

tain, or even a person. However, in a way that was analogous to the need for simplification when numbers became large, as the ideas or objects being represented became more complex, pictograms became so complex that abbreviated forms had to be used. In this way, a pictorial representation evolved into an arbitrary symbol set and eventually into an alphabetic system. Similarly, the preservation of oral information required that some kind of phonogram or written code for uttered sounds had to be invented.

Thus, strong felt needs for both alphabetic and syllabic written languages emerged to represent both tangible objects and abstract ideas as well as serving as a code for the spoken language. During the early evolution of writing, of course, not all the earlier stages were discarded. Highly evolved pictographic symbols are still being used by a large proportion of the world's population, for example in China and Japan. In other cases, for example in classical Egypt and Mesoamerica, pictograms or hieroglyphics represented the pinnacle achievement of their writing systems, only to disappear when these societies vanished from the scene.

Unresolved as the conflict between these two theories of the origins of writing (commercial counting vs. pictorial object representation) may be, so too is the problem of where writing originated. Not surprisingly, the origins of writing are a matter of considerable dispute among specialists in the field. One thing that is generally accepted is that writing of different kinds was most likely "invented" in several places, perhaps nearly simultaneously, but perhaps millennia apart. The writing systems of the Middle East, of China, and of Central America are all sufficiently dissimilar that they must be attributed to their own unique origins.

The oldest and most generally accepted source of European writing is usually[4] attributed to the Sumerians. From about 3300 BCE onwards there was a steady progression from simple pictorial representations of objects, which looked very much like the birds, fish, or pottery that they were meant to represent, to more abstract aggregations of wedge or "cuneiform" marks. The development of the wedge-shaped tool as a writing device was probably a result of practical needs to simplify the inscription of these symbols. It was much easier to punch a set of identical shapes into a clay tablet by repeated use of a handy wedge-shaped tool, often shaped from a reed, then to draw curved lines. Indeed, it was this fact—that the ancient Sumerians used clay tablets as their medium that were subsequently baked, either

---

[4]As we shall shortly see, however, very new evidence suggests that the Sumerian writing system may have been predated by Egyptian developments. Even this may not be the oldest writing. This is a highly controversial area of archeological research. For example, Li, Harbottle, Zhang, and Wang (2003) report the discovery of tortoise shells (reminiscent of later oracle bones) that have 11 different kinds of symbols scraped on their surface. The extraordinary thing about this find is that these shells have been dated to 6000 BCE—more than two thousand years before the earliest Egyptian or Sumerian proto-writing!

purposely or accidentally in building fires—that may be the basis for the conventional, but now contested, attribution that they were the first to invent writing. Even if some other culture had priority, vanishingly small traces of earlier writing have survived.

Egyptian hieroglyphics, dating from about the same time as the earliest Sumerian cuneiform (also around 3300 BCE), are a combination of ancient pictographs and a newer syllable-based system. Although the dates may be similar, the Sumerian and Egyptian pictographic systems are quite different and are obviously based on entirely different foundations. It is difficult, therefore, to substantiate a link that has sometimes been made from hieroglyphics to cuneiform or vice versa, because of the substantial stylistic differences between the two. An additional obstruction to attributing a close relationship between the two types of writing arises from the fact that both seemed to have emerged, each from its own part of the Middle Eastern desert, at about the same time. What seems to have actually been the case is that both were based on simple precursors that evolved into their own individual form of writing as the cultural pressures for efficient communication grew during the time of these early civilizations.

Which form of writing came first? The argument continues. Although there is a substantial bias toward the Sumerian cuneiform, recent data suggest a possible alternative. A very recent discovery in the Egyptian desert at Gebel Tjauti, south of Cairo, of a sample of primitive Egyptian hieroglyphic writing dating from 3250 BCE has been reported by a husband–wife team of archeologists—John and Deborah Darnell. They propose that their discovery is the oldest known sample of any kind of writing and, if so, it would represent a specific date for a definable boundary between the prehistoric and the historic. The inscribed tableau tells the story of a king of ancient Egypt—the "Scorpion King"—who had been thought to be mythical, but who, in the light of new findings like these and those of Dreyer (discussed later), must now be considered to have been a truly historical person. A book by Darnell and Darnell (2002) describing these extraordinary discoveries in detail has recently been published.

Another Egyptian contender that meets the archeological criteria for first known symbolic writing (as opposed to pictographic drawings) has recently been unearthed at the Abydos tombs of the predynastic Egyptian pharaohs by Günter Dreyer of the Cairo based German Institute of Archeology.[5] Dreyer reports finding symbols inscribed on small, square bone tags that he believes are the earliest form of true writing. These "tags," Dreyer suggests, were multisymbol labels indicating the origins of the materials to which they had been attached. He dates them to a period between 3200 BCE

---

[5]Dreyer's discoveries are described in a recent Web site at http://whyfiles.org/079writing/ and in several scholarly publications including Dreyer (1998, 1999) and Dreyer et al. (2000).

and 3100 BCE, in the time period just prior to the first Egyptian dynasties. (It should be noted that this time is almost identical with the antiquity of the Darnells' discovery at Gebel Tjauti.) Dreyer's claim is that these tags represented a symbolic representation of language as opposed to drawings of objects. His argument is that these are not just "pictures" but are closer to what we mean by writing.

In distinguishing between symbolic representation of language and pictures, Dreyer implicitly responds to the interesting question: Are the earliest hieroglyphics really writing? This is an important and subtle point. What is the line of demarcation, he is implicitly asking, between the tags of early Sumeria and the first proto-cuneiform writing? Should *writing* be denoted when the tag does not look like what it is representing? Does it require the additional criterion that several tags be coalesced into a *sentence*? Questions like these add controversy and uncertainties to superficially simple queries such as "who invented writing?"

Thus, the actual origins of writing are now much more uncertain than they were only a few years ago. Whether the Sumerians or the Egyptians should be credited with the invention of this essential aspect of modern western civilization is, however, probably less important than the fact that it was invented about 5,000 years ago and, as a result, provided the basis for recording virtually all aspects of modern civilization.

On the other side of the world, a completely separate and distinctly different kind of writing evolved from its own pictographic roots about 2,000 years later. It is often suggested that early Chinese writing may have evolved from marks made on the so called *oracle bones*, a fortune telling device by means of which the future was supposed to be predicted. However, there is one great unknown. If the oracle bones were the original source of Chinese stroke characters, it is difficult to account for the fact that the questions for which divination was required were actually written prior to the writing on the bones? Furthermore, the script on the oracles bones itself is not that primitive. Obviously there was an even older Chinese history of writing, one that dates back much further than the 1000 BCE date to which the oldest of the oracle bones are usually attributed.[6] Although Chinese writing was later to become a major part of the commercial life of that country under its many emperors, it seems the original motivation for its development was for religious and ritual purposes. This was quite unlike the Sumerian system that grew out of the needs of commerce, but similar to the forces driving the development of Egyptian writing—the recording of religious beliefs and rituals, dynastic histories, and conquests.

---

[6]The oracle bones date from the Shang dynasty period of ancient China. It is likely that the first writing was invented in China during the preceding Xia period. See page 109 for a tabulation of the early Chinese dynasties. However, see page 83 for an even older possibility, one that dates back 8,000 years.

Finally, the writing systems of Central America are totally distinct both in form and concept from those of either Asia or the Middle East. This suggests an independent origin for this essentially hieroglyphic system. Unlike the Sumerian roots, but like the Egyptian and Chinese sources, rather than being primarily a commercial invention, the Toltec, Zapotec, Mayan, Aztec, and other writing styles of Central America seem mainly to have been a means of recording their wars, conquests, and dynasties and, to a lesser degree, their religious ideas.

It is important to appreciate in this brief history of writing that the Chinese and Mesoamerican writing systems both date from a period 2,000 to 4,000 years later than the initial Sumerian and Egyptian inventions of cuneiform and hieroglyphic writing, respectively. It is possible, though very unlikely, that these systems could have been influenced by the earlier developments in those faraway lands. However, no such link has ever been definitively established. It seems much more likely that they were independently "invented."[7]

Thus, it appears that, much like any of the other significant developments of the time, writing was invented in multiple places at different times. The fascinating and still unanswered question is how these early systems metamorphosed into modern alphabetic writing systems. The evolution of the Chinese system found in today's Asian countries is straightforward. The current forms are clearly just modernizations of the archaic ones, transformed by the random uncertainties of history or the need for simplification. However, the trail from the ancient Sumerian cuneiform or Egyptian hieroglyphics to modern alphabetic writing systems is much less clear.

Accepting momentarily for purposes of discussion, the traditionally accepted conclusion that the Sumerians were the first inventors of writing in the Middle East, their system has, until recently, generally been thought to be the root of most Indo-European written languages. The cuneiform system spread rapidly throughout the Middle East, accelerating after the conquest of a large portion of those lands by the Akkadians in 2340 BCE. Thus, it became the basis of the written language of Mesopotamia and the nations that surrounded and ultimately succeeded it. The trail from their ancient pictographs to modern alphabets is not a clear one, however. What we do know is that as the evolution of the original cuneiform system continued, the archaic symbols also became increasingly complex. This eventually led to another very significant invention; a set of a small number of symbols—alphabets—that were to further revolutionize writing. Although not definitive, a plausible theory of the evolution of European alphabets seems to go something like that presented in the following discussion.

---

[7]As we see on page 125, there has been some suggestion that the Mesoamerican writing systems actually originated in West Africa. This "theory" has largely been discredited, but remains a remote possibility.

As we have already seen, the Sumerian cuneiform went through a progressive evolution from simple counting tokens—dated from as early as 5300 BCE—to pictograms to clusters of wedge-shaped "words" consisting of several organized marks, a process that continued until about 2500 BCE. About this time, these pictographic cuneiforms evolved further into a simplified set of a very few marks that are supposed by modern archeologists to represent the oldest known approximation to an alphabetic system. It has been suggested that the alphabetic cuneiform was actually the product of the Ugarit culture (a city in modern day Syria that was the site of an important empire in the period before 2000 BCE), since it was here that the first alphabetic cuneiform samples were found. The roots of our modern alphabetic systems are, on this theory, the evolutionary result of the classic Sumerian cuneiform writing. An excellent chart (Fig. 4.1) developed by Katsiavriades and Qureshi (2001) demonstrate the developmental route of alphabetic writing forms from that early origin to the nearly worldwide dispersion to be found today.

An alternative to this conventional view of the origin of alphabetic writing has recently been put forward. New discoveries at Gebel Tjauti in the Egyptian desert, also made by the Darnells (Darnell & Darnell, 1997) and by Himelfarb (2000) add support to the idea that an alphabet was actually a derivation of Egyptian hieroglyphics rather than of Sumerian cuneiform. The evidence supporting this assertion was found in the form of a simple kind of hieroglyphic graffiti scratched into rocks presumably around 1900 BCE.

Whenever it happened, Egyptian writing eventually evolved into a simplified set of about 20 characters that could be used to represent complex ideas. Either or both (it is still a matter of extreme controversy among archeologists) the primitive but seminal Sumerian and the Egyptian alphabets contributed to the Ugaritic and then to the Phoenician systems of writing. Given the widespread trading activity of the Phoenicians, their alphabet had an enormous dispersion and was, almost certainly, a major key to the development of the many different written languages with which we are now familiar in Europe and Western Asia today.

One chain of development led from Phoenicia to Assyrian Aramaic, and then to other Semitic languages such as the remarkably durable Hebrew and later day Arabic. Another chain of the historical development of writing went from Phoenicia to Minoa to Greece to Etrusca (or, possibly, vice versa from Etrusca to Greece) to the original Roman alphabet.[8] It is likely that all these linguistic chains were also cross-linked; it is, for example, almost cer-

---

[8]Of course, all of these early alphabets were incomplete. For example, the early Roman alphabet consisted of only 21 letters. Of the other five, Q and F were added in classic times and W, J, and U in the middle ages.

The Evolution of Scripts and Alphabets

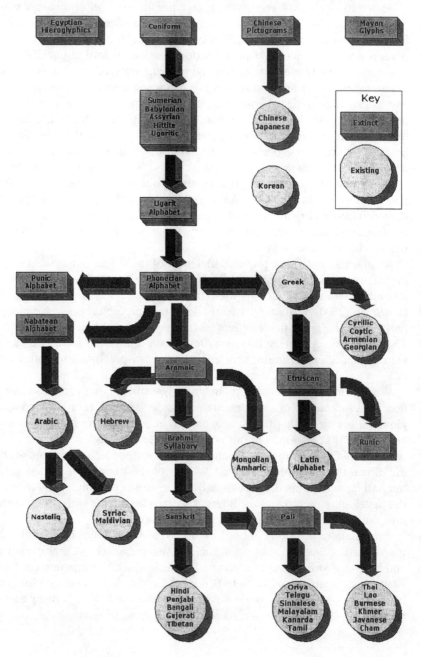

FIG. 4.1. A diagram of the historical relations of written languages prepared by Katsiavriades and Qureshi (2001). Reproduced with the permission of Kryss Katsiavriades.

tain that the Hebrew alphabet influenced early Greek writing and that Aramaic most likely led to Sanskrit and then to modern Hindi and the other writing systems of the Indian subcontinent. It is also generally agreed that Sanskrit, a derivative of the Phoenician written language, was the root of writing in many countries of Southeast Asia. This explains their uniqueness in Asia and the alternative they provided to the Chinese pictographic writing system from their north. The centerpieces of the development of modern western writing, of course, are the Roman and Cyrillic alphabets used today; the former in the Western European tradition and the latter in the Eastern.

The history of writing, to sum up this subject, is a complex subject and still quite a controversial one. The chains of development are overlapping and intertwined. Those of my readers who want to sample other views of how simple Sumerian and Egyptian tokens might have led to the ubiquitous and uniform 21st century alphabetic systems should seek out books by Gaur (1984), Robinson (1995), and Schmandt-Besserat (1996). It must be appreciated, however, that every year new discoveries are made that can drastically change what we know about the history of writing.

Alphabetic writing can be considered to be the great time machine; on the one hand, a gateway to an imagined future is opened up by it; on the other, it allows us to communicate with the past. It, thus, provides us the best possible access to the thinking of those ancient witnesses and respondents who left little or no earlier traces of their cognitive processes. Although those modern societies who still use complex pictographic symbols (e.g., in Japan and China) may dispute the fact, alphabetic systems are much more efficient than those essentially pictographic ones.

With more and more written records now beginning to emerge from the darkness of the past, it is possible to access much more directly the thinking of the people of what has been designated as the Bronze Age—the first of the historic epochs. In addition to the defining invention of this kind of metal processing about this time, the development of writing also marked this new epoch. Writing appeared in many forms throughout this period. However, preservation of writing until our time has, with few exceptions, required that the characters, whether they be hieroglyphs or alphabetic symbols, be inscribed on some more permanent material than animal skins or papyri. Indeed, it is the inscriptions carved into stone monuments, drawn on stone walls, or baked into clay that are among the earliest sources of human history.

Some of the most notable of these objects are the very early cuneiform tablets with long lists of real and mythical kings found at Uruk in ancient Mesopotamia dated to about 3300 BCE. These, as well as the Gebel Tjauti findings (see page 87), are among the leading candidates to be the oldest known examples of writing of any kind ever discovered. It is extremely interesting to note that both of these extraordinary discoveries have been dated to within a few years of each other, 3300 BCE and 3250 BCE, respectively. It may never be possible to determine which of these two civilizations had priority or, indeed, if they were both independent creators of this important tool.

Some of humankind's most treasured historic documents are inscribed in durable stone. The world's museums are filled with many examples of carved monuments containing hieroglyphic writing from, most notably, the older Egyptian dynasties dating from 2600 BCE. The most famous hieroglyphic inscription of all, however, is the relatively new (196 BCE) Rosetta stone, the key to translating this ancient language. (Davies, 1987, is among the most useful of the modern texts on the history of the translation of hieroglyphics.) The classic hieroglyphic writing on this most significant object was translated into two more recent ones—demotic, a simplified writing system used by commoners in the later Egyptian dynasties—and, most important, into Greek, a living language. This triple rendition of the same message honoring the Pharaoh Ptolemaios V permitted Jean Francois Champollion to decipher the hieroglyphic script in 1822.

Another treasure of human written history is Hammurabi's code, a system of laws that had been inscribed in cuneiform on a black basalt stela in ancient Babylonia. Dating from about 1800 BCE, it represented one early law code regulating human social interactions in that ancient society. An even earlier law code dating 300 years earlier than Hammurabi's stela is the law code of Ur-Nammu, a king of the city of Ur in Sumeria. It was written on a clay cylinder that does not have the dramatic power of Hammurabi's fascinating black rock. However, in terms of sheer antiquity, it is outstanding.

Arguably the oldest Hebrew writing so far discovered is a very early form of this script inscribed on a limestone tablet that appears to be a writing exercise of a calendar. It was found in Israel at a location called Tel Gezer. Dating of this calendar is uncertain but it appears to come from about 1000 BCE, the reputed time of King Solomon. A somewhat more recent, but still archaic, Hebrew inscription was found in 1880 in the Siloam tunnel, a project designed to be an aqueduct for the old city of Jerusalem. It is dated to about 700 BCE and is thought to describe the digging of the tunnel itself. In particular, the script mentions the excitement and celebration when the two teams of excavators, coming from opposite directions, met.

Inscriptions attributable to the oldest forms of Greek were found on baked clay tablets written in an archaic version known as Linear B and dated to a period around 1300 BCE from Crete. Linear B was most likely a derivative of earlier Phoenician. The earliest version of anything that can remotely be considered to be Modern Greek script dates from around 800 BCE. In particular, the archaic form of the Greek script on the famous "Dipylon" jug is very similar to Phoenician script. This ceramic pot was apparently a trophy—the inscription reads: "Who of the dancers play the best of all today, he will get this." The most ancient Roman writing known at present is an archaic form of Latin found on a rectangular stela found buried in the Roman Forum. The generally accepted date for this object is around 600 BCE.

In the new world, the Olmec culture of Central America left us a few tantalizing and controversial examples of their writing carved onto stone. They seem to have had both written counting and calendar systems. In some archeological circles, their writing system has often been described as nothing more than a pictographic token system, more akin to the prehieroglyphic Egyptian or the earliest Sumerian tag decorations. Nevertheless, Olmec inscriptions are thought to be the foundation of all later, more sophisticated hieroglyphic systems such as those used by the Mayans and the Aztecs. Primitive Olmec writing, indeed, is now considered to be the parent of all Central American writing systems that have been so far discovered, some of which have been specifically designated as "epi-Olmec."

By far the most convincing evidence that Olmec writing was the ancestor of most other Mesoamerican writing has appeared in the form of a cylinder seal and fragments of a plaque described by Pope, Pope, and von Nagy (2002). Excavating at an Olmec center—La Venta—in western Mexico, these archeologists discovered these two objects contained inscribed glyphs that could be linked to later languages. Radiocarbon dating of charcoal associated with these two finds solidly placed their origins at 650 BC, well before any of the other Mesoamerican scripts were developed. Because of the similarity in style, these Olmec writings are now considered to represent the earliest evidence for the unique origin of writing in the new world. Of course, any such attribution is accompanied by the usual archeological disputation (see Stokstad, 2002).

The discovery of the relatively complete epi-Olmec La Mojarra stela in Mexico in 1986 has been translated by Justeson and Kaufman (1993). Although this stone dates from a period perhaps 1,000 years later (about 150 BCE) than the original Olmec period (900 BCE to 450 BCE), it is considered to be in the direct line of writing development with that more ancient system. It is now considered to be the oldest of the Middle American writing specimens to have yet been translated. The La Mojarra stela tells the story of an ancient king and the rituals he performed in his rise to power. It, too, is a remarkable lithic monument to writing from an entirely different location in the world than the Middle East.

There are only a few treasured examples of writing not done on stone. Among the most notable examples is a copy of the Egyptian *Book of the Dead* (dating from approximately 240 BCE). This important document was written on papyrus and its survival is considered to be almost miraculous considering the ephemeral nature of that plant product.

Another very special example of ancient writing, not executed on stone, is the extraordinary instance of the Dead Sea scrolls. These especially remarkable (because of their relevance to modern religious beliefs) documents were written between 400 BCE and the BCE–CE interface, most often on animal skins but in a few cases, on copper sheets. These very rare examples of nonlithic documents must be considered to be aberrations and their longevity must be attributed to the dry desert conditions in which they were found. Stone and fired clay remains the main repositories of ancient writing during the immediate post-Neolithic ages. Those cultures that left no written record have remained cryptic and poorly understood. Those that did leave a written record that was inscribed on stone are best remembered. The moral of this story obviously is: *If you want it to be remembered, inscribe it on a stone!*

4.2   THE EARLY HISTORY OF DEATH, AFTERLIFE, AND DUALISM

The historic period begins with the invention and dispersion of writing. History, therefore, must be dated from these times, a date uncertain but one that probably occurred between 3000 or 4000 BCE. After this momentous invention, we can examine the cognitive processes concerning death, not by indirect inference about what an artifact or human remain might have meant, but, much to be preferred, by directly reading the expressed intent of witnesses and respondents of those times.[9] I have already indicated that, with the exception of a few fragments, the written record essentially starts with the Sumerians. Therefore, let us begin by examining their ideas about death and the afterlife.

4.2.1   The Sumerians

It is important to appreciate that although written history begins in the fourth millennium BCE, prehistoric events that determined philosophies and religions had been running their course for many years. By the time of the Sumerians, religion had developed to a highly sophisticated level that belies any attempt to describe their point of view as the first of anything or even qualitatively different from the beliefs of their predecessors. During the Sumerian and predecessor civilizations, therefore, many important stages in the evolution of religious ideas had already occurred; that which

---

[9]Once again, it is important to note that even the most precisely written document may not be a valid indicator of what a person is thinking. There are many reasons to intentionally mislead or deceive as well as a host of unintentional self-misunderstandings.

had been "primitive" was now highly evolved, old ideas had been elaborated, and new ideas had been introduced. Where each concept came from is virtually impossible to determine.

The main point of discontinuity is that for the first time, we have records of what was happening, not that anything suddenly novel had happened at this critical point in human history. The major theme of this review is the search for the attitudes of these peoples to death and the afterlife as it was written down in the record of their times. As we now see, there is a remarkable consistency to the beliefs of many of these early historic societies. The rest of this chapter looks at a sampling of the historical polytheistic religions that existed prior to the rise of monotheism in the Middle East.

The Sumerian religion was clearly a polytheism, in that it was a theology of many Gods and Goddesses. Although the earliest cuneiform tablets named Enlil, ruler of the sky, Babbar the Sun God, and Enki, the Earth God, it is now appreciated that by the end of the Sumerian epoch, literally thousands of Gods were counted among the Sumerian Pantheon. Indeed, it seems that simply compiling lists of the names of the deities was a major activity of the Sumerian priestly class (Beek, 1962).

The Sumerian mythology that has come down to us is most notable for its epical tales of Gods and demigods whose adventures make up a major portion of their religious history. One aspect of their religion, oft repeated in many different forms, concerned the death of one or another of the Sumerian Gods. Indeed, death and the search for immortality generally played a central role through the Sumerian epics. What was to happen in an afterlife was fully and confidently described. For example, after death a God would travel to the "Land without Return" across the "Waters of Death" where they would be magically reborn. Indeed, as Eliade (1978) makes clear the deaths and resurrections of the Gods were essential parts of the religious beliefs of the Sumerians as well as the early Egyptians. As I discuss later in this chapter and the next, this same theme reappears in many other, even modern, religions. The metaphorical relation of this cycle of death and resurrection has an obvious connection to the solar cycle of the year—the Gods, like the earth, could die and then be reborn. The earthly annual cycle can be clearly seen as the model from which many of these ancient religions were derived. It takes no stretch of logic or imagination to see this same influence in modern religions.

Despite the fact that the afterlife was designated as "the land without return," a major, albeit inconsistent, part of the Sumerian religion was based on the idea that this supernatural "land" was only a temporary stop before a return to life, even for the human dead. The sense of immortality of the "soul" separate from the body was, therefore, deeply embedded in human consciousness during this early historical period. A dualist theory of the universe was highly developed by the time the Sumerian religion emerged from prehistory. The expression of two kinds of worlds, a natural and a supernatural one, distinguishing between a world of Gods and a world of humans, persists throughout all of the known Sumerian literature.

Both Gods and humans are eventually capable of being reborn according to the Sumerian mythology. The "land without return," temporary abode that it might be, was neither fully pleasant nor fully unpleasant—neither a heaven nor a hell. Rather it was a place for the person's evaluation by the Gods and a place in which it was determined how long a person must stay before returning to a worldly existence. There is dispute among archeologists whether this "return" was meant to be a literal reincarnation or something much less concrete.

Whatever the details of the Sumerian religion as we interpret them through the uncertain veil of cryptic cuneiform writing and linguistic and cognitive differences,[10] there is no question that their religion, one of the oldest of which we have written records, was deeply concerned with death. Fear of death had developed by their time into a rich philosophy and mythology of two quite different worlds, a natural one of life and a supernatural one of an afterlife. Furthermore, like virtually all other religions to come, human existence was divided into a transient corporeal one and a more or less permanent spiritual one. In 4th-millennium Sumeria, the vestigial glimmerings of the Paleolithic and Neolithic fears and concerns became fully manifest in a formal religious structure that left a written record. Nevertheless, the same dualist theme that permeates all other religions is also to be found in this one. The termination of the mind/soul/sprit was denied by separating the indisputable evidence of the death of the body from the hypothesis of an immortal soul and an interesting, if not heavenly, afterlife. Throughout this entire tradition, one senses a gentle, happy, more or less optimistic approach to life that was, unfortunately, not to be maintained in subsequent cultures.

4.2.2   The Egyptians

The Egyptian civilization temporally overlapped that of the Sumerians[11] and both, obviously, contributed parts of their considerable cultural achievements to most subsequent European and many Asian cultures. Egyptian

---

[10]Some artifacts that have been left to us carry meanings that are not all cryptic. For example, the Sumerian Warka Vase, a 3-foot-high stone vessel, has depicted on it what some authorities have argued may be the oldest graphic example of religious rituals. Dating from about 3100 BCE, it is described in Campbell (1974).

[11]The beginning of the first historic Egyptian dynasty has been dated to 3100 BCE. How precise this date is cannot be known with absolute certainty, but it is not far off compared to other contemporary dates. This important event is sign-posted by the unification of upper and lower Egypt by Menes/Narmer, the historic founder of the first dynasty.

history is remarkably well preserved because of their monumental tombs, their culture of preserving bodies, and their special concern for recording the chronology of their pharaohs and their accomplishments. Prior to the sequence of dynastic pharaohs, many of whom were known only through the ancient historical record known as the "King List," Egypt also had what is still a dimly understood predynastic period about which we are only recently becoming aware.

The already mentioned Scorpion King is one particular quasimythical individual who now seems also to have some historical reality. One of the tombs recently excavated in the predynastic burial grounds near the ancient city of Abydos by Dreyer (1998, 1999) is decorated with scorpion signs in a way suggesting that this was the name of an actual person. The Scorpion King is now believed to have lived about 3250 BCE just prior to the first Egyptian dynasties. The Scorpion King, now that his historical validity seems to have been authenticated, is given credit for the unification of upper Egypt—an important precursor of the unification of both upper and lower Egypt by the first dynastic Pharaoh—Narmer or Menes—who is discussed momentarily.

Earlier than that date, the mists of prehistory thicken and Egyptian legends describe god-like rulers who can only be considered to be mythological. The most famous of these god-like predecessors of the pharaonic predynasties and dynasties was the traditional founder of the Egyptian civilization—Horus, the falcon headed—supposedly the offspring of the Gods Osiris and Isis. Horus' contributions, such as bringing agriculture and religion to a barbaric and cannibalistic ancient Egypt, certainly suggest that he personified the Neolithic revolution that must have occurred in the thousands of years of Egyptian prehistory prior to the dynastic lists. The explanation of the rise of their respective civilizations by means of mythical personifications is also a constant theme throughout all the various historic civilizations discussed in this chapter. A God-myth about the origins of, say, agriculture, was a satisfactory answer to the ever-present question—Whence came our tradition of cultivating plants?—to a curious society that had no written or oral history or even memory of the actual event.

The Osiris story is especially interesting because it was not only the basis of subsequent Egyptian theological thinking, but also may have had a strong impact on subsequent Greek and Christian thought. Osiris, either a myth of a predynastic God or a vague recollection of a dimly remembered prehistoric king, is credited with the origins of Egyptian civilization. The Osiris myth of the development of the Egyptian civilization is a bloody and eerie one for our modern tastes. Nevertheless, this early resurrection myth has a curious familiarity even for our times. To understand why, I now present the barest outline of the story. This ancient tale is fully and elegantly described in Frazer's (1911) compilation of the great myths of civilization.

The story goes as follows: Osiris was murdered by his evil brother Set who was jealous of him for his accomplishments in bringing great wealth to Egypt. Nevertheless, Osiris was able, after his death, to father a son, Horus, with his wife, Isis. This inflamed Set's jealousy even more and he cut Osiris' body up into 14 pieces. The devoted wife Isis, however, was able to collect most of the body parts with the notable exception of the genitals. Then, with the help of the jackal God Anubis, she resurrected Osiris who thereafter became king of the dead.

From a modern perspective, the fascination lies in the role that the Osiris myth may have had in later religions. The basic theme of the myth is of the murdered and subsequently resurrected god/king/man. Freke and Gandy (1999) trace this idea through ancient religious histories and discuss how it reappears in the stories of Dionysus (Greece), Attis (Asia Minor), Adonis (Syria), Bacchus (Italy), Mithras (Persia), (all of whom are cited on their page 4) and ultimately in the Jesus story itself. Ancient ideas obviously have extraordinary staying power!

The first historical name (until the recent confirmation of the historicity of the Scorpion King) is the first dynasty Pharaoh Narmer, otherwise known as Menes. The last is the unquestionably historical Cleopatra. Table 4.1 presents a list of the currently accepted sequence of kingdoms and dynastic periods of ancient Egypt.

Narmer or Menes, a historic king of upper (i.e., southern) Egypt, is mainly known through an extraordinary artifact—the "Palette of Narmer." This tennis racket sized and oblong shaped stone object is dated to 3200 BCE just prior to the 1st dynasty. One side of the carving on the palette depicts Narmer's victory over the cities of Upper Egypt and the other side depicts what some believe are his conquests of lower Egypt. This juxtaposition suggests that Narmer was the first ruler to unite the southern and northern regions of the Nile River into a single country—Egypt. As such, he

TABLE 4.1
The Egyptian Pharaonic Dynasties (All Dates in BCE)

c. 3100–2613	Early Dynastic: Dynasties 1–3
c. 2613–2125	Old Kingdom: Dynasties 4–8
c. 2125–2025	First Intermediate Period: Dynasties 9–11
c. 2025–1700	Middle Kingdom: Dynasties 11–13
c. 1700–1550	Second Intermediate Period: Dynasties 13–17
c. 1550–1069	New Kingdom: Dynasties 18–20
c. 1069–945	Third Intermediate Period: Dynasty 21
c. 945–727	Third Intermediate Period: Dynasties 22–23
c. 727–332	Late Period: Dynasties 24–30 and Persian Occupation
c. 332–30	Ptolemaic Period[a]

[a]With the end of the Greek-influenced Ptolemaic period, Rome dominated Egypt and the Egyptian classical period and the Pharaonic dynasties came to an end.

is not only the first Pharaoh of a united Egypt but also the initiator of the dynastic sequence that was to rule Egypt for more than 3,000 years.

In contrast to the uncertainty that still hangs over our interpretation of religious life in ancient Sumeria, perhaps no ancient culture has left behind as complete a record of their attitudes toward death and the afterlife as the Egyptians. The reason for this is obvious; the Egyptians perhaps more than any other culture, before or since, were obsessed with death and dying. Indeed, to an extraordinary degree the centerpiece of their entire culture seems to have been preparation for death—particularly for their God-kings, the pharaohs of the many dynasties. The three huge pyramidal tombs built at Giza by the pharaohs Khufu, Khafre, and Menkaure, respectively, within a 50-year period of the old kingdom (probably between 2550 BCE and 2500 BCE) are among the most famous antiquities of all time. It is sufficient to say they are the largest constructed monuments dedicated to the idea of an afterlife and to the core assumption of the Egyptian religion that it was necessary to preserve the physical remains of a human for reuse in that afterlife.

Although originally it was only the God-kings who were supposed to ascend to heaven and who, presumably, would be in need of their earthly bodies, by the time of the middle kingdom Egyptian civilization (commencing about 2125 BCE) the entire death–mummification–afterlife culture became democratized. From this time on, preparation for the afterlife was prevalent throughout all social ranks. Although the tombs and graves of commoners are on a much smaller scale than the monumental old kingdom pyramids and sometimes their bodies were simply buried in more or less shallow graves, the mummified remains of ordinary citizens are constantly found scattered throughout many parts of modern Egypt. The excavation of an extensive mortuary[12] in the desert at the Bahariya Oasis west of Cairo was characterized more by the range of socioeconomic classes of those buried there than by enormous monuments (Hawass, 2000). This hidden pit burial area, which was in use up until about 300 BCE was filled with Roman as well as Egyptian mummies from their then contemporary societies. Regardless of the complexity of Egyptian burials, whether it be that of a pharaoh in a grand pyramid or these more plebian pit burials shared with dozens of their neighbors, each in its own way provides evidence of a commitment to the basic idea that it was necessary to prepare for immortality by preserving the body.

As noted, our knowledge of Egyptian religious ideas is extraordinarily rich. The main reason for this is that an enormous amount of effort was expended on the decoration of the pharaonic and other noble tombs themselves. Tombs were covered with inscriptions, drawings and paintings, and

---

[12]"Extensive" may be a gross understatement of the reality of this mortuary area. Hawass (2000) suggests it may contain more than 10,000 mummies!

incised carvings of an enormous variety, but all attempting to serve the anticipated needs of the dead in one way or another.

One of the most extraordinary inscriptions was the previously mentioned "Book of the Dead." The "Book" was not a book in the modern sense, but rather a collection of magical spells and embalming techniques to be used more or less as a guide for the dead person in traversing the afterlife. The extraordinary thing about the "Book" is that it was in use virtually unchanged for at least 2,000 years, certainly as far back as the Fifth Dynasty—from approximately 2500 BCE—until the end of the Ptolemaic period of Roman domination. There is some suggestion, indeed, that parts of the Book of the Dead may have been in use in Egypt much earlier. The Book of the Dead actually comes in many versions and subtexts that appeared throughout the entire dynastic history of Egypt.

During the Old Kingdom, the Book of the Dead was, as noted, inscribed on the walls of tombs and, as such, is usually referred to as examples of "pyramid texts." During the Middle Kingdom, the spells and instructions were painted on the inside of coffins and were referred to as "coffin texts." During the New Kingdom, the "Book" was written on papyrus whose survival was strongly dependent on the dry conditions of Ancient Egypt. The most famous of the papyrus texts is the one found in the tomb of Ani, a resident of the ancient capital of Thebes and dated to about 1240 BCE, a date probably within the Nineteenth Dynasty of the New Kingdom. The classic translation of the papyrus version of the Papyrus of Ani was done by Budge (1895) but the best modern version is considered to be the newer one by Faulkner (1994).

The Book of the Dead contains such useful hints for the dead as, for example, how to avoid being burnt by fire:

> Nu saith: I am the paddle which is equipped, wherewith Ra transported the Aged Gods, which raised up the emissions of Osiris from the Lake of blazing fire, and he was not burned. I sit down like the Light-god, and like Khnemu, the Governor of lions. Come, cut away the fetters from him that passeth by the side of this path, and let me come forth therefrom.

Another fascinating part of the Egyptian religion of death was that it did not invoke a simple dualism regarding the nature of the immortal components, but, rather, taught that the soul had many parts: It was a pluralism invoking many different kinds of spiritual realities! According to interpretations of ancient inscriptions, in addition to the mummified body itself, which was intended to remain in the tomb, the "personality" (i.e., soul or spirit) of a person actually consisted of several parts including:

1. The "ka," best thought of as the life force that animated the person while he was alive. It was created at birth. Dreams were manifestations of the ka's mental activity.

2. The "*ba*," an idea that is closer to what later religions referred to as the personality or character of a person.

3. The "akh." After mummification, a new spirit was generated by the re-combination of the ka and the ba. It was this spirit that could communicate with the living that was the form in which the dead existed.

4. The "Swt." This was the shadow or shade of the person.

5. Finally, the person's name itself was considered to be as important as any other part of his personality. It had to be written on walls of the tomb and on papyri for the activities of the afterlife. Obliterating the name of a person—a common practice throughout Egyptian history— could finally destroy the remaining vestiges of the person.

What was the afterlife like according to the Egyptians? One translation (Gardiner, 1935) describes the advice given to the dead in these words.

> Thou shalt come in and go out, thy heart rejoicing, in the favour of the Lord of the Gods, a good burial [being thine] after a venerable old age, when age has come, thou assuming thy place in the coffin, and joining earth on the high ground of the west.
> Thou shalt change into a living Ba and surely he will have power to obtain bread and water and air; and thou shalt take shape as a heron or swallow, as a falcon or a bittern, whichever thou pleasest.
> Thou shalt cross in the ferryboat and shalt not turn back, thou shalt sail on the waters of the flood, and thy life shall start afresh. Thy Ba shall not depart from thy corpse and thy Ba shall become divine with the blessed dead. The perfect Ba's shall speak to thee, and thou shalt be an equal amongst them in receiving what is given on earth. Thou shalt have power over water, shalt inhale air, and shalt be surfeited with the desires of thy heart. Thine eyes shall be given to thee so as to see, and thine ears so as to hear, thy mouth speaking, and thy feet walking. Thy arms and thy shoulders shall move for thee, thy flesh shall be firm, thy muscles shall be easy, and thou shalt exult in all thy limbs. Thou shalt examine thy body and find it whole and sound, no ill whatever adhering to thee. Thine own true heart shall be with thee, yea, thou shalt have thy former heart. Thou shalt go up to the sky, and shalt penetrate the Netherworld in all forms that thou likes. (pp. 29–30)

Death to the Egyptians, in other words, is very much like life, complete with both natural muscular responsiveness and dietary needs, but also buttressed with supernatural abilities to fly above or descend into the earth.

Death, at the worst was a "temporary interruption," a time during which there was transition from one form (life) to another (afterlife).

During this transition period, the dead person traveled on a boat to the Hall of Osiris in the Land of the Gods. It was here that the dead individual was judged and the heart weighed to evaluate the moral (or immoral) quality of the life that had been led. The scale on which the heart was placed was balanced by a feather of the Goddess Ma'at. Those who had led a good life would have such light hearts that the magical feather would weigh more; those who had done evil would be cursed by a heavy heart. Heavy hearts were devoured by the Goddess Amemet depriving the person of any kind of an afterlife. Only those who passed the heart test would return to their bodies to live again.

Beyond these magical tests, an important key to survival in the afterlife according to Egyptian theology was the preservation of the body. The Egyptians, therefore, had developed the elaborate mummification process that, as already discussed, became such a prevalent ritual throughout the history of their civilization. This embalming ritual probably had evolved from observations of the natural mummies that frequently occurred in the dry desert environment of Ancient Egypt, but the process took on a much more important ritual meaning over the millennia. Indeed, not only did the body have to be preserved, but so, too, did the afterlife of the dead person have to be provided for by filling the tomb with the clothing, tools, food supplies, and furniture that would be required to live a comfortable and satisfactory afterlife. For a pharaoh, the few unplundered tombs make it clear that the offerings were usually wildly extravagant. Although most Egyptian tombs had long ago been looted, a few like the famous grave of the relatively minor Pharaoh—Tutankhamen—gives an indication of the wealth that was poured into these royal graves (Carter, 1954). As the centuries went by, some tomb offerings became symbolic rather than real; pictures or models taking the place of the real objects. The arguable burial relics of the Middle Paleolithic and the verified ones from the Upper Paleolithic had by Egyptian times evolved into what was clearly among the most elaborate traditions of burial offerings that ever existed.

The details of mummification and the processing of the organs of the body always represent an exciting story, but the main point of mummification, often overlooked in our fascination for the technical details and the grisly results, was the distinction made between the body and the other aspects of a human that collectively came to be called the soul. Invisible though they may be, the Egyptian idea was that the afterlife provided a time that brought only pleasure and no pain to the virtuous dead. This afterlife was led, not in a heaven or hell, but rather in the middle of the living. The "next world" for Egyptians was coextensive with the present one.

All of this ritual was designed to provide for the needs of an individual that were assumed to continue after death. Perhaps, it has never been as clear anytime in human history how central a role was placed on an entire society by the search for that "escape hatch" from mortality. The economic cost to Egypt was enormous. One wonders what might have been if their natural resources had been directed in other directions?

4.2.3 The Akkadians—The Babylonians and the Assyrians

The Middle East has been referred to as the cradle of western civilization. It was there that many of the most important inventions of the Neolithic period were first created. It was there that writing was first developed as the prepotent communication tool of human history. Civilization in the form of settled communities evolved there when most of the rest of the world was still composed of hunting and gathering cave dwellers. Sophisticated polytheistic religions characterized virtually all of the religions of this area during this early historic period. I have already discussed the Sumerian and Egyptian civilizations and their theologies. I have also noted their monumental contributions to thought and culture in terms of their coincident invention of writing in both its pictographic and alphabetic forms. However, these two societies were not the only ones existing in the Middle East at the time of their greatest prominence. Other cultures arose and fell during the millennia from 5000 BCE to modern times. Some came and went mysteriously and we still have only partial information about their existence, their way of life, and for the purposes of this book, their ideas about immortality and the afterlife. Some of these peoples are now known only by fragments or cryptic monumental remains. For example, the Amorite, Kassite, and Hittite empires,[13] have not left the kind of historical records that the Egyptian and Sumerians did and, thus, have not caught the full attention of either archeologists or the lay public. Table 4.2 depicts the historical complexity of this region by tabulating one view of the historical sequence of indigenous and invading cultures that occupied this small region of land. (Some of these names are subdivisions of the Akkadian and Babylonian dominant culture; some of these dates are still only approximately known.)

---

[13]The Amorites (or Old Babylonians) were a nomadic people from the Arabian Peninsula who moved into and dominated Babylonia from about 1900 BCE to 1600 BCE. The Hittites followed them in controlling Babylonian Mesopotamia from about 1600 BCE to 1200 BCE. (The extent of their domain was much larger, however; the great city of Hattusas in central Turkey gives only an incomplete picture of the extent and grandeur of the Hittite empire.) The Kassites, like the Hittites an Indo-European people, followed and ruled the region for a brief period, all of this occurring during what was nominally the reign of the Akkadian domination.

TABLE 4.2
Historical Epochs of Ancient Mesopotamia

• Ubaid	5000–3500 BCE
• Uruk	3500–3100 BCE
• Jemdet Nasr	3100–2900 BCE
• Early Dynastic I–III	2900–2340 BCE
• Akkadian	2340–2100 BCE
• UR III	2100–2000 BCE
• Isin-Larsa	2000–1750 BCE
• Old Babylonian	1750–1600 BCE
• Kassite	1600–1150 BCE
• Post Kassite	1150–1000 BCE
• Neo-Babylonian	1000–539 BCE
• Achaemenid 5	539–331 BCE
• Seleucid	331–125 BCE
• Parthian	125 BCE–CE 226
• Sasanian	226–637 CE
• Islamic	637–1500 CE
• Ottoman	1500–1918 CE
• Modern Iraq	1918–?[a]

Note. The original source of this table is unknown. I am grateful to whomever constructed it.
[a]It is not yet certain at the time this book was written if domination by the American military will constitute a new epoch in Mesopotamian civilization.

However, other Middle Eastern civilizations did attract attention, sometimes because of their monuments and some because of the role they played in anticipating the nature and content of later religions. Among those that did survive the wasting forgetfulness of history were the Akkadians, a name that refers to what were originally thought to be two distinct cultures—the Babylonians and the Assyrians—but which are now thought by some scholars to be a more or less continuous development in middle eastern history. Collectively the two groups of Akkadians, along with the various intruders, and their descendants dominated the Tigris–Euphrates valleys from about 2300 BCE until about 600 BCE.

About 2300 BCE, the Sumerian civilization had begun to fall apart as repeated invasions disrupted their well-ordered society. The victors in 2340 BCE in this conquest were the Akkadians led by Sargon I and a succession of other unpleasant and, from the Sumerian point of view, barbarous despots. Sargon I had founded the city of Akkad and the dynasty that was to use his city's name only a few years before his conquest. From Akkad he was able to conquer most of Mesopotamia. He persists in history not only because of the extent of his conquests but because of the extraordinary organization of his domain. He is reputed to have formed the first professional army, that is, one composed of full-time soldiers rather than conscripts from the local population.

The history of the Tigris–Euphrates valley was, thus, marked by a succession of cultural changes, some of which were due to the series of conquests, but others occurred as an example of a process of natural societal evolution. The century beginning in 2100 BCE, for example, saw a renaissance of the old Sumerian culture in the Akkadian empire based in large part on the persistence of the Sumerian cuneiform writing system. This must have been a fascinatingly diverse time; the Sumerian culture has been described as being much more highly developed than the Akkadian one that had conquered it and the mixture of many traditions and languages stimulated an enormous amount of cultural change in the years that followed.

Many aspects of Sumerian life, thus, continued to influence the culture of the Akkadians during the next 600 years. However, in a period roughly dating from 2000 BCE to 1600 BCE, the Akkadian culture (including that of invading peoples) finally and completely swamped out the vestiges of the old Sumerian one. In 1750 BCE Hammurabi united the Babylonian empire and began the Babylonian and Assyrian supremacy that lasted, albeit influenced by many foreign invasions, for almost another 1,000 years. His written legal code inscribed on the black basalt stela (see page 90) remains one of the most significant relics of human history.

One particular Sumerian cultural aspect that did not survive these turbulent times, however, was the Sumerian spoken language. Akkadian was a Semitic language that became the dominant tongue of the Mesopotamian region for almost 1,000 years through the time of Babylon and the subsequent Assyrian period. Akkadian (i.e., the new spoken language), however, was written down in old Sumerian cuneiform and it is from records such as those that we have learned so much about Akkadian history.

The dominance of the Akkadian people in the Mesopotamian region was not continuous but was interrupted by invasions, wars, and conquests from outside forces throughout its almost 2,000-year-long history. The later Akkadians, in the form of the Assyrian empire, led by Sargon II, conquered all of Mesopotamia as well as modern day Lebanon and Israel and were even sufficiently strong to dominate Egypt for a short period between 1671 BCE and 1657 BCE. In 586 BCE, the Babylonian King Nebuchadnezzar II sacked the city of Jerusalem, destroyed the Hebrew temple, and sent the Hebrew people into "Babylonian Exile"—the Diaspora—the beginning of a 2,500-year-long exile that was not to end until the 20th century.[14] The power of the Akkadian–Babylonian–Assyrian Mesopotamian empire persisted until the rise of the Persian empire to the East and the Mediterranean superpowers Greece and Rome to the West.

Some of our ideas about the Akkadian religion come from retelling of what were more than likely originally Sumerian myths. The epic tales Enuma elish

---

[14]It is not entirely correct to say that the "Hebrew Diaspora" actually "ended" in 1948. The Jewish people, of course, are still scattered around the world.

(the creation myth) and the Epic of Gilgamesh[15] spell out their views of the origins of the world and the role of humans in it. From the beginning, two levels of reality were dealt with by these Mesopotamian peoples, not only for the Gods, but for the individual. In these epics, however, the Gods were given immortality but humans and demigods generally were not.

The Epic of Gilgamesh is a wonderful tale of adventure and misadventure. Gilgamesh, a king of Uruk, is described as the offspring of a Goddess and a mortal man. In spite of his partially supernatural origin, Gilgamesh is mortal and has an enormous fear of death. The epic relates his search for immortality after the death of his friend Enkidu. The quest ultimately fails but he does meet Utnapishtim, a mythical predecessor of Noah, who is the one mortal to whom the Gods have given eternal life. The bad news is presented to Gilgamesh by Siduri, a tavern-keeper, in what has become one of the most quoted lines from antiquity:

> You will never find that life for which you are looking. When the gods created man they allotted to him death, but life they retained in their own keeping. As for you, Gilgamesh, fill your belly with good things; day and night, night and day, dance and be merry, feast and rejoice. Let your clothes be fresh, bathe yourself in water, cherish the little child that holds your hand, and make your wife happy in your embrace; for this too is the lot of man.[16]

The differences between the Sumerian and Akkadian attitudes toward death, mortality, and the afterlife are significant. Whereas death seems to have been but a brief interlude to the Sumerians who did believe in human immortality for some, there is a gradual increase in a morbid cynicism that was increasingly expressed by the Akkadians. Eliade (1978) suggested that this was the result of an emerging awareness of the fact that life was not fair. He stated:

> This despair arises, not from a meditation on the vanity of human existence, but from the experience of general injustice: the wicked triumph, prayers are unanswered; the gods seem indifferent to human affairs. (p. 81)

How this despair and cynicism was expressed in the daily life of the Akkadians cannot be known for sure. However, their society lasted for a remarkably long time although interspersed as it was by outside invasions and

---

[15]The Epic of Gilgamesh was originally found on a set of clay tablets inscribed in antique Sumerian cuneiform. Until the recent discovery of the Gebel Tjauti tableau it was generally considered to be the oldest complete written story of any kind.

[16]These lines are reputed to have come from the Xth tablet of the Gilgamesh Epic by Eliade (1978). Curiously, although quoted in several sources, some translations do not contain these famous lines. This may be because of their explicit rejection of human immortality and the conflict it, therefore, raises with many subsequent religions.

then their own reconquests. War was continuous, enhanced by the lack of any natural defenses of the Tigris–Euphrates valley. It appears very likely the gentle optimism of the Sumerians was replaced by a time of turmoil and both social and personal disappointment. It is this unsettled time that obscures our knowledge of some of these cultures that may have had significant civilizations at that time.

4.2.4 The Indus River Valley Civilizations

North Africa and the Tigris–Euphrates valleys were not the only places in which recorded civilization with rich religious traditions were developing from 3000 BCE to the BCE–CE interface. China and the Central and Southern Americas also are now known to have been going through similar cultural revolutions and to have developed what are clearly high religious cultures of their own about this time. Somewhat less well known, however, was the civilization that developed in the Indus River valleys of modern day Pakistan and India. Perhaps this is because of the less direct line of influence on western civilization exerted by the Indus River valley peoples. Whatever the reason, it is worthwhile looking at the development of writing and religion in this region in addition to the ones already discussed.

The ancient history of the Indus River valley people goes back to a time that is as least as ancient as that of the Nile and Tigris–Euphrates valley peoples. Why these regions should have been the ones to produce civilizations is a well-discussed issue. Suffice it to say that they provided what Gordon-Childe (1945) described as an "optimum challenge"—one that was neither too harsh nor too easy to stimulate the growth of a complex civilization. These fertile valleys allowed agriculture to develop and flourish so extensively that many workers in the population could be spared to partake in the development of other aspects of civilized life, like furthering the development of theological ideas.

The oldest remnants of Neolithic villages in the Indus River valley at Mehr Garh are dated back to about 7000 BCE. More highly developed cultures dating from 3300 BCE have been discovered at Kot Diji. By 2800 BCE, these early cultures seem to be completely replaced by the Harappan civilization, a much more complex society that, like the Egyptian and Sumerian civilizations to the west, also developed their own form of written records.

The Harappan cultures are named after one of the most important of the Indus River communities—Harappa, the first to be excavated. Harappa was probably settled as early as 2800 BCE. The peak of the Harappan culture is estimated to have thrived between 2800 BCE and 1900 BCE. Other cities sharing this culture and this time have also been located including the much larger Mohenjodaro, an extraordinary city equipped with baths, indoor toilets, and a central citadel, among many other wonderful architectural delights. Both of these ancient cities seem to have been wiped out by invasions from the north about 1500 BCE. A classic book on the Indus River valley civilizations was written by Wheeler (1966); a more recent history can be found in Kenoyer (1998).

Before discussing the prototypical Harappan religious cultures and the development of the Indus valley style of writing in general, it is worthwhile to mention another early Harappan site known as Dholavira. It was here that one of the earliest examples of a totally unique form of writing was discovered—the famous "signboard" of the citadel. This collection of 10 large letters of the Harappan script may have been a welcome sign or the name of the gate on which it was placed. Whatever it actually represented, it is now thought to be the oldest item of a large-scale publicly displayed writing ever found.

The nature of Harappan civilization is better known, however, through the sites at Harappa and especially at Mohenjodaro, both enormous and surprisingly modern communities. Both cities were first[17] professionally excavated in the early 1920s. The archeological remains suggest that centralized support of agricultural activities was the main reasons for these huge settlements.

The Indus River civilization was both extensive in size and heavily populated. Indeed, it is assumed to have covered an area of more than one half million square miles. Recent estimates suggest that the population of either one of these Harappan cities very likely had exceeded those of the Sumerian, Egyptian, and Akkadian cities that were its contemporaries.

The first examples of Indus valley writing were found on pottery shards dating from about 3000 BCE. These were simple tree-like marks, perhaps indicating the name of the potter. The Harappan-era writing system is better known to us primarily through the medium of small seals and tags. Inscribed on these small tags and seals are the symbols of a written language consisting of 60 syllables that can be combined into several hundred compound signs. Almost all of the written inscriptions were very short—the longest being only 7 to 10 characters. This has led to great difficulty in deciphering their written language.

Although the Indus language has long been considered to be undeciphered, several recent publications claimed to have finally been able to translate them. One by Jha and Rajaram (1996) suggested that the language is akin to Vedic Sanskrit. A second viewpoint has been expressed by Winters (1989, 1990); he believed the Harappan language is more closely related

---

[17]An interesting story of colonial empire suggests that the ruins at Harappa had, in fact, been discovered in the 19th century by a deserter from the British army—Charles Masson. Surprisingly, given his status as a felon in Victorian England, he was able to eventually write a book (Masson, 1842) in which he discussed his observations there and gained a certain fame, if not infamy, for his earlier behavior.

to the Dravidian languages that emerged from the Saharan region of Africa. Although both sources claim they have been able to decipher this ancient language and that some translations are now available, the purported decipherments have come under severe criticisms from other scholars. Witzel and Farmer (2000) and Parpola (2000), for example, believed that Jha and Rajaram (1996) did not provide a convincing argument for decipherment and may have "fudged" some of their data. The topic has been fraught with controversy. Indeed, Possehl (1996) has written an entire book debunking the many attempts to decipher the ancient Indus River valley texts.

The germane question to the topic of this book is: What did these Harappan fragments have to say about the religion of the Indus River valley peoples? Even in the absence of a specific translation of their script, the pictographs suggest their religion was deeply reverent toward animals and plants. Many of their tags display pictures of bulls, a feature in common with many of the religions of the Mediterranean region. Cobras, unicorns, tigers, elephants, and horses all appear on various fragmentary samples along with mythical creatures. Another theme is represented by branching geometric structures that seem to represent trees, much like those found on the earlier mentioned shards. One thing is for certain; the Harappans used their writing mainly for religious representations, as a way of concretizing their prayers rather than for commercial accounts as did the Sumerians. They were talismans, prayers, and invocations, not bookkeeping accounts!

From these seals, Winters (1989, 1990) concluded that the Harappans were, like all religions discussed in this chapter, polytheistic. It is unclear whether they actually considered animals to be their Gods or whether the animals depicted on the tags and seals were simply symbols (i.e., names) for more humanoid Gods. There also appears to have been a cult of a mother Goddess as well as frequent depictions a bull-like horned human. The use of the bull as a symbol again dimly reflects the Neolithic religions of Jericho and Catal Huyuk and suggests some kind of a cultural link. The existence of any direct communication between these cultures is problematical, at best; we shall probably never know whether this was an example of convergent cultural evolution or an influence from further west in the ancient Middle East or Turkey.

It is now generally agreed (e.g., see Eliade, 1978) that the Harappan religious system was a direct antecedent of the Hindu religion that evolved in India in the centuries that followed. There are many common features including an early version of the Hindu Goddess Siva and the reverence for the phallic lingam. Yoga was also practiced in the Harappan cities and this, too, suggests connections with the Hindu religion of the successor Indian cultures.

The Harappan peoples practiced simple burial rituals that were nowhere as complex as those found, for example, in Egypt. The Harappans simply placed food in clay jars alongside the wooden coffins of the dead. Few other objects were placed in their tombs, certainly nothing that was of great value—again, quite unlike the Egyptian tradition. However, the indications of their complex supernatural world and the fact that grave offerings were made at all strongly support that these early Indus River valley people believed in an afterlife and, thus, either explicitly or implicitly believed in a separate kind of existence for the mind/soul and the body, respectively. Dualism was as major a part of their life as that of any of their neighbors to the north and west.

4.2.5 Ancient China

The antiquity of Chinese religions is sometimes obscured by the fact that two of them—Confucianism and Taoism—are still very much a part of modern Chinese culture. Another mitigating factor is that both are, from one point of view, philosophies or quasi-religions more concerned with the relationships among humans than with the relation of humans to the Gods. In chapter 5, I consider these two persistent quasi-religions in detail.

The task before us now, however, is to describe the ancient Chinese beliefs about death and the afterlife as indicators of their dualist approach in the times prior to the widespread adoption of the two great philosophical systems. To appreciate the history and religious attitudes of the predecessors, contemporaries, and successors of Confucius (who lived from 551 BCE to 479 BCE) and Lao-Tzu, the founder of Taoism (who probably lived from about 600 BCE to 530 BCE) we have to turn to the archeological, mythological, as well as secondhand copies of written records. It will help to understand the historical sequence by reference to the dynastic periods of China prior to the time of Christ (see Table 4.3). Between the Neolithic Chinese people (see page 72 for a fuller discussion of those times) who date from a period as far back as 8000 BCE, on the one hand, and the now generally agreed to be historic Xia culture, that dates from 2200 BCE on the other, only mythology guides our discussion. At best, this "mythology" is available only in written records that were recopied about 2,000 years ago from earlier, and now lost, documents.

These ancient myths speak of three "Cultural Heroes"—Fu Hsi, Shen Nung, and the Yellow Emperor—each of which was reputed to have invented major items of Chinese culture. To Fu Hsi is attributed writing, hunting, and fishing; to Shen Nung is attributed agriculture and commerce; and to the Yellow Emperor is attributed government and commerce. Once again, the three "heroes" might better be thought of as embodiments of cultural memories personifying these important cultural developments, rather than as real historical individuals. However, they are said to have lived between 2800 and 2600 BCE, dates that are so recent and so specific that it at least leaves open the possibility of their historical reality.

TABLE 4.3
The Early Chinese Dynasties

Prehistoric Period	?–2200 BCE
Xia	2200–1776(?) BCE
Shang	1776(?)–1050 BCE
Western Zhou	1050–771 BCE
Eastern Zhou	770–221 BCE
Spring and Autumn Period	770–476 BCE
Warring States Period	475–221 BCE
Qin	221–207 BCE
Han	206 BCE–220 CE

Only slightly more likely to have actually existed, as opposed to being pure myths, are the three "Sage Kings"—Yao, Shun, and Yu. These three have been much more specifically dated (than the three "heroes") to the century between 2300 and 2200 BCE. Indeed, the last of the three has more than just a tentative historical existence; King Yu may well have been a real person. Recent archeological evidence suggests that he may have been the same person as the founding emperor of the Xia dynasty. To him is attributed at least the partial control of the floods that decimated China throughout its history.

For years the Xia dynastic period was itself considered to be mythological and of doubtful historical reality. This skepticism existed despite the fact that later historical records listed a very detailed and specific chronology of its kings. Even today, there is still is considerable controversy whether the Xia period was sufficiently well organized and broad enough in the extent of its power to represent a unified state in the sense in which the later dynasties dominated vast regions of China. Currently, the clouds of ancient mythology have parted sufficiently so that the Xia Empire is now considered to be one of the true historical periods of ancient China. Archeological excavations at the community of Erlitou (dated with some uncertainty to about 2000 BCE) and other locations along the Yellow River have revealed large buildings that vastly eclipse the proportions of the earlier Neolithic villages. Because of its size and the nature of the remaining constructions, there is little doubt that Erlitou should be considered to be a city in the true sense of the word. Whether it was a powerful enough city to have conquered a large "empire" is still a matter of debate. However, a consensus seems to be developing these days that the Xia culture, represented by finds at the Erlitou settlement, was in all possible ways a "centralized territorial state" (Liu & Chen, 2003).

Of one fact, however, there is no doubt; this period saw the dawning of the great Chinese accomplishments in bronze metallurgy. One tale related to this technological contribution supporting the notion that the Xia Empire did have true imperial extent is that of the bronze cauldrons. King Yu, the reputed founder of the Xia dynasty, the story goes, cast nine great bronze cauldrons ("The Auspicious Bronzes of the State") to represent the nine lands he had conquered. What gives credence to these otherwise mythical cauldrons is that they are repeatedly referred to throughout the historical records of the Shang and Zhou dynasties; each succeeding culture reporting that the cauldrons were among the booty gained during their respective conquests. This historical record is strongly suggestive evidence that the Xia Empire was a major player in early Chinese history regardless of the historicity of the cauldrons themselves.[18] Nevertheless, the history of this early dynastic period remains shrouded in doubt and myth and the significance of the Erlitou finds remains controversial (Thorpe, 1991).

Another important contribution of the Xia dynasty that has a considerable logical and chronological credibility is the invention of the earliest form of Chinese writing. Given that sophisticated writing found on the so-called "oracle bones," on inscriptions on bronze artifacts, and in the form of red lettering on ceramic pottery of the successor Shang dynasty, it is almost certain that an archaic form of Chinese writing had existed and most likely was first developed during the Xia period.

The exact dates of these earliest dynasties of Chinese history are at best uncertain and, in fact, there may not be sharp lines of temporal demarcation between them and their prehistoric predecessors. These archaic dynastic periods may represent the outcome of very arbitrary lines of demarcation suggested by later historians in place of a continuous evolution of cultural styles. It is much more likely that from the time of the Neolithic settlers, there was a progression of cultural stages occurring almost continuously in China. The Lanshao and Lungshan peoples described on page 72 may simply have represented milestones along the way from even earlier prehistoric people that eventually culminated in the Xia and Shang societies. Each of these early stages of Chinese history and prehistory had its own material culture as reflected in its archeological remains, but one may have simply fathered the next one.

Like the Xia, the Shang dynasty was first considered to be only a figment of mythology and fantasy by Chinese historians. It, too, has now taken on a concrete reality as excavations at the very early Shang site of Zhengzhou and at the last Shang capital at AnYang (Chang, 1986) have produced the remains of indisputatively large cities as well as written lists of the Shang kings. Amazingly enough, the ancient lists replicated some of those that had been copied centuries later and had independently survived to modern

---

[18]Repeated historical reference to the cauldrons, of course, may be in their symbolic sense. At later times they may have come to represent the conquered territories rather than actual physical objects.

times. We now know that the Shang dynasty lasted until the reasonably precise date of 1027 BCE when it was overrun by the Zhou nomads from western China. This last date and the facts of the conquest are specific enough to clearly separate the times of the Shang and the Zhou. From this point on, dates of specific events and of the lives of a few people, at least, become much more certain.

The Zhou people controlled a substantial portion of China for 800 years. However, from 770 BCE on, the Zhou Empire began to disintegrate. At first it was a gradual reduction in the area under their control produced by attacks from "barbarians" from the north and west. The Zhou Empire was greatly reduced in size to a remnant in East China during a time referred to as the "Spring and Autumn" period. From 475 BCE until 221 BCE, China fell in chaotic disorder. This period was so terribly disruptive as various warlords contested who would dominate China that it came to be called the "Warring States" period.

The Warring States period was followed by an enormous sociopolitical event—the unification of China under the Emperor Qin. The Qin dynasty, although very short-lived (221–207 BCE), marked a period of enormous cultural and political vitality and, as we see later in this discussion, left the world with one of its greatest cultural treasures.

This brings us to the point of this brief history and to the culmination of what had been a developing Chinese burial culture[19] that was eventually to rival that of the Egyptians in the splendor of its contents if not in the blatant obviousness of its above ground monuments. Much of this archeological record, however, is little known to westerners. There are several reasons for this obscurity. One reason is that Chinese history is generally not well known in Europe and the Americas. Citizens of the "west" tend to look for their roots in the ancient lands of the Mediterranean. Another very important reason is an architectural one. Although many of the most famous Egyptian tombs were built above ground (it was only in the later dynastic periods that tombs were hidden to avoid plunders), almost all of the Chinese tombs were initially hidden underground in pits. Only late in Chinese history did the use of earthen mounds become widespread. Furthermore, many of the most famous Chinese tombs were only discovered after World War II and most have not yet been full excavated, whereas there had been extensive discovery and excavation in the Mediterranean in the 18th and 19th centuries. Nevertheless, those Chinese tombs that have found their way in popular western consciousness are equally as extraordinary as the

---

[19]An excellent guide through the sequence of Chinese burial styles can be found in the website maintained by the University of Washington designated as http://depts.washington.edu/chinaciv/archae/tmarmain.htm. It has been an important source in much of the following discussion. Even more important to me have been my personal visits to the tomb museum of the Marquis of Yi and to the amazing terra cotta soldiers at Xian.

western ones. They also make it clear that the ancient Chinese had a dualist worldview that differed only in detail from those of the West. In both societies, the foundation assumption was that an important and separate aspect of the mind or spirit continued after the death of the body and that it was necessary to provide for its needs, both in terms of materials goods and, as we see shortly, in terms of "support personnel."

From the dawn of Chinese history it is clear that their early religious beliefs were strongly committed to the idea that there was some spiritual continuation of earthly life. However, the details of the afterlife were not well defined. Indeed, the oldest Chinese traditions barely distinguish between the body and spirit. When a person died, several different kinds of spirits or breaths (Ch'I) persisted and continued to have an active role in the world and activities of the living. Indeed, the famous oracle bones were messages sent seeking advice from one's ancestors rather than from Gods. The situation, of course, did not remain static, many different belief structures developed over the long history of China. At one time, it was taught that the spirit or soul had two components—the "Hun"—restricted to the nobility, which became a part of the Heavenly court, and the commoner's "P'o," which descended into some ill-defined kind of netherworld. A more detailed discussion of these early Chinese theologies may be found in Seidel (1987).

The ambiguous and equivocal line between life and death meant that the needs of the dead had to be provided for by material goods as well as "support personnel." The number, variety, extent, and contents of Chinese tombs and burials that have already been discovered are extraordinary even in the bright light of the Middle East. As the burial history of China is being progressively revealed by modern archeological excavations, the major observable trend is in the increase in the value and amount of goods that were interred with the dead person. The Xia graves discovered at Erlitou contained some of the earliest evidence of Chinese bronze casting. Some of the pieces are obviously reproductions of earlier Neolithic stone implements; others are objects of graceful simplicity that speak to the early stage of development of bronze metallurgy as early as 2000 BCE. Nevertheless, chemical analysis has confirmed that the construction of these objects was based on a sophisticated knowledge of the metal. However historically significant and charming in their simplicity the grave goods of this time were, they were only pale harbingers of what was yet to come.

Very recently (1997–2000 CE) additional Xia gravesites have been excavated at Donglongshan in northwest China. The objects found there included some that were closely related to the Erlitou artifacts and some that seemed to have come from an earlier and simpler culture. The findings at Donglongshan are now thought to represent an early stage of development of the Xia. Among the discoveries there were 37 tombs, none of which contained any extraordinary objects, just a few simple stone implements, and some pottery. The absence of bronze implements in this early Xia settlement anchors speculation about the invention of bronze casting to the Xia period. Its early stages did not have any; its later stages did. Therefore, Chinese bronze casting was invented during the Xia dynasty.

The artistic and technical development of bronze objects reached a very high level of sophistication during the subsequent Shang dynasty. The enormous variety and beauty of the Shang bronzes were harbingers of what was to come in the later artistic history of early China. The Shang development of bronze casting from its primitive Xia beginnings was truly amazing. Drums, bells, cups, and cooking vessels of many kinds, all decorated with intricate designs filled the Shang excavations. The catalog (Anonymous, 1980) of the 1980–1981 exhibition "The Great Bronze age of China" only begins to indicate the scope of Shang bronze work.

In one of the best known tombs at AnYang (dated to 1250 BCE), that of Fu Hoa, the wife of one of the Shang kings, more than 400 bronze objects were found along with more than 700 jade objects. However, only a few pieces of pottery were found in this honorable lady's grave. Most interesting, in terms of the perceived need to serve the needs of the dead, was the fact that 16 human skeletons and six dog skeletons were found arrayed around her coffin presumably to provide support for this noble lady in her afterlife! For an unknown period of time prior to Fu Hoa's death, human sacrifice had obviously been an important aspect of preparation of the deceased for the afterlife. Other indications that it was an afterlife for which these objects and sacrifices were specifically being prepared was that Fu Hoa had been given a new name—Si Mu Xin—when she was buried, a name that presumably was to be used in her afterlife. The Fu Hoa site as well as other Bronze Age burials in ancient China is described in Chang (1986).

Other Shang dynasty tombs suggest that human sacrifice was widely accepted during this period. For example, at Xiao Xuanqiao, mass burial pits were found that contained dozens of skeletons as well as other pits with only scattered body parts. Many of these were severely mutilated and most seemed to be the remains of young men. Thus, it is possible, as archeologists have suggested, that these were the remains of captured soldiers or slaves that were not deemed worthy of the extravagant ritual burial of the nobility such as those that attended that of Fu Hoa.

At Xibeigang, a Shang town near AnYang, Ayers (1998) reports that 11 tombs, possibly those of 11 AnYang kings were also found with many dismembered human sacrifices. Parts of bodies and decapitated corpses were found scattered through the tombs. Additionally, a wide variety of offerings including food, clothes, and useful utensils were present supporting the conclusion that a belief in an afterlife was also very important during the Shang period.

The idea of human sacrifices was continued by the Zhou invaders that conquered the Shang dynasty, although in a more modest fashion. The Zhou tomb of the Count of Yu, who was buried around 400 BCE, even though much larger than the Shang tomb, had "only" seven associated skeletons. What was reduced in human remains was made up in Bronze objects—more than 2,700 objects made from this metal were interred with the Count and his wife and possibly, his favorite concubine—a happy family group indeed.

Another important aspect of these early burials was their size. Fu Hoa's early Shang gravesite was relatively modest. It was a pit only about 5.6 m by 4 m and entirely below ground level. The Zhou tomb of the Count of Yu was considerably larger measuring 8.4 meters by 5.2 meters, but buried 12.2 m deep. The tombs became progressively larger, buried deeper, and filled with greater and greater numbers of grave offerings as the centuries passed.

It was also to this Western Zhou period (1050 BCE–771 BCE) that the earliest Chinese writing other than the oracle bones is attributed. In particular, Shujing—the book of documents—is the leading candidate for being the oldest Chinese written history. It is a collection of speeches and edicts describing and justifying the conquest of the Shang by the Zhou as well as describing some of the religious rites of the time.

By the time in the Warring States period when Zeng Hou Yi, the Marquis of Yi, died (his tomb is precisely dated to 433 BCE), the tombs were even larger and filled with even more ornate treasures. The Yi tomb itself was not discovered until 1977; a beautifully arranged museum now holds the objects found within it. In 2002, I had the opportunity to visit the Yi tomb at Hubei near Shanghai. The tomb was also in the form of an underground pit but, unlike the earlier ones, it consisted of a suite of several large rooms. It was also much larger than either of the two earlier tombs just described. Its dimensions were irregular but it stretched 21 m in one direction and 16.5 in the other at a maximum and was buried very deeply (13 m) into the ground. Every effort had been made to preserve these tombs and it contents. The whole pit had been filled with charcoal that had become waterlogged over the centuries. This combination of charcoal and water meant that the tomb contents were in an excellent state of preservation when it was finally discovered and excavated in 1978 CE.

The Yi tomb was filled with many wonders. Human sacrifices were found here too; 21 young women had been buried with the good Marquis. The grave goods consisted of some extraordinary objects including articles of bronze, gold, and jade. However, by far the most imposing were two remarkable musical instruments, one a carillon of 65 bronze bells of sizes varying from very small to quite massive (a meter or so in height) and the other a similar percussion instrument made of 32 marble slabs. Details of the contents are described in a book by the Hubei Museum Staff (written in

1995). During my visit I had the opportunity to hear a concert played on these two bells sets and on other instruments that were found in the tomb. It was an extraordinary experience, carrying many in the audience back to a time in a way that was totally unexpected yet profoundly touching. The bells and the slabs performed as well 2,300 years later than when they were first constructed. Many of the other Yi tomb objects indicated both an exquisite aesthetic sense as well as a technical mastery of bronze and jade fabrication.

By far the most impressive of the Chinese tombs, however, is the world famous Qin mausoleum at Xian in central China. Here, size and contents have evolved to a level that has few peers anywhere in the world. The story is a fascinating one told well in books such as the one by Cotterell (1981). However, this is also one of those places that must be seen to be fully appreciated. No book can convey the magnitude of this archeological wonder. My two visits to it in 1983 and 2001 were among my most important archeological experiences. Qin Shih-huang-ti, revered as the first emperor to unify all of China, must have been a remarkable man. Although his rule, and indeed, that of his dynasty was brief, during the 14-year period that he ruled China his many accomplishments included the standardization of the many different legal, commercial, and writing systems of the Warring States period that had preceded him. He was also able to carry out major construction projects including irrigation systems, an elaborate system of roads, and, most notably, at least the continuation of the construction of the Great Wall that had been an ongoing project for the previous two centuries. His armies were well organized and effective. Unfortunately for his regime, his armies were unable to overcome the Peasant's Rebellion that overthrew his dynasty almost immediately after he died.

What he did leave us in those few years (beyond the sociopolitical contribution of a unified China) is now considered by all to be one of the true wonders of the ancient world. As soon as Qin became Emperor, he had begun the construction of a mausoleum that rivals in many ways the Pyramids of Egypt. The historical record is detailed (see, e.g., Cotterell, 1981, p. 17). 700,000 workers were reported to have built an elaborate underground city that is described as having "rivers of mercury," "models of buildings," and the bodies of concubines and workers. Exactly what is actually contained in Qin's tomb is still unknown because the mound in which it is buried is yet to be excavated. What has been excavated from a series of pits in the neighborhood of the tomb mound, however, is stupendous in its own right—a stunning army of terra cotta warriors. Their existence and the magnitude of this find suggest that the interior of Qin's tomb itself may actually be as marvelous as it was described in the ancient literature.

The story of the discovery of the terra cotta army is well worth a few paragraphs. In 1974, some local farmers were digging a well approximately

3 km from the tomb mound of the emperor. These farmers discovered a life-sized head formed of terra cotta, a rough clay used for millennia by potters everywhere. The head was taken to a local schoolteacher who brought it to the attention of the authorities and the archeological community. Preliminary excavations revealed a most extraordinary archeological find—an entire army of individually designed, clay models of Chinese soldiers who had stood frozen in ranks for more than 2,200 years!

The site at which the first terra cotta soldiers were found was but the first of what eventually has turned out to be three vast underground pits. The largest, Pit 1, had been buried 5 meters below the farmer's field. It was enormous, extending 210 m in length and 60 in width. Although only partially excavated, the army consisted of 11 ranks of life-sized soldiers. In all it is now estimated that there were more than 3,200 of these soldiers guarding the Qin tomb! Pit 2 is still in an early stage of excavation but seems to be mostly associated with chariots and their riders—a mobile force whose raison d'etre was the protection of the Emperor's tomb in his afterlife as his living army had done in his life. Pit 3 was much smaller and seems to have been a headquarters detachment. When I visited the excavations in 2002, three sturdy and architecturally pleasant protective buildings had been built over these three pits making it one of the grandest museums in the world.

There are so many interesting aspects to this "army" that it would take (and has taken) many books and articles to describe it fully. Briefly, it is of special interest to know that each of the terra cotta warriors is individually sculpted—both faces and clothing were individually formed. In addition to the soldiers, the remains in the pits include a number of chariots as well as many life-sized reproductions of the horses that drew them. Many bronze weapons were also found, but most of the soldiers had been carrying wooden implements that had long ago deteriorated. Although uniformly gray nowadays, traces of color suggest that individual warriors were originally painted with bright colors.

All three of the pits and their contents have been badly damaged over the years. Shortly after the death of Emperor Qin, soldiers of the Peasant Rebellion pillaged and set fire to the terra cotta warriors in their trenches. Obviously the location of the terra cotta warriors was still well known in the years immediately following their construction. Over the years, earthquakes had also damaged the wood beams holding up the ceilings and considerable amounts of earth had collapsed inward fracturing most of the warriors, their chariots, and the horses into pieces. Everything had been damaged to some degree and it has been a continuing task for Chinese archeologists to reconstruct those that have been excavated from what are sometimes badly fractured shards. Nevertheless, the museum now displays large numbers of the reconstructed soldiers, horses, and chariots; it is quite a sight!

The Qin tomb, despite its magnificence and the extent to which it departs from earlier tombs in terms of size, still shares many of the same characteristics exhibited by it predecessors. The basic logic behind the presence of the army is based on the dualist assumption that the Emperor will need the services of these fighting men in his afterlife just as he did in his life. As likely as it is that the tomb itself contained food and concubines for his future needs, so too was the army a lasting symbol of his needs to defend an unearthly afterlife empire. The suggestion in the written records of human sacrifice in the main tomb (although no real skeletons have been found in the three pits of the terra cotta warriors) supports the suggestion that the Chinese rituals of that time also invoked the dualist concept of an afterlife with service needs that must be satisfied. It is, perhaps, an indication of improving social and ethical standards that the terra cotta replicas could serve that need in place of what otherwise might have been an army of sacrificed living humans.

This archeological story of tombs and graves, of offerings for the dead, as well as the written records that do survive from these early Chinese dynasties, provide us with a picture of an indigenous Chinese religion that continued to develop during the early dynastic periods. Despite the turmoil of conquests and overturned dynasties, this religious tradition is surprisingly well preserved and relatively continuous even to our times. The archeological evidence indicates a strong element of veneration, if not worship, of ancestors who are supposed to influence the daily life of the living long after they are gone. These ancestral spirits represented a supernatural level of existence, distinct from the natural one of the body. Clearly, there is in this philosophy, like that of all other religions, a commitment to the dual nature of existence—the transient body and the perpetual spirit.

There is a certain familiar constancy to the sequence of Chinese discoveries that I have reviewed here compared to the others discussed in this chapter. That constancy is the pervasive influence of dualist thinking arising out of the fear of death, the general acceptance of the persistence of the mind/spirit/soul, and the persistent reverence for ancestors.

4.2.6 Minoa, Mycea, and Classical Greece

As discussed earlier, in the millennium prior to the time that the Xia and Shang dynasties dominated East Asia, European and Middle Eastern societies were also in the process of developing their writing systems and recording the events of their colorful histories. The Egyptian, Mesopotamian, and Indus River valley societies all developed thriving civilizations in the period of 3000 to 2000 BCE. About the same time as the first Xia city of Erlitou (about 2000 BCE) was settled, other developments were occurring in the Mediterranean Sea area to which I now direct my readers' attention.

Among the earliest of these Mediterranean civilizations was that of the Minoans that emerged on the island of Crete. Named after its best remembered King—Minos—this was a land of great palaces and, apparently a luxurious life style. The classical archeological study of the island was written by Evans (1964), who carried out the most complete excavations of the Minoans' great palaces. Although Crete was definitely inhabited by early Neolithic peoples as early as 6000 BCE, the golden age of the Minoan palaces dates only from 2000 BCE. Elaborate palaces were first constructed at Knossos and other locations on the island about this time, only to be repeatedly destroyed and rebuilt for hundreds of years. Ultimately, the eruption of the great volcano on Santorini in 1450 BCE led to the final decline of the Minoa civilization.

Minoan burials varied over the long history of the island; caves originally were used and then constructed tombs. Unfortunately, no written records have been recovered from the earliest times in Crete. In their absence, pottery, bronze, and other grave offerings give us a picture of a society dominated by a mother goddess (often associated with snake worship) and the persistent story of man against bull—better known as the myth of Theseus and the Minotaur—the latter being a super strength creature, half man and half bull.

Writing did evolve in several distinctive stages during the ascendancy of the Minoan people. Originally a kind of hieroglyphic system emerged that suggests a link with Egypt, a not unlikely speculation given the fact that Crete was an island nation close to the coast of North Africa. These hieroglyphics either evolved into or were replaced by two sequential stages of syllabic forms of writing. The first—Linear A—probably imported from Phoenicia remains undeciphered; the second—Linear B—was deciphered by a young architect—Michael Ventris—in 1954 who unfortunately died before being able to publish his work. Subsequently, his outstanding cryptographic accomplishment was described by Chadwick (1959). Linear B, unfortunately for our purposes, holds few clues to the religious life of Crete. Like their Sumerian predecessors, the Minoan palace administration mainly used writing as a method of keeping agricultural and other product distribution records and inventories. Thus, most archeological reports from this area in recent years have been more concerned with Mycenaean Cretan economics rather than their religious cultures. For example, see the work of Killen (1984, 1985, 1993), one of the most prolific scholars of Minoan history whose extensive corpus of scholarship is almost completely dedicated to Minoan economic history.

Linear B, however, served one additional very important historical purpose; it was probably the first writing to be used on the continent of Europe and is considered to be the root source of modern writing there. This momentous event occurred during the Mycenaean period, the immediate predecessor to ancient Greek society. According to Ventris, Linear B represented an archaic form of Greek writing.

There was, however, one residual problem that probably contributed greatly to the long delay in the decipherment of the Linear B script. The Mycenaeans invaded Crete in 1450 BCE, adopted the indigenous Linear A, and were probably responsible for subsequently developing it into Linear B. As residents of the Greek peninsula they brought Linear B back to their home where it was used as a written language for more than a century. However, for reasons that are still not well understood, it disappeared completely along with any other form of writing from the archeology of Greece. For more than 500 years—from about 1200 BCE until 800 BCE—the preclassical Greek societies now held in such high intellectual repute were functionally illiterate! Given the reputed historical connection between Linear B and the Greek alphabet, this was an extraordinary dark period and served to hide many of the connections that would have led to a timelier decipherment of the earlier form of writing. Explanations of this literary Dark Age in Greek history are varied. However, the most prevalent and reasonable was that the continuing chaos of the wars between the Mycenaeans, the Dorians, the Ionians, the Aeolians (collectively the ancestors of the Greek peoples), and subsequent invaders reduced the amount of cultural attention that could be given to writing and its uses.

The Mycenaeans, who had lived on the Greek mainland from as early as 1900 BCE, were in control of that historic land until 1100 BCE when the local Dorian, Ionian, and Aeolian tribes, finally overwhelmed them. Around 800 BCE the earliest versions of what are direct antecedents of the Greek alphabet appear. The Greek literature that evolved from these earliest beginnings brings us a fairly complete idea of the religious beliefs that were to dominate Greece throughout its Golden Age. It is also from this time that the Homerian epics—The Iliad and The Odyssey—were thought to have been first told by minstrels, if not yet written down in what was yet to become the Modern Greek script.

Given their rich philosophical heritage, it is not surprising that a naturalist skepticism and a deeply rooted dualism challenged each other throughout the history of Greece. I have already alluded to Plato's quotation of Socrates' musing at the time of his death about what lay ahead. Socrates cum Plato predates the thoughts of modern agnostics who argue that we simply cannot know about such things as an afterlife.[20] However, this was a very

---

[20]There are two meanings to the word agnostic that should be kept separate. The first is the one alluded to here—agnosticism—the philosophy asserting that although we *do not yet know* about the supernatural world, it is possible that we might someday. The second, often referred to as strong agnosticism, argues that we *cannot know*, suggesting the existence of an impenetrable epistemological barrier. Both must be distinguished from atheism, the belief that there is no supernatural world with which we must deal.

sophisticated idea and not one that characterized the belief of most Greeks of the time. The common Greek's theology was of a supernatural world (located on Mt. Olympus) inhabited by a bickering family of immortal Gods who not only interfered in the lives of mortals, but also, on occasion, interbred with them. These unions produced the demigods, the most famous of whom was Hercules. Starting from this polytheistic premise and a determined belief in the supernatural existence of other kinds of entities, the Greek built a complex mythology and with it, an elaborate thanatology of death and the afterlife.

A significant difference between Greek thinking and Egyptian on this subject was that the early Greeks did not believe that deceased bodies were important after death. Cremation, therefore, was widely practiced early in Greek history. Burials were used infrequently in those ancient times. Indeed, some scholars have suggested that cremation was preferred just because of the belief that the hypothetical psyche or soul was released from its worldly constraints more quickly that way than through the natural processes of decay and putrefaction.

Although there is little question that over the hundreds of years of Greek civilization ideas about death and the afterlife changed considerably from what may have originally been Mesopotamian (via Minoa) roots, there were some constancies that remained from one historical period to the next. According to Greek mythology, once freed from the body, the psyche began a long journey into a subterranean world of the dead. After much traveling, including the crossing of the River Styx, the dead shades or spirits, arrive at a "Plain of Judgment," much like the judgment chamber of the Egyptian mythology. It was there, according to their theology, that the individual's future was evaluated. This Plain of Judgment was considered to be a part of the domain of Hades, the Greek God who took over the underworld when the three domains—Earth and Heavens, Ocean, and Underworld—were distributed to Zeus, Poseidon, and Hades respectively.

Hades' domain was made up of three possible afterlife destinations: Tartarus, a hell-like place, is the destination of the unjust or those who have committed specific inappropriate acts in their lives. The ordinary folk went to the Plain of Asphodel, whereas, the exceptionally just or great heroes were sent off to Elysium. Tartarus was described as the lowest place on earth, surrounded by a river of fire in which many punishments were exerted upon the undeserving shades, the spiritual remnants of the physically dead.

Elysium, on the other hand, was a place of pastoral beauty in which people danced, sang, and lived in pleasant groves under a sky complete with sun and stars. Most important of all, Elysium could also be a gateway for some of the dead to be reincarnated and returned to their earlier lives. The reincarnated, however, had no recollection of their previous existence having drunk too much of the River Lethe, the river of forgetfulness, which ran through Elysium.[21] Asphodel was thought to be much like the Christian purgatory, but more so a place in which ordinary citizens with no great claim to fame and no great sins or crimes spent their afterlives in reasonable, but not the extraordinary comfort of Elysium.

There is within this Greek model of life, death, and the afterlife, an apparent conviction that life is very much a cycle. Not only do the unborn start off in Elysium but so, too, do many others who have been through the cycle of life and death and are destined to repeat it. Clearly embedded in this theology is a dualism in which the psyche and the body are subject to quite different sets of rules and laws.

Avoiding the inevitable aspects of physical death was an enormous part of Greek life. Philosophers and priests were all concerned about this problem, to a degree that is comparable with any of the other world cultures I have already discussed. Although filled with complex myths and rituals, with its panoply of Gods, Goddesses, and demigods, Greek theology and mythology represent a way of responding to the same primitive fears that drove the earliest *Homo sapiens sapiens.* Curiously, some of the most sophisticated philosophical questioning about the nature of the psyche and of the human relationship to the physical world was also to develop alongside these deeply held religious beliefs.

4.2.7 Classical Rome

Rome's origins, like those of most of the other ancient cultures discussed in this chapter, are shrouded in mythology and mystery. The classical story of Romulus and Remus founding the city in 753 BCE is an obvious fabrication mainly created to explain the otherwise mysterious origins of the name of the city. In point of fact, some authorities suggest there was no need to look very far for the origins of the city name. "Roma" (it has been suggested and, as usual, disputed) was an Etruscan name and may very well have been the name of a small village along the Tiber River that grew into the great city Rome has become.

However, the story of the twins was not the only myth; other ancient stories suggested that Rome was settled by refugees from the Trojan wars, thus implying that Roman culture was simply an evolutionary byproduct of Greek history. The chronology of those times, however, does not support such a myth. A period of more than 400 years separated the Homeric times

---

[21]Thus, although reincarnation was possible, no one would have any memory of their previous existence. This is an interesting form of immortality (in the form of the reincarnation of the spirit) while serving as an explanation why the individual has no recollection of previous lives. Current enthusiasm for hypnotic regression to the previous lives suggests that this pseudo-theology still has some undeserved persistence even in modern times.

from the generally accepted date at which the city of Rome began to grow and the Roman Empire set out on its path toward world domination.

What we can be reasonably sure of is that prior to 700 BCE both Greek and Etruscan influences were very strong on the emerging Roman identity. Greek outposts along the Adriatic coast and on the island of Sicily and Etruscan land settlements to the north of Rome were well entrenched. It is likely that the Greeks and Etruscans were constantly both at war and trading with the indigenous tribes that were to coalesce into a distinct society in that little village on the Tiber River. It is likely that the first "Roman kings" who ruled during the so-called Regal period (753–509 BCE) were actually Etruscan.

In 509 BCE, however, the Roman people finally overthrew the monarchy in a rebellion that unseated the last Etruscan king—Tarquin. From the ashes of this rebellion arose the foundations of the Roman republic that came to dominate first the Italian peninsula and, ultimately, the entire Mediterranean world. Nevertheless, continued warfare was waged among the occupants of the peninsula: the Romans, Etruscans, and Greeks, eventually culminating in the Etruscan society's final and total collapse in 396 BCE. It took another 200 years, however, before Rome completely extinguished Etruscan influence in Italy. Although the Greeks and Etruscans no longer were important powers in Italy, they did not leave without bequeathing many important cultural characteristics to the new empire. Many aspects of what we identify as characteristics of Roman culture and style actually were derivatives from these earlier people.

The Roman Republic lasted for more than 300 years, a period continually marred by the Punic Wars (264–146 BCE) with Carthage, a powerful city-state located in North Africa. In 27 BCE, the republic was transformed into a dictatorial empire with the coronation of Octavian as emperor. The empire lasted until 476 CE when the "barbarians" from the north finally overran the city of Rome itself.

Of all these borrowed cultural aspects, it was the Greek religious ideas that are most germane to our present discussion. The Roman Pantheon of Gods is almost identical to the Greek Olympians, however, with different names. Much of the burial rituals and traditions were also quite similar. The early Romans, like the Greeks, cremated their dead. After 300 BCE, however, elaborate burials were more frequently carried out. There is no doubt from the extensive written records, that the Romans, like most of the other world cultures, believed strongly in an afterlife and the continuing influence of the dead over the lives of the living. Grave offerings were common, but often with what has been interpreted as a felt need to appease the dead rather than to provide for their needs in the afterlife.

In most respects, the Roman view of the afterlife was a carbon copy of the Greek one. Like the Greeks they believed that the River Styx must be crossed by paying the boatman Charon. The dead were then judged and, depending upon the deceased's position in life, led to the Elysian Fields, to the Plain of Asphodel, or to Tartarus. As with the Greek thanatology, the postdeath residence was Elysium for warriors, Asphodel, for good citizens, and Tartarus for those who had committed some legal or social crime while alive. The Roman underworld was presided over by the immortal Pluto or as he was otherwise known—Dis. His dual Roman names should not obscure the fact that Dis or Pluto was identical in every way with the Greek God of the underworld—Hades.

In Rome, we once again encounter a literate society in which there are strong beliefs in the immortality of the soul, of an elaborate subterranean world controlled by the Gods and shades in which the dead led afterlives that are dependent upon their worldly behavior. More details of the Roman religious attitudes to the dual nature of reality can be found in Toynbee (1971).

4.2.8 The Americas

4.2.8.1 South America. Finally, in this discussion of those ancient religions with which sufficient historical information exists to understand their theologies and belief concerning death and the afterlife, I turn to the New World—the Americas. The great South American civilizations can be disposed of rather quickly because there is relatively little original written information[22] about the Inca (who ruled Peru and surrounding regions from 1450 CE until 1532 CE) and their predecessors (various cultures who left archeological traces dating from 1400 BCE until the advent of the Inca empire). Not only did the Inca leave no written records, but also their great buildings at Cuzco and Machu Picchu are devoid of the kind of decorations and inscriptions typically found in Central America. This does not mean that they were not a highly cultivated people; many beautiful gold and silver objects and textiles have been found in their burials. Indeed, the technical quality of the stonework in the Incan ruins definitively classifies them as a "highly developed civilization" albeit a nonliterate one.

What we do know of the Inca religion comes mainly from the records of the Spanish invaders who conquered the Incan nation in 1532 CE and from such wonderful tales as those told by Prescott (1936), a reprint of his classic two separate volumes (1847 and 1865) on the Conquest of Mexico and Peru,

---

[22]The Inca did, however, have a system of recording numbers—the Quipu—a system of knots tied in strings. It worked well enough as indicated by the vast domain over which the Incas ruled during their hegemony. Their society and culture, including their extensive roads, their magnificent architectural constructions, and their highly effective administrative system were remarkable achievements for what might otherwise be denigrated as a "preliterate" society. An excellent description of the Quipu system has been written by O'Connor and Robertson (2001).

respectively. The Spanish histories of Peru describe a society in which the religion and the government were totally integrated. The Sun was both the God (Apu Inti) and, in its human manifestation—the Inca—the Chief of the Empire. Otherwise there was a Pantheon of many Gods at the top of which stood Virachocha. Secondary Gods had specific responsibilities. For example, rain was controlled by Chiqui Illapa and the fertility of soil was monitored by Pachakama. Many of the Gods were associated with agriculture and the yearly cycles.

Sacrifices of animals were common in the Incan culture, but human sacrifices did not play an important role unless a truly extraordinary event occurred. For example, humans were sacrificed in times of famine to propitiate the Gods. A curious aspect of the Inca religion reported by the Spaniards was the belief in two kinds of spirit jointly inhabiting the body, rather than the simple body–soul dualism of many of the other religions. The first spirit accompanied the body into death while the other went off to one of two kinds of afterlife—a heavenly one or one in which the restless dead could continue to exert influence on the living.

It is interesting to speculate that the natural conditions of Peru, some dry coast and some high mountains, which led to the natural preservation of dead bodies, also led to an unusual (for the Americas) custom of dealing with dead bodies—mummification. The Inca goal was to preserve bodies rather than allow them to decompose. Recent finds of thousands of mummies underneath the streets of present day Lima underscore this important difference with most other pre-Columbian American societies. This find is so new that the only reference to it that I can find is the May 2002 issue of *National Geographic.*

Even the humblest burial included some kind of grave goods. On the other hand, when the Inca, the descendant of the Sun God himself died, he would be buried with a great wealth of items. A modern discussion of the history of the Incas and their predecessors can be found in Keatinge (1988).

4.2.8.2 Central America. Several of the pre-Columbian societies in Central America have, quite unlike their South American contemporaries, left sufficient written information for us to understand their religion as well as their burial rituals and traditions: the Olmec, Mayan, and Aztec being among the most prominent. Of course, there were many other Native Americans about whom we know much less, but these advanced Mesoamerican civilizations left more traces of their religious practices than did the predominately Neolithic and preliterate contemporaneous cultures of North America.

It is now thought that the first of these great pre-Columbian, Central American civilizations was the one developed by the Olmec of Southern Mexico. I have already briefly discussed their contributions to the subsequent written languages of Mesoamerica, but it also seems clear that their religious beliefs also seeded those of the societies that followed. The Olmec civilization lasted from 1150 BCE until, arguably, 200 or 300 CE after which the societies are generally classified as epi-Olmec by archeologists.

The Olmecs were master carvers of stone. In particular, the huge stone heads that remain from their culture raise one of the great mysteries about ancient Mesoamerica. These heads appear to some scholars to represent people who may have migrated from Africa! If this hypothetical linkage between the New World and the old could be authenticated (see the work of Winters, 1977, 1979, its most active advocate), it would establish a link between African cultures and the New World. Indeed, such a link would provide an alternative explanation of the conceptual similarity of the pyramids of Egypt and ancient Mexico, as well as why their hieroglyphic languages have such similarities. Of course, this is also a highly controversial topic with others (e.g., Follensbee, 1999), arguing that the Olmec people were not Africans, but the descendants of the same proto-Americans who came across the Bering Strait and who eventually populated the two Americas. It is an interesting and controversial story, however, that still leads to vigorous discussion.

A much more compelling explanation of the similarities between different cultures may lie, not in a history of cross-cultural exchanges, but rather in terms of the natural forces and cognitive logics to which each culture must respond. The particular slope of a pyramid, for example, is likely to have been mainly defined by the physics of the situation. Too small a base to support a structure of a particular height (and thus too steep a angle of the pyramidal slope) could lead to catastrophic collapses as evidenced in the remains of the bent pyramid of Sneferu in Egypt. It would not take many such trial and error attempts to establish the angle that permitted the optimum balance between the amount of building materials and the obtainable height. Similarly, complex hieroglyphic scripts may both emerge from a simplified token or tag representation that virtually dictated the multiplication of pictographic symbols.

There is one other issue: Despite the arbitrary judgments of those who see similarities between the pyramids of Africa and Mesoamerica, they are really not that much alike once one passes beyond their basic shape to examine the details of their design. Similarly, no one would consider the hieroglyphics of the Mayans and Egyptians to be very similar, again, once one passes beyond the basic fact that they are both pictographs. To assert that the Mesoamericans needed the influence of distant cultures is to denigrate the enormous and unique contributions made by these people.

Wherever the Olmec people came from, there is ample evidence that some of the most important symbols and aspects of their religion were transferred to the Mayan and Aztec societies that followed the decline of the Olmec civilization. The Olmec winged serpent God, Quetzalcoatl, and the Jaguar Gods that play such an important role in the later religions, also had predecessor origins in Olmec times.[23] Archeologists studying these early Olmec people have found ample evidence that they were sacrificing humans on special platforms at this time. Human sacrifice is also a common feature of the later Mesoamerican religions. Like most of the other peoples we have discussed, Olmec graves were usually filled with various kinds of grave offerings, another indication of their society's commitment to a spiritual afterlife following bodily death.

As I indicated earlier in this chapter, only a few samples of Olmec writing have been discovered and deciphered. (See page 91 for a discussion of the Olmec La Venta fragments and the Epi-Olmec La Mojarra discoveries and decipherments.) Therefore, little is known of their specific burial rituals and philosophy about death beyond these limited archeological remains. We do get a better picture of what they believed from the cultural remnants that were preserved in subsequent cultures, in particular, among the Maya who flourished after the Olmecs had disappeared from the historical record.

As the Olmec culture vanished into the Central American jungle about 300 or 400 CE, the Mayan civilization arose to take its place carrying along many rituals of the earlier religious traditions. The Mayan civilization was spread over a much more extensive region than the original Olmec domain. Huge cities evolved from El Salvador north to the Yucatan in Mexico with monumental buildings, pyramids, and an exquisite architectural style that rivals any found elsewhere. The Mayans also developed a much more extensive writing system than the precursor Olmec hieroglyphics.

It is not possible to specify exactly when the Mayan culture disappeared or even that it actually has. A decline in their society had long been underway by the 16th century when the Spanish conquistadors arrived. By 900 CE, their influence was sufficiently diminished to allow a succession of other peoples to take over much of the land they once dominated. Despite their early heavy losses, there were Mayan cultural remnants in the 19th century (a time of uprisings and rebellions) and even into the 20th century. Some of these uprisings are the basis of political unrest in Central America even now in the 21st century and reflect a persistent continuation of a Mayan sense of community. Clearly, however, these vestiges are but pale reflections of the great pre-Columbian Mayan civilization.

After long and contentious argument between different groups of pre-Columbian archeologists, Mayan writing was finally deciphered by the Russian ethnologist Y. V. Valentinovich. Amazingly, he had never been to Cen-

---

[23]One supernatural entity, however, was quite particular in the Olmec pantheon. Both their hieroglyphic writing system and many carved objects describe a uniquely Olmec God—a "wer-jaguar"—a composite character produced by a mixture of a jaguar and a human baby.

tral America or had he visited any of the Mayan sites. His story, and much of the rest of the controversy surrounding the decipherment of the Mayan language is well told in Coe's (1999) history. The salient aspect of Valentinovich's insight that permitted him to successfully translate the Mayan language was based on the realization that, like the Olmec writing, the Mayan script was a combination of symbols, some of which represented whole words and some of which represented syllables. Clearly, Valentinovich's decipherment of the Mayan language was not, by any sense of the word, complete, and it still remains an active project of archeologists.

There are three main sources of Mayan writing available for current archeological study. The rarest (only four are known to exist) are original Mayan codices written on animal skins or plant materials. The most famous of these is the Dresden Codex that was painted on tree bark. It is primarily an astronomical calendar with what are quite accurate predictions of eclipses. The rarity of this kind of document is explained by the fact that almost all others were destroyed by the Spanish conquistadors (and the Catholic priests that accompanied them) in an effort to stamp out the indigenous native American religions.

The second and somewhat less rare source of information about Mayan writing are the copies of original Mayan documents made by the Spaniards. One of the most famous of these documents was transcribed by the second Bishop of the Yucatan, Diego de Landa, infamous not only for his brutality toward the Mayan people at the time of the Spanish conquest, but also as the individual who was mainly responsible for burning the largest mass of pre-Columbian codices. His work originally entitled "An Account of Things in the Yucatan" is available in English translation (Landa, 1937).

The third and much more numerous sources of Mayan writing, not surprisingly, are to be found engraved on the stones of the temples and monuments that remain from their time. Magnificent remnants of their writing can now be observed at such sites as Palenque, Cjichen Itza, Tulum, and Tikal, extensive developments that were most likely religious shrines rather than residential cities. Surprisingly, most of the Mayan writing does not deal specifically with religions and rituals. More likely are to be found chronologies of kings and their conquests, notable births and deaths, as well as astronomical and mathematical charts. What we have been able to glean about their religions suggests that the Mayans were, not surprisingly, also polytheists with many Gods and spirits filling out their panoply of supernatural beings. Gods such as Hunab Ku, the creator God, Kinich Ahau, the Sun God, Chaac, the God of Rain, and Yum Cimil (or Ah Puch), the Lord of dead and the underworld, among many others, were all important parts of their theologies. Not to be forgotten, either, is Quetzalcoatl, the winged serpent that appears again and again in many Mesoamerican cultures from Olmec times on.

The Mayans also exhibited an elaborate form of animism in which each natural object had its own spiritual essence. These spirits, whether in humans, animals, or inanimate objects were part of a supernatural world that had to be "kept in balance." This was accomplished by ceremonies that included human sacrifices, either an entire human or in the form of ritual bloodletting by the Mayan nobility. (As we see later, this carnage was carried to a far bloodier extreme by the Aztecs.) This need to assuage the Gods was particularly important to the Mayans because a major part of their religion was based on their belief in the repeated destruction and resurrection of the Universe. According to their myths, creation had occurred five times and destruction four times. Avoiding the fifth destruction demanded satisfying the Gods with the blood of humans.

The Mayans, like their predecessors in Mesoamerica and the Mediterranean, had both a heaven and a hell (Xibal), but heaven was not for everyone. Only a special few were to enjoy that kind of an afterlife and then only after passing through a 13-step process that finally permitted them to arrive in the Mayan heaven. Infants who died in childbirth or their mothers, those who died in wars, priests and the nobility, humans who were sacrificed (including the losing captain of ritual ball games), and most surprising of all, suicides, immediately entered heaven. Indeed, there was a special Goddess for Suicides—Ixtab. Such a special place for those who took their own lives made suicide extremely common in Mayan society. The method of choice was hanging, represented by the fact that Ixtab is usually depicted with a noose around her neck.

In sum, the Mayans, like most of the historic cultures discussed in this chapter, have a richly dualist view of the world with both supernatural and natural levels of existence going on simultaneously. People move between the two realities through the doorway of death. A variety of entities inhabit the supernatural world and provide order to the natural world by virtue of a system of rewards and punishments that depend on one's behavior while alive.

Coincident with the Maya was another much less well-known society— the Zapotecs. Although the ancestors of the Zapotecs have been identified as living in the region that was to be their home for almost 2,000 years, the Golden Age of Zapotec culture did not develop until the years between 250 and 700 CE. It was at Monte Alban in the Pacific coast state of Mexico— Oaxaca—that their architectural achievements in the form of extensive monuments, palaces, and underground tombs, were to be found. After 700 CE the Zapotec society declined and other, even less well-known, cultures took over the domination of the west coast region of Mexico. The Zapotec religion was typical of the others that arose and fell in Mesoamerica. Marcus and Flannery (1994) described it as having been based on "four principal features":

1. An animism "which attributed life to many things we consider inanimate."
2. "... the worship of natural forces, such as lightning and earthquake."
3. "... reverence for human ancestors, especially royal ancestors."
4. Reciprocal relations between humans and the supernatural: "... each supernatural blessing required an appropriate sacrifice by the recipient." (p. 57)

Zapotec writing is known mainly through inscriptions found on the ruins and in the tombs of the settlements in the Oaxaca region. Like the Olmec and Mayan writing system, it was made up of a system of glyphs, in some cases, however, quite a bit more ornate. Those that have been deciphered suggest that it was mainly used to describe historical rather than religious concepts.

With decline of the Mayans, which had begun as early as 900 CE, other Mesoamerican cultures appeared and subsequently disappeared. Between 800 and 1200 CE the Toltecs were a major influence particularly in the region to the north of what is now Mexico City. After 940 CE, the Mixtec people arose in the northern part of Oaxaca state. They persisted there until 1600 CE well after the Spanish invasion.

Around 900 CE, however, a profound historical development occurred. There arose in Mesoamerica a civilization that is now known as the Aztecs, but was originally called the Mexica, who were able to maintain their cultural style until the arrival of the Spanish conquistadors. This is also a story that is elegantly told in Prescott's (1936) great book, the excellent modern edition of his classic 1843 work. The Aztecs set up their city, complete with monumental structures, at Tenochtitlan, the site of modern Mexico City.

The religious ideology of the Aztecs is in the main sequence of Olmec and Mayan religious beliefs. The somewhat restrained use of human sacrifice by the Mayans evolved into a bloody Aztec cult to appease the Gods (and assure that the sun would rise the next day). Although there were several different means of ritually killing people, the best known was characterized by the removal of the heart of the living victim. The prevailing Mesoamerican myth of the cycle of destruction and recreation of the universe was also a part of the Aztec religion as was the winged serpent God, Quetzalcoatl.

The Aztec writing system seems to have evolved from that of its local predecessors. Both phonetic and hieroglyphic meanings were attached to an elaborate vocabulary of glyphs, not identical, but closely related to the Mayan and other earlier Mesoamerican scripts. For example, the poorly understood Zapotec writing system (which itself reflects its Olmec ancestry) is likely to have been the precursor to the Mixtec glyphs. From there it probably made its way to later cultures by the various routes used by trade and war.

The close relation of all Mesoamerican writing systems is obvious on visual inspection. There are undoubtedly significant differences in the meanings and specific design of the glyphs, but the familial relationships of the different glyphs are easily discerned. According to some scholars, all are closely related and differ mainly in the degree to which particular phonetic sounds were associated with particular glyphs. Thus, it may have been possible for the glyphs from one culture to be read for their meaning by another people even though they may have not spoken the same language.

Given the size and continuity of the isthmus of Mesoamerica, the similarity of the theologies and written languages of all of these cultures are not surprising. The northernmost regions of Mexico are only 1,000 km from the Yucatan peninsula. There are no major mountain ranges or other geographical barriers that separate the societies that we have discussed. Only time, and it is clear from the chronologies that there was plenty of that, for common theological and architectural styles to diffuse throughout Central America. If one looks at a map showing the regions in which each of these societies lived, it is clear that distance was hardly a constraint on cultural diffusion. The ancient Olmec people who set the linguistic and architectural styles were only a couple of hundred km from their successors and close enough in time for the various peoples to have actually intermingled. The relatively small size of the Central American domain obviously played a significant factor in explaining their similarities and the common debt they all owed to the original Olmec society.

4.3 CONCLUSION

This chapter has briefly sampled the traditions and theologies of some of the ancient religions for which we have written records. This is the time of history, of written records, and of continuing challenges to decipher the ancient scripts. This period of written accounts differs considerably from the previous preliterate one because of this single, but dominatingly important factor—the ability to directly transmit ideas, free of the need for the archeologists' indirect inferences and interpretations.

Writing is, of course, neither complete nor totally accurate; it is subject to many kinds of misinformation just as is any other kind of communication. This misinformation may be intentional or it may be due to the original authors' expressed or repressed confusion about what was actually going on in their thoughts. Furthermore, a considerable portion of the writing considered here had political or religious goals that led to the expression of propaganda designed to influence rather than history designed to explicate and illuminate. Given the inaccessibility of human mental processes and the well-known fallibility of introspection, writing probably is best thought of as a means of communicating ideas about what people think they are thinking than what they are actually thinking.

Nevertheless, and in spite of the fact there may well be constraints on the true expression of what people are really thinking, writing provides a uniquely direct means for humans to communicate with each other beyond the boundaries of time and space. Nothing else, not even spoken face-to-face conversations, is as information rich. The increment of knowledge is enormous when one moves from indirect interpretations of archeological remains to written records.

There is another aspect of writing that should be considered. Human existence is personalized by writing. That is, the excavated tombs and graves contain the remains of people who are no longer anonymous. We became privy to their names and even the life experiences of at least a small number of those who preceded us for the first time when written records became available. We can understand what they believed in detail rather than having to limit ourselves to the extremes of either the obvious or the inferred aspects of remains and artifacts.

What we see throughout the enormous geographic range of cultures that are discussed in this chapter is a surprising amount of constancy and similarity in beliefs. From the oldest cultures we considered here, those that provided us with the first rudiments of written communication, to those that lasted into the third millennium of the common era, many of the theological and ritual ideas seem very much alike. Of course, the languages, scripts, and specific details differ substantially, one society to the next, but there is a commonality that becomes clear when we peel away the details and compare their central assumptions.

Before I begin to tease out these common ideas, a brief note of explanation concerning the interpretation of historical events is appropriate. Many of the detailed inferences from the events mentioned in the brief histories presented here are, without doubt, still controversial. Interpretive theories are just as much a part of archeology as they are of any other science and are, likewise, always subject to change as new data appears. Each new discovery adds to the complexity of the story and often serves as a potential seed for disagreement and controversy, as well as consensus. Sometimes these controversies are bitter and prolonged, even long after a convincing case has been made for one or the other positions for reasons that transcend the purely scientific and objective. Agreement is sometimes hard to find even among the experts whose responsibility it is to deeply study these matters.

Whenever possible, I have tried to keep clear when controversial issues were raised. However, I am sure that the opinions of others as well as some of my own expressed here may not always be generally accepted. Myth can turn into reality and reality into myth all too quickly with the uncovering of an ancient object, a new transcription of some piece of ancient writing, or, most unfortunately, a change in the prevailing contemporary political ideology. One notable example is how much the interpretation of Chinese history and religion varied from the early days of the People's Republic to the views held among current Chinese archeologists. Undoubtedly, political and religious preconceptions greatly influenced the interpretation of artifacts and even the meaning of written records.

As I discovered during the course of writing this book, one does not have to go very deeply into the literature to discover enormous controversies and sometimes highly personal antagonisms over such technical matters as the original source of writing or the decipherability of a particular script among scholars. The main reason for this disagreement is clear. Although writing is an enormous step forward compared to even the best of preliterate sources, it is not completely transparent, and the potential for different interpretations of the *meaning* of what are often cryptic comments emerging from a vastly different cognitive style are enormous.

It should also be mentioned that when one undertakes to review the history of a topic as sensitive as attitudes toward death and the afterlife, one does not only encounter serious religious scholars and scientists interested in an objective analysis but also the ranting of crackpots, fanatics, and charlatans, many of who ignore the scientific data or the basics of logic in their effort to prove a point. Unfortunately, it is not always possible to distinguish the drivel from the serious.

In spite of these difficulties, there is enough transparency for us to discern the common features that permeate the religious expressions of virtually all the peoples whose ideas have been reviewed here. I now undertake the task of extracting these common features from the previous discussion.

 Of all the features of the literate cultures examined in this chapter, three interacting ideas stand out as universal: polytheism, dualism, and spiritual immortality. There are many ways to give priority to these three great concepts. I have already expressed my view that the search for an "escape hatch" from the cessation of personal consciousness was the prime mover in the development of primitive dualisms and eventually of full-blown religions, but others may have different interpretations of how religious ideas evolved.

Let us consider the ubiquitous presence of polytheism first. Without exception, each of these religious philosophies discussed in this chapter was totally committed to the belief in a multiplicity of supernatural Gods and their lesser attendants. Each of these entities was endowed with different roles in regulating the events of human society. From the earliest written records of Egypt and Sumeria to the classical periods of Greece and Rome, from Mesoamerica to the Indus River valley, Gods were numerous and distinguished by their separate responsibilities in the world. All of the cultures surveyed here were committed to the idea that their respective families of Gods were organized in a manner much like human families or early societies. Thus, the family of Gods, led by a dominant figure, reflected nothing other than the organization of the society of that time. That is, the pantheon of Gods, led by a major God, mirrored the only kinds of social organization known to the founders of these religions: tribal communities, families, or clans under the domination of some king, warlord, or other type of powerful leader.

A related aspect of these polytheistic families was that each God had a place in a hierarchy of power. Usually, one was identified as the dominant God or Supreme Being and contention and compromise among the lesser Gods was a major part of each mythology. The origins of polytheism can be seen in the expressed needs of people to explain those aspects of their lives that required their attention and effort. Thus, early on arose the Gods of weather and agriculture, as well as the creation myths to explain the great unknowns.

Why all of the religions of those times should have developed in this manner will probably never be known with certainty. One can speculate, however, that polytheisms evolved from a primitive awareness of the individual's interaction with multiple objects in the environment in different ways. Because of this intrinsic partitioning of the world into components, the interaction of individuals with various objects or conditions might easily be interpreted to result from their intrinsic independence of each other. This kind of observation could have led directly to the proposition that each object had a "personality" or "spirit" of its own. In such a situation, individuals and, therefore, societies, came to attribute "spiritual" independence to the various entities and thus a necessary multiplicity of responsible Gods. This, then, resulted in a deification of objects and events as well as animals. According to this hypothesis, the early animisms naturally gave rise to the concept of a number of different supernatural entities, each responsible for some aspect of our life.[24]

The logical chain need not even be that specific. There may be something about this partitioning or modularization of the world around us that is fundamental to human cognition. It is far easier for humans to deal with the

---

[24]Needless to say, even this relatively straightforward hypothesis is not without its critics. Some religious scholars have suggested that monotheism actually preceded polytheism. The multiplication of Gods, on this theory, resulted from the multiplication of languages: People simply forgot that their different words referred to the same entity and, thus, evolved a multiplicity of Gods. Such an argument seems to be heavily influenced by the desire to justify the properties and tenets of modern monotheistic religions, rather than to deal objectively with the historical record.

parts of a complex system than to understand the much greater complexities of a unified and holistic process. Perhaps, humans are intrinsically "linear" thinkers and it takes a considerable intellectual development to even begin to appreciate the basic "nonlinearity" of a unified natural world. If this speculation is correct, polytheism initially arose as a direct result of the state of cognitive evolution during the time period covered in this chapter.[25]

There are, of course, several other possibilities. An alternative explanation for the origin of polytheistic religions may be that the many Gods reflect an unwritten community memory or realization of the enormous cultural breakthroughs that occurred during the Neolithic period. Gods of agriculture, of hunting, of the home, of rain, of fertility, and many others may simply instantiate and personify a kind of societal appreciation of these momentous events or an awareness of the very important and distinctive role that each of these activities play in human life. Each event was so significant that it tended to be separately deified in the form of an individual God.

The second, nearly universal, aspect of the religious customs described in this chapter is their division of the world into separate visible natural realities and invisible supernatural realities. This fundamental dualism was mainly necessary, as I have argued, to assuage the fear of death. However, the evolution of this central idea in all religions may have been driven by dreams, hallucinations, and other inexplicable and mysterious mental phenomena. This first-hand evidence of different voices from a "supernatural world" leaking through to consciousness must certainly have played a profoundly influential role in stimulating the rise of early views concerning multiple realities. The role of such "divine" revelations has been substantial throughout the history of all types of religions from the earliest Neolithic shamanisms to much more recent ones.

Another possible contributing cause to the postulation of dual realities may have been the same one supporting supernatural beliefs today—a lack of appreciation of the role of chance and coincidence in our lives. The compelling human tendency to attribute significance to random events has been a source of supernatural ideas throughout our history. Unfortunately, it has also been the source of some bizarre psychological theories. (See Uttal, 2003, for a discussion of the origins of "Psychomyths" in psychological science.)

Finally, among the three universal features of these early literate polytheisms is the omnipresent concept of some kind of an afterlife following bodily death. This feature, however, does not characterize these ancient religions alone; all theologies, in one way or another, are based on the foun-

---

[25]There is nothing unique about this hypothesis. As discussed later in this book this tendency to break up unified entities into smaller modules or components influences theory making in scientific psychology as well as in the thoughts of ancient peoples.

dation belief of some kind of an afterlife and thus a personal immortality. What does, however, stand out among those discussed in this chapter is the uniformity of the specific details of that afterlife. Several common details of the world into which we go after death become obvious as a result of the review made here. These include the concept of an underworld composed of different kinds of afterlives, of an evaluation of the decedent's life by a panel of supernatural beings, and of punishment for what sins or transgressions may have been committed before death.

Although polytheism, dual realities, and the persistence of some aspect of the personality after death are the major features of these religions surveyed in this chapter, there are several other aspects that repeatedly appear in their archeological remains as well as in their written records. For example, it is interesting to note just how pervasive the idea that the realm of death is underground has been throughout our entire discussion. The relegation of afterlives, usually hellish, but occasionally heavenly, to subterranean locales is a common property of many of these ancient religious systems. Why the underground should be the residence of the dead is also something about which we can only speculate. However, there are several cultural and linguistic forces that may have led to this idea. One was the simple fact that burials, from the earliest evidence we have, are generally made in or under the ground. Thus, there was an a priori association between a "hole in the ground" and the residence of the dead. As primitive, preliterate religions evolved during the Neolithic era, in particular, this cognitive association may have been irresistible.

Another force toward linking the afterlife with the underground may have been a simple psycholinguistic phenomenon. Death is a dark and gloomy affair much unlike the life of the living in the bright sun. The darkness of the underground may have become synonymous with the gloom that pervaded the community following the death of one of its members. Whichever of these psychological forces drove the afterlife underground, the notion that the underground abode of the dead was mainly a place of punishment for the wicked probably occurred much later. In many of the cultures discussed in this chapter, both the wicked and the innocent originally spent their afterlives in the underground.

Another ubiquitous characteristic of virtually all the early polytheisms is the progression toward the increasingly elaborate nature of the goods that were buried with the dead over the course of history. As discussed in earlier chapters, funereal offerings were certainly not a new idea. We have seen how relatively simple, and predominantly decorative grave offerings were found in upper Paleolithic and Neolithic graves. The quantity and quality of the grave offerings became more and more extravagant as the centuries passed, ultimately including the most extreme offering—the sacrifice of the living to attend the dead in their afterlives. The efforts of the late

Chinese and Egyptian civilizations to entomb luxury as well as practical items stand at the apex of this tradition.

What interpretation are we to make of this enormous "waste" of material and human "goods"? Most obviously, it attests to the deep conviction throughout the history of these ancient civilizations that there was an active afterlife. This afterlife had to be stocked with the same kinds of necessities (or their replicas) that were necessary for life before death. Life and death, therefore, was merely parts of a sequence of stages in the continuing existence of a separable and immortal part of human existence: the mind/soul/spirit/psyche.

If death was to be denied for one's self, then logically it could not be denied for one's ancestors. If some aspect of their consciousness was preserved, then it is but a short logical step to the idea that they may very well play an important role in the life of the living. Thus, there is also a compelling logical pressure exerted toward ancestor worship, another frequently encountered property of these early religions.

The review carried out in this chapter also demonstrates another ubiquitous property of the religions I have surveyed. That is, the continuity of ideas from earlier cultures to later ones. For almost 2,000 years, the Mesoamerican cultures show continuous development in which one set of ideas builds on the preceding ones. Concepts introduced by the Olmecs were still to be found in Aztec culture. Their theologies were not identical, but the later ones were clearly based, and not just influenced, by the cultural heritages of the earlier ones. There is, perhaps, no clearer evidence of the continued influence of one society on the next than that observed in the history of writing. Although there remain many questions of priority or of particular script, there is little question that writing evolved in an orderly way from simple beginnings as the concept was passed from one society to another.

Finally, there is another important aspect of this review of early religions that should not be overlooked: their role in social control. The idea that an individual's life was to be judged upon death is pervasive throughout all of the discussion. What better system of rewards and punishments could have been devised than heavens and hells? Obedience and loyalty to one's king or emperor and behavior codes comparable to the Ten Commandments are only two examples of how society could be kept in moderately good order by adherence to the tenets of religious doctrines about a life after death.

In conclusion, we see in this chapter a steady progression from what we deduced about the simpler Paleolithic and Neolithic proto-theologies to what are documented examples of complex historic polytheisms. The next stage of our examination of the evolution of dualist ideas about reality takes us into a new epoch, one in which the polytheisms undergo what, from a historic point of view, can only be seen as a surprising theological simplification—the emergence of monotheisms. This is the topic of the next chapter.

CHAPTER

5

Modern Religious Dualisms

5.1 THE RISE OF MONOTHEISM

The historical review[1] carried out in this book makes it clear that there are two great themes of religious history. The first theme is the ever-present continuity of current religious thinking and earlier concepts and doctrines. Despite the repeated allusion to a "new divine revelation," older ideas serve as precedents for later ones in religion as well as science. The Toltec theologies percolated down throughout the religions of Central America for 1,000 years or more. The Sumerian religious principles can be discerned in many of the cultures that followed in the Middle East. Greece and, subsequently, Rome had almost identical theological doctrines, both of which were heavily influenced by their Middle Eastern antecedents. For example, the River Styx, a mythological entity that plays a major role in both of these relatively advanced cultures' eschatologies is very likely to have been a vestige of Egyptian and even Mesopotamian ideas. It is well known that many of the pharaohs of ancient Egypt were physically transported across the Nile River for burial in the Valley of the Kings. Perhaps this historical reality became the root of the mythological River Styx. Similarly, the modern Christian religion seems to have roots in the ancient mythology of the mar-

---

[1]The brief capsules of religious history and interpretation presented here are done so with the full appreciation that there is an enormous literature on every one of the topics on which I touch so briefly. I ask my reader's forbearance and patience as I head toward the essential point of this book. This is necessary background material for the thesis that pervasive dualist ideas influence psychological theory.

tyred and resurrected demigod Osiris and current Muslim beliefs are, in part, derivative of early Jewish and Christian ideas.

The second great theme of religious history is that its intellectual and doctrinal evolution parallels the process of biological evolution. In addition to the preservation of old ideas, there has been a continuing evolutionary development of religious thought. The progression has been, in turn, from animisms to polytheisms, and, as demonstrated in this chapter, to religions that are increasingly extreme in their monotheistic doctrine.

The point is that both archeology and history attest to the fact that, contrary to the teachings of most religions, specific theologies do not arise as a result of abrupt divine revelation, but rather as the result of a continuous process of intellectual development and absorption of preexisting ideas. Every religion, indeed every intellectual endeavor of any kind, carries within itself the traces of earlier thought and tradition. Sometimes the influence of the earlier belief is very explicit (e.g., the use of the Old Testament by Christians). However, sometimes these vestiges are deeply embedded in a cryptic and unrecognized fashion (e.g., the story of the Christian resurrection, a new rendition of the Osiris myth).

Another example of the persistence of an earlier tradition is the story of Moses, abandoned in a basket and subsequently pulled from the bulrushes by a royal princess. Interestingly, this tale is almost identical to the one told about Sargon, the founder of the Akkadian dynasty, almost 1,000 years earlier. In the interim between Sargon and Moses, according to Rank (1909/1990), many other intervening heroic leaders were also the subjects of nearly identical myths.

Perhaps the best known of these persistent vestigial tales is the epic of the worldwide flood, as originally told in Sumerian mythology and then retold in the Old Testament. The compelling suggestion is that many of the myths and revelations of late religious histories are retellings of ancient oral narratives. The concept of a continuity of religious ideas (as well as any other kind of human thought), therefore, compellingly arises.

In chapter 4, I traced the history of a group of religions that were almost entirely characterized by a polytheistic pantheon of Gods and Goddesses. The families of Gods described there, I argued, were natural intellectual (evolutionary) developments from the more primitive animisms and pantheisms of the prehistoric past. Specialized deities arose in substantial numbers in virtually all of those early religions to represent natural forces of one kind or another or to personify the events of human existence. Gods of the sun, agriculture, the dead, storms, and many other specialties reflected the tendency of peoples of those times to modularize the world into natural and then supernatural components.

Today there is a diverse mixture of religions of many kinds to be observed throughout the world's successful societies. Some polytheisms have

TABLE 5.1
Number of Adherents to the World's Major Religions

Christianity	1.9 billion
Islam	1.1 billion
Hinduism	781 million
Buddhism	324 million
Sikhism	19 million
Judaism	14 million
Baha'ism	6.1 million
Confucianism[a]	5.3 million
Jainism	4.9 million
Shintoism	2.8 million

Note. From the *Christian Science Monitor* (August 4, 1998).
[a]The estimate for Confucianism may be very low. Other sources place the number of followers of this and other "traditional Chinese religions" to be very much higher.

persisted into modern times. However, if we were simply to count adherents, it is clear that for the last 2,000 years or so, monotheistic theologies of one kind or another have dominated religious doctrine. A recent estimate of the number of adherents to the world's major[2] religions is shown in Table 5.1. The numbers presented in Table 5.1 are probably underestimates (the total world population is now estimated to be about 6.3 billion) and almost all religions have grown in membership since the year 2000. However, the likelihood is that approximately the same ratios exist now as then. For the purposes of this discussion it is important only to note that at least two thirds of the adherents of modern religions claim to be monotheistic.[3] This number is to be contrasted with the overwhelming proportion of polytheists among those religions discussed in chapter 4. Clearly there was an enormous change in the nature of our beliefs concerning the supernatural between the times described in these two chapters.

This chapter deals with beliefs about death and the supernatural that characterize many, but certainly not all, of what I have collected together under the rubric of "modern religious dualisms." Modern monotheistic dualisms, it might well be reiterated here, did not spring *de novo* from poly-

---

[2]I have arbitrarily chosen to limit the "major religions" to those with a known or claimed constituency of a million or more. There are obviously many other minor groups that are derivative from these major groups that claim their doctrinal independence. There are also some interesting and truly novel cults and sects derived from the major religions that will not be covered here. The estimates of the number of adherents to each religion are, of course, based on very flimsy data. However, the orders of magnitude are as accurate as we need for the following discussion.

[3]As we see later, this too is a very soft estimate. Some monotheisms invoke auxiliary supernatural entities; some that superficially seem to be polytheisms, argue that all of their gods are, if theological fact, manifestations of one Supreme Being.

theistic predecessors any more than any of the other doctrines can claim a discontinuous novelty. Rather, there is a history of predecessors that have to be understood to appreciate the evolutionary processes that led so many of the major modern religions from polytheism to at least a nominal monotheism.

Because the dates of the three main contenders for the role of "first" monotheism are critical in our understanding of what happened prior to the Common Era, it is useful to provide a brief chronology of the critical events surrounding the time of each of the contenders for priority in inventing this important idea. The dates mentioned here, however, like any other ancient chronology must be taken lightly, as many different dates have been suggested for each of these events. For better or worse, there simply is no valid date for most of the events discussed in this section. Therefore, it is best to think of them only in relative terms and as "best current" estimates. An even more fundamental caveat is the fact that at least some of the people alluded to in these stories may themselves have only been mythological and the events may never have actually taken place. Nevertheless, traditions such as these die slowly and, given that our purpose at this point is to seek out possible original sources of monotheism, let us use the best estimates for the dates shown in Table 5.2 to continue the discussion.

What is certain is that approximately 3,400 years ago, the first historical indications of monotheistic thinking begin to appear in the recorded and oral histories of those times. Perhaps it arose as a result of the earlier practice of having a chief God for each village, thus suggesting the possibility of a rank ordering of Gods and, therefore, the dawning of an appreciation of the possibility of a supreme one. Perhaps, the idea of a single all-powerful deity arose as a natural development of the hierarchy that seems to have been a characteristic of most of the earlier polytheisms. Whatever the intellectual sources, priority for the first recorded monotheistic religion almost certainly has to be given to Akhenaten; no earlier version has any credibility among archeologists or historians of religion and none earlier has left any record of its existence. Later renditions of reputed earlier monothe-

TABLE 5.2
Proposed Dates for the Emergence of Monotheism

1367?–1350?	BCE	The reign of Pharaoh Akhenaten (Amenhotep IV)
1290?	BCE	Traditional time of the Exodus[a]
628?–551?	BCE	The time of Zoroaster

[a]The exact date of the Exodus, if it actually happened, has proven to be extremely difficult to determine. Dates that range from 1447 BCE to 1290 BCE have been suggested for this important event in world history. It is almost as difficult to determine the exact date of Akhenaten's reign. Suffice it to say the most probable times for each of these two events are very close and could, conceivably, have overlapped.

isms, for example, those reported in the first five books of the Old Testament, are unsupported by any archeological evidence.

The story of Akhenaten's attempt to create a monotheistic religion is a very interesting one just because his early attempt to change the course of religious history failed so completely. Akhenaten proposed a sudden and drastic change in the entire religious and priestly culture of dynastic Egypt. His plan was to replace the entire pantheon of hundreds of Egyptian deities with a single sun God—Aten. This scheme not only included the establishment of a new city—Akhetaten—but, also, the diminishment of the role of the substantial priestly class that had long dominated Egypt in the name of the Pharaohs. Needless to say, the entrenched traditions and political influence of the priests, as well as the subsequent role that is purported to have been played by Horemheb, a general of the Egyptian army, led to the overthrow of the new monotheism and the return to the old Egyptian polytheism immediately following Akhenaten's death. At this point not only were the monuments to Akhenaten and his city demolished, but he was declared a criminal and efforts were made to remove his memory from Egyptian history by the literal defacement of his monuments. Thus perished the first attempt at monotheism reported in history, presumably a victim of powerful traditional values, the persistent religious ideas of most Egyptians, and the overwhelming influence of the powerful priests of dynastic Egypt.

However, there is a remote possibility the effort to destroy Akhenaten's religion and place in history may not have been as completely effective as the bare bones of this tale suggest. If one examines the short chronology presented in Table 5.2, it is clear that only a few years passed between the ill-fated Aten-based monotheism and another event of questionable historicity—the Exodus. As few as 60 years separated the death of Akhenaten from a generally accepted date for the departure of the Hebrews from Egypt. It is also possible, because of the uncertainty of dates that the two events occurred much closer in time—perhaps even simultaneously!

The unusually enigmatic prophetic leader of the Exodus—Moses—remains one of the most problematical individuals of human history. His personal history is told in great detail in the Old Testament and, regardless of his actually historicity, has been engrained as fully as any other myth in human annals. Nevertheless, his mysterious origins have suggested to many (most notably to Freud, 1939) that he may actually have been an Egyptian; perhaps the illegitimate son of the royal princess who snatched him from the bulrushes. Old Testament tradition tells a different story—that he was by birth a member of the Hebrew tribe that had already been enslaved in Egypt for several hundred years prior to his birth. Whatever his origins, if we are to believe the story of the Exodus, this extraordinary individual did lead the Hebrews out of Egypt and gave them a code of conduct and the core of a monotheistic religion that was to become the root source of the religious beliefs of the majority of the world's future population.

The residual doubt raised about the continuing influence of Akhenaten's aborted monotheism is based solely on the brevity of the interval between his reign and the generally accepted date of the Exodus. Is it possible that the Aten cult had persisted in some form in Egyptian culture and that Moses was actually promulgating a version of it to the Hebrew people at Mt. Sinai? Questions like this can probably never be definitively answered, but whatever the reasons, it is now Moses who is considered to be the original source of many of the key ideas prevailing among contemporary monotheist religions.

What is uncertain is how much influence Akhenaten's supreme God Aten had on Moses' El, or as he was otherwise known, Adonai or Yahweh. The brief period of time and the geographical propinquity at least raise the possibility of such an influence.

There are several interesting alternatives to the hypothesis of Akhenaten's influence on the Hebrew religion. One, already mentioned, is that the polytheisms discussed in the previous chapters were actually derivatives of long lost monotheisms. Most scholars have rejected this hypothesis. The Old Testament descriptions of a single God going back to the origins of humanity in Genesis and the other four books of the Pentateuch were written at a much later time[4] and, therefore, can neither rule in an preexisting monotheism nor rule out the possibility or a major theological change about the time of Moses. The other equally untenable, but fascinating hypothesis is that Moses and Akhenaten were actually one and the same person! This intriguing idea is based on several factors: (a) the fact that the two personalities, if they lived at all, lived within a few years of each other. The uncertainties of dating those times make the minimal 60 odd years between the two only the briefest interval in recorded history. (b) The philosophies expressed by the two were sufficiently similar, even though they did differ in detail, at least to raise the possibility. (c) There is some suggestion in Egyptian history that Akhenaten and his followers also fled Egypt in the troubled times that followed his official reign. Perhaps, even if Akhenaten and Moses were not the same person, Moses was an Egyptian prince who led the Hebrews (or some other minority group) out of Egypt in order to preserve the Atenist religious ideologies in the same way that the Puritans

---

[4]The discovery of the Dead Sea Scrolls provided an extraordinarily complete version of at least parts of the Old Testament. A sample of these documents was dated by the University of Arizona using a carbon dating procedure to the period ranging from 150 BCE to 5 BCE, a time period that overlaps with other evidence of the presence of the monastic community of Essenes who are assumed to have written them. It is estimated that other relevant documents were written over a period from 300 BCE to as late as 70 CE. A slightly earlier, but very incomplete, record of a few excerpts from the Old Testament is known as the Nash Papyrus (Cook, 1903) and is now believed to date from as early as 200 BCE (Albright, 1937). The oldest known fragment of the Old Testament was inscribed on a silver amulet and is dated to about 700 BCE (described in Hoerth, 1998). Because of these late dates, none of these fragments can authenticate any earlier monotheistic belief. Abraham's monotheism can, therefore, well be taken as apocryphal.

left England in the 16th century. The best read on such speculations is still Freud's (1939) *Moses and Monotheism*.[5] Others, for example, Redford (1987), believe that the two religions are so dissimilar in their basic teachings that they cannot possibly be related. What is indisputable is that Atenism disappeared while the Hebrew monotheism went on to stimulate what are the modal forms of religion in today's world.

Is there any reason to believe that monotheisms predated Akhenaten and Moses? Unfortunately, there is no evidence, solid or otherwise, to support such a hypothesis. The biblical patriarch Abraham of Ur lived in a Mesopotamian society that archeology tells us had thousands of Gods. The biblical stories of his relationship with a single God were all written long after his time and in an obvious attempt to provide an ancient foundation for the primary monotheistic tenet of the Hebrew religion. It is most likely that Abraham, if he existed as a historical personage, worshipped some if not all of the Gods of his time and place.

I have already discussed the archeological remains of the Neolithic Middle East and their universally polytheistic religions. Without exception, all of the other cultures of the Middle East display shrines dedicated to deities of many different kinds. Monotheism, for all of its implications for later years and all of the *ex post facto* literature, left no archeological or literary signs of its existence prior to the Akhenaten–Moses era. It is, indeed, startling (given how widely the story is accepted) to realize that there is precious little to authenticate the entire Moses–Exodus story or, for that matter, the ancient histories of any other religion. The search for historical or archeological confirmation of a particular biblical figure or event 2 or 3 thousand years in the past has generally been fruitless.[6] Nevertheless, the ideas that have emerged from those times have monumentally influenced the modern world and have to be taken very seriously.

It is also of interest to ask why the Mosaic Law had to start with such a strong admonition to worship only a single God? Why should this have been necessary if the Hebrews of the Exodus had a preexisting tradition of monotheism? Rather, according to the biblical epic, it was necessary for Moses to make this admonition and the ones against idolatry and "taking His name in vain" primary, even before the prohibition of murder or theft. We can also ask, why in a time of doubt, did the Exodus Hebrews so promptly regress to idol worship if it had not been a part of their religious

---

[5]Freud (1939) draws many other parallels between the Egyptian Aten religion and culture and that of the people of the Exodus. Egyptians, he points out, also practiced circumcision; there is a curious linguistic similarity between "Aten" and "Adonai"; and, of course, Moses' name is Egyptian.

[6]However, as we saw in chapter 4, it is not impossible. Some myths have become realities on the basis of archeological evidence. The problem is very much complicated, however, when one is seeking evidence of specific individuals who are central to deeply held religious beliefs.

beliefs for many years? Could it be that they were in flight not only from bondage but also from a polytheism that had, for one reason or another, become unsatisfactory to either the masses or their leaders? All of this, of course, is fantastic speculation. All that we do know for sure is that a new form of religion—monotheism—emerged from the Near East about 1300 BCE. The basic idea of a single omniscient and omnipotent Supreme Being was to have enormous influence in the future world.

The other candidate, often cited as the original disseminator of monotheism, was the Persian Zoroaster. The date of the birth of Zoroaster (also known as Zarathustra Spitama) is uncertain. It has been suggested, but unsubstantiated, that he was born about the time of the Exodus. This myth has led to his often being associated with a very early, if not the first, articulated monotheism. However, as the history of his time has unfolded, most modern scholarship now supports the idea that Zoroaster was actually born around 628 BCE and died around 551 BCE. This places him nearly 1,000 years later than Akhenaten and Moses. On its face, this dating strongly disputes the theory that he was the original source of monotheism. On the other hand, Zoroaster may have been the codifier of a pre-existing monotheistic religion of which we know nothing or, alternatively, an independent inventor of a type of religion that he did not know existed elsewhere.

That Zoroaster's religion was monotheistic, however, is indisputable. Its single God, Ahura Mazda—the Wise Lord (also known as Ormazd), had an evil antagonist, Ahriman (conspicuously like the Christian Devil). This dual Godhead suggests that a vestige of an ancient Persian polytheism crept into Zoroaster's teaching. However, it should also be remembered that the presence of auxiliary supernatural entities other than the "one God" is a feature of all other monotheisms as well.

The possible correspondence between the accepted time at which Zoroaster lived and the most likely time of the Hebrew empire in Judea and Israel also raises the possibility that the Persian Zoroaster may have been the recipient of some of the ideas that had emerged to his west in what was by that time a flourishing Hebrew nation-state. However, it is not beyond the range of possibilities that the flow of ideas may equally as well have gone in the opposite direction. Zoroastrianism is well known to have influenced Greek philosophy and it is likely that it also fed back some of its ideas to the development of the ancient Hebrew and more recent Christian religions that were to follow. In particular, the dual nature of the God Ahura Mazda presages the distinction between God and the Devil in Christian theology.

Again, my readers must be reminded that we are in the realm of the speculative, a realm in which no definitive archeological or written records are available to confirm or deny any of these theories about the origins of monotheistic Zoroastrianism or its interaction with other religions. Like Judaism, Zoroastrianism has been remarkably persistent and is still practiced by a substantial number of people in the Middle East and South Asia. The religion of the Parsees in India, for example, is closely related philosophically to this ancient religion.

Zoroastrianism may also have had another route into early Jewish and Christian thinking; it has long been suggested that the Hellenistic Gnosticism may have been strongly influenced by Zoroaster's ideas. Furthermore, some of the Dead Sea Scrolls, for example, contain documents that seem to reflect teachings of Zoroastrianism. In particular, the scroll entitled *The Manual of Discipline*, containing the rules for entering the Qumran Essene community, seems to be strongly influenced by the teaching of Zoroaster. The "Manual" includes a discussion of the duality of good and evil that reflects Zoroastrianism's theology and presages Christian doctrines. Whether this represents another example of convergent evolution of ideas or a direct or an indirect influence on the ancient on the less remote is, as usual, hard to determine.

A final introductory comment, like many of the other dichotomies around which such emotional scholarly wars have been waged, the distinction between monotheism and polytheism is not always clear-cut. Porter (2000) edited a collection of articles that deal with this problem of definition of these two key words. It may well be that the argument is a red herring that depends on the emphasis. There is always some doubt if a single "God" is being revered to the exclusion of all others, or is simply the dominant one in a pantheon. Virtually all nominally monotheist religions involve some sort of demigods or angels. Like many other such debates, the graduations between different religious doctrines may be subtler than the extremes of the polytheistic–monotheistic dichotomy suggest.

Whatever the differences in their origins or doctrinal detail, monotheistic religions are the modal form of those religions that have survived to or that have emerged in the past thousand years. The purpose of the rest of this chapter is to continue our survey of their respective beliefs about death, the afterlife, and the foundation ontological assumption of all religions—that there are two kinds of reality that distinguish between the fundamental natures of the mind/soul/spirit and the material body respectively. The thesis of this book continues to develop; deeply imbued dualist thinking leads to an erroneous cognitive science that tends covertly to treat the mind as an object composed of identifiable parts that is separate from the brain rather than as an inseparable process of that organ.

5.2 MODERN RELIGIONS

The discussion that follows is ordered on the basis of different criteria than those used to organize Table 5.1. In that table, sheer membership size was the single parameter used to rank order the various religions. In the discussions in this section, however, two intermixed criteria for ordering the discussion are simultaneously used. The first is simple antiquity. The most ancient religions are discussed first. The second criterion, however, is composed of philosophical relationships and historical sequences. Thus, Judaism, Christianity, and Islam, three great modern religions that flow along a common course, are discussed together even though the roots of Judaism, as we have already seen, date at least to the second millennium BCE and both of the others are much more recent. Only Hinduism, probably an outgrowth of the Indus River proto-religions of the second and perhaps even the previous millennia, has a greater antiquity. For this reason, I commence the discussion with a consideration of this ancient religion.

5.2.1 Hinduism[7]

Hinduism has an outstanding attribute: It is arguably the oldest religion still being practiced on the face of the earth today. This is evidenced in chapter 4 where the early Indus River civilizations are considered. It is shown there that the proto-religions practiced by the Harappan culture were very important in the development of modern Hinduism. The Hindu practice of Yoga is preceded by certain Harappan rituals in that fertile land. So too are deities that are now believed to be predecessors of Hindu deities. For example, Siva, the ancient Sanskrit name for the Hindu God Shiva,[8] may be, for all theological purposes, identical figures in both the Harappan and Hindu religions. As we see shortly, Siva or Shiva plays a very important role in the devotions of current Hindus. The Harappan respect for many kinds of animals, as indicated in their early religious tokens, is also reminiscent of the strong respect for animals, especially cattle, that is such a central belief in contemporary Hinduism.

Another important contribution to modern Hinduism came along with the so-called "Aryan" or Vedic invasion (probably proto-Persian people from the region now known as Iran) when they overwhelmed the indigenous Harappan culture about 1500 BCE. The Aryan people brought with them a war-like, polytheistic religion with many Gods representing various aspects of life. These Aryan Gods included Indra—the God of War—after whom India may have subsequently been named.

---

[7]An aspect of historical Hinduism is that, unlike virtually all other extant religions, with the additional exception of Shintoism, there is no human prophet or leader to whom the original religion is attributed. All of its "founders" are mythological beings and deities. This is probably due, simply enough, to its unusual antiquity as well as to the fact that some of its roots were to be found in what were originally foreign and alien doctrines.

[8]There is a suggestion in some of the material I have studied that the Siva was originally the main Harappan God, a role now played by the trichotomy of Brahma, Vishnu, and Shiva embedded within the supreme Saguna Brahman of modern Hinduism.

The main Vedic God, however, was Brahma, and this name, if not the detailed theology, became that of one of the most important of the subsequent Indian beliefs—the triumvirate of Brahma (the God of creation), Shiva (the God of destruction and transformation), and Vishnu (the God of preservation and stabilization). One can speculate that the Indian triumvirate may reflect the historical amalgamation of the ancient Aryan Brahma, the Harappan Siva (*sic*), and some other as yet unknown source for Vishnu as the cultures' religions came into conflict and then merged to produce modern Hinduism.

Although I have been unable to find any reference to a pre-Hindu equivalent to Vishnu, this manifestation of the triumvirate is often depicted riding on the bird God Garuda. Garuda, half man and half bird, is especially revered in Southeast Asia. A perfectly ungrounded, but interesting speculation is that Vishnu became an important figure in Hinduism as a result of the immigration of or conquest by people from the southeast just as Brahma was integrated into the local religion by people from the northwest. It must not go unmentioned, however, that some historians suggest that Vishnu was also of Vedic origins.

The Aryan religious hymns, the Vedas, were also amalgamated into the indigenous Harappan religion and became the basis of the holy books of Hinduism. Indeed, Hinduism is distinguished from its less orthodox descendants, including the other great Indian religion—Buddhism—and the more recently founded Jainism—by the acceptance or rejection of the Vedic literature. The Vedic holy books include the four main texts (Rig-Veda, Jajur-Veda, Sama-Veda, and Atharva-Veda) written between 1500 BCE and 1000 BCE. These Vedic texts were supplemented by commentaries (the Upanishads) written about 700 BCE.

Other holy books were introduced into the Hindu liturgy over the centuries including the Mahabharata epic (about 300 BCE) that includes the Bhagavad-Gita, a poem supposedly told by Krishna detailing how one should go about achieving self-realization. Another very important piece of Hindu religious literature is the Ramayana, which was written about 200 BCE. This is an extraordinary love story describing the rescue by Rama of his kidnapped wife Sita that is often found carved on Hindu monumental structures. I personally have seen it on both the great temples at Borobudur near Jagjakarta in central Java and Ankor Wat in the town of Siem Rep in Cambodia. It is a delight to see a romantic love story become such an integral part of the religious literature of any culture.

The Vedic Aryans also made another important contribution to the Indian subcontinent; they introduced an extensive literature written in the Sanskrit script. In this manner, they provided the basis of the subsequent written language of both India and Tibet, as well as many other countries of Southeast Asia (see Fig. 4.1 on p. 88).

The exact links between the components of these earlier faiths and modern Hinduism, of course, are still subject to considerable uncertainty and, thus, vigorous dispute. Other contributions may have been made by other indigenous sources, but for the most part they are lost to history. By 800 BCE, Aryan Vedism had begun to disappear and an orthodox form of Hinduism that, nevertheless, accepted a considerable portion of the Vedic teachings began to appear in the form we know it today.

One does not have to travel very far in India or Bali to begin to suspect that modern Hinduism has maintained many features of the Vedic polytheism. Temples dedicated to various Gods and images of many different supernatural beings dot the landscape. However, the actuality of modern Hindu interpretations of the nature of their deity or deities may not be that simple. Despite the presence of diverse monuments and temples dedicated to a huge pantheon of Gods and Goddesses including the main triumvirate of Shiva, Vishnu, and Brahma, there is a strong tone of monotheism expressed by modern Hindu theologians. Each of the many Hindu Gods, including the dominant triumvirate, is often described, not as a separate entity, but rather as a manifestation of a different attribute of a single omnipotent God—Saguna Brahman. On the other side of the coin is the undeniable polytheistic fact that the individual Gods of the triumvirate (as well as other lesser well-known divinities such as Ganesha, the God of wisdom depicted with an elephant's head) are, in some situations, the main object of the prayers of individual Hindus or particular communities.

Hindus, if not explicitly monotheistic, do tend to deal with one God at a time—a tradition known as *Kathenotheism*. Closely related is the term *Henotheism*, the worship of one main God without denying the existence of others. Indeed, any attempt to rigorously characterize Hinduism by a single word or phrase is also complicated by the fact that this very important religion is considered by some scholars to actually be an amalgamation of many different traditions attesting to its Harappan and Vedic roots as well as to later developments. The complexity of the situation is further enhanced by the centuries of theological evolution that have taken place since 1500 BCE, the time that classic Hinduism is supposed to have emerged from its ancient predecessors. Although there are certain core beliefs, uniformity of religious expression among the nearly billion people who consider themselves to be "Hindus" is even less likely to be found than among those who would identify themselves with some of the more homogenous religions—if such a thing exists.[9] Dom (1999), for example, suggests that

---

[9]In writing this paragraph and searching for a counterexample of a more homogenous religion than Hinduism, it occurred to me that every religion that has been around for more than a few centuries has already fragmented into subdivisions of one kind or another. This appears to be a characteristic of theological evolution as much as it is a part of biological evolution.

there are at least six divisions of the central core Brahmanistic Hinduism including the Vedanta,[10] Samkhya, Yoga, Mimamsa, Vaiseshika, and Nyaya sects along with many others such as Vaishvanism and Suryaism. Clearly the word "Hindu" does not just refer to a single religion, but rather to the many subreligions of India that still share some residue of belief in the validity of the ancient Vedic writings. In this context, Dom also cites Theertha (1992) who argued that:

> Frankly speaking, it is not possible to say definitely who is a Hindu and what is Hinduism. These questions have been considered again and again by eminent scholars, and so far no satisfactory answer has been given. Hinduism has within itself all types of religions such as theism, atheism, polytheism, Adwitism, Dwaitism, Saivism, Vaishnavism, and so forth. It contains nature worship, ancestor worship, animal worship, idol worship, demon worship, symbol worship, self-worship, and the highest god worship. Its conflicting philosophies will confound any ordinary person. From barbarous practices and dark superstitions, up to the most mystic rites and sublime philosophies, there is place for all gradations and varieties in Hinduism.

For the purposes of the present discussion, however, our major concern is with the Hindu attitudes revolving around death and the afterlife. If we can generalize a bit from the complex Hindu religion in general without doing too much damage to the varieties of the various subreligions, it is possible to discern that Hinduism, like virtually all other religions, is dualist with regard to the relationship between the soul or spirit (the Atman) on the one hand and the body on the other. The body is transitory in Hindu eschatology, being composed of five traditional elements (fire, earth, water, air, and ether) that, most properly, will be recycled. For this reason, cremation is considered to be the appropriate means of disposing of the body by Hindus. The essence of the self, the Hindu spirit or soul, however, is much more persistent. After death, the soul or Atman continues to exist but in a temporary reflective state, which for most people ends with reincarnation— the soul being once again reborn in living form.

Even though this proposed cycle of death and reincarnation may seem to provide another one of those supernatural escape hatches from physical death, the central idea in Hinduism is that this is not the ultimate state of affairs to be desired. Rather, the true goal of human life is to avoid being born again. That is, the ultimate "heaven" is a state of wisdom and understanding and purity of soul (Nirvana) that is finally attained in the form of an individual's spiritual enlightenment. Once that sublime state is achieved, the individual soul will become a part of the existence of the Supreme God, Saguna

---

[10]Vendanta Hinduism, itself, is made up of nine or more subsects, thus adding to the difficulty of identifying the unique doctrines of a religion that has been around in various forms for over 3,500 years.

Brahman, and not return to the endless pains, discomforts, and frustrations experienced by those who have to return to the living world. For those who have achieved Nirvana, the links to earthly life are cut away completely and the cycle of death and reincarnation ends.

Early Hindu writings, in particular the four Vedas, did not deal with either heaven or hell in detail. A God of the dead—Yama—was discussed but only vague comments were made about the nature of the afterlife that was to be encountered by the good and the wicked, respectively. It was not until much later, about the time the Mahabharata was compiled (about 350 CE) from oral histories, that more explicit statements were made about heavens and hells. In the interval between one life and the next reincarnated one, the individual Atman may travel through many different kinds of heavens and hells according to the Hindu eschatology, each appropriate to the life previously led by the dead person. In each case, however, there is an intended educational purpose in which the individual is being prepared for the next cycle or reincarnation. Eventually, the goal is to have learned enough as one passes through the multiple reincarnations to achieve the state of Nirvana and to be excused from rebirth.

The main concept of Hinduism is best summed up by considering the etymology of the word *Nirvana*. It derives from the Sanskrit word "The act of extinguishing." My dictionary defines Nirvana as:

> The final beatitude that transcends suffering, karma [causation], and samsara [the cycle of death, misery and reincarnation] and is sought . . . through the extinction of desire and individual consciousness. (*Merriam-Webster's Collegiate Dictionary*, 2000)

In such a context, heaven and hell can, at best, be temporary way stations on the road to the deeply desired state of Nirvana.

In summary of this brief discussion of what is, even after so many millennia, still one of the dominant religions on earth, it is hard to reject the statement that Hinduism is, at its roots, a polytheism. However, in its modern version, Hinduism avows that the single Supreme Being is unique although capable of being manifest in many different forms.

Whatever the theological details, Hindu dualism is explicit in the belief that the human soul or Atman is a manifestation of a separate and distinct supernatural kind of reality from the physical world. The Atman, however, is caught up in a cycle of death and rebirth until the individual achieves a state of enlightenment or self-realization in which it is possible to appreciate the meaningless of both pleasure and pain. Although it professes its religion by means of rituals and doctrines that are very exotic to western eyes, Hinduism is no different in fundamental doctrine than any other religion in this regard: It is dualist in accepting two levels of reality and the persistence of some aspect of the human mind/spirit/soul after death.

5.2.2 Buddhism

The Indian subcontinent was also the home of what is currently the fourth largest religious group in the world—Buddhism. Although the proto-Hindu and Hindu traditions dominated the area from about 1500 BCE and 800 BCE respectively, around 535 BCE a strong reaction to some of the traditional Hindu cosmology and eschatology occurred. In addition to this theological rebellion, there was also a humanistic reaction to the gloomy despair that the Hindu philosophy projected about the endless cycle of misery and reincarnation and the difficulties in escaping from that cycle. The reaction was embodied in the thoughts and teachings of one of the most extraordinary historical personalities, an individual who was among the very few who can truly be said to have shaped the course of human destiny—Siddhartha Gautama (563 BCE–483 BCE), later to be known as The Buddha. The teachings of Buddha spread from India to much of the rest of Asia during the centuries after his death. Busy economic activity along the Silk route provided a channel through which many of Buddhist teaching came to China and, eventually, into Japan, Tibet, Korea, and the countries of Southeast Asia.

Siddhartha Gautama's role in Buddhism was originally that of a secular teacher, rather than a religious prophet, who was to lead others to enlightenment by a philosophy of contemplation and good acts. Later in Mahayana Buddhism and other more theistic sects, he became a kind of deified savior through whom individual humans could escape the cycle of death and reincarnation. Regardless of which of these two roles he was believed to play, all current Buddhist sects classify him as the greatest of the Bodhisattvas: those who lead others toward the ultimate enlightenment. However, he is not alone in this role. Other great teachers can and have also achieved this important state according to Buddhist doctrine.

Siddhartha Gautama proposed something quite new: a philosophy that emphasized the quality of this life rather than the next one; a philosophy that proposed rules of conduct that made for a good and honorable life here rather than there; and most important, a philosophy that offered a semblance of contentment in this life. It was, in many ways, a radical departure from the austere and pessimistic Hinduism that preceded it.

The philosophy–protoreligion that Siddhartha Gautama originally enunciated was, therefore, very unusual in originally not having an explicit theology; that is, classic Buddhism did not teach or pay much attention to the existence of supernatural Gods,[11] either in the form of a polytheism or a

---

[11]This is not universally true for all kinds of contemporary Buddhisms. Mahayana Buddhism, which began about the time of Christ, is replete with Gods. Siddhartha Gautama, himself was deified and given manifold kinds of representations that are hard to distinguish from some of the Hindu Gods that preceded him. My trip through Tibet alerted me to the fact that the Buddhist Gods have multiplied substantially over the centuries. The Tantric Buddhism flourishing there is replete with supernatural beings of many different kinds.

monotheism. Rather, in both its original and increasingly popular form in current western society, attention was directed at the ultimate enlightenment of the individual and the development of an ethical and moral behavior in this life. Early Buddhists did not deny the existence of an afterlife; it was just not a matter of the utmost priority. Living a good life was deemed to be very important not only for its own value, but also because what is to happen in the next life is "caused" by the quality of life in this one. This principle of causation is referred to as Karma and is a universal tenet of virtually all modern Buddhisms.

The foundation teaching for what was essentially a humanistic description of a moral and ethical life was recorded in the Tripitaka, the written rendition of Siddhartha Gautama's oral teachings, themselves known as the Sutras. As Buddhism evolved, it changed and adopted a more theological tone. Nowadays, one is more likely to read religious pronouncements into the Sutras than social commentaries.

Some of the basic ideas of the Buddhist religion nee philosophy described there are obviously closely related to the Hindu source from which it evolved. Buddhists, like Hindus, came ultimately to believe in reincarnation and the ultimate release of the soul from the cycle of death and rebirth. However, the world of the living is not as terrible or hostile a place to the Buddhists as is the one described by Hinduism. To the devout Buddhist, the good and the bad of life are, in any case, merely illusions, and moderation and inner peace could be attained temporarily in life and permanently when enlightenment was achieved. The life goal of the individual, according to Buddhist, as well as Hindu, teaching is to achieve a state of understanding of the meaninglessness of worldly existence and to transcend to a state of "cosmic harmony," Nirvana, or enlightenment. To accomplish this goal, one had to learn how to get rid of desire for material things.[12] When this state of enlightenment or Bodhi is achieved, Buddhism teaches that the individual would be released from the eternal cycle of life and death as well as from any sense of self or desire.

The original Buddhist philosophy was, as noted, a reaction to the extremes of both Hindu asceticism. Even though it was initially devoid of any concept of supernatural beings such as had been incorporated in the pantheon of Hindu Gods, the same pervasive dualist theme regarding the mind–body dichotomy observed in all other religions is undeniably present in classic and modern versions of Buddhism. The body and the soul were considered to be independent expressions of two different kinds of reality: one permanent (the spirit) and one transitory (the body).

---

[12]The Buddha, himself, accomplished this lofty aspiration. He was born into a wealthy family but by the end of his life had divested himself of virtually every material thing with which he had been endowed.

Whatever else may be said about the *philosophy* of Buddhism, the key idea of the Buddhist *religion* is that the soul/mind/spirit does not terminate at death even though the body decays repeatedly during a cycle of birth and reincarnation. The shared Hindu and the Buddhist doctrine of the reincarnation cycle is another highly refined example of the effort to develop an "escape hatch" from total spiritual annihilation and the complete loss of personal identity. A major difference between the early forms of the two religions was that the early classic Buddhism dealt with the permanence of the spirit in the absence of any cadre of supernatural beings whereas Hinduism was replete with many Gods and demons.

Some modern versions of Buddhism (e.g., the Ch'an or Zen Buddhism that emerged about 500 CE) still maintain this essentially atheistic, meditative, person-centered, worldly tradition. However, other schisms (e.g., Mahayana and Tantric Buddhism) developed elaborate polytheisms in response to what appears now to be a deep need for more concrete expressions of the supernatural among the common people of Asia. This tendency toward more formal "theist" religions was also buttressed by the needs of the Chinese nobility to create a divine basis for their dynasties and positions. Sometime during the long history of this ancient religion, what had originally been memorial monuments to Buddha and the other important historical figures began to metamorphose into representations of them as Gods including the deified Buddha himself. What had begun as a sophisticated philosophy of life, thus, evolved under social pressures into a religious school of thought much like the polytheisms of ancient times. Siddhartha Gautama was transformed from a wise scholar to supernatural status in what is a curiously familiar way. Like the Hindu and Christian Godheads, he was assigned a kind of triple reality made up of three manifestations, Shakyamuni (the historical Buddha), Amitabha (the Buddha of the "Infinite Light"), and Vairochana (the eternal Buddha) in the Nichiren version of Buddhism.[13] One can only speculate what common forces could have driven prophets and scholars toward this triple manifestation or what channels of intercultural contact might have existed that could account for these doctrinal similarities throughout the various religions.

The Buddhist Gods came in many other guises in the numerous sects and divisions of this ever-changing religion. Although, as just noted, some represent different manifestations of the Buddha himself, other personages who have also achieved a high degree of Bodhi—enlightenment—were also

---

[13]Each of these versions of the Buddha plays a distinctive role in other sects of Buddhism. The superficial simplicity of this statement should not be taken as a complete rendition of the Gods of this very complex religion. For example, in some sects Amitabha is a dominant, rather than coequal figure, and Vairochana is relegated to the role of guardian of the inner shrine of a Buddhist temple. This particular concept of a trinity is only an example of many different and often contradictory beliefs and not a definitive feature of all versions of Buddhism.

partially or fully deified in some sects. Others represent supernatural pro-
tectors (e.g., Sakradevanam) or devils (e.g., Papiyan) that seek to lead the
potential Buddhas away from the path to enlightenment and, thus, subvert
them back to the cycle of death and reincarnation and illusions of both the
good and bad aspects of life.

The Buddhist pantheon has grown enormously over the years. Boeree
(2002) lists the very large number of Gods, titans, ghosts, and demons that
are alluded to in the Buddhist literature. He also raises a very interesting
psychological point concerning how these supernatural beings are dealt
with by Buddhists. Boeree's suggestion is that many adherents to this faith
or philosophy do not take them seriously as all-powerful Gods, but, rather,
consider them to be purely "metaphorical or mythological entities" to
whom they need not succumb or propitiate in the same way required by
the Gods of other religions. Indeed, Gods and their fellow supernatural trav-
elers such as demons, saints, and other avatars in the Buddhist religion are
not dominating creatures, but often are described as secondary and subservient to the human Buddhas who have achieved enlightenment.

Although Buddhism originally did not teach anything specific about a
heaven or a hell (the afterlife was a vague sort of interval between death
and reincarnation) many of the later sects did describe some places in
which the righteous would be rewarded and the evil punished. Indeed,
Sadakata and Sekimori (1997) described dozens of different kinds of Buddhist heavens and hells. The most desirable one, of course, is the one for
the truly enlightened in which all desires for worldly goods are removed
from consciousness. This paradise is restricted to those who have accumulated sufficient Karma in their earthly lives by their good deeds and con-
templations. For those with insufficient Karma, one of several kinds of hells
awaits. The afterlife led in the various kinds of Buddhist heavens and hells
differs, but the goal to which all must continually strive is the state of "indescribable bliss" (Nirvana) of the truly enlightened.

In summary, it would be presumptuous to suggest that these brief comments on a religion as complex and diverse as those beliefs and tenets included within the word "Buddhism" could ever be distilled to an essential
credo. Nevertheless, Buddhism does have some general properties. All
Buddhists believe in the cycle of death and reincarnation and the desirabil-
ity of escaping from it by the achievement of an enlightened state—Bodhi.
Because of its diversity, it is difficult to conclude whether Buddhism is atheistic, monotheistic, or polytheistic; different sects and different times have
affirmed one or another of these positions throughout the course of Buddhist religious history.

What is uniform throughout Buddhism and every other school of
thought that can be called a religion is that it is dualist with regard to the
persistence of the individual's soul or personal identity. However much the

details of ritual may vary, all agree that the individual consciousness or spirit continues to survive after the death of the body. The concluding point, once again, being that all religions of the world ascribe to the notion that mental processes have an existence that is independent of the body— that the two attributes of our existence are governed by essentially different laws, one kind in accord with the rest of natural science and the other in deep contradiction. As developed later, this raises serious questions for psychology: the science dedicated to understanding mental processes in the terminology and laws of the natural world.

5.2.3 Jainism

Another ancient religion arising in the first millennium BCE on the Indian subcontinent was Jainism. Jainism shares great antiquity with Hinduism and may actually have overlapped with some now defunct religions of the time. There are probably about 4 million followers of Jainism today, mainly in India. Current Jainist mythology suggests that the details of their religious philosophy developed as early as those of Hinduism. If this is correct, then Jainism did not evolve in reaction to the dissatisfaction with Hinduism but coexisted with it for a thousand years before the great Jain teacher Mahavira (599 BCE–527 BCE) revitalized whatever traditions had existed in those earlier times. However, this extreme antiquity of Jainism is counter-indicated by the relatively well-established dates of Mahavira's life.

In any event, regardless of what happened in the dim light of an even more ancient history, it is from Mahavira's lifetime that the beginning of Jainism is usually dated. If there were more ancient prehistoric roots, they may well have been associated, like Hinduism, with the Harappan and Aryan peoples who lived in the Indus River valley at that time. Like those of China, Egypt, Mesopotamia, and other ancient lands, many of the earlier contributors to Jainism, such as Rishabhadeva (the reputed founder of the religion in 1500 BCE) may be more mythological than historical. It is more likely that the same social and political conditions that led to the Buddhist religious revolution also led to that of the Jains in the 6th century.

The Jain religion has a holy book or, rather, a collection of them—the Agamas. The Agamas are composed mainly of the writings of the historic teacher, Mahavira. Many of the written beliefs of Jainism are comparable to those of Buddhists. Jains, however, have a much more aesthetic, strict, and rigid view of the world than do the Buddhists. This is summed up in the five vows that are supposed to be taken by all Jains:

1. Ahimsa—Never to destroy any living thing
2. Satya—Never to lie

3. Asteya—Never to steal
4. Brahmacharya—Chastity
5. Aparigraha—Never to own or desire any thing

Of course, a total, complete, and extreme devotion to these vows (particularly #4) would have decimated the Jain population, but the principles are noble. Furthermore, Jains are well known to typically be among the wealthiest Indians so adherence to the fifth vow is, presumably, also perfunctory.

The Hindu and Buddhist belief in the cycle of death and reincarnation is also a central part of the Jain eschatology. Jains teach that this cycle had to be broken by an extinction of worldly desires and the destruction of Karma. However, this latter term—*Karma*—is used in a different sense than it is by Buddhists. To the Jains, Karma is not just an intangible "causation," but, to the contrary, an actual substance that has to be destroyed by contemplation and good deeds. When it is sufficiently destroyed, the individual can achieve Nirvana, the state in which the individual's personality in this world is also totally destroyed, eternal bliss is achieved, and the person, himself, becomes a God.

This brings us to one of the most interesting and perplexing aspects of Jainism. Like the early Buddhists, but quite to the contrary of classic Hindu religion, Jainism does not express even the remotest semblance of a belief in either a single supernatural supreme creator or a multiple pantheon of specialized Gods. Rather, Jainism, perhaps reflecting a vestige of some earlier animism, as befits its ancient origins, asserts that everything, organic and inorganic alike, has a soul or spirit. Furthermore, all humans who achieve the enlightenment (Kevalajnana) that permits them to rise above their mortal constraints become Jinas (Tirthankaras) or god-like teachers themselves. Thus, the number of supernatural deities constantly increases as more and more people achieve relief from the cycle of death and reincarnation and become Jinas. With this relief comes both infinite knowledge and infinite power, although that power is limited: Jinas cannot influence human existence.

For Jains, both the supernatural and the natural realities coexist in a permanent world; the task is to rise from the constraints of the natural to the god-like status of the supernatural. This is the ultimate afterlife. Other forms of afterlife, however, are possible. If a person has been particularly bad, there are hells to which they may be sent. Even worse is that the Jains believe that you can be reincarnated as a (much) lower animal if you have been particularly bad.

In conclusion, Jainism is a rigorous, demanding religion in which austere demands are made on the living in the quest for the relief of an indescribable state of bliss—Nirvana. The conceptual link between Jainism and its sister religions, Hinduism and Buddhism is clear-cut—the cycle of birth and reincarnation. The differences between the religions are mainly couched in terms of the doctrinal issues about how one achieves Nirvana. Classic Buddhism and Jainism share an almost atheistic view with regard to a single supreme God; Jainism populates its universe with huge numbers of humans turned Gods.

Without a doubt, however, all share a common belief in dual realities, the natural one that we endure or enjoy while alive and the supernatural one to which we gain entrance by virtue of our good or bad works.

5.2.4 Shintoism

Another ancient religion that has survived to the present time is one native to the island nation of Japan. Originally, the early inhabitants of Japan practiced a kind of animism in which all objects were imbued with some kind of an ill-defined "spirit." In this regard, early Shintoism probably differed little from other shamanistic nature worships that dominated thinking about the relationship between humans and the world during Neolithic and, perhaps, even as far back as Paleolithic times. Originating back in the prehistory of Japan, probably in the thousand years before the Common Era, Shintoism was originally devoid of a noble founder, a sacred text, or even (until much later) a name for this life style. Rather, it was a general expression of a belief in the supernatural inherent in every living object.

The primary Shinto deity is Amaterasu, the Sun Goddess, reputed to be the principle offspring of Izanagi no Mikoto and Izanami no Mikoto, the male and female "first principles." Amaterasu, however, was only one of many Kami, some who were god-like entities, but others more expressions of good and evil forces. In short, early Shintoism was the naturalist expression of a people who lived comfortably within a relatively nonhostile environment and did not concern themselves too greatly with issues of the afterlife. When a person died, he simply became another Kami and joined the many other spirits that pervaded human life. If a "good" life had been lived, the person became a good Kami, whereas the person who had led a "bad" life became a destructive one.

Herein lay the roots of a Japanese ancestor veneration (if not worship) that has persisted to modern times. Shrines were set up to express appreciation of and seek propitiation from the Kami, particularly those who were one's ancestors. In a certain sense, its role in defining an accepting and gentle, more or less contented, style of life may have been more characteristic of Shintoism than the enunciation of a particular controlling theology or of a divinely revealed religion in the manner so typical of most other religions.

This state of affairs did not continue, however. In the 6th century CE, Japan began to interact with other countries of the world. Two main additional contributions were made to Japanese culture at this time. One was the already highly evolved Buddhist religion and the other was Chinese writing. Remarkably, Shintoism was not overwhelmed by the invasion of the new religion. Rather, it developed a kind of symbiotic relationship that has persisted to this day as many Japanese eclectically follow both religions. The simple joy of the Shinto emphasis on this world was combined with the Buddhist concern with the attainment of enlightenment so that the individual could escape from the cycle of death and reincarnation. Thus, families would be married in Shinto shrines and buried from Buddhist temples. Many religious Japanese have shrines in their homes to both religions. After having visited and lived in Japan for some time, I still find it hard to distinguish between Japanese attitudes toward shrines and temples. Perhaps modern Japanese attitudes toward religion should best be considered as an amalgam of both traditions. Indeed, the situation is even more complex than this. The Japanese attitude toward religion is so relaxed that it is possible for one to be actively involved in this duplex religion, some of its cultish offshoots, as well as other religions, such as Christianity—all simultaneously.

There were, nevertheless, substantial changes that occurred in Shintoism with the 6th-century arrival of Buddhism and Chinese writing. One obvious development was that the heretofore-unnamed naturalism was for the first time referred to as Shin-to or Shin-do—the "Way of the Gods." The naming of the ancient Japanese religion was also an explicit effort to distinguish it from the newly arriving Buddhism. In being so distinguished, however, it also helped to perpetuate the older traditions and customs. Quite remarkably, the strategy worked and Shintoism still plays an important role in contemporary Japan. Another important development was that for the first time an effort was made to write down a record of Shinto history and mythology. This was accomplished between the years of 683 CE and 712 CE in the form of the Kojiki—the "Record of Ancient Matters."

The role of Shintoism has not been static throughout Japanese history. During the 19th century, there was a major upheaval in Japanese society. For hundreds of years, the military Shoguns had ruled Japan relegating the emperor to a minor role. In 1868, during the so-called Meiji restoration, the country returned to its classic imperialism and the Meiji emperor, who had long been considered to be the lineal descendent of Amaterasu and, thus, a divinity himself, returned to power. At the same time, Shintoism became the state religion, moderated its gentle naturalism, and thus provided the basis, some say, for the aggressive militarism of Japan's national policy after that date. Shintoism became closely associated with emperor worship and Bushido, the very strict code of conduct followed by the feudal Samurai or warrior class since the middle ages of Japan. The combination of a state religion and the militarism of the Bushido code were, undeniably, among the most important factors leading to the disaster of World War II for the Japanese people.

After World War II, Emperor Hirohito renounced his divinity and Shinto-ism mainly returned to the role of an unofficial cultural tradition. Bushido metamorphosed from a warrior's code to a system of ethics for business-persons. Many of the old feudal traditions of hierarchical loyalty and group responsibility that are now found in the Japanese corporate culture were clearly vestiges of the Shinto and Bushido traditions. This is not to say that such a tradition has remained inviolate. Japan, around the turn of the mil-lennium, has continued a process of cultural change as large corporations no longer felt a need to offer lifetime job security. One result of this change is the popular trend away from a tradition of group responsibility to west-ern style individualism.

Regardless of the specific role of Shintoism in ancient and modern Japan, its attitudes toward death and the afterlife have remained both relatively minimal and relatively constant. As noted earlier, Shintoism is a religion of life and nature. It simply supported the idea of a continued spiritual exis-tence of the individual in the form of a Kami. The Kami, like all the other Shinto spirits and Gods, continued to participate in human life. Thus, addi-tional seeds of ancestor worship and the need for ceremonies to satisfy one's predecessors were planted. After the 7th century CE, interpretations of the Shinto religion were heavily influenced by Buddhist ideas. Reincarna-tion became a part of Shintoism as well as the Buddhist ideas of heaven and hell. An excellent discussion of the Shinto religion and the cultural tradition it embodies can be found in Littleton (2002).

In summary, Shintoism originally emerged as a pantheistic animism in which all objects of nature were imbued with a life spirit. There was, there-fore, a huge multiplicity of these spirits (which might be considered to be proto-Gods) thus identifying the original Shinto religion as another example of the polytheisms already surveyed in chapter 4. Shintoism also exhibited the near universal acceptance of the idea that both a natural world and an unseen one existed, further characterizing it as a proponent of a dual real-ity. Although it was unusual in the minimal amount of concern that it ini-tially paid to what happened after death, from the inception of Shintoism a deep commitment to the idea that the spirit or personality or soul of the in-dividual continued after death was expressed. In later versions, Shintoism adopted a substantial part of the Buddhist eschatology, easily maintaining its supplementary emphasis on leading a satisfactory life in this world.

5.2.5 Confucianism and Taoism

Although listed among the great belief systems by almost every scholar of religious history, it is by no means certain that the original pristine forms of Confucianism and Taoism, two ancient but persistent Chinese philosophies, should be included in this present discussion. In their original formulations, both, like classic Buddhism, were much more devoted to the development of a system of human-to-human interaction rather than human-to-God interaction. It was only much later that the two systems of thought were conjoined with (usually) subsequent Buddhist religious thinking and diverged into the many different sects and interpretations with which we are familiar today. It was these descendent groups that can more properly be considered to be religions and to incorporate ideas about the supernatural, death, and the afterlife. Because of this major role in modern Asian thought, however, it is appropriate to briefly discuss both the history of these two philosophies and their modern religious instantiations.

K'ung-fu-tze or Confucius (551 BCE–479 BCE) exemplifies another one of the privileged class of his time who, toward middle age, rejected the violence and special privilege that characterized Zhou dynasty society. In so doing, he proposed a new philosophy that promised to provide an ideology and a code of conduct for human interactions. Confucius was born and lived just prior to the turmoil of the Warring States period of Chinese history. Even during his lifetime, the Zhou Empire was in disarray and in decline from the pinnacles of the power it had enjoyed for hundreds of years. The Zhou dynastic period was a time of fearful Gods, human sacrifices, and an almost pathological commitment to preparations for the afterlife rather than with a concern for the conditions and needs of the population or the opportunities for ethical government.

It is interesting to note that Confucius was not alone in proposing a retreat from the strife of society at this time. At almost exactly the same time, Siddhartha Gautama—the Buddha, was also presenting his social agenda to the world in India. However, where Buddhism adopted much of the theology of the Hindu emphasis on the achievement of an escape from the cycle of birth, pain, and reincarnation (Nirvana), early Confucianism emphasized relations among people in this world almost to the exclusion of such transcendental concerns.

Confucius lived most of his life as a member of a feudal society in which the ideal person had hitherto been considered to be someone born into the line of nobility. The God-Kings who ruled prior to his time were idealized as persons as well as deified. It was Confucius' insight and philosophical intuition in reaction to the arbitrariness of this system and the injustices that it produced that led him to propose a very different set of criteria to define the "superior man." His main point was that merit should be dependent upon behavior rather than on heritage. Considering that even modern society is still afflicted with aristocracies and hereditary monarchs or dictators, this was a prescient interpretation of what could be a better world, a world of justice and equality that was not to be more fully realized for nearly 2,500 years.

The criteria laid down by Confucius for the ideal to which each person should aspire were based on virtue and wisdom, rather than any accident of birth. Confucius proposed the four main themes of human virtue: "sincerity," "benevolence," "filial piety," and "propriety." Each of these was further detailed in his teaching to provide a plan for a humanitarian form of human interaction that many would consider deeply idealistic and optimistic in these and previous times. The Confucian ideal of "wisdom," although not synonymous with education, did ultimately stimulate an admirable respect for learning that continues today into modern Asian society.

Confucianism, as noted, was not originally deeply concerned with divinities or the afterlife. It is generally agreed, however that it was not patently atheistic. The early Confucian writing (e.g., Li-Ki—the Book of Rites) expressed a vague notion of a supreme creator or heavenly ruler (Shang-ti), but had little to say about a heaven or hell, or an afterlife. The Li-Ki, one of the most complete of the Confucian classics, goes into exquisite detail about the conduct of many of the activities of daily life including marriages, burials, and ceremonial feasts without invoking god-like presences or the rewards or punishments of an afterlife. Clearly, the emphasis in Confucianism is on living a good life in this world rather than being rewarded in the next one.

The implication of the philosophy of an ideal and ethical humanity, especially among its leaders, as opposed to the divine rights of a hereditary nobility brought Confucianism into conflict with the reigning dynasties of China. During the 2nd century BCE, major efforts were made to suppress his philosophy. This suppression included the burning of most of his books, a tactic that has repeatedly been used throughout history by many societies with minimal effect, ideas having their own kind of immortality. Much of this antagonism to the teachings of Confucius came from what has been called the Legalist or Fa-chia school of thought. Legalists were not primarily philosophical or religious, but political, theorists and were mainly concerned with perpetuating the dynastic power of the nobility. Unlike Confucius' teachings, they were convinced that the masses were both evil and intrinsically incapable of governing themselves.

However, only a few years hence, in the latter part of the 2nd century BCE, Confucianism was declared the official philosophy of the Han dynasty. The antagonism of the Legalists had been overcome and substantial efforts were made to combine ideas from all preceding philosophical schools into a single or "Syncretic" interpretation. In this regard, the Han philosophers succeeded remarkably well.

Because of its emphasis on this world, there was more discontent expressed by another, somewhat unexpected source, however. The lack of emphasis on the supernatural, with its attendant Gods, demons, and the afterlife, did not sit well with the public for whom Confucian teachings were much too sophisticated. Thus, from very early times, there are strong indications that Confucius' social philosophy was increasingly pressured to combine with both the Buddhist and Taoist theologies to produce a combined philosophical–religious program. There was pressure for dictates that more fully met the needs of those who required the supernatural to explain the meaning of their existence and to reward them for the tribulations of this life. Indeed, in 136 BCE Confucianism was transformed from the state philosophy into the state religion. Its role in Chinese civilization has been continuous since then. The heavy emphasis on education and equalitarianism permeated Chinese society for millennia. The long tradition of civil service examinations to choose administrators persisted into the 20th century, as did the veneration of parents and ancestors. It was only in the 20th century that many of these traditional ideas fell victim to the deprivations of the Red Guards.

At about the same time that Confucius was seeking to pacify the fundamentally warlike hostility and the chaotic social conditions of the Zhou dynasties with his ethical system of the "Superior Man," another Chinese teacher was also active—Lao-Tzu (604? BCE–531? BCE), also known as Lao-Tse and Lao-zi.[14] Lao-Tzu was reputed in some quasi-mythological stories to have actually met and debated with Confucius. It is hard to tell whether this story is true or not (as are the exact dates of his birth and death). Nevertheless, Lao-Tzu proposed another very Chinese-style philosophy suggesting that solutions to political and social problems of the feudal world in which he lived would come, not from defining a virtuous and well-educated "superior man" à la Confucius, but rather from a return to Nature (with a capital N) from that world.

Taoism, as Lao-Tzu's philosophy came to be called, did, therefore, have a more theological bent to it than did Confucianism. It was expressed in terms of a vague kind of pantheism in which Nature represented a kind of intangible and indescribable heaven that controlled and regulated the entire world. The Tao *is* Nature, heaven, and, in some very abstract sense, God itself. Taoists referred to it as the "Great Ultimate." The proper role of people in this world was to seek a return to a union with the world of that natural entity. This was accomplished, Lao-Tzu taught, by the conscious effort to simplify one's life to the extreme and to achieve good physical health and mental contentment. The individual had to adopt the Tao[15] or "way of life" in which satisfaction and fulfillment would be obtained from simple pleasures and activities, as well as regular exercises such as Tai chi. Exceedingly important to this world was the concept of wu-wei, the philosophy of nonaction. Wu-wei has also been, along with Confucian teachings

---

[14]"Lao" is the usual honorific for an older person in the current Chinese language.

[15]In my studies in preparation to write this section, I have found two different definitions of the term *Tao* or, as it is often also written, *Dao*. The first is synonymous with the indescribable heaven and the second is used as a definition of the desirable life style that leads to the good life. It is acceptable that it be used in both ways.

one of the subliminal forces throughout Chinese history. Subservience, rather than rebellion, was considered the ideal. One should not fight nature, but rather allow it to "run its course." Current traditional style Chinese medical practices are in large part influenced by Taoist thinking about the potency of "natural" pharmaceuticals.

The main texts of Taoism are the I Ching (*The Book of Changes*), a book that may have been adopted from Lao-Tzu's contemporary, Confucius, and the almost untranslatable Tao-te-Ching (*The Way of Power/Virtue*) in which Lao-Tzu is reputed to have spelled out the essential details of his naturalistic philosophy.

Throughout the recorded history of China there has been an ebb and flow of interest and dedication to Taoist ideas. As also happened in Confucian doctrine, there was an increasingly theological overtone to the two life styles as Buddhist ideas and other religious ideas were eventually incorporated into what had originally been proscriptions for this world's life style.

In 424 CE, this new amalgam of Confucian and Taoist philosophy and Buddhist religion became the official religion of the Wei dynasty. In the centuries that followed all three religions exhibited enormous influence on Chinese civilization. All three shared many common ideals such as respect, if not worship, of one's ancestors, a respect for education, and, to a surprising degree under the many emperors and rulers who followed, a respect for ability over birthright. All three have been adopted and accepted without substantial internal philosophical inconsistency in subtle ways that influenced Chinese thought, even when the details of their specific rituals did not persist.

In addition to the Confucianism–Taoism–Buddhism tradition that dominated Chinese civilization over the centuries, there were many other schools of thought that have come and gone leaving lesser marks on the course of Chinese thought. The "Moist" tradition grew up in the same epoch of Confucius and Lao-Tzu; it was fathered by Mo-Tzu (traditionally considered to have lived from 468 BCE to 376 BCE). The differences between Moism and Confucianism were mainly procedural. The Moist were appalled by the attention paid to rituals and rites in the Li-Ki as opposed to a reverence for the rules and influences on living. However, these were but slight difference and, like its contemporaries, Moism was also very much concerned with the problem of how people might go about living the good life.

A common attribute shared and influenced by all of the philosophical and religious traditions in China was the idea of the Yin and Yang. The essential assumption, expressed in the familiar half black and half white interlocked symbol, is that two forces, one negative and one positive, must be balanced to provide for a satisfactory way of life.

It is still debated whether Moism, Taoism, and Confucianism are religions or philosophies. Perhaps the best way to look at them is through the window of history. Originally, all were more concerned with developing a style of life in which the respective criteria of virtue, universal ancestor love, or "disentanglement" could guide the individual to establish a harmonious relationship with fellow humans. As I noted, however, all have changed enormously over the years. Theological and supernatural concepts continuously fed into the original dictates for establishing an optimum life style. Where they may have been worldly philosophies at the beginning, the enormous pressure exerted by the human fear of death has led these schools of thought to adopt ideas of the supernatural that have made them more religious than philosophical. Whatever they have become, it is clear that any specific designation of them as dualistic, monotheistic, or polytheistic would miss the point that their founders intended to make.

5.2.6 Judaism

Today, much of the world follows another great tripartite system—the Judaic–Christian–Muslim religious tradition—otherwise collectively known as the children of Abraham. Perhaps half the people in the world are followers of what have long been referred to as the Abrahamic theologies. All three religions look back to a remarkably specific time and place for the roots of their religions—the Middle East of 4,000 years ago. According to tradition, the founding Patriarch of all three religions was Abraham, a citizen of the Chaldean city of Ur in Mesopotamia. The exact dates of this remote ancestor cannot be exactly known, of course, but biblical scholars have calculated (on the slimmest of evidence) that he must have lived (if he was actually a historical figure) within a century or two of 2000 BCE. From details spelled out in the Old Testament, however, his supposed life story is especially well known to most of the world's population. The story of his migration in the book of Genesis from Mesopotamia (including periods of residence in both Ur and Haran) to Canaan and then to Egypt only to return finally to Canaan is replete with exact detail. His movements among the various towns and cities during his migration are described almost to the week.

The biblical story continues with equally complete details of the lives of Abraham's descendants through the years of Hebrew power and influence in Egypt and then the years of slavery. The biblical story finally comes to a head in the great tale of the Exodus led by the cryptic character Moses.

The story of Abraham is so much a part of Western culture and the Judaic–Christian–Muslim tradition, the religious choice of so many people, that it is sometimes hard to acknowledge that it was recorded, at the earliest, more than 1,000 years after the events described may have occurred. In such a situation, ideas (such as monotheism) that actually may have arisen many years later are sometimes reflected back onto a history that may or may not have ever occurred and that invoke people who may or may not have ever lived. Certainly, if Abraham was a real historical person, he was much more likely to have been a follower of one of the Mesopotamian polytheisms of his time rather than of the demanding monotheism of the Old Testament that originated much later.

In the final analysis, we cannot know for certain what is myth and what is an extraordinary well preserved oral history. It is most likely that we never will be able to know whether any individual of those times actually existed. The raw fact of the matter is that little well substantiated direct archeological or historical validation or confirmation of any of the biblical tales prior to the 7th century BCE has ever been found. In the absence of such objective data, Abraham probably should be best considered to be as much a myth as Gilgamesh, Osiris, Poseidon, Ixtab, or Quetzalcoatl!

What Abraham and the other personages of the Pentateuch do represent is the personification of ideals and principles as well as some of the actual events that occurred much later when the Old Testament was written down. Finkelstein and Silberman (2001), in their up-to-date discussion of biblical archeology, suggest that the Abraham story is really a reflection of prehistoric events dimly remembered in oral histories of population movements and other aspects of social history instantiated in the life of a single individual.

Although the absence of any specific archeological evidence for the existence of any of the biblical patriarchs is a terribly unpleasant fact for the devout to acknowledge, it is generally agreed by biblical archeological scholars that such a negative conclusion is warranted. Hoerth (1998), a beautifully illustrated and thoughtfully written book on the archeology of the Old Testament, is also (along with Finkelstein & Silberman, 2001) an intelligent review of the archeological findings that are contemporary to the early Old Testament stories. As one reads Hoerth's book, however, it becomes quickly evident that he is actually telling two almost totally independent tales—one a chronology as it is recorded in the early books of the Hebrew bible and the other a discussion of the archeological finds from approximately the same times those people were thought to have lived.[16] The documented historicity of the second tale, the archeological one, does nothing to authenticate the mythology of the first.

What Hoerth does very successively accomplish is to tell us about the world as it existed at the approximate time that Abraham and the other biblical patriarchs may or may not have lived. This does not overcome the classic problem to which I alluded in chapter 1—namely, that it is not possi-

---

[16]My readers cannot be reminded too often that the dates of all of the people mentioned in Genesis are subject to dispute among biblical historians. Because there is no correlated archeology, the birth or death dates of the major figures, even the fact that they lived, or the time of certain events is uncertain.

ble to infer the thoughts of a people from their artifacts any more than it is from their behavior. Hoerth (1998) put it this way:

> There is the tendency by some Christians to assume too much from archeology. Sometimes the words *confirm, prove, authenticate,* and *substantiate* can be employed. It can be proved that historical conditions were such that Solomon could have been as powerful a king as the Bible says he was; but this does not prove that God gave Solomon wisdom. It can be fairly well substantiated that there was a census when Jesus was born; but this confirmation hardly proves his divinity. No archeological evidence will ever prove the atonement. (p. 20)

So much for what archeology can do even for these relatively recent religious figures. The archeological evidence necessary to establish the existence of some of the more ancient people cited in the older portions of the Pentateuch remains elusive, if not unobtainable.

The next problem that arises in the search for concrete evidence of the existence of the figures mentioned in the early books of the Old Testament is the ambiguity of the few records that have survived from that time. Prior to the time of the Egyptian captivity, there is absolutely nothing in the archeology of either Egypt or Palestine that even suggests the existence of a Hebrew people. A few papyri from Egypt dating from the pre-Exodus period mention slave lists with names that are seemingly Hebrew (Hoerth, 1998, p. 149). However, the word "Habiru," which may be nothing more than an Egyptian near homophone of the word "Hebrew," does not appear on any monument or in any record until the time of the writing of the Tel El-Armana cuneiform tablets. These letters, presumably communications from the kings of Babylon to the pharaohs of Egypt, have been, with a high degree of certainty, dated to approximately 1380 BCE to 1350 BCE. Among the tablets are letters from Ashur-uballit I to the monotheistic pharaoh Akhenaten, which, as we have already seen, places them not too distant from the time frame of the Exodus. However, as Hoerth points out (pp. 216–217) there is great uncertainty whether "Habiru" (or the closely related term "Apiru") really refers to the Hebrew tribes. It may well be a general name for any enemy or invader or, even, bandit. Links to a specific Hebrew people are very weak even at this relatively late date, and nothing earlier exists. As Finkelstein and Silberman (2001) suggest, it may have been a name for a lawless band of outlaws, mercenaries, or even "hired laborers working on government building projects" (p. 103) *in Egypt!* This does not, of course, mean that the Apiru were not the progenitors of the ancient Hebrews—the outlaw life of an itinerant piratical tribe may have been their early existence. The Old Testament, written hundreds of years later, may simply have "laundered" this unpleasant history into the biblical tales. Indeed, the tales of migration and conquest so eloquently and poetically told in the Pentateuch are not that fundamentally different in kind from the reports of the outlaw Apiru if one reads just a little between the lines. In the one case, the invasion and conquest are treated as a noble venture. In the other, nearly the same activities are treated as a potential disruption and criminal intrusion into an otherwise stable existing state.

Unfortunately, there is an almost complete absence of even the most tenuous archeological links to the early existence of the Hebrew people, much less to the detailed genealogy of biblical personalities, and certainly to any putative monotheism prior to the time of Akhenaten and Moses. As I noted in chapter 4 (see page 90), the oldest Hebrew writing dates from no earlier than 1000 BCE. Thus, there is a period of several hundred years from the arrival of the Hebrews in Canaan following the best estimate of the date of the Exodus until the Kingdom of David that is, for all practical purposes, an archeological lacuna in terms of any specific reference to the ancient Hebrews.

The marginal historical status of Abraham, Moses, and the Exodus are not too difficult to accept. They existed hundreds of years before the Old Testament was written. Finkelstein and Silberman (2001), however, remind us of something that should be even more intellectually challenging than those quasi-mythological events. The biblical tales of David and Solomon, the golden city of Jerusalem, and the sequence of kings prior to the 8th century BCE are *equally unsupported by archeological evidence!*[17] Indeed, Solomon's supposedly grand temple left no archeological traces. What evidence has been accumulated about the status of Jerusalem at that time indicates that this was no more than a small village of at the most a few hundred people around 1000 BCE. Even by the 7th century BCE, when the Old Testament was first written down, Jerusalem was still a small village half the size of the current Old City.[18]

Nevertheless, the long adopted and deeply believed story is that armed with a dogmatically monotheistic religion dictated in the divinely inspired tablets of the Ten Commandments and led either probably by an Egyptianized Hebrew (Moses) or, improbably, a Hebraized Egyptian (Akhenaten), a band of ex-slaves of unknown number made their way from Egypt into a land they were told had been promised to them by their fierce and demand-

---

[17]As usual, the facts change very quickly in archeology, especially with the advent of new techniques. Bruins, van der Plicht, and Mazar (2003) recently reported that radiocarbon dating of a site in modern day Rehov, Israel links the conquest by the Pharaoh Shoshenq in 925 BCE with biblical references to the time of David and Solomon. Although, there is still no mention of these individuals, Egyptian records do report that there was a substantial community there at Rehov at this time.

[18]One interesting hypothesis cited by Finkelstein and Silberman (2001) is that the Hebrew people were actually neither "invading raiders nor infiltrating nomads" (p. 104) but actually a consolidated hill tribe that had moved there from the cities of Canaan in a time of social strife or agricultural failure. This theory of the origin of the Hebrew people, first put forward by Mendenhall (1962), would mean that rather than being the conquerors of Canaan, the first Hebrews were themselves Canaanites!

ing God. Regardless of the details, it seems certain that the pure monotheism that they practiced was the first to survive to modern times. If Akhenaten's single Sun God predated their theology by a few years and even if it
did influence the Hebrew religion to some degree, it did not last. Not only
did the Hebrew people and their religion persist, but their ancient traditions and scriptures gave rise to the other Abrahamic religions that now
dominate so much of the world, both east and west.

However unclear may be the prehistory of this influential band of Semitic people and how much dispute about the details of those early times
there may be, there is little argument over the central core of their beliefs.
Judaism, as the religion of the ancient Hebrews is now called, serves but
one God. The central watchword of every Jewish religious service is the
"Shama": "Hear O Israel, The Lord our God, The Lord is One." Whether Reform, Conservative, or Orthodox this monotheistic centrality dominates the
worldview of any religious Jew.

The singular Hebrew God is omnipresent and omnipotent, as well as
wise and deeply involved in human affairs. He rewards the good (e.g.,
Noah) and punishes the wicked (e.g., the residents of Sodom and Gomor-
rah). Idols to this one God are forbidden and there cannot even be any secondary Gods to provide support and counsel or to conflict with Him. The
Ten Commandments, given by that all-powerful God to Moses, are designed
to provide a core of social ethics and behavior as well as to proclaim a pure
form of monotheism. These are the central tenets of Judaism.

Beyond that point, however it gets a little dicier to tease out the specific
beliefs of the Jewish people concerning an afterlife. Throughout the ages,
there has been a tendency toward individual choice and responsibility and
this has led to a variety of interpretations about the afterlife and the possibility of a heaven and a hell. Reform, Conservative, and Orthodox doctrines
often conflict with each other.

Jewish attitudes toward death and the afterlife have, therefore, always
been quite variable. Although originally there was relatively little concern
with a specific heaven or hell, Jewish tradition did promulgate the idea of
an ultimate resurrection of the dead "sometime in the future." It is not clear
whether this was intended by all of the adherents to this faith to be a bodily
resurrection or a spiritual one in which the individual would attain an intangible "fellowship with God."

In Old Testament times, the concept of a place in which an afterlife was
spent prior to the resurrection—the She'ol—played a relatively minor role in
the Jewish eschatology. It was interpreted, without great detail, as an underground place in which the souls of the dead awaited the coming of the
Messiah. After the resurrection, the Book of Daniel suggests that

> . . . many of those who sleep in the dust of the earth shall awake, some to ever-
> lasting life, and some to shame and everlasting contempt. (Daniel 12:1–2)

Thus, the idea of a spiritual, if not bodily, immortality seems to have been a part, albeit of secondary importance, of the Jewish religion from its earliest times. The idea that heaven represented a rewarding future life only became popular during the centuries around the time of the birth of Jesus Christ. Life in the world of that time had become increasingly terrible for the inhabitants of Israel. The Roman domination, the destruction of Jerusalem and the second temple by Titus, and the mass suicides at Masada, all may have contributed to the idea that miseries of this life ought be balanced by rewards in a heaven to follow. It is also possible that the ideas of otherworldly rewards and punishments may have fed back from the early Christian beliefs onto the more traditional Jewish ones. Like the Chinese peasants, ordinary Jews of those times may have needed something more concrete than a distant resurrection to assuage the potential loss of personal identity.

In spite of this relatively low level of concern with eschatology, debates about the exact nature of the resurrection (e.g., whether it provided for corporeal regeneration as well as a spiritual revival or whether it would happen to all people and not just the just) have kept scholars busy throughout Jewish history. As one reviews the last 2,000 years of Jewish history, it becomes clear that internal theological and social debates concerning this topic have played a very central role. The Mishna, for example, is a commentary and discussion of ancient Jewish oral law first written down around 200 CE. The Mishna provides interpretations and detailed proscriptions supplementary to the Old Testament. The Talmud, which followed, however, is a series of debates and discussions that are intended to explore and clarify the internal logical inconsistencies of the Mishna. Two versions of the Talmud are known to exist: the Palestinian and the Babylonian Talmuds.

The writing of the Talmud became a major preoccupation of Jews in the centuries after 200 CE. Only parts of the Palestinian Talmud remain. It was written during the period 250 CE to 425 CE and much of it was lost in later years. The more complete Babylonian Talmud was written in the period from about 200 CE until about 500 CE in Mesopotamia in the years following the scattering of the Jews after the destruction of the second temple in Jerusalem in 73 CE. The Talmud established a tradition of scholarly debate on Jewish religious doctrine that has been added to continuously by scholars over the last millennia and a half.

Over the years, more detailed cultural traditions of heaven and hell were appended to the originally vague ideas of a Jewish afterlife just as they had been appended to the early teachings of Confucius and Lao Tzu. We can only speculate whether or not this increasingly explicit eschatology arose out of the same needs of a populace still horrified by the unavoidable evidence of bodily death. In any event, traditions of heaven and a kind of hell became an increasing part of the Jewish tradition during and after the 1st century BCE. Paradise or heaven (Gan Eden) became the ultimate destination of the just, whereas hell (Gehenna) became a place of punishment for those who had led a less than holy life. There is so little in any of the scriptures about the immortality of the soul that many of the ideas revolving around the nature of the afterlife are left up to the individual. In modern times, most Reform Jews have rejected both of these ideas as well as the idea of a personal Messiah. On the other hand, Orthodox Jews still accept these as important parts of their interpretation of Judaism.

The Mishna and the Talmud speak more explicitly than does the Old Testament of Olam Ha-Ba—the afterlife or world to come. The Mishna likens it to an ever-lasting banquet, but one of considerably greater pleasure and satisfaction. The Talmud builds on this metaphor by considering issues such as who will be admitted and who will be denied heaven and directed to hell, respectively.

It is not easy to sum up in a few words the eschatology of the Jewish religion either as it was originally described in the Old Testament or in the many other books in which it is known today. Like all other religions discussed in this chapter, Judaism has evolved and incorporated ideas from many of the cultures with which it has interacted over the years. Traces of Mesopotamian, Egyptian, and even Christian ideas are not too difficult to tease out of the varieties of current Jewish thought. Accepting the fact of the basic monotheism is easy, but the centuries have added many other ideas and concepts that complicate any answer to the posed question of the detailed philosophy of a "Jew." However, of one other basic fact we can be sure. Like all other religions and vague though it may be, there is an intrinsic dualism built into Judaism. To devout Jews, the body and the soul are not manifestations of one and the same reality and one can survive the other.

In summary, the Jewish religion's formal concern with life after death and the details of what happens and where, is secondary. Individuals are pretty much free to believe what they will. An interesting history of the concept of death in Jewish history can be found in Gilman (1997).

Another incontrovertible and definitive aspect of Jewish theology is the rejection by all factions of Judaism of the idea that a Messiah has already arrived. It is this particular act of faith, more than any other doctrine that led to the great schism between Judaism and its next major offshoot—Christianity.

5.2.7 Christianity

As already noted, the Jewish religion began to change substantially in the last years before the birth of Jesus. These years were a time of enormous turmoil and crisis for the small nation that were in many respects even worse than the previous centuries that had passed since the supposed reigns of David and Solomon (around 1000 BCE). It is worthwhile to understand a bit more of the history of the crossroads of conquest and reonquest that this region represented to appreciate what happened in the first century BCE. In 922 BCE Israel was divided into two separate countries (Israel in the north and Judah in the south) that were to be ruled, off and on, by distinct, though related, dynasties. From about 900 BCE, one conquering people after another marched over the land and sacked the major cities of the region. The Assyrians came in the 8th century BCE; the Babylonians in the 7th century BCe; the Persians in the 6th century BCE; the Greeks in the 4th century BCE; and the Syrian Seleucids in the 3rd century BCE. During these years, the two kingdoms phased into and out of existence as one or another of these conquerors made it a part of their much larger empires. After the return of the Hebrew people from Babylonian captivity, the southern region of Palestine around Jerusalem was referred to as Judea.

In 164 BCE, the Judean people, led by Judah Maccabee rebelled against the Seleucid rule and restored a Jewish dynasty—the Hasmoneans—which lasted until 63 BCE. At that time, internal conflicts arose between Hellenist and traditional Jews as well as among the different Jewish factions over control of the priesthood, among other issues. To resolve those conflicts, a fateful and terrible decision was made to invite in the Roman Legions to provide some kind of order. The Romans installed a puppet government eventually placing Herod on the throne of Roman Judea. Herod reigned from 37 BCE to 4 BCE, which brings us to the main topic of this section.

Herod might have gone down in history as a highly accomplished leader. He rebuilt the Jerusalem temple that had been destroyed in 581 BCE by the Babylonians and directed many other impressive construction projects in Judea. However, he also instituted some policies that locally exacerbated the internal stresses on the Judean population. It should be remembered that the region in general was in a confused state. A major war between the Hellenized Ptolemaic dynasty of Egypt and the Roman Empire was occurring on their doorstep. Herod's reign overlapped with the battles between Mark Antony and Cleopatra, on one side, and Octavian, the Roman Emperor on the other and the latter's ultimate victory. The heavy hand of the Roman Legions, freed from the demands of its Mediterranean war, was then to fall on the people of Judea. During this chaotic international situation, Judea was also involved in numerous internecine contests, often abated by outside invasions, for example by the Parthians in 40 BCE.

More fundamental than the international crisis, however, for the present story is the intellectual turmoil that beset the Jewish religion at this time. There was continued debate over the imminent arrival of the long predicted Messiah who, it was hoped, would free the Judean people from the terrors of Roman oppression. Life was so bad, as noted earlier, that an added compelling tendency was exerted for the population to look to a life after death to replace the pains of the present one. This conflicted strongly with traditional Jewish thought.

Control of the priesthood also became a contentious issue among the various Jewish sects—the Pharisees (primarily a group of common people who accepted some aspects of Hellenism), the Sadducees (primarily an upper class, priestly group in support of Hellenism), and the Essenes (a group of aesthetics vigorously opposed to Hellenism) among many other less well-known groups. All of these sects were jockeying for religious and political power at the time. Issues of free will and predestination, as well as the specific nature of the afterlife were also vigorously, to say the least, debated by the contending groups. Another issue that also divided the Jews of Judea concerned whether or not the Old Testament was the divine and literal revelation of God or just a historical interpretation of times-gone-by by mortal scholars.

Much of what we know of the religious ideas and conflicts, as well as their political agendas, of the time comes from the writing of Josephus (1999), a Romanized Jewish historian who was born in 37 CE and died somewhere around the end of the first century CE. His second volume, *The War of the Jews* discusses the political and theological issues that split the various contending groups. The other major source of the history of the times is, of course, the New Testament. However, like the Old Testament, Josephus's book and the Gospels of the New Testament had particular causes to support and, in the case of the latter, a specific theology to promulgate. Many of the historical details spelled out in all of these books may, therefore, be strongly biased by the message they were seeking to send.

Thus, in addition to the tyrannical Roman occupation, two major themes of contention rent the intellectual fabric of Judea—Hellenization and specific theological issues. However, there were also universally held beliefs that tied the contending Jewish groups together. One, of course, was their view of God as a vengeful and angry figure who actively interfered with people's lives, rewarding some and punishing some. Another was the notion that people were generally born good instead of carrying the burden of Adam and Eve's original sin. Entry into any kind of heaven or hell (if one accepted that there were such places) was regulated by the quality of one's life on earth. Circumcision was universal among all Jews as part of the Covenant with God. Finally, though many thought that the arrival of the Messiah was close at hand, Jews, in general, did not yet accept any of many claimants of that role and the offered hope of relief from Roman oppression and the social and theological chaos that reigned at that time.

Into this mélange of contending ideas and belief came another remarkable teacher and prophet, Jesus of Nazareth. Jesus or Jeshua,[19] a Jew, taught a

---

[19]Few archeological or concrete evidences of the existence of Jesus exist. A search for the "historical" person, therefore, has continued for centuries. In 2002, a remarkable ossuary, was discovered that bears the inscription: James, son of Joseph, brother of Jesus" dating from 63 CE. If this unique artifact can be associated with the family of Jesus, it will be the oldest evidence of

revolutionary new philosophy of man's place in the universe that contradicted much of the traditional Jewish teaching of the time. It was a religion of a forgiving God and the certainty of an ultimate judgment and an actual bodily resurrection for true believers. Many of the ideas that surrounded his person are now appreciated to have historical precedents (Freke & Gandy, 1999). I have already mentioned the similarity of the Osiris legend of the murdered and resurrected Man-God in both Christian thinking and even the mystery cult of the Hellenized Jews. Indeed, as Freke and Gandy (1999) argued, it may well have been the philosophy of the Hellenized Jews who, in departing from the standard beliefs of their old religion, evolved into what came to be called the Gnostics. These authors suggested that early Christianity originally carried many of the characteristics of the Hellenic Gnosticism. Indeed, they go on to argue that Christianity actually arose from that source rather than directly from traditional Judaism. Only later, did the Christian literalists overcome the Gnostic tradition of ascribing hidden and symbolic meaning to the New Testament to produce the theological core of the modern, literally interpretive Christianity we know today.

To say that Judaism and Christianity differ in many respects is probably the understatement of the last two millennia. Although one is the intellectual descendant of the other and the two have been tied together for better or for worse since the time of Jesus, there are many general principles of the respective religions that are completely incompatible and are likely to remain so. The acceptance of the divine life story of Jesus is but one fundamental difference. To Christians, he was not only a man, but is one part of the tripartite nature of a God that Christians believe is expressed in three manifestations—The Father, Son, and Holy Ghost. Jesus, Christians believe, was (or is) the Messiah and his death was a form of atonement for the sins of mankind. He is expected to return in the second coming at some unknown, but to some of the faithful, imminent time.

Furthermore, the roles of heaven and hell have been in the past far more important to the Christian religion than they were to Judaism. To many Christians, Hell and damnation are the destiny of anyone who does not accept the teachings and divinity of Jesus; all will be judged at the time of their death to determine their fate. Catholics, in addition, believe in the intermediary stage of Purgatory, a kind of lesser Hell, from which a person can ultimately be transferred to heaven. The only salvation from Hell or Purgatory is through acceptance of Jesus as a manifestation of God as evidenced by the act of baptism and a demonstrated acceptance of his teachings. Those who

---

his existence yet uncovered. Unfortunately, the most recent examination suggests it is not authentic. There is a curious mix of script-types (the latter allusion to Jesus is done in a different style with unusually sharp edges than the names of the James and Joseph) and the region of the ossuary on which the inscription has been written seems suspiciously smooth.

do believe, according to Christian doctrine, will earn eternal life, including bodily resurrection, again at some unknown time in the future. Those who do not so believe, it is taught, can expect only eternal damnation.

Another widely held Christian belief that differs from Jewish teaching is that humans are inherently evil and cursed by the original sin (Adam and Eve's devouring of the forbidden fruit). This predetermined evil has to be overcome by good works and particular rituals in this world. Finally, among the almost universally held tenets of Christianity, it is believed that Jesus himself was born of a virgin conception; that his mother, Mary, was impregnated by God without an act of physical intercourse through the action of the Holy Spirit. (The concept of a virgin conception, or as it usually inaccurately called—the virgin birth—is another ancient idea that has been incorporated into successive religions. Tales of virgin conceptions are told in ancient Egyptian, Mesopotamian, and Greek mythologies.)

The Christian God is also quite different than the Jewish one. Whereas the latter was demanding and often angry, the former is a forgiving, heavenly Father. To Jews, God is constantly involved in worldly affairs, rewarding the good and often wreaking havoc including such extreme punishments as the physical destruction of the wicked. The need for a personal savior is alien to Jewish thought, but a centerpiece of the Christian religion. Because of its emphasis on this world, Judaism teaches a more active participation and, from some points of view, a greater tendency toward rebelliousness that is less emphatic in the more docile Christian cultural tradition. The admonition to turn the other cheek is very Christian and much less Jewish.

Many Christian beliefs are universally held by all members of this huge worldwide religion; the divinity of Jesus and his oneness with God is accepted by virtually all adherents to this faith. However, there is enormous diversity on other points. The Catholic belief in the literal transubstantiation of water and bread into the blood and body of Jesus is not followed by most Protestants. Practitioners of the Roman Catholic faith have traditionally accepted pontifical and church authority in all matters ecclesiastical as well as secular. Protestants, in accord with their name, have a far less rigid line of authority from their leaders to the laity.

The role of Heaven and Hell is also quite diverse among the Christian denominations.[20] In the past thousand years the Christian concept of heaven, hell, and purgatory have been repeatedly and specifically defined by various writers including Dante and St. Thomas.

---

[20]Whatever the differences, the idea still holds a significant amount of popular appeal. According to a recent article in *Newsweek* magazine (August 12, 2002, p. 47) "76% of Americans believe in heaven, and of those, 71% think it is an actual place." This should be compared with the previously mentioned fact (see page 22) that 95% of the general public believes in the existence of God in some form.

There has, however, been a recent reduction in teachings about the specific nature of hell, in particular, among modern Protestant theologians) For reasons that may be associated with the state of the present world, some Christian theologians seem currently to be moving away from the old "fire and brimstone" version of hell and the specifics of heaven to a less well-specified version of an afterlife. This new approach suggests that rather than a garden flowing with delights of many kinds, heaven is a kind of spiritual communion with God. Indeed, this view is becoming increasingly similar to some of the older Jewish views. Judaism satisfied the popular need for an otherworldly life only in the later centuries before the birth of Jesus due to the tribulations of those times. The Jewish solution was to add somewhat vaguely defined otherworldly abodes for the dead. For the most part, the details of that afterlife were left for the individual to determine. The Christian concept of an afterlife seems to be moving, at least in some circles, in the same direction.

Christianity, despite its claims of monotheism, does accept the existence of other supernatural beings than the tripartite God in its most fundamental teachings. Satan, the embodiment of evil, is said to be a fallen angel. Many attempts have been made to explain the complex significance of the trinity and, in particular, the role played by the Holy Spirit. It has often been suggested that the Holy Spirit's main task is communication with mankind. For example, traditional Christian doctrine has suggested that the revealed divinity of the bible arises from the fact that it written under the direction of the Holy Spirit, albeit by the human scribes of the New Testament.

Finally, fundamental Christianity is much more concerned with what is perceived as an imminent end of the world than are most other religions. For fundamentalists, the second coming, the War of Armageddon, the rapture in which the faithful will physically arise to heaven, and the ultimate resurrection of believers in Jesus is near at hand. This is all predicted, they argue, in the last book of the New Testament—The Book of Revelations. Some scholars see this writing as a metaphor for the return of the Jewish people to Judea after the destruction of the second temple. Other more literal readers believe it is a prophecy of the end of the world. Paragraphs like the following make it amenable to many different interpretations.

> And I stood upon the sand of the sea, and saw a beast rise out of the sea, having seven heads and ten horns, and upon his horns ten crowns, and upon his heads the name of blasphemy. And the beast which I saw was like unto a leopard, and his feet were as the feet of a bear, and his mouth as the mouth of a lion: and the dragon gave him his power, and his seat, and great authority. (Revelations 13:1–2)

Needless to say, such metaphorical writing leaves many doors open to diverse interpretations, only some of which suggest an imminent "End of

Times." Historical figures are all too easily identified with some of the demons. Armageddon, the prophesied place of the final battle between Good and Evil, has been specifically located in the town of Megiddo in modern day Israel.

Another interpretation is that the tale is simply a coded historical rendition of what was going on at the time. That is, the seven heads are the seven hills of Rome and that the "beast" is nothing more than an allegory (not too far removed from reality) for the terror of Roman rule. Whatever the meaning of its authors, it is quite different than the other books and some Christian scholars question just how tightly the apocalyptic Book of Revelations should be linked to the New Testament.

Christianity, in its 2,000 years of history has, like virtually all other religions, evolved, adopted new interpretations, and, perhaps more than any other religion, fragmented into an innumerable number of denominations. Each of these subdivisions has continued to spin off new sects, some of which have survived and others of which have disappeared from ecclesiastical history. From the Anglican to the Baptists to the Greek Orthodox to the Quakers and Unitarians, an enormous variety of points of view can be detected in their liturgies as well as their eschatologies.

A major historical event in the history of Christianity was the division of the Church into Catholic and Protestant segments. This monumental schism can be attributed to two contemporary but completely different historical figures: Martin Luther (1483 CE–1546 CE) and Henry VIII, King of England (1491 CE–1547 CE). These two historically significant figures were antagonists on virtually every issue: their commonality existing only with regard to their respective roles in the breakup of the Catholic Church. Luther, an Augustinian monk, was disgusted by the corruption of the Catholic Church of his time. In particular, two issues—the selling of papal indulgences and a dispute whether faith alone was sufficient for salvation—led him to severely criticize the Pope and the Church. In 1517 CE, he went so far as to post his famous 95 theses on the door of the church at Wittenberg. These theses argued that the pope had no right to absolve sins and that the individual could only find salvation through his faith. Ultimately, this led to Luther's excommunication.

However, the historical effects of Luther's protest were enormous. Because of popular support for his position and antagonism to the Italian papacy, Luther's rebellion led to the reformation and the founding of the Protestant schism, perhaps one of the most significant events in Western history.

His contemporary, Henry VIII was no friend of Luther's; the two knew of and even had attacked each other in published letters over matters involved with the sacraments. What Henry VIII did that was so influential in further weakening the Roman church was to create the Church of England, one of the first Protestant Christian denominations. Clearly, his motives were far different than were those of Luther. Luther's motives had been based on theological principle. Henry's schism was based on his desire to divorce a wife (or at least to secure an annulment) who had not provided him a male heir—Catherine of Aragon. By so doing, the Church also excommunicated him. Henry called his parliament into session in 1529 CE in order to pass a number of modifications of church law. He completed the creation of the English version of the Protestant reformation by declaring his church separate from the Catholic Church in Rome and making himself its head. From those heady days in the 16th century and from such disparate reasons as motivated Luther and Henry VIII arose the two major divisions of modern Christianity.

In summary, the Christian religion is also deeply committed to a dualist theology in which bodily and spiritual aspects are considered to represent two kinds of reality. With regard to monotheism, all Christians argue that their idea of the trinity is monotheistic and that Father, Son, and Holy Ghost represent three different manifestations of a single God. The acceptance of angels and demons by many Christian denominations, however, suggests some residual belief in multiple forms of supernatural beings. In a much more practical sense, Christianity appears to be more concerned with the next life than is Judaism, a faith in which the traditional emphasis has been on this life.

5.2.8 Islam

This brings us to the third member of the Abrahamic monotheisms—Islam—the Muslim religion.[21] The history of Islam[22] begins in the Arabian Desert during the lifetime of another of those prophetic figures who was to exert enormous influence on the subsequent history of the world. This prophet was Muhammad, who was born about 570 CE and died in 632 CE. In the 62 years of his life he accomplished an extraordinary amount both in the secular and the religious worlds. Arabia, at the time of Muhammad, was a land inhabited by a relatively homogenous majority of Arabic city dwellers and wandering Bedouin tribes as well as a minority of Christians and Jews. The

---

[21]The exact definitions of the words Islam and Muslim are elusive. One explanation is that the noun "Islam" is a derivative of the Arabic word "Salamma," the Arabic word for peace. It is now generally interpreted to mean "submission to the will of God." Muslim is also a noun with a slightly different meaning—"one who surrenders to God." I use the word "Muslim" in the following sections as an adjective (as in—*Islam is the Muslim religion*). The usage is further complicated by the recent tendency to use the word "Islamic" to refer to the extreme fringes of the religion—those who have declared an active war (Jihad) on the western world.

[22]An excellent history of the Arab people from the time of Muhammad to modern times can be found in Hourani (1991). This book has been my main guide to the early history of the Arabian Peninsula.

indigenous Arab people were mainly followers of vaguely defined polytheistic animisms. Shrines were set up to honor idols representing Gods of many different kinds, some special to the local environment and some more generally revered.

Although the people of the central Arabian Peninsula were enjoying a relatively quiet time in their own history, wars were being fought all around them at the time of Muhammad. The Byzantine and Sasanian empires were fighting over control of the Middle East: The Sasanians had occupied the eastern part of Arabia and the Byzantines the north. This occupation was to be quite temporary for in the few years of Muhammad's life the Arab people began to spread out, first in a forced amalgamation of the isolated and relatively untroubled (by outside events) central cities of Arabia. Then, as the years went by and Muhammad's message became more widely spread throughout Arabia, in terms of a conquest by force of arms under the banner of the new Muslim religion. In only a few years, this new wave of Muslim Arabs was to overrun most of the Middle East including Egypt and Persia and even the home of the Sasanians—Persia or, as we know it today, Iran.

In what must be considered from a historical point of view a remarkably short period of time, by the middle of the 8th century Arab and Islamic conquerors controlled the world as far west as Spain. The political conquests were accompanied by a spiritual conquest; the Muslim religion was adopted by a large number of the people who had been overrun by the Arab invaders.

The success of the Arabian conquest depended in large part on the deeply held beliefs that had evolved from the desert animism with its many Gods and its admixture with some of the Judaic and Christian precursors into what must now be considered to be among the most orthodox monotheisms now extant in the modern world. How this new religion emerged from the desert is primarily the story of Muhammad the prophet.

Muhammad, a resident of Mecca, his reputed place of birth, had married a rich widow who, according to legend, was willing to support him as he pursued his scholarly and religious studies. The venue of these studies included annual isolated retreats into remote desert caves. One night in the year 610 CE, Muhammad is said to have had a revelation from God communicated to him by an angel. This critical event in Muslim history is referred to as "The Night of Power." During the revelation he was told by an angel that he would be the prophet of God and he was directed to preach subsequently revealed angelic dictations or recitations to his people. In years to come, the elements of this originally oral tradition were written down in the book that has become the Holy Scripture of the Muslim religion—the Qur'an or Koran. There is still some dispute over when the actual transcription into the written version of the 114 suras or chapters occurred. There is also some question (as there is for any ancient writing that has been copied and recopied) concerning the origin and authenticity of some of the material that is included. Nevertheless, the Qur'an is the holy book guiding the Islamic religion much as the older "peoples of the book" depended on their Old and New Testaments, respectively.

After a 3-year hiatus following the Night of Power, Muhammad began to teach what he believed was the essence of a new religion. His goal, remarkably well achieved, was to replace the idolatrous desert polytheisms with a single, all-powerful God. It is clear that he was heavily influenced by other peoples with whom he must have come into contact during his early days in Mecca. Both Judaism and Christianity had some followers in that ancient city and Muhammad adopted the prophets of both religions into his own theology. Specifically, he traced the origins of Islam back to Abraham, although not to the Hebrew lineage through Isaac and Jacob, but to Abraham's other son, Ishmael.

Anyone starting a new religion has to expect that adherents to the old ways will object. Indeed, this is what happened and in 622 CE, the situation became so bad in Mecca that Muhammad and his followers moved to the city of Medina. It was subsequent to his arrival there that he became involved in a number of battles with the people from his old hometown—Mecca. The motives for these interurban wars were complex. They were fought both over the control of trade routes as well as an effort on the part of the Meccans to further punish Muhammad for teaching a religion that was in such contradiction to their traditional theologies. The Meccans lost the battle, however, and Muhammad returned with an ever-increasing army of devoted followers and took over the city. His political and military success was parallel by a religious one; there was a total conversion of the inhabitants of his old hometown to the new religion.

Further battles were fought with the residents of Ta'if, another central Arabian town, but after a decade the entire region fell under his control and Islam became the single, widely accepted religion of the area. From there, as I have already noted, it took less than 100 years to conquer most of the Mediterranean and the Middle East. Muhammad was not only the founder the new Islamic religion, but he was also the founder of a powerful and expansionistic state.

Many of the older traditions of Judaism and Christianity were accepted into the new Muslim religion. Although the idea of the trinity was absolutely rejected, Jesus was accepted along with Abraham, Moses, and David as prophets who had communicated with God in earlier times and had brought forth His word in their respective holy books—the Pentateuch, the Psalms, and the Gospels. Indeed, these earlier prophets are still held in high regard by devout Muslims. Many of the particular teachings in the Old and New Testaments, however, were considered unacceptable or out of date. The Qur'an, being the most recent was considered to express the most appropriate (i.e., "full and final") word of God. (For readers who would like a more extensive introduction to the Muslim religion, I suggest the work of Lippman, 1995.)

By the time of Muhammad's death in 632 CE, the fundamental tenets of the new religion of Islam and an accompanying social code had become clear. He had incorporated some very unpopular ideas and some that were more easily accepted. Alcohol and gambling were prohibited,[23] for example, but in accord with ancient desert tradition, multiple wives were allowed. The consumption of pork was prohibited and, in a radical form of anti-idolatry, all representations of humans were forbidden.[24] However, these are only rules of everyday life. The specific Islamic religious obligations are based on the observance of the five basic "pillars":

1. The first pillar is testimony to the basic monotheistic premise of the Islamic faith. Whereas the Jews would recite the "Shama" as their central watchword, devout Muslims similarly pronounce the "Shahada" as the testimony of their faith. It avows: "I bear witness that there is no deity (none truly to be worshiped) but, Allah, and I bear witness that Muhammad is the messenger of Allah." Usually this is shortened to "There is no God but Allah and Muhammad is his prophet" or "I bear witness that there is no God but the Almighty God and that Muhammad is a messenger of God." The slightly different constructions convey important theological distinctions that cannot be reconciled here; they remain controversial issues among Muslim scholars. The important fact about the Shahada is that it need only be said once in a lifetime for a person to become a Muslim. Nevertheless, it is regularly recited by the devout in many different situations.

2. The second pillar is the requirement that every good Muslim should recite "salat" or prayers five times a day while facing Mecca.[25]

3. The third pillar requires devout Muslims to fast from dawn until dusk on every day of the holy month of Ramadan.

---

[23]"O you who believe! intoxicants and games of chance and (sacrificing to) stones set up and (dividing by) arrows are only uncleanness, the Shaitan's [Satan's] work; shun it therefore that you may be successful. The Shaitan only desires to cause enmity and hatred to spring in your midst by means of intoxicants and games of chance, and to keep you off from the remembrance of Allah and from prayer. Will you then desist?" (Qur'an 5:90–91)

[24]The Muslim prohibition of human images provided an impetus for one of the most beautiful forms of architectural art in the long history of humanity. Muslim mosques and palaces (e.g., the Ottoman palace in Istanbul) are among the most pleasing and exciting artistic environments I have had the opportunity to visit. The calligraphy and the plethora of geometric designs of Islamic art make up one of the greatest tangible treasures of human history.

[25]Originally, the direction one should face when praying was toward Jerusalem. During the early days of Islam, there was so much disagreement with the Jewish inhabitants of Medina in particular, that it was decided to change the holy direction so that the prayers were directed to Mecca.

4. The fourth pillar is the requirement to contribute a certain portion of one income to charity. The figure of 2.5% is often stated as the bare minimum donation, but it is expected that additional monies should be given to the poor to the limits of one's economic capability.

5. The fifth pillar is not an absolute, but given sufficient wealth and health on the part of each potential pilgrim, a good Muslim is supposed to make a pilgrimage to Mecca at least once in their lifetime.

As with any other religion that has been around for more than a millennium, Islam has divided itself into sectarian divisions. The two most important are the Sunni and Shia sects. The schism in this case was the result of a very early division between two contending forces seeking to control the succession following Muhammad's death. Even though these two sects make up most of the Islamic world there are many others that are still active including the mystical Sufi, the Isma'ilite, and the Deobandis, the latter otherwise known as the Taleban. Disagreements about tradition, ritual, the degree to which Islamic law must be followed, and secular goals are replete among adherents to each of these sects, a not atypical situation for evolving religions in general.

The central theological core of Islam, of course, is its emphasis on monotheism. Not only is acceptance of the unity of God the first pillar and the key to conversion to the Muslim religion, but also any suggestion that He might have manifestations other than His essential unity would place a believer outside the umbrella of any kind of Muslim tradition.

In spite of this radical monotheism, Islam, like Judaism and Christianity, makes allusions to other supernatural entities. In the case of Islam, these entities are known as jinns and angels. Satan also plays an important role in Islam, but is counted among the angels, albeit the most disobedient. The jinns, according to the Qur'an, are not quite angels, but a form of consciousness between human and angels that are also especially prone to disobedience. Given that a basic idea of Islam is "submission" or "obedience" to God, the very act of disobedience is taken very seriously in Muslim teaching as a major form of bad, even sacrilegious, behavior.

The existence of other kinds of supernatural entities (other than God) such as angels, demons, devils, or jinns is a concept tracking through all three of the Abrahamic religions. Such a proposition stimulates at least a bit of concern about the essential expression of the fundamental monotheism of all three religions. Where did these supernumerary, supernatural entities come from? What are they? How do they interact with humans? Although these questions are not dealt with in detail in Judaism and Christianity, they are in Islam. Muslim theology suggests that humans are formed from clay, jinns from fire, and angels from light. One possible answer to the historical (as opposed to the theological) question of their origin is that all such entities are vestiges from the ancient polytheisms from which the newer monotheisms seem to have evolved. It is interesting to note that the two levels of Muslim supernatural beings—jinns and angels—always operate in a secondary role. Sometime they serve as a communicator of important tidings from God, sometimes in the role of a servant, and sometimes as a nuisance disrupting the smooth flow of life and tempting humans to one kind of blasphemy or another.

Muslim eschatology is also much more specific about the nature of Heaven and Hell and the afterlife than are either the current Jewish or Christian traditions. The concept of an eventual resurrection is shared by the deeply religious of all three faiths. However, the details differ significantly. To a Muslim, on the Day of Judgment, God will decide the eternal fate of each person. Those who have accepted God's omnipotence and singularity and who have lived a responsible life in serving his agenda will be sent to heaven.

The Islamic heaven or paradise is best described in the words of the Qur'an.

> And convey good news to those who believe and do good deeds, that they shall have gardens in which rivers flow; whenever they shall be given a portion of the fruit thereof, they shall say: This is what was given to us before; and they shall be given the like of it, and they shall have pure mates in them, and in them, they shall abide. (The Qur'an, Sura 2:25)

Traditions outside of the Qur'an speak of "all of the beautiful things from the whole universe and things we can not even imagine." The idea of "unimaginable pleasure and delight" is an oft-repeated phrase in Muslim descriptions of Heaven. Food and drink of outstanding taste, leisure time spent reclining on couches, and, most of all, closeness to God, are repeated again and again among the various characteristics of Heaven. The Qur'an has other things to say about the joys of heaven. Speaking of the righteous "servants of Allah":

> Therefore Allah will guard them from the evil of that day and cause them to meet with ease and happiness; and reward them, because they were patient, with garden and silk, reclining therein on raised couches, they shall find therein neither (the severe heat of) the sun nor intense cold. And close down upon them (shall be) its shadows, and its fruits shall be made near (to them) being easy to reach. And there shall be made to go round about them vessels of silver and goblets which are of glass. (Transparent as) glass, made of silver, they have measured them according to a measure. And they shall be made to drink therein a cup the admixture of which shall be ginger, (Of) a fountain therein which is named Salsabil. And round them shall go youths never altering in age; when you see them you will think them to be scattered pearls. And

when you see there, you shall see blessings and a great kingdom. Upon them shall be garments of fine green silk and thick silk interwoven with Gold, and they shall be adorned with bracelets of silver, and their Lord shall make them drink a pure drink. (Qur'an, Sura 76:11–21)

Heaven is spoken of elsewhere as a place with many levels (I have encountered estimated numbers varying from 100 to 500 in my research). Although the inhabitants of all of the levels of heaven are able to stay in touch, inhabitants of lower levels are restricted to whatever pleasures that are available there and not to those from higher levels.

Other Suras speak of the "Houris" who will attend the males and youthful servants who will attend both males and female. Who are these entities? The Qur'an refers to them in the following way:

Thus (shall it be), and We will wed them with Houris pure, beautiful ones.
And pure, beautiful ones, the like of the hidden pearls:
A reward for what they used to do. (Qur'an, Sura 44:54 and 56:22–24)

The Qur'an goes on to suggest that they are of "special creation." It is not clear from the text of these Suras what the role of the Houris is intended to be. The allusion to them as virgins ("hidden pearls") suggests a sexual relationship, however, sex is not supposed to happen between humans and jinns or angels. On the other hand, how else would one explain the phrase "We will wed them"? The exact nature of the human–houri relationship is, therefore, somewhat uncertain as described in the Qur'an. In the last 2 years since the beginning of the Intifada in Palestine and Israel, the promise of 72 Houris to Palestinian suicide bombers has been repeatedly evoked, but no such specific number appears in the Qur'an. Like many other supplementary materials to holy books of all kinds, additional material has become part and parcel of the Muslim religious teaching.

A fascinating side issue concerning the Muslim version of heaven is that it reflects the worldly desires of the desert people from whom the religion sprang. The allusion to rivers and gardens reflects the ever-present problem of finding sufficient water to irrigate and, especially, the extreme luxury of being able to "waste" water on decorative rather than consumable plants. Muslim gardens are famous wherever there was sufficient water, for example, in those parts of Spain that marked the limits of Muslim expansion.

The Muslim concept of Hell is also spelled out generally in the Qur'an:

Surely hell lies in wait, A place of resort for the inordinate, Living therein for ages. They shall not taste therein cool nor drink But boiling and intensely cold water, Requital corresponding. Surely they feared not the account, And called Our communications a lie, giving the lie (to the truth). And We have recorded everything in a book, So taste! for We will not add to you aught but chastisement. (Qur'an, Sura 78:21–30)

And:

Surely the tree of the Zaqqum is the food of the sinful Like dregs of oil; it shall boil in (their) bellies, Like the boiling of hot water. Seize him, then drag him down into the middle of the hell; Then pour above his head of the torment of boiling water. (Qur'an, Sura 44:43–48)

Other details of the Muslim vision of Hell are expressed elsewhere. Infidels and evildoers will be continually burned in a never-ending fire. Beatings and insect bites, corruption and disfigurement, repellant smells, and the eternal burning make it a very unpleasant place indeed. There does, however, seem to be some contention about who will suffer this endless torture. In one Sura of the Qur'an, hell is specifically alluded to as the fate of all nonbelievers:

Surely those who disbelieve from among the followers of the Book [Jews and Christians] and the polytheists shall be in the fire of hell, abiding therein; they are the worst of men. (Qur'an, Sura 98:6)

However, what about devout Muslims? One school of thought is that they will ascend directly to Heaven. The Qur'an, however, is ambiguous about this point saying:

(As for) those who believe and do good, surely they are the best of men. Their reward with their Lord is gardens of perpetuity beneath which rivers flow, abiding therein for ever; Allah is well pleased with them and they are well pleased with Him; that is for him who fears his Lord. (Qur'an, Sura 98:7–8)

The other point of view is that everyone will spend some time in Hell. Perhaps, some Islamic teaching holds, even the devout will not go directly to heaven. Rather, everyone, Muslims included, will receive some punishment. Eventually, however, all Muslims will ascend to paradise. Whatever happens is predetermined by the life you led. Indeed, one of the principles of Muslim eschatology is that there are no second chances. Your life and your submission to God have already determined your ultimate fate at the moment of your death.

Before summarizing this brief discussion of Islam, I must reiterate an important point that may have slipped by unnoticed. That is that Islam, like other religions, is extremely diverse in the 21st century. Even the Qur'an is translated somewhat differently by different groups and sects. Furthermore, even when the translations are close to each other, they may be room for significant interpretive differences of what the various statements mean. I would not be surprised if other interpreters of this and other religions arrived at quite different understandings than have I.

Given that caveat, Islam clearly is in the same line of theological development as are Judaism and Christianity. This paternity is clearly indicated in the Qur'an, but not without a clear renunciation of many of the specific tenets of the other two religions. The major point of difference with Christianity is the role of Jesus in history. Christians have made him a part of God; Muslims deny this and consider him only a mortal who served as one of the continuity of prophetic links to God's message to humankind that was to culminate in Muhammad's message.

In Islam, the basic monotheistic creed is carried to the extreme. Polytheism, with the exception of the supernatural angels, jinns, servants, and Houris, is long gone from this theology. These auxiliary figures are all secondary. Any suggestion that God shares his uniqueness and supreme power with any other being, natural or supernatural, is considered the utmost blasphemy.

On the other hand, Islam shares with all of the other religions we have discussed a total commitment to a dualist ontology. That is, there exists a world of here and now, but also another world for spirits and souls to inhabit after bodily death. Implicit in this are two kinds of reality, the second of which is designed to provide for continuation of the mind/soul/spirit. Thus, like other religions, this expression of duality provides an escape from the frightening consequences of bodily death and the promise of eternal consciousness.

We turn now to two other popular but relatively recent religious traditions to complete this chapter.

5.2.9 Sikhism

Throughout this chapter, there have been repeated demonstrations of the fact that religions evolve and develop much as do organic species. Even those religions that have persisted from early times have either been modified or have spun off new sects and theologies in response to social, economic, theological, or political needs. For example, Hinduism's dark view of life was supplemented by alternative theologies with brighter views of human existence. From such a grim foundation, Buddhism arose as an antidote to what was deemed to be too harsh a view of life.

The trend of spinning off new religions differing in significant ways from their predecessors continued into the second millennium of the Common Era. In the latter part of the 15th century, in the Punjab region of Northwest India, the world of religion was once again deeply influenced by a charismatic and prophetic leader. In this case it was a guru or teacher by the name of Nanak Dev ji (1469 CE–1539 CE) who proclaimed the new religion now known as Sikhism. In spite of the fact that Sikhism is less well known in the west than other predominantly eastern religions, it is currently estimated to be among the world's largest religions. Indeed, it is the largest after the four giants: Christianity, Islam, Hinduism, and Buddhism.

Sikhism arose as a reaction to and yet an amalgam of many of the ideas, traditions, and tenets of both Hinduism and Islam and many of the fundamental tenets of those two religions remain a part of its teachings. From Hinduism, Sikhs have adopted the idea of a never-ending cycle of death and reincarnated rebirths. Sikhism asserts that this cycle of life continues until one "learns" the true meaning of life and escapes the cycle to join with God. Indeed, the word "Sikh" means student or learner and much of the religious activities of the daily life of practitioners of this faith are directed toward achieving understanding through study and contemplation. From Islam, and in particular the mystical version known as Sufism, came an emphasis on meditation as the main route to the understanding necessary to escape from the cycle of reincarnation. Meditation and learning are substituted in Sikhism for rituals, dietary laws, fasting, asceticism, confession, or celibacy or any other kind of comparable extreme asceticism. In the Sikh religion, there are none of the ceremonial or ritual activities that many other religions offer in the hopes of earning salvation. Therefore, there is no special Sabbath and rituals are minimal.[26]

With regard to the nature of God, Sikhism is much more extreme in its monotheism than are any of the other theologies already discussed in this chapter. This is a religion without angels, jinns, demons, or multipart Gods and one that most emphatically condemns the use of idols of any sort, including photographs and paintings of its historic teachers. In fact, in its present version, it is a religion without priests or other holy men other than readers appointed to lead the temple studies.

Following the proclamation of the new Sikh ideology by Guru Nanak Dev ji in 1498 CE, there was a succession of 10 great teachers or Gurus. However, the tenth and final human Guru, Gobind Singh (1666–1708) declared that there was no further need for human teachers or priests of any kind. Rather, he proposed, and his coreligionists accepted the idea, that the human Guru should be replaced by the holy book of the Sikh religion—the Guru Granth Sahib. (Note that the title "Guru" is applied here to the book itself as well as to its 10 human predecessors.) It is the book, rather than a human priest or cleric that has now become the "teacher" in the Sikh religion. Contemplative study of the Guru Granth Sahib is considered to be the

[26]The tradition of wearing five symbols (long hair—kes, a knife—kirpan, a steel bracelet—kara, a comb—kangha, and a specific kind of underwear—kachcha) is associated with membership in the "Khalsa Brotherhood," a status that does not include all Sikhs.

route to what Sikhs consider salvation. Most of the contents of this holy work are poems, chants, and hymns (some drawn from Muslim and Hindu works) that are intended to help the Sikh learn the fundamental religious requirements—truth, harmony, and wisdom—of the good life. According to the Sikh religion, these are also the virtues necessary for escape from the cycle of reincarnation and the union of the individual with the ineffable and dimensionless God.

Sikhism also teaches that there is a natural progression of reincarnation from primitive life forms to the human. However, during the progression, some aspect (the soul?) of the individual moves to ever-higher stages finally achieving humanity. Given that God has created all life, therefore, all life is precious and every effort must be made to protect even humble insects. Furthermore, Sikhism is much less ethnocentric than other religions. They teach that there are no chosen people or others who deserve special treatment because they are a member of one or another religion, sect, or cult; everyone, regardless of their religious affiliation, achieves the ultimate union with God. Most laudatory, there is an explicit rejection in Sikhism of racism or any other form of discrimination of other peoples or of women. Another important feature of the Sikh religion, given its location in the Indian subcontinent, was its early and explicit rejection of the caste system.

For this life, Sikhism teaches that normal family life and service to one's community are important attributes that define the just person. A considerable amount of attention is made of the nobility of honest work and of charitable contributions. There are no attempts to sanctify or in any other way identify particular holy people. The seeds of conflict with the Hindu religion (which espoused concepts of caste and ascetic holy men) in the region in which most Sikhs live can easily be discerned here. In 1984, rioting between Sikhs and Hindus exploded after Indian army troops were sent into the Golden Temple at Amritsar, the holiest shrine of Sikhism. Shortly thereafter, the prime minister of India, Indira Ghandi, was assassinated by her Sikh bodyguards in retaliation. Thousands were killed in the terrible sectarian violence that followed.

With regard to the Sikh view of the afterlife, it is pleasantly simple in light of the highly specific details propounded by Christianity and Islam, among many others. There is no special place called heaven and hell. If there is a hell, Sikhs believe that it is embodied in the Hindu influenced cycle of death and birth in which each human is entangled. If there is a heaven, it is in the mystical union with the indescribable God once one escapes from the cycle.

All in all, Sikhism is a high purified and refined form of religion that has minimized many of the attributes, rituals, and beliefs of other more complex religions. Its teachings of human equality and the opportunity for all, regardless of their commitment to any other religion, to achieve "salvation" are especially notable in a world where so many of the teachings of other religions are discriminatory and hostile toward nonbelievers.

Sikhism, however, does share with all other religions, a fundamental acceptance of the dual nature of reality. The body and the mind/spirit/soul are manifestations of two different natures. Throughout the cycles of death and reincarnation, there is a succession of bodies that decay and are lost. Beyond that bodily death, Sikhism teaches that there is a perpetual aspect of human existence that persists from one life to another until it is finally absorbed in God. This dualism is another expression of the one universal concept that can be found in every religion. Why is this so? The thesis of this book is that these supernatural (i.e., extra-physical) concepts are driven by a deep fear on the part of humans, ancient and current, of the loss of personal consciousness—of death. Dualism arises out of that fear and pervades many different aspects of human life in this world, including, as we see in chapter 7, psychological theory.

5.2.10 Baha'i

The emergence of new religions has continued into modern times. The last of the great religions to be discussed in this chapter, Baha'i emerged very recently—in 1866 CE. Baha'i is, like Sikhism, an attempt to find a basis for a more eclectic religion that incorporates all (or, more appropriately, many) religions under a single umbrella. Unlike Sikhism whose roots were mainly in Hinduism, Baha'i arose primarily out of the Muslim tradition. Today, Baha'i presents a remarkable open mindedness about other religions, denying neither many of the tenets of Islam nor even the divinity of Jesus.

The key person in the history of this new religion was Siyyid 'Ali-Muhammad (1819 CE–1850 CE) a merchant living in Shiraz, Iran, who came to be known by his followers as the Bab. Unfortunately, the ministry of the Bab was quickly cut short; he was executed after several years of imprisonment for what the Muslim community of Iran (including both the religious leaders and the Shah) considered to be his blasphemy against Islam. During the years around 1850, as many as 20,000 of his followers were also killed because of their apostasy from Islam.

After the Bab's execution, his work was carried on by Mirza Husayn 'Ali-I-Nuri (1817–1892) who also received a new name—Baha'u'llah—in his role as the successor leader of the new religion. Baha'u'llah is considered to be the actual founder of the Baha'i faith; it was he who was the purported recipient of the revelation that led to the formulation of their teachings in their several holy books, most notably *The Most Holy Book* (al-Kitab al-Aqdas) and *The Book of Certitude* (Kitab-I-Iqan). Baha'u'llah also spent much of his life in prison or exile, finally dying in the city of Acre in present day Israel. For this reason, the holiest shrine of the Baha'i faith is located in nearby

Haifa. It is, again, like the Vatican, the Mosque at Mecca, and the Golden Temple at Amritsar, one of those especially beautiful architectural achievements that religion has bestowed on the world. A long string of stairs ascends through spectacularly beautiful gardens to the shrine of the Bab.

Baha'i is also an extreme monotheism, carrying the idea even further than did Islam. The Baha'i ineffable, unknowable, omnipotent God created everything and directs everything. According to Baha'i, all religions, regardless of the details of their rituals and specific beliefs, are actually expressions of the same religious experience. The long string of prophets extending from Adam and Abraham up to the Bab and Baha'u'llah are all conveyers of the intentions of God. Although they are human, they speak with the words of the deity.

The Baha'i religion shares with Sikhism a strong conviction to the equality of all humans, especially of men and women, but also including peoples of all races. They have supported universal education for all children and have proposed that their religion is uniquely capable of bringing world peace. Indeed, they have been long time proponents of a single world government (which, unfortunately in terms their otherwise ecumenical approach, must be based on acceptance of the Baha'i organizational plan[27]) and restoring some modicum of economic equality between the world's rich and poor. Furthermore, like the Sikhs, they have no identified clergy. Rather, spiritual assemblies are elected at each location and at their headquarters in Haifa to administer the Baha'i faith. A useful introduction to the Baha'i faith can be found in Momen (1999).

Discrimination against adherents to their faith is still rampant in Iran and probably became much more severe with the overthrow of the secular modernity of the Shah and the installation of the radical Islamic theocracy in 1979. Many Baha'i adherents escaped to other countries at that time.

The Baha'i eschatology joins with all others to proclaim an intrinsic dualism of mind/spirit/soul and body. The body is temporary and decomposes according to Baha'i beliefs. However, the soul is immortal and upon death is freed of bodily concerns. It does not go to a specific heaven or hell, but rather to another "plane of existence." In fact, Baha'i writings are very explicit that their image of an afterlife cannot be described or understood in the ultra-concrete way that is attempted in, for example, Christianity or Islam. The closest approximation to a "hell" is that a person who has not been both devout and just will simply not be able to attain this new "plane of existence."

---

[27]In what many believe is a misguided and fruitless attempt effort to purify the beliefs of their religion, the Baha'i controlling spiritual assemblies have placed some limits on freedom of expression. Their punishment for unapproved writing by their members is of the same genre as excommunication in the Catholic or shunning in the Mormon religion.

5.3   INTERIM SUMMARY

This brings us to the end of our review of the 10 largest (in terms of the number of adherents) religions active in today's world. It should now be clear that there are enormous differences among the beliefs and philosophies discussed here as well as significant similarities. Among these similarities, one attribute stands out as the universal and ubiquitous foundational belief common to each and every one of these religions, as well as with all other smaller groups that have not been mentioned in this chapter. That universal belief is the commitment on the part of all extant religions to a fundamental dualism, the acceptance of the premise that there is a separate and perpetual state of existence for the spirit/soul/mind, on the one hand, and the transitory nature of the body and its material parts, on the other.

My view is that this fundamental assumption is based on the strong human need to find an escape hatch for one's personal awareness or consciousness as an alternative to the terrors of mental as well as physical death. A guiding premise of this book, therefore, is that notion of spiritual immortality is a natural human response to the ultimate horror—the cessation of the intrapersonal consciousness that emerged sometime in the course of organic evolution. The rest of religious doctrine and ritual, including the possibility and nature of a supreme creator—a God—and other supernatural entities, is decoration and extremely diverse decoration at that!

It is also important to appreciate that there is no evidence of any kind for such a state of spiritual immortality. Rather, the fundamental assumption is, according to religious axiomatic principles, not subject to debate, argument, or the rules of evidence that govern scientific inquiries. One either believes or one does not! I have never observed any debate on such matters to change the opinions of any of the participants. The absence of irrefutable physical evidence rarely negates a dedicated belief in an afterlife on the part of a believer.

The broadly accepted, fundamental idea that the "soul" continues after death in one way or another immediately raises questions of tremendous import for philosophers, scientists, scholars, and theologians who ponder the nature of human existence. The premise of spiritual immortality is the foundation assumption on which the theological, ritual, and eschatological details particular to each religion are based. Some, for example Sikhism and Baha'i, do not go much further than the acceptance of individual immortality. Others, for example the three Abrahamic religions, go far further in elaborating the implications of that core belief. Given the universal acceptance of this assumption, prophets, gurus, priests, rabbis, reverends, and religious leaders of all kinds are compelled to ask questions about the implications of such a profound statement of belief. The questions that must be answered are varied and plentiful. For example, what is the nature of the afterlife? Where is it? Who controls it? What is the nature of this controlling entity? How do we get there? Is there a heaven of rewards and hell of punishment? Do we need a "savior," a teacher, or can individuals find salvation independently? What is the final state of the individual's spirit/soul/mind in this afterlife?

An important property of all these questions is that each is secondary and becomes meaningful only in terms of the acceptance of the fundamental assumption that some aspect of our personal consciousness continues on after the obvious decay of our physical bodies. Without the assumption of the continuity of some aspect of mental life after death, all of the rest of the questions just posed become moot if not meaningless, and the pressure to ask them would be much reduced. Indeed, even the hypothetical nature of one's God or Gods becomes secondary to the assumption of personal immortality. In other words, without the urgent need to provide for our own continuation, there would be no compelling reason to develop any of the rest of the panoply of religions—the Godhead, the rituals, the shrines and temples, the saints and holy persons, and the details of the afterlife. Clearly, the essential assumption of mind–body dualism is the foundation of all religious beliefs.

The secondary questions I have just posed have been answered in many different ways by others than the religious faithful. Allusions to ghosts or spirits can help to fulfill the need of those who are afraid of death by providing a kind of evidence of the existence of an afterlife without invoking Gods of one kind or another. These "psychic" solutions to the problem of "what happens after death?" serve the same deep needs of people fearful of a complete discontinuance of their own conscious awareness as does religion. The advantage of such psychic beliefs is that such "evidence" may be provided without the sometimes cumbersome requirements on conduct that are demanded by formal religions.

Thus, the fundamental dualist principle of two kinds of reality (one for the body and one for the soul/spirit/mind) has enormous influence on the way most people in the world think. Such a dualism engenders a schism between the measurable physical and the immeasurable supernatural worlds.

Among the most disconcerting corollaries of the dualist hypotheses is the suggestion that the laws of the natural physical world do not apply in the supernatural one. In the latter, time may be irregular and paradoxical. Events such as precognitions, revelations, or prophecies become not only possible, but are accepted as commonplace. Events can have influences at great distances and with minimal, if any, expenditure of natural energy in the supernatural world. The spirits of the dead, as well as objects, can occupy little or no space and processes can go in the absence of any tangible mechanism to actuate them. Despite the protestations of those who seek an entente between science and religion, there remain profound differences of worldview between the two approaches that cannot be reconciled.

This chapter has demonstrated the enormous variety of putative answers to the questions impelled by our belief in immortality of the soul or mind. The God or Gods of each religion have profoundly different personalities, one from the other. The angry Hebrew God is very much unlike the warm, welcoming, and supportive God of the Sikh religion. Similarly, heaven differs greatly, varying from a highly tangible place very much like the homeland of their respective original prophets to ineffable feelings of bliss. In some cases, heavens and hells are concrete places with specific furnishings and climatic conditions; in others they are only the most intangible states of awareness.

A common historical feature of most heavily accepted religions that have persisted into modern times is that they usually pay homage to a charismatic prophetic figure who typically acts as the interlocutor between humankind and the Gods.[28] In some religions, this prophet may assume the divine role himself; in others, he is human but has had the knowledge of the divine revealed in a mystical experience communicated by an angelic figure. The prophet is then directed to dispense the revealed word to the world using whatever communication lines are available at the time to a population which may or may not be, for some social, economic, or theological reason, receptive to this new message.

Unfortunately, the new prophet inevitably comes in conflict with preexisting points of view regarding the divine and is very often martyred by those who have preceded him. In many cases, this martyrdom becomes a part of the theology as well as the history of the religion. An interesting and ubiquitous fact about martyrdom is that the idea of the dying and then resurrected God-man has been one of the main themes of the history of religion. It is not a new idea that sprang full blown from the hill of Golgotha, but rather an idea that had it roots in traditions at least as far back as the Egyptian mythology and perhaps into the darkness of the preliterate religions discussed in chapters 3 and 4.

Nevertheless, most religions (and all of the most recent ones) pay honor to a human who served as the conduit between God and humankind. In some logical arena, this could be considered to be an especially controver-

---

[28] Two possible exceptions to this generality are Hinduism and Shintoism. Tracing their roots back further than any of the others of the "Big Ten," it appears that there is no human figure who can be identified as a founder of these ancient religions. Perhaps mythological deities (such as Brahma, Vishnu, and Shiva) represent a cultural memory of a long lost great teacher or leader. The antiquity of Hinduism and Shintoism completely clouds this issue; we are unlikely to ever confirm such a speculation.

sial link. If there is an omnipotent God, why could he not have spoken to all mankind? What is the need or purpose of the interlocutor? One very unpopular hypothetical answer to this question is that religion is a product of human invention rather than divine revelation. A further kind of contributory support for such a hypothesis is that the heavens and hells of many religions often closely approximate the countryside (or an idealization of it) from which a particular theology emerged. Of course, the main thesis of this book, that fear of death leads to a compelling pressure to invent immortality, also raises another argument in favor of the hypothesis of human invention into religion.

However dogmatic may have been the teachings of their original prophets, religious doctrine does not remain constant. Like all other organic activities, religions have displayed continuing tendencies to evolve and change over the course of centuries. There has been a progression from early polytheisms to quasi-monotheisms (which often invoke the existence of supplementary figures such as angels, demons, and jinns) to extreme monotheisms denying all of these supernumerary entities. Hinduism, despite some modern protestation to the contrary, should properly be considered to be the best existing example of a classic polytheism. Christianity, on the other hand, complicates its professed monotheism with the doctrine of the trinity, the three manifestations of an otherwise singular God and other supplementary angels and demons, [f saints]

As the centuries have passed, however, there has been a tendency for newly emerging religions to become more explicitly and rigorously monotheistic. The case is most strongly made for the most recent of the Abrahamic religions—Islam—and for the newest expressions of the deep human need of the supernatural—Sikhism and Baha'i.

There are many other indications that do attest to the evolutionary development of religions over time beyond the great animism–polytheism–monotheism trend. In some instances, this has been a form of regression from a more abstract or human oriented position to one that adds supernatural details to the basic philosophy. As I discuss in this chapter, both Judaism and Confucianism responded to their times and popular pressure for more explicit statements of the nature of heaven and hell, both in the centuries before the Common Era. However, changes have also gone in the other direction. Many modern forms of Protestant (in particular) Christianity have retreated from highly specific descriptions of the afterlife to increasingly abstract ideas that are reminiscent of the original Old Testament pronouncements.

No clearer evidence of the continuous evolution taking place in religions is their history of begetting new denominations and sects. Each and every one of the original versions of the religions described in this chapter has

branched, segmented, and diverged into different interpretations and schis-
matic subdivisions. Even within the confines of a single historical religious
tradition there is a continuing trend to modify and reconstrue the significance of earlier teachings. Each religion's scholars find different meanings
in their respective holy books at different times in their histories.

Another line of their evolutionary development has been the increasing
willingness on the part of religions to be more ecumenical toward the beliefs of other religions. Whereas the ancient past was characterized by an
extreme dogmatism (unbelievers, infidels, or apostates are repeatedly said
to be irretrievably doomed) a kind of universality or ecumenical enlightenment has increasing credibility in some doctrines (e.g., Baha'i and Sikhism)
in recent times. This does not mean, of course, that the level of sectarian
disagreements and wars has ended, particularly in the light of the terrors of
the last half-century, but rather that the trend in some circles seems to be
away from the ultra-dogmatism and theological ethnocentrism of the past.

Why should this promising trend be happening? One reason is that the
modern world is much more heavily interconnected than ever before. People do not live in isolation to the extent they did as recently as a few decades ago. Awareness of the philosophical and theological positions of other
peoples and other cultures has been greatly enhanced. Furthermore, we
are in the latter stages of an enlightenment that has changed views of the
world and of how people living in that world now must interact with each
other. Population movements have dispersed different people around the
world in a way that would have been unimaginable until the 20th century.

Social and political norms have also evolved. It is far more acceptable to
accept diversity and acknowledge human differences than in earlier times.[29]
Certainly the condition of women in the modern world has vastly improved
in most places, if not in southern Asia, Africa, and other parts of the world.
Overt expressions of racism also trend downward, even if it has not been
completely exorcised from the thinking of many of the people and peoples
of the world.

Similarly, modern economics and, in particular, global economics, even
though polluted by some exploitive tendencies on the part of large corporations, has tended to bring people together. The disasters of recent wars
have also led at least a few people to think of breaking down political barriers. The United Nations exists, if not thrives, in 2004 in a context that was
not possible in 1918. International coalitions now have replaced unilateral
activities in at least a few cases. The idea of a single world government ex-

---

[29]It is necessary to point out in defense of these optimistic statements that improvements
such as these are not constant. Inhumanity still exists and sometimes seems to reign supreme
(consider the Holocaust of the 20th century). However, I argue here that the trend is for the
better and, in general, the slope of enlightenment is upward.

plicitly propounded by the Baha'i religious doctrine now reflects the world-view of a broader sampling of humanity than ever before.[30]

It also has to be acknowledged that there is a measure of self-centered-ness about the drive toward ecumenical convergence. Many oppressed people have now found a voice in the new world. Their strivings for equal-ity and justice provide another reason for the spread of a sense of religious equality and a kind of theological equivalence among the many world reli-gions. To the extent that an appreciation has grown that ritual and doc-trinal detail are secondary, there also has been an appreciation of the ways in which religions share a common foundation. All of these factors contrib-ute to a continuing reformulation of religion as a basis for dealing with the afterlife—the common concern of all.

Finally, it is also necessary to point out that even though religion has evolved mainly to provide a basis for dealing with the fear of death and the hope of immortality, the afterlife, and the supernatural, it is one of the most important factors in regulating society. From the earliest codes of conduct to the most recent recommendations to how one should lead a good, noble, and just life, religion has provided proscriptions for guiding a harmonious society. Whether it be the Ten Commandments, the Sura of the Qur'an, or the Sikhs' Guru Granth Sahib (to mention only a few), virtually all religions have adopted a code of conduct that assists people to reside side by side with minimum conflict difficulty. This code is often enforced by raising the possibility of punishment or reward in the afterlife, but the additional pur-pose of the regulation of human society cannot be minimized. Religion has always been a tool to accomplish that noble end. It should be noted and ap-preciated that organized religious rituals also bring solace and closure to situations that seem otherwise inexplicable such as the death of a young person. This is not a minor contribution, but it, too, is derivative of the foundation dualist assumption of immortality.

In conclusion, this brief survey of current religious thought demon-strates that they share a number of common features. The huge majority of the population of the world that accepts religious doctrine of one kind or another, as well as even the most cursory reading of world history, testifies to the overwhelming impact that religious thought has had and is having on human life. The core of this ubiquitous style of thinking, I argue, is the fun-damental assumption of a dual reality. In the next chapter I explore atti-tudes about dualism outside the realm of religion. The main question asked is: What does nontheological philosophy have to say about Dualism? In pre-

---

[30]As I write these words, the United States of America is involved in one of those regressive periods of aggressive unilateralism that makes this kind of optimism seems Pollyannaish. I hope that the trend toward reason will return and this current state of affairs will turn out to be a mo-mentary historical aberration.

view, it is clear that even technical philosophies are not immune to the historical pressures of dualist thinking. In many instances, the continuity from the most primitive fear of death to the modern philosophical arguments can be clearly discerned. In particular, there has been an evolutionary trend from animisms to polytheisms to monotheisms; we now move into a domain in which the Gods have been exorcised but dualism survives.

6

Modern Philosophical Dualisms[1]

6.1 THE "DETHEOLOGIZING" OF DUALISM

So far in this book, the discussion has mainly concentrated on the history of religion, both ancient and modern. In the course of this work, I have shown how religions evolved from primitive animisms to polytheisms to monotheisms to highly sophisticated and increasingly abstract forms of belief in the supernatural. In this and the next chapter, however, I digress from religious history to consider some closely related secular views of the dual nature of reality held by students of philosophy and psychology. At the outset of this chapter it is important to note that the evolutionary sequence exhibited in religious history continues even into these supposedly naturalist and secular endeavors. The argument I make in these two chapters is that ancient dualism continues to influence even these two approaches to understanding human nature.

For modern philosophy of mind, this has resulted in an enterprise in which Gods have been expurgated but which is still explicitly concerned with dualist ideas about the nature of the mind–brain. Psychology, on the other hand, in its aspiring to be a natural science, has attempted to purge dualism completely from its exploration of the nature of human mentation.

---

[1]In this chapter, I once again change the notation used to represent the chronology. With the exception of a few pre-Christian Greek philosophers, I now deal with the last two millennia. Therefore, the designation "CE" is no longer necessary, but is understood throughout this chapter.

Unfortunately, we see in chapter 7 that dualist ideas persist implicitly and cryptically in mentalist approaches to the study of cognitive function.

The previous chapters support the contention that the defining criterion of all religions, without exception through their diverse history, is that they are, at their most basic roots, dualist. That is, their dogmas, rituals, and beliefs are based on the fundamental assumption that there are two kinds of realities that operate by dissimilar laws and are subject to different causal forces. One reality includes the obviously impermanent physical body and the other tangible material aspects of the world; the other encompasses the presumably enduring, but intangible, mental aspects of human existence. The concept of a persisting and immortal soul or spirit or mind, I suggest, provides an important "escape hatch" for the terrors of an impermanent personal consciousness. Not even the central theological idea of an omniscient and omnipotent God is as universal as is that of personal immortality in the various theologies that have evolved over the millennia.

My argument, so far, has been that this basic fear of death has led human thought through a series of intellectual evolutionary steps to the modern religions and their respective theologies. However, at this point the path splits. Chapter 5 discusses a few of the many versions of modern religious thought (most of which are now monotheistic) that still find so many adherents. The present chapter considers another fork in the path—modern studies in the philosophy of mind, an intellectual endeavor unfamiliar to most people.

The converse of the observation that all religions are dualist, however, is not true. Not all dualisms are overtly religious. On the contrary, a number of philosophical schools of thought have emerged over the years that argue on what are intended to be nontheological grounds that mind and body represent two different kinds of reality and are controlled by different kinds of laws. Although it may be argued with some credibility that some of these philosophical positions actually may be vestiges or derivatives of preceding theological ideas, many modern dualist philosophies are presented in the form of logical arguments that do not allude to any theology per se.

A new question thus arises to replace the age old ones such as: What is the nature of God? What is the nature of the afterlife? This new question is: What is the nature of the relationship between the mind[2] (or, as some would further particularize it—consciousness) and the body (or, more specifically, the brain)? Opposing the dualist point of view are various kinds of naturalist, materialist, and physicalist theories that there is only one kind of

---

[2]In the following discussion, I use the words "soul," "consciousness," and "mind" interchangeably as the situation requires. All, I believe, have the same denotative referent. Similarly, *brain* is just a more specific term for what had previously been referred to as the *body* and either may be used as appropriate for the comments at hand. Furthermore, *brain*, to be technically accurate, is a part of the *nervous system*, the latter term also including the peripheral nervous system.

reality—a physical one that produces, in some as yet unknown way, the mental life of which we all have first-hand knowledge. This opposing view, which also comes in a wide variety of guises, falls under the rubric of material monism.

In this chapter, as well as throughout this book, the emphasis in our discussion is, however, on the history of dualism and its influences on philosophy and cognitive psychology. Therefore, no effort has been made to comprehensively review the various forms of monism appearing in the philosophical literature to the same extent that I delve into dualisms. Only a few pages at the end of this chapter describe a bit of the modern history of materialist thinking and the several different ways it has been structured in current philosophical thinking.

This emphasis on dualism must not be misunderstood to reflect my own views. My personal philosophical and scientific predilections and evaluations of the scientific scene have led me to be a supporter of a monist ontology. However many constraints there may be on our ability to explain and reduce cognitive processes to the terms of the neurophysiology, I argue that this inability to solve the mind—brain problem is only an epistemological problem. The arguments for a physicalist, materialist, and monist ontology are compelling from my point of view. Ontological monism, combined with epistemological dualism, characterizes a point of view that has been called "monism (or materialism) without reductionism." A number of philosophers share this perspective with me (in general, if not in detail), including Broad (1925), Boyd (1980), and Horgan (1993).

Chapter 5 makes it clear that religious dualism is not extinct: It is not only still with us, but it represents the foundation beliefs of the vast majority of humans in today's world. Nevertheless, there has also been in the last several hundred years another evolutionary step forward, one in which secular philosophies have begun to supplement (but certainly not replace) religious beliefs. The net effect of this has been the detheologizing[3] of philosophical studies of the nature of the world and of the relation between the mind and the body/brain. This is the story told in this chapter—the modern consideration of the nature of psychobiological reality by philosophers (and some scientists prone to philosophizing) and the secular dualisms onto which a considerable portion of them have converged.

In a notable discussion of the mind—body problem, the deeply committed monist philosopher Mario Bunge (1980) performed an extremely useful service in tabulating what he believed are the main historical arguments

---

[3] I also use the words *detheologize* and *secularize* as synonyms. Philosophy may not have overtly set out to remove theology from its discussion, but that is what has happened. Questions about the nature of the relationship between humans and Gods have been replaced with logical arguments about the relation between the mind and the brain as demonstrated later in this chapter.

supporting dualism. There is no better way to introduce this chapter than
to list the produalism arguments he has identified. His counterarguments
against dualism are listed in a brief comment about the alternative monist
points of view on page 241.

1. Dualism is a part of religion, in particular of Christianity.
2. Dualism explains personal survival and ESP.
3. Dualism is enshrined in ordinary language.
4. Dualism explains everything in the simplest possible way.
5. Mind must be immaterial because we know it differently from the way
   we know matter: the former knowledge is private, the latter public.
6. Phenomenal predicates are irreducible to physical ones, so the mind
   must be substantially different from the brain.
7. Whereas neurons fire digitally, we can have continuous experience
   (e.g., we can perceive a gapless green surface).
8. There must be a mind animating the brain machinery, for machines
   are mindless.
9. There is ample evidence for the power of mind over matter (e.g., vol-
   untary movement and planning).
10. Dualism squares with emergentism and the hypothesis of the level
    structure of reality. (Bunge, 1980, pp. 10–16)

These arguments, only one explicitly theological, some linguistic, some
logical, some neurophysiological, are all challenged by Bunge both in the
text interspersed between the items in his list and in later portions of his interesting book. However, I do not join him in pursuing these counterarguments here. The task of this chapter is to understand the various nontheological philosophical dualisms, the evolution of their fundamental
axioms and principles, and their influential role in current thought.

6.2 TRADITIONAL DUALIST PHILOSOPHIES[4]

What has historically been designated as the mind–body problem was by
no means an exclusively modern development. The mystery of mind's
emergence from matter was explicitly discussed as a conceptual issue at
least as early as the classic Greek period 2,500 years ago. Both Anaxagoras
(500 BCE?–428 BCE.) and Plato (427? BCE–347 BCE) were among the many
philosophical dualists who championed the notion of the separate exis-

---

[4]A few selections in the following discussion have been updated and expanded from Uttal
(1978).

tence of the mental and physical domains. Curiously, their arguments sound much more modern than some of their immediate successors based as they were on what was clearly more a scientific or technical philosophical basis than a theological one.

In a similar nontheological vein, the great naturalist–philosopher Aristotle (384 BCE–322 BCE) fathered the closely related theory of vitalism: the philosophy that animate organisms differ from inanimate objects by virtue of the possession of some unique life fluid, process, or principle that was itself not reducible to the terms of the material world. However, this concept of a separate life force was, even for Aristotle, an epistemological statement and not an ontological one. Both he and Democritus (460 BCE–370 BCE) probably can be considered to be outside the main stream of historical dualisms and to presage some early monist ideas. In this regard, they were somewhat unusual.

Plotinus (205 BCE–270 BCE) was a Hellenized Egyptian who was strongly influenced by the writing of Plato and Aristotle. Plotinus proposed a neoplatonic dualism that was essentially free of references to theology. His reference to the "highest principle" may still reflect a kind of religious concern, but in most ways the remnants of his writing suggest a more secular view of this particular problem of the nature of reality than was common, particularly in the early days of Christianity.

This proto-scientific-philosophical approach to the mind–body problem did not last and was not resurrected until almost 2,000 more years had passed. Virtually all of the philosophy that has come down to us from postclassic Greece until the enlightenment (the Age of Reason) of the 17th and 18th centuries was written from the point of view of theological as opposed to philosophical or secular dualists.

For example, the writing of such philosophers as Aurelius Augustinus (Saint Augustine), who lived from 354–430, was, therefore, mainly directed to the clarification and justification of Christian theology. The Middle Ages (usually defined as the period from 500 to 1600) saw the emergence of such scholars as Peter Abelard (1079–1142) and Thomas Aquinus (Saint Thomas) (1124–1274). Like many of their brethren of the time, both these philosophers were clerics who also, as did Saint Augustine, used philosophy as a tool mainly in an effort to deal with the theological problems raised by Christian dogma. John of Fidanza (otherwise known as Saint Bonaventure, 1217–1274), also a theological dualist, wrote about the nature of the soul and its independence from the body as a necessary foundation of Christian thought.

Non-Christian philosophers, mainly living in the lands to the East of Europe, were also contributing to similar discussions concerning the central issue of the relationship between the soul and the body. Maimonides (1135–1204), a Jewish Spaniard who spent most of his life in Egypt, suggested that "immaterial intelligence" (i.e., the immortal soul) could be acquired and had to be distinguished from the "material soul." In Persia, Avicenna (980–1037), an Ismali Muslim, wrote about the nature of the dualism of the soul and the body from a non-Christian point of view. Although emerging from a considerably different culture, none of his ideas about the soul–body issue conflicted in any major way with the dualisms that had originated in the west. Both of these two "eastern" theological philosophers, Maimonides and Avicenna, contributed to the thinking of other notables such as John Duns Scotus (1266–1308) who was concerned with the difficult challenge of "proving" or "demonstrating" the survival of the soul following death.[5]

In general, therefore, western philosophy, especially to the degree that the soul/mind–body conundrum was an issue, was the exclusive province of religion up until the 14th century. Religious dualism reigned supreme during this period. To say there was a controversy between dualism and monism during these times would be an overstatement of the actual situation: Everybody was a dualist then. However, times changed, and during the following 200 years, the world went through an intellectual revolution that was to modify, to an unimaginable degree, the perspectives of all of the scholars, theologians, and philosophers involved in determining something about human nature. This is not to say theologians did not remain active after those times, but rather that a revitalized stream of secular philosophy that had not been seen since classical Greek times reemerged following the Middle Ages.

During the Renaissance, secular and humanistic thinking began to supplement, if not replace, concern with theological matters. Although some of these new approaches were often clothed in traditional, religious vocabularies (e.g., see the discussion of Descartes' work), a new kind of philosophy appeared, one that was more concerned with an understanding of human nature than with providing a justification for particular religious beliefs. The remainder of this chapter presents the story of the various forms of philosophical, nontheological dualisms that arose in a period that roughly encompasses the last half millennium.

6.2.1 Descartes' Interactionism

The modern history of philosophical, as opposed to theological, solutions to the mind–body problem is usually dated to the 17th century beginning

---

[5]The preservation of teaching of all kinds in the "east" and in Ireland during these times was an exceedingly important aspect of European history. During these years, a "dark age" had descended on Europe. Illiterate Germanic peoples had destroyed the literate Roman Empire and little attention was paid to literature of all kinds. The story of how the Irish monasteries became the repository of written thought is engagingly told by Cahill (1996). Nothing emphasizes the "darkness" better than the fact that Charlemagne was himself illiterate.

with the writing of René Descartes (1596–1650). Descartes was an extraordinary man who contributed to both philosophical theory and to more practical matters of mathematics, physiology, and physics. His invention of analytic geometry—the union of algebra and geometry—was instrumental in the enormous growth of technology and science in subsequent centuries. In the context of the present chapter, his role as a philosopher and, more specifically as an ontologist, is of primary interest.

In 1641, Descartes' metaphysics was presented in a work, the title of which most clearly defines the residual theological slant of his dualist perspective—*Meditations on First Philosophy, in which the Existence of God and the distinction between Mind and Body Are Demonstrated.* In this book and his other works, Descartes spelled out a persistent dualist solution to the mind–body problem that has come to be called *interactionism,* a theory that continues to this day to be a foundation of dualist thought. However, Descartes' main contribution was not so much to propose a new universally acceptable solution to the mind–body problem as it was to sharpen the questions that had to be asked. For example, How can minds and bodies interact? What is the nature of the mind and the body? Where do they interact?

Mind, to Descartes represented a fundamentally different kind of reality than that of the body, but it was a natural reality as much as was that of the body. Thus, he made an exceedingly important step forward from the theological interpretations of the scholastic philosophers (most recently represented by Maimonides and, earlier, by the writings of St. Augustine) that had dominated thinking in the previous millennium. That step was to formulate the problem (regardless of his apologetic title) in the language of the natural rather than the supernatural domains. Although still clothed in a protective theological vocabulary, Descartes was one of the first to distinguish between the soul and the mind. Some have even gone so far as to suggest that the theological tone of his title may well have been an intentional subterfuge to avoid conflict with the church that he believed was bound to occur during his lifetime.

The main premise of mind–body interactionism, that mind and body are distinct and separate entities, is the essence of Descartes' dualist point of view. The key to his particular rendition of dualism was the nature of the interaction between the mind and the body. From Descartes' time onward, as we see later in this chapter, one of the main issues dividing the different kinds of dualism was the nature of this interaction. The challenge faced by many subsequent dualisms was to define how the two domains interacted in order to explain the many observed instances of correspondences between observable behavior and thought. It was his thesis that mind and matter did interact with each other and that either one is capable of "causing" effects in the other. Just as the body could affect mental processes, the mind was also capable of affecting physical processes.

A major philosophical perplexity for the Cartesian philosophy of interactionism, however, lies in the challenge of achieving a precise definition of "causation." Descartes' interactionism, however, was straightforward enough, even to the point of his suggesting a site at which the mental and bodily processes might actually carry out their mutual causal interaction. The site he proposed was the pineal gland, even then well-known through anatomical studies and certainly centrally enough located in the human brain to appear to be of special significance.[6]

Although strongly influenced by his contemporary religious environment (he once stopped publication of one of his books because of possible conflict with church teachings), the work of Descartes, particularly his concept of dualist interactionism, is considered to be the starting point of most modern (nontheological) dualisms. Many of the later theories of mind–brain interaction were specific reactions or supplements to Descartes' ideas. Thus, his importance as a seminal contributor to the philosophy of dualism is unquestioned.

Descartes' dualist answer to the question of the mind–body relationship did not go unchallenged, however, even in the 17th century. A school of skeptical critics quickly arose in the next century including Simon Foucher (1644–1696). Foucher attacked both Malebranche's occasionalism (see the next section) and Cartesian interactionism on what can, from some perspectives, actually be interpreted as a preliminary kind of monism. Foucher argued that if mind and matter were totally different kinds of "essence," then they could not interact, as had been suggested by Descartes. Furthermore, since it was obvious they did interact, he proposed they could not be essentially different.

Lest it be misunderstood that interactive dualism is long buried, my readers should be aware that even as late as the 1990s some current philosophers have argued for a theologically cleansed version of Cartesian dualism. Hart (1988) and Foster (1991) both present the case for a two-way interaction between mind and brain. Hart, in particular, argues that the mind–body problem faces no more serious difficulties than that faced by interactions between physical objects.

6.2.2 Geulincx and Malebranche's Occasionalism

In the late 17th century there was another reaction against the Cartesian interactive version of dualism from scholars who believed in alternative forms of mind–body relationships. Arnold Geulincx (1624–1669) and Nicolas Malebranche (1638–1715) introduced what may best be considered to be a throwback to a theologically oriented philosophy. It is somewhat imprecise

---

[6]It was not until centuries later that the pineal gland was appreciated for what it really is, a vestigial photoreceptor that has mainly secretory (endocrine) functions in mammals.

to refer to their view, which they called occasionalism, as dualist because it actually involved three separate forms of reality. Nevertheless, to avoid neologisms such as "trialisms" or to misuse old ones such as "pluralisms," let us expand the concept of dualism to include philosophies that invoke two or more levels of reality.

Geulincx and Malebranche's idea, like that of the classic dualist positions, was that a complete distinction be drawn between the realities of mind and body, respectively. The two domains, indeed, were so distinct that, in fact, they could not interact; that is, they could exert no influence on each other. Nevertheless, there were sufficient similarities and correspondences between the respective activities in the two domains that some accounting had to be made of their parallel behavior.

The issue confronting them, therefore, was to determine what explained the parallel behavior of bodily matter and mind in the absence of any mutual influence. Malebranche and Geulincx proposed that the parallel operation of these two levels of reality was accounted for in terms of a third level of reality—an actively involved God who was neither mental nor physical. The simplest interpretation of their ontological theory was that it represented a continuous miracle (i.e., the perpetual intervention of an actively intervening God) to explain the observed correspondence of mind and body. The role of God in this tripartite universe was to coordinate the actions of the physical and mental domains so that they were concurrent.

Malebranche and Geulincx proposed that although the two domains of mind and matter appeared to causally interact, in fact, they were totally independent and did not exert any influence on each other. Instead, their correspondence occurred only on the "occasion" of God's intervention. According to this occasionalist point of view, the mental and physical domains followed their own set of laws, whereas God followed another set of natural laws that were not interpretable in terms of the nature of either mind or body. God was sufficiently powerful to juggle all of the mind–body balls in the universe simultaneously.

Occasionalism may best be appreciated in terms of its exceedingly close relationship to classical theology to a degree that was unlike the essence of Cartesian interactionism. Although the formulation of this particular perspective is a more technical form of philosophy than the traditional church might have been willing to support at that time, occasionalism is clearly a theological theory.

However, from another point of view, the nature of God in this theory is secondary. Occasionalism is not a theory of God; God's role is merely to provide an explanation of parallel mind–matter behavior. Occasionalism was, in terms of its most fundamental goals, quite unlike classical theological philosophies that were aimed at the justification and explication of the nature of God, per se. The notion of a continuous miracle and the omnipresent and ever-influential intervention by a supernatural force is, nevertheless, quite distinct from other, much more naturalist, philosophies with which we are concerned in this chapter.

Descartes, Geulincx, and Malebranche, for whatever their political reasons may have been, were among the last wave of major philosophers to attribute the nature of the difference between the mind and body realities to the influence of God. Even then, as mentioned earlier, Descartes seems to have done so only to assuage then current opinion in the church. In the centuries to follow, a new wave of philosophers began to write and speak in a very different language, a secular one in which God played a much-reduced role in defining the nature of the world. Rather, their philosophies dealt with reality in terms of analogous mechanisms—such as clocks—even though the respective philosophers themselves may have been personally religious. It is possible to discern here the beginnings of what has continued to be a serious conflict situation for many scientists and philosophers.

6.2.3   Leibniz and Hartley's Parallelism

The main thesis of another classic dualist philosophy—parallelism, is originally attributed to Gottfried Wilhelm Leibniz (1646–1716) and was more fully developed by David Hartley (1705–1757). Like Malebranche and Geulincx, their parallel philosophy asserted that the dualist cleavage between mind and matter is so great that the two domains are totally incapable of causal interaction in the manner proposed by Descartes. Leibniz, Hartley, and the succeeding parallelists were, therefore, confronted with the same problem faced by the occasionalists: How do we account for the similarity of behavior between two domains that can't interact (since they are manifestations of two different kinds of reality) without introducing the "continuing miracle" proposed by Malebranche and Geulincx?

Rather than the hand of God, Leibniz suggested that mental processes and bodily functions usually correspond because both are identically affected by the same stimuli. In reality, he argued, the correspondence between the two is only fortuitous; it is definitely not causal in whatever sense one would like to use the word. Neither the mental aspects nor the physical aspects cause or produce the other, but, as Leibniz analogized, they are in agreement just as two clocks would be in agreement if they had been started at the same time and were reasonably accurate. The agreement between mind and body is due not to interaction, causal relationships, or to the intervention of the deity, but quite to the contrary, it is a very natural response of two independent systems that respond to a common history.

The common history could come in several forms; one of the most often cited is Leibniz' concept of a "preestablished harmony." According to this idea, a supernatural power (or, preferably, some other natural force) had set into motion a sequence of events. The effect of which was to synchronize the independent mental and physical events that guided the behavior of mind and matter. Leibniz' parallelism, therefore, describes a dualist relationship between mind and matter that can be characterized as noninteractive and, unless one wants to theologize preestablished harmony, nontheological in terms of how it runs it course. That is, both are natural processes. The role of the supernatural, if any, was only to initiate the sequence. Whatever that initiating force was, it simply removed itself and let the two natural processes run their parallel course. This kind of parallelism was among the first to minimize, if not exclude, the role of the supernatural and theological, a role that had been quite explicit in most of its predecessors.

Leibniz stands with other great scientist–philosophers of his time in accelerating the progression from theology to natural explanations of mind and body, even if his personal solution remained dualist. Most modern philosophical monisms or materialisms, arguably the currently preferred philosophy among philosophers and scientists, share the properties of being nontheological, No longer was the soul–body problem primarily concerned with finding some way to justify the concept of an afterlife or to consider the role of God in every aspect of human life. Although dualisms, including that of Leibniz and Hartley, may be motivated to some degree by vestiges of the desire to provide some kind of a theory of cognitive immortality, this issue was subordinated in this approach to the ontological problem.

Leibniz was by no means an atheist; however, his religious opinions were certainly subordinated to his concerns with natural issues of physics, mathematics, logic, and the nature of the human mind and body. The idea that God must play a continuing role in determining the parallel behavior of either the mind or the body was anathema to Leibniz. In most of his discussions, God is present in the background, but does not appear in the center of things as in earlier theologically oriented philosophies. One exception to the absoluteness of this statement is that Leibniz frequently referred to the "author" of the "preestablished harmony," that synchronized the clocks of mind and matter, a theological notion if we have ever encountered one.

In more ways than not, however, Leibniz was an early natural philosopher who was concerned about some of the same issues that had challenged past theologians, but his approach to these issues was very different. His point of view can be contrasted with that of his contemporary, Benedictus (Baruch) Spinoza (1632–1677), who had earlier proposed a philosophy of mind and body called double aspect theory. Double aspect theory was a monism proposing that the mind and the body were simply the distinctive results of two kinds of observations of a single kind of reality, an underlying reality that had priority over the method by means of which it was observed. That single dominant reality was God. Thus, unlike Leibniz, Spinoza's philosophy was dominated, as were most of his predecessors, by the need to justify and explain a theological issue—the role of God. Even though parallelism and double aspect theory have many properties in common, their respective raisons d'être were totally different.

6.2.4 Rehmke's Ontological Dualism

By the latter part of the 19th century, many philosophers had forgone any explicit connection of their dualisms with theology. In doing so, they turned to logical arguments as they developed their respective philosophies concerning the mind–body problem. This was often done in spite of their personal religious training. Indeed, it was not atypical for ontological philosophers to be trained as clerics and then, later in their lives, become more technically oriented philosophers. The reasons for these frequent transformations are obvious. As I noted earlier, there is a considerable overlap of the most important problems confronted by theologians, philosophers, and psychologists. That early training in theology should have alerted individuals who later became philosophers or even psychologists to certain of these shared problem seems obvious.

It is not always possible to trace the specific roots of an individual's thoughts, so we cannot always know whether early religious training actually stimulated particular interest in dualist ontologies. Nevertheless, there is a strong suggestion that, like later psychologists, many of these ordained philosophers actually were responding, however indirectly, to their early training.

One philosopher who fit this description perfectly was Johannes Rehmke (1848–1930). Rehmke was unusual in being an ontological dualist and an epistemological monist. The more usual reverse ideology is one that assumes an ontological unity of brain and mind, but then occurs the practical necessity to study these two kinds of reality separately (epistemological dualism or nonreductive materialism).

According to Rehmke, we can study the physical but are blocked from "measuring" the mental because consciousness does not have any extent or even place. Thus, we have to assume that this critical difference argues for two kinds of ontological reality, one measurable and one immeasurable. This barrier to direct examination and measurement does not deny the existence of the mental or its unity with the material; it only poses a problem of knowledge acquisition, a situation that can be interpreted as requiring different tools to measure the mind and the brain (i.e., epistemological dualism).

6.2.5 Polten's Contemporary Interactionism

Polten (1973) is a modern idealistic dualist who embodied his arguments for a modern interactionism within the framework of a critique of identity theory: the radical monist idea that there is but one kind of reality and that it is material. He presented, as his alternative to the identity hypothesis, an updated form of interactionism that involves two forms of reality—the inner mental world and the external physical world, respectively. Furthermore, he proposed that two distinct levels of perceptual experience existed. The first level was that of an "inner sense" reflecting our awareness of inner mental states, and the second was an "outer sense" that reflects our awareness of the material universe in which we are physically embedded.

Polten's proposed form of interactionism between mental and physical realities appears to be more or less the classic one. The crux of the interaction question for him is: Can the mind affect the brain? However, as is characteristic of so much of the philosophical wrestling with this question, the argument becomes circular and it becomes difficult to tie down the exact meaning of Polten's particular answer. For example, in rejecting the results of some hypothetical Gedanken experiment in which corresponding brain states were shown to be present on a one-for-one basis for all psychological processes, Polten (1973) said:

> For it might be the case that every private mental event in the inner sense, even spaceless mathematical thought, continuously has brain events as its effect, and that a brain event which seems to be the cause of a subsequent mental event is really itself the effect of a prior mental event. (p. 242)

This logical problem permeates many other interactionist dualisms that have descended from Descartes' original exposition of the idea.

6.2.6 Ornstein's Multiple Aspect Theory

Ornstein (1972), writing in specific apposition to the mind–body identity theory as well as to Ryle's dispositional monism (discussed later in this chapter), proposed in their stead a "multiaspect theory" of the relationship between the mind and the brain. He suggested a theory of the mind–brain relationship lying halfway between Cartesian dualism and the extreme reductionist versions of identity theory. However, in developing his notion of a universe with multiple aspects that must be studied relatively independently and in which the linguistic terms of one aspect help little to explicate the other, Ornstein described what is essentially a pluralistic view of reality rather than an intermediary between monism and dualism.

Specifically, Ornstein suggests that there are four aspects of mind. They are the *experiential* (what we feel), the *neural* (what is going on in the nervous system concomitant to the experience), the *behavioral* (what the organism is doing), and the *verbal* (what a man [*sic*] [uniquely] may say about what he is doing). The identification of each of these aspects, Ornstein suggests, is necessary for assuming that mind exists in any given situation. A fifth aspect of his pluralism is the body, composed as it is of the organic states that underlay the four levels of mind. This "body category," according to Ornstein, also includes the receptor responses to stimuli from the external world.

The main thrust of Ornstein's theory is that reductionism from one of these levels to another never works; it only leads to infinitely smaller categories that are themselves equally inexplicable. In thus rejecting reductionism and turning to this sort of pluralism, Ornstein multiplies many of the difficulties that are generated by the dualist position. Rather than causal mind–body interactions alone, a whole new collection of dynamic interactions between all of his five aspects become problems demanding solution. Whether this is an expression of the ultimate nature of reality or merely a philosopher's invention, it is difficult to say. In any event, most contemporary philosophers would be unwilling to accept his fourfold taxonomy of mental processes.

6.2.7　The ESP and Psychic Connection

Henri Bergson (1929) proposed a dualism on the basis of what he referred to as "pure" memory—the record of all of our experiences. Unfortunately, the data that he used to support his theory was based in substantial part on the totally refutable observations of ESP—extrasensory perception—including remote brain-to-brain communication, telekinesis, and communications with the departed through "mediums." Bergson argued that the complete record of our past experience would overload human consciousness unless it was expressed in some manner. One way, according to him, in which this expression could occur was to project it out so that it could be picked up by other brains and other objects thus flushing the memory banks of all of this excess information. This is an interesting piece of poetry, but a very dubious interpretation of what was then known in the brain and psychological sciences.

Given the preponderance of studies suggesting that such paranormal phenomena are unlikely to have any substance, Bergson's notion of a complete recording of personal history and of an ESP basis for a dualism has been totally rejected by most current philosophers and scientists. Others who have attempted to make similar ESP arguments for dualism include Thouless and Wiesner (1948). Otherwise distinguished and well-known philosophers (e.g., Broad, 1925) also fell victim to these same fallacious supernatural arguments.

The psychologist, William McDougall (1911), quite to the contrary of what we may refer to as standard scientific dictum, had also proposed a dualist theory of mind and spirit. McDougall was also an active supporter of parapsychological research and thus may have been subject to the same intellectual pressures as those working on Bergson, Thouless, and Wiesner.

In any event and whatever the causes, he proposed that there were two kinds of reality—one of spirit and one of matter. His discussion, like many others described in this chapter, was not explicitly based on any theological axioms, but reflected a pure kind of "psycho-physical" interactionism in which the "spirit" was able to influence both the mind and the body.

Regardless of one's attitude toward dualism, parapsychological arguments should long ago have succumbed to their frequent debunking. ESP is a particularly fragile foundation on which to base any kind of a theory of reality. None of the parapsychological-based theories discussed here have any notable creditability today even among those philosophers who lean toward dualisms.

6.2.8 Eccles and Popper's Tripartite Reality

Lest it be misunderstood that pluralisms are more or less antique philosophies that grew out of classical philosophy or medieval scholasticism and subsequently faded completely from the philosophical scene, I next direct my reader's attention toward what many believe is a neurophysiological–philosophical curiosity. I have repeatedly asserted in my writings that modern cognitive neuroscience must be monist if it is to make any scientific sense at all. In fact, any ontology of mind–body unity has to be inexorable in its search for the physiological mechanisms associated with mental processes, whatever the constraints on such a quest may be. To do otherwise would make a travesty of this very complex science. In spite of this admonition, a modern dualism, or more correctly, a tripartite pluralism, was eloquently championed by a scientist–philosopher who, perhaps as much as any other, might well have been called the dean of modern neuroscience. John C. Eccles (1903–1997) received the Nobel Prize in 1963 for his distinguished work in neurophysiology. In short, his scientific credentials are impeccable and his scientific achievements outstanding in all regards. Yet Eccles' personal philosophy, as summed up in his books (Eccles, 1970, 1973), indicated that this very important neurophysiologist read out of his experimental results a very different interpretation than have most contemporary neuroscientists.

Eccles' goal was to provide a neurophysiological basis for a view of the universe suggested by the philosopher Karl R. Popper (1902–1994). Popper's philosophical theory invoked three levels of reality. The first level of reality, which Popper called "World 1," is the world of physical objects and states including the material portion of the nervous system. "World 2" is the world of mental activities, or as he termed them, "states of consciousness," and "World 3" is the world of human culture and knowledge. To Eccles the essence of Popper's mind–body–culture tripartite reality revolved around the possible manner in which these three levels of metaphysical reality interacted with each other. Just as with the dualisms we have already discussed, the degree of interaction became the critical issue in his proposed solution to the mind–brain problem.

As a neurophysiologist, Eccles went far beyond most philosophers in pointing out the specific anatomical structures that he believed played significant roles in this pluralist universe. He backed up his theory with what he believed to be relevant neuroscientific data in a way that is quite unusual in the history of mind–brain theory. On the other hand, he found it easy to accept, in exactly the same manner as Polten, the notion of two classes of sensory perception: an inner sense responsive to World 2 mental processes and World 3 stored memories, and an outer sense responsive to the stimuli emanating from the external World 1. The central interpreter of all these sensory impressions was accepted by both Popper and Eccles as a form of "pure ego." As incongruous as it seemed in a modern neurophysiological text, Eccles referred specifically to this pure ego as being in many ways equivalent to the theological use of the word "soul."

Eccles proposed that the link between World 1 and World 2 occurred at extremely microscopic levels. He argued that the mind could influence the brain because it (the mind) exerted an influence over the probability that a marginally stimulated neuron would or would not be activated. The uncertainty of firing was analogous, if not identical, to the uncertainty in quantum interactions in his interpretation of mind–brain interactions. Thus, by shifting the probabilities, even the minimal energy exerted by the mind could take over control of the entire brain and, more generally, the behavior of the organism.

It is important to appreciate that unlike some of his dualist predecessors, Eccles was not asserting that the brain and the mind obeyed different kinds of laws. Rather, his linkage of mind to the microscopic quantum effects and his invocation of the random uncertainty found in other kinds of material systems assumed that both were responsive to the laws of the new physics. In this manner, he hoped to overcome one of the most effective criticisms of earlier dualisms—the reluctance on the part of many scholars to accept the fact that, undetectable, invisible, immeasurable, and unknown forces were necessary to explain mental activity.

Over the years, Eccles was particularly interested in the idea that there is a "Liaison Brain" that is sufficiently competent to mediate the interaction between the World 1 brain states and World 2 mental states.[7] Based primarily on Roger Sperry's work on the split-brain preparation, Eccles argued that the liaison brain is probably some part of the dominant cerebral hemisphere, a region then thought to be most concerned with verbal and conscious behavior.

---

[7] The similarity between Eccles' "Liaison Brain" and Descartes' use of the pineal gland should not be overlooked.

The importance of Eccles' version of dualism was the very specific physiological associations that they made. However, it is exactly in this specific association that Eccles' neurophysiological reductionism ultimately failed. Nowadays, there is precious little support for his proposed triple kind of reality or for minuscule quantum effects in determining the probability of neuronal activations. It is nevertheless, a fascinating aspect of the history of dualist thinking arising as it did from the thoughts of a scientist who behaved otherwise so thoroughly as would have been expected of an objective, modern neuroscientist.

6.3 A SAMPLE OF MODERN DUALIST PHILOSOPHIES: THE NEW LOGICIANS

Somewhere in the middle of the century, perhaps after World War II, study of what was increasingly referred to as the mind–brain problem underwent another evolutionary change. The main change was the increasing acceptance of the materialist or monist explanation of how the brain produced mind. It was becoming increasingly acceptable that the two kinds of observations did not represent anything comparable to different levels of reality. However, there were also changes occurring in the various kinds of neo-dualisms that still permeated a nonnegligible portion of philosophical thinking. One area where these changes can be found is in the progression of terminology that made up the vocabulary of mind–brain studies. Indeed, the very use of the word *mind*, which had been held in such disrepute by the behaviorist psychologists of the mid-20th century, began to emerge again as a major issue. Mind, particularly in terms of our self-awareness, or as it often designated by a word of unquantifiable vagueness—"consciousness"—began to reappear in the titles of many books and articles. This section reviews many of the new philosophical studies of mind and brain, especially those that have turned to logical and quasi-logical arguments to make their case.

There was another, perhaps even more fundamental change occurring: the increased application of what was purported to be logical or conceptual analysis to "prove" the existence of dual realities. Although this approach was not entirely novel (it appears in the literature in a somewhat subdued form throughout the last several centuries) syllogistic and quasi-syllogistic reasoning came into its own late in the 20th century very often in support of dualist theories. Axiomatic statements are stated and their logical consequences determined.

The problem, as we see shortly, is that in many cases the axioms themselves are without adequate foundation. Often they are "intuitive" (whatever that means) and, in other cases, they represent a kind of circular reasoning depending on what is sometimes a cryptic version of the conclusions to which the logic is supposed to lead. This situation becomes evident as I consider some of the most notable of the 20th-century "logical analysis" approaches to dualism in this chapter.[8] However, before doing so, it is worthwhile to look at some of the new vocabulary that has recently evolved in studies of the philosophy of mind.

6.3.1   Some New Terminology

The philosophy of mind, and in particular, the relationship between the brain and the mind—the mental and the physical—has reemerged as one of the main topics of current science. What had previously been only speculative is now being supplemented by extraordinary developments in the neurosciences. The development of the microelectrode permitted us to look at the action of individual neurons; the development of the averaged evoked potential permitted us to look at the collective actions of many neurons when a sensory modality was impulsively stimulated; and, most recently, the Positron Emission Tomography (PET) and Magnetic Resonance Imaging (MRI) techniques[9] have revitalized the hope that direct comparisons could be made between thoughts and brain activities. To many, it seemed the day of the materialist and monist theories had arrived. Dualist philosophers, however, responded to this developing state of affairs by seeking to restructure the problem. Classic Cartesian dualism was scrutinized anew to tease out its fundamental assumptions and to see how it could be distinguished from the developments in materialist theory. Mainly, however, a new vocabulary was invented that incorporated some of the following terms:

Substance Dualism.   As I just noted, the very vocabulary used to discuss the issue began to change about halfway through the 20th century. Descartes' dualism, in which mind and brain were considered to be two totally different kinds of material reality (the classic dualist position), came to be characterized as "substance dualism." That is, the mind and the brain were instantiated in two different substances or, even more specifically, as two different kinds of objects. The mind, from the point of view of substance

---

[8] The discussion presented in this chapter is, of necessity only the barest and most incomplete sampling of the enormous amount of activity in philosophy of mind studies. An appreciation of how extensive such studies have become can better be obtained by examining the recent collection of important articles edited by Chalmers (2002).

[9] Although these new methods are powerful and wonderful tools, there is at least a question of how effective they can be in achieving the goals that many cognitive neuroscientists have set for themselves. They may represent the fulfillment of a long anticipated hope or simply a new phrenology. I refer my readers to Uttal (2001) for a full discussion of this issue.

dualists had no less concrete reality than the material aspects of our bodies and could, therefore, not only exist independently of the brain/body but also could interact with it. Substance dualism, however, began to lose its charm in light of the unobservable nature of the hypothetical mental substance.

Property Dualism. That there should exist an intangible, immeasurable, mental substance, thus, has always posed a problem for dualist philosophers. The idea of an intangible substance raised very difficult logical problems for philosophers of science if not for theologians.[10] As modern science progressed, the ideas of measurement and experimentation became more and more a part of both the scientific and philosophical Zeitgeist. Modern dualists, therefore, sought to finesse this problem by redefining the nature of the entities involved in the mind/brain dichotomy. Descartes' mental and physical substance dualism was replaced by a new idea—"property dualism." On this theory, both the mental and the physical aspects of an object are independently assayable, but these properties do not represent different kinds of "things" à la Descartes, but rather only aspects or attributes of "something else" (e.g., the "person"). Thus, according to property dualists, there may be two kinds of properties, attributes, or characteristics that are characterized by two kinds of measurement. Implicit in many property dualist theories is the idea that, for reasons of deep principle (e.g., incompatible measuring tools) it is not possible to explain mental activity in terms of neural actions. Mind "emerges" from brain but in a mysterious way that poses an intractable challenge.

This kind of property dualism obviously comes very close to certain kinds of material monisms, for example, double aspect theory. The distinction between the two is mainly between alternative explanations of how this mystery should be explained. Property dualists would typically argue that the reason is ontological; there exist two fundamentally different kinds

---

[10]How difficult the logical problem of intangible entities can be was summed up in a recent article by Estling (2002). He said:

> For this is the logic that dare not speak its name, the logic that says, I believe in something completely incredible, improvable, irrational, and with no evidence to support it, but never mind all that. Just show me where I am wrong. *Prove* that my (fill in favorite belief system) doesn't exist. (p. 58)

I am also reminded of a brief encounter in an elevator. A young man announced that he was going to a meeting exploring the role of the spirit in everyday life. I asked what was that all about and his response was "If you don't know, I can't tell you." This further reminded me of the oft-quoted line "For those who believe in God, no explanation is necessary. For those who do not, no explanation is possible." The conclusion to which one is inexorably drawn is that it is impossible to discuss or even communicate on matters like this with many of the deeply committed on either side of the issue.

of properties with which we have to contend as far as we can see into the future. Double aspect theory, proposes there is only one kind of reality but that we are forced to look at it with different measures of the material and the mental, respectively. Monists of the school that argues we can have ontological mind–brain identity without mind–brain reduction argue that the mystery occurs only because of epistemological constraints on our abilities to analyze complex systems. All, however, agree that this obstacle to reduction is not temporary, but is likely to be permanent.

Property dualism, comes in several different forms, most of which differ on the basis of the nature of the interaction between the two kinds of properties. Debates now rage over the causal influences of the two kinds of properties on each other. It is clear that, in many instances, the issue of the directions and efficacy of causal forces (of the brain on the mind or vice versa) has largely replaced considerations of immortality and the nature of God in modern philosophical studies of mind. This is not to say that older theological views have not had some impact on thinking in philosophy or psychology (see chap. 7) but that the detheologizing of modern philosophy of mind continues apace. Furthermore, the flood of new information from the neurosciences has laid to rest many of the older speculative answers to some of the great conundrums of human history. In their place, questions of the limits of knowledge, of causality, and of logical methodology and axioms, have grown considerably more central to the discussion of the mind–body problem in modern philosophy.

As discussions among philosophers of mind have become more and more technical in recent decades, there has been a continuing change in the ongoing discussion of dualist theories. In place of references to the theological or to God, attention has been directed at what are hoped to be more precisely defined concepts that had only been implicit in the work of the earlier scholars. In many ways the transition from substance dualism to property dualism is a change from concentration on ontological issues to epistemological ones. It, thus, represents a diminishment of age-old efforts to discuss the nature of the unobservable supernatural and an enhancement in philosophers' attempts to determine what may be the limits on understanding natural events.

Qualia. Another new term that has received a significant play in recent years is *quale* or, in its more frequently used plural form, *qualia*. The invocation of the word qualia is an attempt to sharpen up the general idea of mental experiences beyond the hitherto inadequately precise definition of the word *phenomena* or the phrase "raw feel" reputedly introduced by Feigl (1958). Qualia are postulated as the properties of our experience, the mental attributes of which we as individuals are introspectively aware, and which we as individuals are able, depending upon one's attitude toward mental accessibility, to access and, possibly describe.

The range of the dimension along which qualia are ordered is increasing. Qualia were originally defined in terms of sensory and perceptual properties; nowadays the concept has been expanded to refer to emotional experiences as well. A useful and articulate appreciation of what philosophers mean by qualia has been provided by Searle (1992). His definition was by exclusion but still is a helpful means of establishing the connotation, if not the denotation, of the term.

> There are certain quite specific qualitative experiences in seeing a red object or having a pain in the back, and just describing these experiences in terms of their causal relations leaves out these special qualia. (p. 62)

Thus, Searle suggested that qualia are "qualitative experiences."
In a similar vein, Dennett (1991) proposed that qualia are "intrinsic qualities" (p. 65) and gets only slightly more specific when he answers the rhetorical question: "Just what are 'phenomenal qualities' or *qualia*?"

> They seem terribly obvious as first—they're the way things look, smell, feel, sound to us—but they have a way of changing their status or vanishing under scrutiny. (p. 338)

Dennett then sharpened this definition by also listing examples of what Qualia are not (e.g., visual phosphenes and filled in "blind spots"). Any distinction drawn between such qualia and the redness of a response to long wavelength light, however, is fraught with the usual difficulties.
Both Searle's and Dennett's definitions, however, leave much to be desired, not so much by their use of the exclusion method of defining a term (i.e., saying what it is not rather than what it is), but rather because they are essentially nonoperational. That is, they cannot be functionally defined (as Dennett appreciates on page 459 of his 1991 book). The discussions, therefore, typically revert to the accessibility issue or any attempt to define subjective states such as those incorporated within that highly problematic word "consciousness." Thus, although, the word qualia appears more and more often in the philosophical literature, it is not at all certain that it adds (or for that matter can add anything) to the denotation of mental or cognitive events.
Whether one wishes to argue that the parameters of mental experience are of the same nature as the material parts of the brain is another matter. However different the measurement techniques appropriate for each may be, there is no question that thoughts have some parameters that are comparable to the physical ones. It takes a certain amount of time to do or think something; our thoughts do change over time, and it is virtually certain that whatever the procedure is, our thoughts are instantiated in the same physi-

cal location in which our brains are to be found.[11] The problem is that defining a strategy for the *interpersonal* communication (i.e., measurement) of *intrapersonal* qualia, whether they exist or not, is synonymous with the problem of cognitive accessibility. (See Uttal, 2000, for my personal argument against the accessibility of mental processes.)

The important role that the concept of qualia might have played in the discussion would have been to provide dimensions and values for the otherwise all-too-vaguely defined entity we know as consciousness. Their nonfunctionality and inaccessibility, however, relegates them to the same bag in which we keep other such ill-defined mentalist terms. That we are epistemologically handicapped (in defining and measuring qualia) should be a warning that efforts to either dissect them into or define them as mental modules may be a far more daunting task than it may at first have seemed.

The ontological reality of mental processes or qualia, or whatever other ill-defined mentalist term one chooses to use, however, is a completely separate issue. Of the reality of qualia there is hardly any question. Unless we are to make the entirety of our experience, if not our very existence, illusory and meaningless, it is hard to reject the first-hand evidence that each of us has of the existence of mental processes. Mind must exist, and qualia (or some other aspect of its dimensions) must have some kind of reality. To go beyond that and to seek precision of denotation or explanatory reduction is a far greater, if not an impossible, challenge.

Indeed, this inherent difficulty in achieving a satisfactory definition of any mental process lies at the core of the epistemological focus of controversy about dualism. The bare-bones ontological assumption of some kind of reality of our mental experiences is the foundation axiom that all of the individuals, theologians, philosophers, and psychologists have depended on from the beginning. The reality of qualia, mind, mental activity, or whatever else one wishes to call this intrapersonal experience each of us enjoys must be accepted or all the rest of human activity is irrelevant and we all become automata.

Nevertheless, the relationship between qualia and the brain is considered by some philosophers to represent a novel point of view compared to ideas of mentation that were popular only a few decades ago. There is precious little to suggest, however, that even in this new form, the uncertainties of the relationship between brain and mind are likely to be resolved in the near future. A simple renaming of the mental activities or entities does not resolve such ticklish matters in the mind–brain debate as their causal influence, their accessibility, or the reducibility of one to the other. As a re-

---

[11] This does not mean that specific cognitive components or modules are localized in particular parts of the brain, but rather that the brain and our minds appear to be in the same general location—our heads.

sult, many philosophers still deny the epistemological identity of qualia and the material brain.

Another problem with the concept of qualia becomes obvious at this point. A close examination of what is meant by the term suggests that they may be another example of a continuing effort to perpetuate and justify dualisms. Qualia contain a number of implicit ideas that seem to set mental processes apart from material objects. By intent, qualia are, at the very least, divisible properties, dimensions, or modules of our experiences. As such, there is an implicit assumption that, despite the accessibility constraint, they are subject to evaluation, measurement, and, therefore, represent real subdivisions of what may otherwise be considered a more molar "consciousness." As we see in the next chapter the very real problem of the modular versus the holist nature of mental activity may be being prejudiced by the simple act of defining isolatable qualia. The similarity between "qualia" and Wundt (1894) or Titchener's (1899) structural concepts of "elementary conscious experiences" is not to be overlooked. Indeed, the modular tone of much of current cognitive psychology makes one wonder if the idea of qualia is a philosophical corollary of psychological divisibility. If it is, its very definition is a kind of cryptic substitute for cognitive modules—an idea that also may have emerged out of dualist roots.

Supervenience. Another "new" idea that has very recently been injected into philosophy of mind discussions is "supervenience" (Davidson, 1970). The concept of supervenience was intentionally introduced to provide a precise logical language to discuss the possible relationships between different domains. Its presence in current mind–brain discussions by philosophers is ubiquitous, but it also has been applied to physics, especially in the relation of the microscopic and macroscopic properties of matter.

At first glance, supervenience, in at least some of its forms, appears to be a corollary of monist identity theory. It describes a relationship between the mind and the brain that is extraordinarily tight, much like the dual aspect nature of mind and brain supported by some early philosophers. However, the concept has taken on a broader applicability in the sense that the actual relation or dependence of mind on matter may be considered to vary in terms of the tightness of the relationship. In the strongest sense, supervenience supports materialism; the mind is totally dependent (i.e., supervenient) on the material brain. In some of the weaker meanings of the term, however, it is used as an argument for various kinds of dualisms; the mind depends on but is not exclusively identifiable with brain states. In this latter example—weak supervenience—it is often suggested that there are logical arguments that the same physical laws that "explain" the physical universe do not necessarily operate in determining the nature of mind.

It has also been suggested (e.g., Klee, 1997) that supervenience is an intentional effort to soften the tight relationship between matter and mind by permitting a kind of dependency that is not totally materialistic, yet at the same time, not totally dualist. Supervenience permits, but does not require, causal relationships and does permit the use of laws. Supervenience is, furthermore, not reductive: It discusses dependencies without making any effort to explain the mechanisms that could account for those dependencies. In this manner, supervenience permits us to retain some semblance of dualism in an increasingly materialist world.

In order to make the concept more precise, let us phrase it in the brain-state mental-state language that philosophers now so frequently use. Weak supervenience argues that if two brain systems are in the same state, then the resulting mental states (if any) may or may not be identical. A corollary of this foundation assumption is that if two mental states are different, then they may or may not be instantiated in two different brain states.

Unfortunately, weak supervenience does not deal adequately with the problem of multiple brain states encoding the same mental state. That is, two identical mental states may be produced by quite different brain states. As we see, some philosophers (e.g., Chalmers, 1966) have denied the premise of identical brain states always producing identical mental states when they proposed that identical physical states might produce different mental states. This, I argue is a crypto–dualism.

An alternative "strong" view of supervenience argues that if two mental states are indistinguishable, then the brain states *must* also be indistinguishable. A corollary of this position argues, contrary to Chalmers' view, that two identical brain states must produce identical mental states. Thus, mind supervenes entirely on brain and only the details of that relationship remain to be discovered. In attempting to fill a gap in weak supervenience, however, the strong version creates a situation in which the one-to-many problem is ignored. That is, it is possible that there are many different reductive explanations (i.e., brain states) that could produce the same mental state. In other words, indistinguishable mental states may be produced by distinguishable brain states.

As suggested by the various meanings of supervenience, it has also been invoked by philosophers of mind in support of antithetical points of view that sometimes cannot be distinguished from either traditional dualisms or material monisms. Kim (1993), for example, although going through a continual metamorphosis of his interpretation of supervenience, argues that supervenience implies that mental activity cannot influence brain activity and, therefore, the physical or material domain is primary. In his case, the issue of dependency (Does the mental state depend completely on the brain state?) is considered primary and the answer arrived at is that mind absolutely "depends" or, in other words, strongly supervenes on the brain.

Thus, the material world is not only dominant, but it is all there is. Clearly, this is a version of material monism.

Others see the great practical difficulty, if not complete impossibility, of ever being able to reduce the mental states to the brain states in order to support logically such a material monism. The problem in this case is the extreme complexity of the brain state. Here, again, the absence of an ability to go from the formal dependent relations of supervenience to specific neural or even operational terms led others to suggest that the two worlds are at least separate epistemologically, if not ontologically.

The hook upon which those who believe supervenience argues for dualism is another corollary of the foundation assumption that different machines can produce the same behavior—the one-to-many problem just mentioned. That is, if two mental states are the same, they need not be expressions of the same physical state. This, of course, is the specter that haunts all attempts at neuroreduction and creates the resulting difficulty in going from mental or behavioral observations to neural "causes." That is, the possibility exists that there are many different brain states that can produce identical mental experiences or, at least, experiences or qualia that cannot be distinguished from each other.

There is at least a suggestion that the modern supervenience movement is but another product of the persistent influence that classic dualist ideas may still be having on modern thinking. Supervenience and qualia might be considered to be modern attempts to sharpen the debate by crystallizing the differences between monisms and dualisms. By defining them, subtle differences between these extreme views, it was hoped, could be detected. The empirical difficulties that have always muddied the waters of this controversy, however, remain as impenetrable as ever. The very nature of the concepts has itself introduced new controversies and disagreements into philosophy of mind debates. It is not at all clear, therefore, that the introduction of such concepts has, in fact, brought any clarity to the question of the relation between the mind and the brain. It may simply be providing "new bottles" for the "old wine" of the very recalcitrant brain–mind problem.

Functionalism. The classic dualist position was formulated as a substance dualism. A new form of dualism, however, proposes that mind represents a distinguishable set of properties of a single physical substance—the brain. This approach—functionalism—has achieved a substantial amount of prominence in modern studies of the philosophy of mind. The current version of philosophical functionalism is derivative from the functionalist school that was, and to a certain degree still is, a major theme of scientific psychology. Indeed, the change from substance dualism to property dualism such as is embedded in functionalism in many ways reflects that change from the classic structuralist psychology (such as that propounded by Wundt, 1894, and Titchener, 1899) to the functionalist school championed by John Dewey (1886) and William James (1890) to name only some of the most prominent of the respective leaders of these two fields.

As Marx and Hillix (1963) pointed out, structuralism was modeled by its proponents on the science of chemistry. The elements of consciousness were to be identified and examined and then the goal was to determine how they were synthesized into mental activity. The functionalists, on the other hand, saw mental activity, not in such terms of isolatable components or elements, but rather as a means of explaining the manner in which stimuli and responses were connected together. Thus, the emphasis was on the way that inferred mental processes served the "function" of connecting or linking the observable "inputs" and "outputs" rather than dealing with them as tangible entities.

Philosophical functionalism emerges, if not directly from this same line of thought, at least as a prominent example of convergent intellectual evolution. As the vulnerabilities and inconsistencies of substance dualism became obvious, philosophers such as Putnam (1988), Armstrong (1968), and Smart (1971) argued that any attempt to specifically define or to provide a definition of mind in terms of its structural components should be eschewed. Instead, they argued, mental process should only be defined in terms of the "functions" they served in transforming stimulus conditions into appropriate behavioral responses. On this theoretical point of view, mental processes became more like mathematical transforms rather than things.[12]

According to this view, there is nothing we can say about the nature of mental processes except to formally define them in their crucial functional role. In fact, a committed functionalist would argue there is nothing further to say about them: They are fully characterized in such transformational terms because of their fundamental inaccessibility and intrapersonal privacy, characteristics that preclude any further attempt to define, measure, analyze, dissect, or even describe anything like qualia or phenomena.

Should functionalism be considered to be a dualism or a monism? The answer is not at all clear. My initial feeling is that it is clearly a dualism, not

---

[12]Sometimes understanding descends upon us like a ton of bricks. As I read more about this new functionalism, I discovered that like the little boy who had been talking prose his whole life without realizing it, I had been talking functionalism without "realizing it." In Uttal (2002) I described how a theory of form recognition must be limited to answering a class of "scientifically tractable" questions such as:

What is the functional (i.e., transformational) relationship between the parameters of the stimulus and the parameters of the response? (p. 125)

Little did I appreciate it at that time (even though I used the word "functional") that what I was proposing was also already known to be the core of modern philosophical functionalism.

because it has specific things to say about the mental, but rather because it suggests that mental states, whatever they are, are of a different genre and cannot be measured or examined using the same tools that work so well for behavior or neural responses. By defining them as relations, mathematical formalisms, or otherwise, the question of their ontological nature is simply finessed. In this case, we see the ontological question is ignored within the confines of a theory in which epistemological dualism is accepted.

On the other hand, there is a strong tone of monism throughout the functionalist literature. Mind is dealt with as process or intermediary between the sensory and behavioral domains. The open question (which is probably answered differently by different functionalists) is whether this is simply a strategy to avoid dealing with the "soul" and other aspects of the supernatural or is an expression of a monist ontological position. At least, functionalism is neutral with regard to that which cannot be examined.

In this regard, it shares with behaviorism the effort to finesse or even to ignore the role of what both points of view agree is a system of inaccessible mental states. Behaviorism argues that whatever they are, mental states are the observed tendencies or dispositions based on a long series of selective reinforcements to respond in a particular way. Thus, we really don't have to talk (and, in principle, cannot talk) about mental states. Like functionalism, of which it may be considered to be a part, behaviorism sees mind as merely a set of transformations or dispositions as far as objective science is concerned.

What does emerge from a consideration of the evolutionary sequence of dualist thinking from ancient to modern times is an increase in the progression from raw supernatural explanations to a kind of hands-off effort to avoid the profound issues of mental independence from the body–brain and immortality that still confront so many thoughtful people. The shift has been in terms of emphasizing the prevalent epistemological problems and assumptions while simultaneously leaving unresolved the ontological or metaphysical issues. One can see this being expressed in the words of many dualist philosophers are reviewed in this chapter; there is a certain reluctance to confront the challenges to dualism that have emerged in the modern world of physics and other experimental sciences.

In this century dualism has been continuously challenged by the objections of empiricism (an attitude transcending even the empirical facts themselves) more than at any time in its history. Nevertheless, the response of those who still adhere to dualist theories has not been surrender and acceptance. Instead, it has turned the battlefield upside down by simply redirecting the issue away from the ontology of the mind to epistemological questions of what we can and cannot know. The alternatives we have been considering here no longer concentrate on the nature of the soul–mind, but rather with the accessibility of mental processes and the transformations

⌊they represent. Whether this is a "cop-out," an attempt to finesse the very difficult problem of defining mind or consciousness, or the next evolutionary step toward a purely monist, physicalist, materialist perspective on human nature is yet to be seen.

Causal Influences. Next, it is appropriate to consider an issue that was once the core of classic Cartesian dualism—interactionism. The Cartesian point of view, as seen earlier in this chapter, was based on the idea that the mind and brain were two different substances that mutually interacted. Indeed, according to Descartes, mind was as capable of influencing brain nee body as brain was of influencing mind. Much of the recent history of brain–mind philosophy has been concerned with the nature of the causal influence that one could exert on the other. This issue was raised in Uttal (1978) and is reproduced here (Fig. 6.1) because it makes the causal influence force clear. Three kinds of measurements are denoted: the physical nature of stimuli, neurophysiological activity, and psychological (or behavioral) responses. In this figure I identified the task domains of psychology, neurophysiology, and psychobiology in terms of how one studies the causal relationships among them.

Traditional experimental psychology, more specifically psychophysics, is concerned with the relation between stimuli and psychological responses; current neurophysiology is concerned with the relation between stimuli

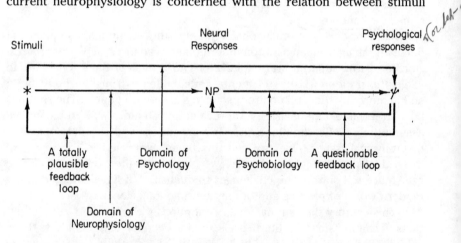

FIG. 6.1. A diagram depicting the possible interactions between physical stimuli, neural responses, and psychological or mental responses. Although it is clear to modern science that stimuli can affect the nervous system, and through the brain, stimuli can also affect the mind and thus behavior, there remains considerable uncertainty whether mental experiences can affect the nervous system and behavior. This is the free will problem expressed in scientific terms. Mind is either influential or epiphenomenal; we have yet to answer this important question.

and measured neural responses; and what was then called psychobiology (and nowadays cognitive neuroscience) was concerned with the relations between neural and psychological responses. Each of these sciences was defined in terms of the causal influence; stimuli on neural responses; stimuli on psychological responses; and neural events on psychological responses, respectively. The one path of potential causal influence that I tagged then as being a "questionable feedback loop" was the one from psychological responses to neural responses. In other words, I was challenging the efficacy of a potential causal link from the mind to the brain.

It turns out that the uncertainty of this questionable loop (i.e., mind influences on brain) plays an important role in the modern philosophy of mind studies. If, on the one hand, one accepts there is a causal influence of mind on matter and the distinction that the two represent different substances, clearly a traditional dualism is the logical outcome. If, on the other hand, one assumes there is no causal influence of "mind" on brain physiology, one might be led directly to a kind of epiphenomenalism, a concept that is usually (but not universally) associated with monisms. Epiphenomenalism proposes that mind is generated by the brain but cannot feed back causal influence on it. Obviously, how one interprets causality in this case will be extremely influential in determining the outcome of debates between monism and dualism. Causality issues of this genre arise, as we see later in this chapter, in many guises.

The Explanatory Gap. Another new term that has come in prominence in recent years is "The Explanatory Gap," the first modern use of which is attributed to Levine (1983). The meaning inherent in this phrase is that consciousness has never been explained and we are not making any progress in our efforts to explain it. Block and Stalnaker (1999) put it more definitively:

> Consciousness is a mystery. No one has ever given an account, even a highly speculative, hypothetical, and incomplete account of how a physical thing could have phenomenal states. (p. 1)

The fascinating thing to me is that this statement of scientific fact is not simply accepted on its face, but rather has become another focus of contention in the dualism–monism controversy. One side argues that because consciousness and other aspects of phenomenal experience have not been reduced to physical terms, this reflects a true difference in the respective realities of each and, thus, by itself is an argument for dualism. Antagonists to this point of view argue, on the other hand, that this "gap" is only an epistemological issue and is not relevant to the ontological problem of any distinction between the ultimate natures of the mind and brain, respectively. Either because we simply do not have the tools available to study these phenomena or because there is an in principle (i.e., epistemological) barrier, we simply do not have and may never have the ability to explain the emergence of consciousness from neural activity.

The explanatory gap due to inaccessibility, however, is not tantamount, from my point of view, to dualism. Indeed, it is not even suggestive of it. Tye (1999) expressed this point very well in pointing out the "gap" is but an illusion:

> A failure to appreciate that the special and a priori irreducible character of phenomenal concepts misleads us into thinking that there is a deep and puzzling explanatory gap for phenomenal consciousness, but this is an illusion. There is no such gap. Those who see in the alleged gap a reason for supposing that phenomenal qualities are special qualities, different in kind from anything physical or functional are *doubly* mistaken. (p. 723)

Others have argued that there is a possible path to understanding the mind (i.e., that the "explanatory gap" is but a momentary problem) and that by ignoring it or by not studying it adequately, we are reneging on a major scholarly responsibility. This is, of course, the famous "baby and bath water" argument. Without minimizing the difficulty of the task, philosophers such as Searle (1992) argued that we should at least attempt to leap the gap by studying consciousness. Although rejecting a firm commitment to both monism and dualism, Searle argues that a proper study of mind is possible. He went on to suggest that by attending anew to studies of consciousness, it is possible to arrive at deep new understandings.

Unfortunately, Searle does not provide us with any strategy to achieve the goal of studying consciousness and leaves us with another example of how great are the dual problems of how the brain produces mental experiences (the ontological issue) and how we can study those mental experiences (the epistemological issue).

To sum up this discussion, it is clear that there has been a shift in modern philosophical studies of mind. Whole new vocabularies have been inserted into the discussions; many of the ubiquitous terms are very recent, emerging as topics of discussion only in the last few decades. There has also been a subtle shift in the emphasis of these discussions. Increasingly, scholars are concerned with the epistemological issues and the detailed logic of their arguments. This is not to say that conclusions about the mind–brain relationship are not being drawn but rather that contemporary scholars do seem to be more open to an appreciation of alternative interpretations of the implications of their logic. There are still numerous and influential dualists about who carry their logic to what they believe are tenable conclusions concerning the mind–body relationship. The following sections discuss a few modern logical dualisms and concentrate on these epistemological issues. Once again, it must be reiterated that the selection of authors in the following sections is not suggestive of my agreement with them, but rather this presentation is made in order for my readers to understand their arguments.

6.3.2 Lovejoy's Spatiotemporal Proof of Dualism

Arthur O. Lovejoy (1873–1962) was a relatively recent dualist who sought to justify the existence of two different kinds of realities—objects and experiences—on the basis of their difference in time and space. He argued that, given that we can have ideas about objects that have occurred or will occur at different times other than the present and that these objects may be located at different places (than here), there must be some kind a fundamental difference between ideas and the objects they represented. Lovejoy (1930) published his ideas in a badly mistitled book—*The Revolt Against Dualism: An Inquiry Concerning the Existence of Ideas* in which he argued for, not against, a kind of ontological dualism as his ill-chosen title might have otherwise suggested.

Lovejoy's main point was that ideas and objects, because of their respective spatiotemporal incongruity, cannot be identical and, therefore, ideas and objects must have their own separate nature. In some instances, ideas or sensations may reflect some of the qualities of objects, but he felt that this was not necessarily true and, in any case, he argued that there is no way to establish the relation.

I see in his formulation of a dualist philosophy a precursor of the assumption that mental processes are inaccessible and, for this reason, he argued, they were not directly comparable or reducible to physical objects and their properties. However, this epistemological constraint, as I hope I have already made clear, does not necessarily lead to or justify ontological dualism.

Of particular interest is that by Lovejoy's time, the philosophy of mind was, for many philosophers, progressing rapidly in unburdening itself from any theological baggage. By then, philosophical assumptions were increasingly based on logic and empirical observations in a way it was hoped would be compelling and irrefutable. This was a very important step simply because it provided a means of making all of the arguments subject to refutation—within the limits of the validity of the premises and axioms, of course. Bald statements of faith, by Lovejoy's time, were having progressively less influence in philosophy, even though in quite a different arena theologians persisted in this kind of argumentation. Unfortunately, it is still sometimes very hard, indeed, to distinguish some of the "premises and axioms" of a technical philosopher from the creedal statements of a religion.

See p. 233A!

6.3.3   Chalmers' Naturalistic Dualism

Chalmers (1996) has been one of the most prolific and articulate of contemporary dualist philosophers. His approach to the controversy is increasingly one emphasizing a formal logical analysis. He formulated the basic approach to his personal solution of the mind–body problem as a logical sequence of the following form:

1. In our world, there are conscious experiences.
2. There is a logically possible world physically identical to ours, in which the positive facts about consciousness in our world do not hold.
3. Therefore, facts about consciousness are further facts about our world, over and above the physical facts.
4. So materialism is false. (p. 123)

This syllogistic reasoning exhibited here is very typical among today's nontheologically oriented philosophers. Certain premises are stated or assumed and their logical consequences deduced.

Chalmers' argument depends, I am sure he would agree, entirely upon the assumption implicit in his Premise 2 that there exist, as he referred to them, "zombie worlds" (Chalmers, 1996, p. 94) [without consciousness] or alternative worlds with "inverted conscious experience" (p. 124). In his book, Chalmers defended this premise in several ways, first by noting that conceivability is "central" to "matters of explanation" (p. 110). That is, simply being able to conceive of, for example, a Zombie world is tantamount to its possible existence and, thus, its relevance to the mind–brain problem. The "relevance" accrues to the hypothetical inverted worlds, he argues, because they demonstrate that the mind is not strongly subservient on the brain. In other words, it is "conceivable" that the same brain state could produce two or more different mental states. The logical analysis that Chalmers presents, therefore, may only be an illusion of impeccable logic, based as it is on a premise (conceivability is tantamount to possibility) that can no more be substantiated than the dualist conclusion to which it ultimately leads.[13]

The fact that there is no empirical evidence of any such world, Zombie, inverted, or otherwise, is more or less ignored; for Chalmers the very possibility and conceivability of such a world is sufficient to justify its use as a premise in his logical analysis. However, in doing so, he runs counter to the logic of the entire modern scientific enterprise. His logic, therefore, con-

---

[13]As we see later on page 233, Chalmers' logic also can be criticized on the basis of being circular; that is, its assumptions (number 2 in particular) contain within themselves the conclusions.

fronts any potential critic with the necessity to prove something's nonexistence, an impossible logical task. One is reminded of the more openly theological expression:

> There are more things in Heaven and Hell that man doth dream of. (Shakespeare, in Hamlet)

Here Chalmers is arguing that the realization of even our wildest dreams is, in fact, unlimited and all that is necessary is to dream to create axiomatic realities. To paraphrase Hamlet: Man can dream of more things than are in heaven or hell (or on earth for that matter)!

As we further scrutinize this second premise of "conceivable possible worlds," it is crucial to appreciate that Chalmers' philosophical proposition of their existence is actually as supernatural a statement of belief as that proposed by any theologian. There is no way to establish or deny the existence of these alternative universes, to constrain or limit them, or, for that matter, to go beyond just their conceivability any more than the existence or nonexistence of any of the classic Gods of the Mayans or Sumerians can be adjudicated. Chalmers' pronouncement of "conceivability" as a premise is of the same quality as the assertions of faith made by any religious persons who intone their own version of the Shama or the Shahada.

The argument concerning the relation between conceivability and possibility is an old one. Its history and arguments for both affirmation and negation are well spelled out in a very thoughtful article by Yablo (1993). He points out that such a controversy actually existed back to the time of Descartes' "Meditations" and of Hume's philosophy. Yablo cites Hume's famous remark:

> That whatever the mind clearly conceives, includes the idea of possible existence, or in other words, that nothing we imagine is absolutely impossible. (Quoted in Yablo, 1993, p. 1)

Antique though it may be, the argument concerning conceivability and possibility continues on. In Yablo's own words:

> Yet throughout this complicated history [of controversy] runs a certain schizophrenia in which the theoretical worries forgotten, conceivability evidence is accepted without qualm or question. (p. 2)

Indeed, after a long and high technical discourse on the various arguments pro and con conceivability as a justification for possibility, Yablo inserts the "qualms and questions" into the debate. The question of his title ("Is conceivability a guide to possibility?") or any of the other reconceptualizations of it that he formulates is not specifically answered in his article.

Nevertheless, his criticism of the idea that conceivability is tantamount to possibility is sharp and to the point.

Chalmers (1996) went on to defend his dualism in his quasi-syllogism on the basis that "Conscious experience is not logically supervenient on the physical" and, thus, "materialism is false" (p. 161). Opposing views are raised (by him) against this logic, but then discarded in favor of a property dualism that Chalmers calls "Naturalistic Dualism." This version of mind–body dualism is defined by Chalmers as the idea that:

> Consciousness supervenes naturally on the physical, without supervening logically or metaphysically. (p. 162)

To appreciate this argument and the meaning of his naturalistic dualism, it is necessary to understand what Chalmers meant by both "natural" and "logical supervenience." We have already seen that supervenience comes in several forms varying along a continuum from *weak* to *strong*. Logical supervenience invokes the mere conceivability of alternative states (e.g., mental) given identical physical states. No reductionism of any kind is necessary in logical supervenience, merely the imagined possibility (i.e., conceivability) of one state or another. "Logically possible worlds" are, therefore, nothing more than an explicit statement of conceivable possibilities.

Natural supervenience, to the contrary, goes beyond the possible to the real. It asserts that the mental properties (to the extent that they are real) are lawfully dependent on the physical properties. The distinction between logical and natural supervenience is summarized by Chalmers (1966):

> It seems very likely that consciousness is naturally supervenient on physical properties, locally or globally, insofar as in the natural world, any two physically identical creatures will have qualitatively identical experiences. It is not at all clear that consciousness is logically supervenient on physical properties, however. It seems *logically* possible, at least to many, that a creature physically identical to a conscious creature might have no conscious experiences at all, or that it might have conscious experiences of a different kind. (pp. 37–38)

Chalmers' dualism is based strongly on what he believes is the necessity to deal with consciousness. Some of us would argue, on the contrary, that since consciousness is arguably inaccessible, immeasurable, and unobservable except through mediated communications that are terribly polluted and penetrated by distortions of one kind or another, any attempts to deal with it can only confuse and distract. In other words, the presence of a current "explanatory gap" is an epistemological issue that cannot be used to justify the ontology of dual realities.

Given that he feels we[14] must deal with consciousness, Chalmers goes on to argue that in doing so one is driven to a naturalistic dualism of the type he champions. Indeed, his position here is understandable if not fully acceptable to the material–monist community; he would argue that since the physical reality of consciousness is at best elusive and at worst inaccessible, it is appropriate to postulate a separate or distinctive nature for it. Ipso facto, some kind of a dual nature of reality is the best solution to the mind–brain problem and materialism must be rejected.

The problem, inadequately faced by all consciousness based dualists, is that consciousness by its very obscurity and ill-defined nature pushes one in the dualist direction. Nevertheless, this powerful impulse may be terribly misleading. Obscurity and mystery can be compelling intellectual forces, akin to the primeval fear of death of which I have spoken so often in this book. Forceful though they may be, such arguments represent a kind of pragmatic, yet potentially incorrect, response to what is only a boundary between the empirically knowable and the empirically impenetrable—two domains that do not necessarily differ in any ontological sense.

Finally, a specific comment must be made about Chalmers' "naturalistic dualism"—the conclusion to which his logic has led him. Although he repeatedly argues that his solution to the mind–brain problem is a dualism (as well as specifically naming it such), a close examination suggests that his theory, by any name, comes surprisingly close in all but the final conclusion to some materialist monisms. There are subtle inconsistencies within his writings concerning this matter. His natural dualism is distinguished from logical (or "possible world") dualism, yet the foundation premise (Number 2 on page 228) of his logical argument can be interpreted as nothing other than a necessary antecedent of the logical dualism he rejects. If I may generalize a bit from what appears to be Chalmers' view, this internal inconsistency seems to be very common among dualist philosophers who sometimes struggle so hard to arrive at their final conclusion. Is it possible that deep down they are fighting the materialist tide in what some would argue is a last-ditch dualist defense? Is this, too, an unacknowledged crypto-dualism?

I have spent quite a few more pages on Chalmers' view of the mind–brain problem than I had originally intended. There are several reasons for this; first, he himself has been an articulate and particularly comprehensive spokesman for his point of view. Second, his logical analysis is a representative example of what is going on in modern philosophy. Third, his work il-

---

[14] The increasing attention being made to mentalism in the form of "consciousness studies" among cognitive psychologists represents one of the most distressing developments in the history of psychology and philosophy of mind. Could it be that we are sliding back into a kind of "pseudotheology" in which consciousness has replaced "soul"? See chapter 7.

lustrates how completely wrong one can go based on erroneous premises even if the logical sequence that follows is impeccable. It is this powerful effect of a priori assumptions that is at the heart of much controversy in sciences of all kinds. It is also the core of the thesis of this book and, thus, deserves every bit of attention directed to it.

6.3.4 Kripke's Dualism

Kripke (1980) is another contemporary dualist who has sought to challenge the materialist philosophy on a logical basis. His position can be contrasted with that of Chalmers in an interesting way. Chalmers argued that, because of the possibility of conceivable alternate worlds in which identical brain states do not produce identical mental states, one cannot strongly link brain and mind within the confines of a single reality. Therefore, one is compelled to accept a dualist philosophy.

Kripke arrives at the same conclusion but along a different path. He argues that mental states (in particular experiences like pain) might, just possibly might, exist without the necessary neural substrate; that is they might exist without equivalent brain states.[15] That is, he raises the possibility of disembodied pain or, at least, of a disembodied personality experiencing a pain. Such a drastic separation of mind from any material substrate is an astonishing and quite unacceptable idea for materialists even if it is acceptable to theologians, dualists, and most of the religious people living in this world of ours.

Both Chalmers and Kripke, regardless of the details of their argument, are essentially making the same case, namely, that the necessary bond between the mental and the physical is irretrievably broken in at least some plausible, possible, and conceivable worlds. Therefore, both come to the conclusion that there is no necessary bond between mind and brain and, therefore, materialist–monist theories posing a tight relation or strong supervenience of mind on brain cannot be correct.

---

[15]Kripke prefers to use the neural activity of C-fiber (small diameter peripheral axons) as the vehicle for discussion of the relation between the mind (i.e., pain) and the nervous system. Work suggesting that C-fibers specifically conveyed neural information associated with tissue damage was carried out in the 19th century and later formulated into a theory associating fiber diameter with specific somatosensory experiences. (See Uttal, 1973, for a complete discussion of this topic.) The generally accepted (due to the absence of any viable alternative) theory now is the one proposed by Melzak and Wall (1965) in which it proposed that C-fiber activity driven by painful stimuli can be gated or overridden by larger diameter A fiber activity. The neural activity produced by the painful stimulus is then conducted by T fibers to the brain where it is "interpreted." In any event, no neurophysiologist ever asserted that it was the activity of the C-fibers in the periphery that was the psychoneural equivalent of pain. Rather that activity was conveyed to the brain where we still have no idea how the transmitted sensory signals are converted to experiences. The point is that pain does not reside in the skin, but in the brain.

In a cogent critique of both Chalmers' and Kripke's dualisms, Perry (2001) argued that both share a common fault. That fault is that both take plausible, conceivable possibilities (alternative mental manifestations of identical brain states on the part of Chalmers versus mental states without corresponding brain states on the part of Kripke) and assume that they actually exist. In effect, they have created Gedanken universes and transformed (i.e., reified) implausible possibilities into what they argue are realities. The reality of either brainless minds or mindless brains, however, may not exist in other than the assumptions of Chalmers' and Kripke's theories. If not, both approaches to dualism fail, even though they may be based on what are presumed to be consistent logical arguments. The key problem in this case is that these two distinguished dualists have not avoided the logical fallacy of *petitio principii* (circular reasoning or begging the question). For example, Kripke argues that since disembodied experiences can exist, therefore dualism is proven. However, if dualism is true, then disembodied experiences become realizable. This reasoning is circular because the assumption of disembodiment carries within it the seed of dualism and vice versa.

I believe that Kripke also, almost in passing and without intending to do so, raises another important caveat about the foundation premises of his dualism. In his book, highly regarded by many as an important foundation for the new look in dualism, he makes the following remark:

Materialism, I think, must hold that a physical description of the world is a *complete* description of it, that any mental facts are "ontologically dependent" on physical facts in the straightforward sense of following from them by necessity. No identity theorist seems to me to have made a convincing argument against the intuitive view that this is not the case. (p. 155)

The disconcerting and revealing item in this comment is the word "intuitive"! I am convinced that many dualist philosophers, in particular but not exclusively, are subject to the same subtle and ancient intuitive pressure. We all live in a culture that has been dominated throughout human existence by certain ideas: fear of death, the persistent soul, tribalism, heavenly rewards for good behavior during life, and a host of other long and deeply held ideas. Kripke's use of the word *intuitive* suggests that the force of these ancient ideas is still with us. Although, we may have moved onward from explicitly associating our modern philosophies with such ideas, they still implicitly lurk in our shared cultural and individual desires. Similar ideas are fundamental assumptions of whatever enterprise in which we are engaged. Furthermore, they motivate us to "think" along certain lines, lines that can lead to dualisms or monisms depending upon the individual's fundamental assumptions. (Don't forget, making this case for scientific psychology is the ultimate goal of this book. Read on, we are getting close.))

6.3.5 The Dualism of Carrier and Mittelstrass

Another eloquent, spirited, and unusually complete argument for a dualist solution to the mind–body problem was published by Carrier and Mittelstrass (1991). Their version is an interactionist dualism, but one quite a bit more advanced than Descartes' original version. To these philosophers, dualism is definitely not a substance dualism, but rather one that emphasizes the "independence and autonomy of mental states and events" (p. 153), presumably from brain events. Yet, this "independence and autonomy" does not prevent the two sets of events from influencing each other. They summed this up when they stated:

> Mental events like goals and beliefs influence our actions, or so it seems; conversely, the dependence of the psychological condition on neurophysiological and somatic states also suggest a causal relationship. (p. 158)

Carrier and Mittelstrass (1991) further contend that it is up to monism to prove itself. This, they argue, can be accomplished in three ways:

1. The actual reduction of all mental events to their neurophysiological equivalents.
2. The empirical proof of mind–brain equivalence.
3. General principles (i.e., logical analysis). (Paraphrased from p. 283)

However, they argue that the empirical option does not exist and that:

> ... there are no principles that are both logically strong enough to preclude dualism and logically weak or flexible enough to assure that they will not interfere with the progress of science. (p. 283)

Thus, it is only a successful reduction to neurophysiological underpinnings that is left as a possible argument for a monist interpretation of the mind–body problem. Unfortunately for monism, they argue a point (with which I completely agree) that no neuroreduction or eliminative monism is likely. Therefore, Carrier and Mittelstrass contend that we are left in a position in which dualism is proven by exclusion: There are no arguments in favor of the alternative. The residual problem is that there may be other reasons for the absence of reductive explanation rather than different realities. For example, simple complexity or numerousness may block reduction for practical reasons that have nothing to do with a dualistic ontological reality.

It is interesting to note that although these two philosophers and I agree on the irreducibility of mind to neurons, we do so for very different reasons. Carrier and Mittelstrass believe that neuroreduction is unlikely because such reductions have never worked in the past and that current neurophysiology is not moving in the direction that would make us optimistic. My view, on the other hand, is neither historic nor evaluative of current efforts. Rather, it depends on arguments from other fields of science to make the case that reduction is, in principle, impossible, not just unlikely (see Uttal, 1998).

What we are left with, in the context of these rejections of arguments for monism in the Carrier and Mittelstrass theory, is, therefore, merely a default judgment for dualism. That is hardly a compelling proof in any terms.

As they apply their ideas to psychology, they see this situation leading to a tension between psychophysiology and cognitive psychology. Cognitive psychology, they point out, is an alternative strategy for the failed attempt to "explain" cognition in terms of neurons or neural nets. Carrier and Mittelstrass (1991) went on to argue that neither approach, solves the mind–brain problem. In an extraordinary concluding remark, they say:

> A dualistic interpretation alone does not teach us much about the nature of mind; we have not yet understood the psychological mechanisms, if we emphasize the autonomy of mental phenomena. Dualism shares this fate with monism, which also needs to be supplemented by a theory of psychological functions. In fact, the problems in this domain are largely independent of ontological commitments. (pp. 285–286)

These comments suggest that these two scholars, despite their concern with the ontological monism–dualism issue, are not metaphysicians, but are functioning solely as epistemologists. They are not really distinguishing between the two great alternative theories of mind–brain, but really are concerned with the doable, the relevance to modern science, and the emphasis on developing a sound psychology. Although, my final ontological conclusions and theirs are diametrically opposed, all three of us have focused in on one of the great problems faced by a serious psychology— "imaginary neurophysiologies and neuropsychologies." Their final call for a "pragmatic, interactionist dualism" (p. 286) is actually a strategic device rather than a philosophical conclusion. Although Carrier and Mittelstrass define themselves as dualists, and I classify myself as a monist, this apparently is not the essence of our difference. That essence is to be found in their support of a nonreductive, cognitive, mentalist point of view, whereas I stand for a nonreductive behaviorism.

6.3.6 O'Leary-Hawthorne and McDonough's Dualism

Perhaps the most recent modern comprehensive dualist theory has been offered by O'Leary-Hawthorne and McDonough (1998). They initially define their version of property dualism as follows:

The central tenet of property dualism, as we understand it, is that mental properties (or a certain class of them) are not intelligible in terms of the properties of an ideal physics. (p. 350)

That is, mind cannot be understood in, even in the sense of being weakly supervenient on physical terms, in the manner already described. More formally, they define property dualism as being defined by three axioms:

1. The mind is either essential or accidental to the brain.
2. If the mind is essential, then the brain can be heterogeneous (i.e., be simultaneously in two different states).[16]
3. If the mind is accidental, then the brain has a property that is not an intelligible accident.

They then go on to describe how logic can lead one from the axiomatic form of property dualism to a full-blown dualism, by which they presumably mean a substance dualism. Their argument continues on as follows. They consider the following two propositions to be axiomatic. Therefore they must be integrated into the definition of property dualism given by the first three propositions.

4. Brain properties that are accidental are intelligible accidents.
5. The brain cannot be in two states at the same time.

They then argue from 4 and 3:

6. The mind cannot be accidental to the brain.

And then from 5 and 2:

7. The mind is not essential to the brain.

They then go on to conclude from 6, 7, and 1 that:

8. The brain does not "have" mind.
(All eight points are abstracted and translated from O'Leary-Hawthorne & McDonough, 1998, p. 364)

The concluding proposition (8) is interpreted by these authors as asserting a full-blown dualism. Although they do not use the qualifying word "sub-

---

[16]This second axiom seems particularly frail to me.

stance" in defining their dualism, their argument comes very close to it. Their conclusion is that:

> Property dualism [propositions 1–3], when combined with certain *intuitive* axioms [propositions 4–5] leads, we say, to the conclusion that there are nonphysical beings in the sense of beings that are unintelligible by way of the microphysical ground floor (*sic*), these beings enjoying coincidence but not identity with beings that are physical in every sense. (p. 368, italics added)

Without any pejorative intent, it sounds very much like O'Leary and McDonough have defined angels! On a more critical level, their logic is based on "intuitive maxims" or axioms that provide logical coherence, but much like Axiom 2 of Chalmers' logic (see page 228), these intuitions also contain the crux of the conclusion at which they finally arrive.

It is disturbing that intuition plays such a large part in the logical analyses of modern dualist thinking. Some of these intuitive axioms or assumptions, I argue, bear within themselves the logical conclusions at which their proponents ultimately want to arrive. Could it be that the whole logical analysis effort is perverted by subterranean assumptions that are, in fact, postulated in order to guarantee the dualist conclusions? This is a strong criticism, however no one can deny the tremendous importance of the problem at hand. It has come down to us from the most remote portions of human prehistory and it would be surprising if its influence was not operating both consciously and unconsciously to dictate current philosophies of mind. At the very least, cryptic assumptions about the dual nature of reality may be flavoring much of the logic and illogic of the philosophers discussed in this section. At best, they are still considering the monism–dualism issue rather than ignoring it, as psychologists are prone to do.

6.4 A BRIEF TAXONOMY OF DUALISMS

In this chapter, I have reviewed the history and present status of a few nontheological, philosophical dualisms that emphasize a more or less formal logical analysis of the great problem of the relationships between brain and mind. This new trend, growing from the somewhat theologically compromised and prelogical philosophy of René Descartes, deals with the mind–body (or, in current terms, mind–brain) conundrum as a natural problem, not necessarily corroborating or authenticating the corresponding theological issue of the existence or nonexistence of God or the soul. Underneath much of the abstract philosophy, however, lies the cryptic message of all dualisms that do not, at least, reject the possibility of spiritual immortality. How great a role this possible influence plays in the formulation of dualist theories cannot be exactly determined. At the very least, some of the theologically cleansed logical approaches of recent years offer tangential assuaging of the age-old fear of personal extinction. More serious is the possibility that much of philosophical dualism is, once one has peeled away the surface and translated the words, nothing other than a crypto-theology.

My concern in this section, however, is to organize and categorize the various kinds of dualisms that have been encountered in this review. Such a taxonomy cannot be definitive, because any such effort to develop a cladistic arrangement of a set of objects or entities that are defined by multiple dimensions and attributes is bound to leave uncertainty in its wake. Specifically, some of the philosophies of mind that have been produced over the course of these historical discussions have been alternatively presented as examples of either monisms or dualisms or, even in some cases, of both. Nevertheless, some order can be brought to the discussion by presenting what is at least the preliminary taxonomy shown in Table 6.1.

Until this century, substance dualism was the main theme of the philosophies of mind. Although each philosophy differed with regard to the degree of causal relation between the mental and physical domains, each adhered to the main metaphysical premise of dualism, namely, that the mind and the brain are manifestations of separate levels of reality. This separation is expressed in terms of their fundamental nature and not just in terms of the operations or language that must be used to examine each. In addition to the consistency with classic theological thinking that such a perspective afforded, substance dualisms also reflected the age-old idea that mental and physical processes operate at two different levels of reality and were not bound by the same laws. The basic problem facing substance dualism was to account for the apparent correspondences or interactions between the two different domains and the manner in which they interacted. Noninteractionism carries this idea to its extreme, proposing that any correspondences between the mental and physical substances are illusory and that, in fact, they do not interact in any manner.

TABLE 6.1
A Brief Taxonomy of Dualisms

Substance Dualisms:
    Non-Interactionism
    Interactionism
    Parallelism:
        Occasionalism
        Preestablished Harmony
Property Dualisms:
    Epiphenomenalism
    Emergent or supervenient dualism:
        Naturalistic Dualism

Most modern philosophical approaches to the mind–brain problem, on the other hand, are characterized as property dualisms: They look upon the relationship between mental and neural activity (the latter having replaced less specific anatomical associations) as being driven by the need to determine how the observed coordinated features, measurements, or properties of mind and brain can be explained. The degree of the supervenience (in several different forms) of mind on brain activity has become a central core of modern philosophical investigation; logic (or as it is otherwise known—conceptual analysis) has become the methodology of choice.

Epiphenomenalism, a term that was arguably introduced by Thomas Huxley (1825–1895), is the theory that mental processes cannot and do not have any interactive influence on the operation of physical material, specifically the brain. Epiphenomenalism is considered by some to be an early form of property dualism implying a total, in principle, inability for the mind to exert any influence on brain neurophysiology even though mind may properly be considered to be a direct product or function of the brain.

In terms of this perspective, epiphenomenalism can be best understood as a kind of monism. From other points of view, epiphenomenalism is nothing more than a statement that the emerging properties of a physical entity cannot feed back on that entity because they are of two kinds of reality. From this perspective, epiphenomenalism appears to be a kind of dualism. Certainly, there is an enormous amount of ambiguity in the definition of this term—as there is for almost all of the other terms used to characterize the nature of mind. Because the various interpretations of epiphenomenalism can place it in either the monist or dualist categories, I enter it in both of the minitaxonomies presented in Table 6.1 (dualisms) and Table 6.2 (monisms).

No brief taxonomy, for that matter, can begin to do justice to the many different dualist theories that have been proposed over the years. I have only touched some of the most notable. Some are cryptic, some border on the incomprehensible, some are obviously vestiges of theological times, and some are just downright loony. The reason this should be the case is simple: Most people alive today are believers in (or at least hopeful for) some kind of mental immortality—the continuity of their own consciousness. There is an enormous amount of peace and solace in believing that the inevitable is not quite as definite as a deteriorating corpse suggests. In the absence of any credible explanation of how mind can be produced by brain, it is all too easy to fall back on mysterious, even magical, dualist explanations that help us to confront the potential loss of personal identity. Moderated, as they are by a kind of formal logic and by existing and potential failures of neuroscientific progress, modern dualisms, although still polluted by ill-defined axioms or circular reasoning, provide a means of buttressing the hope of persisting human consciousness beyond death.

6.5   A BRIEF TAXONOMY OF MATERIALIST MONISMS

As I have noted several times, this is a book mainly aimed at the examination of various forms of dualism. It is not my intent to delve deeper into the arguments against dualism or those supporting my own personal philosophy—a monism that can be as best by the phrase "materialism without reductionism" (see page 246 for a discussion of this point of view). In other words, I am comfortable accepting an ontological materialism (mind is the product of the brain—nothing more and nothing less) and an epistemological dualism that asserts that for both practical and "in principle" reasons, there is no way to explain how mind is produced by the brain. Therefore, we must be content to live with both kinds of measures. Ontological monism implies that the fundamental nature of everything (including consciousness as a process or property) can be accounted for, *in principle*, in the language, terms, and measurements of the material world. Epistemological dualism implies there are fundamental and perhaps intractable problems with accessibility and both cognitive analysis and neurophysiological reduction. Therefore, the hoped for "accounts" of how mind emerges from brain may not be forthcoming even if one is actually the product of the other.

Although my purpose in this chapter is to identify the principal tenets and principles proposed by the major figures in the philosophy of mind who have offered dualist theories, the story told would be incomplete if it did not at least mention the contributions of the many philosophers who have built what they are convinced are internally consistent monist theories of mind.[17] Therefore, I now present a brief discussion of the materialist—monist point of view. In brief, a material monism gives priority to the material objects of our life and proposes that, in principle if not in practice, all phenomena of the mind or the soul are explicable in terms of the nature of that physical material and the processes that material undergoes. It is monist in the sense that it argues there is only one kind of reality. In applying such thinking to everyday life, material monism obviously denies any kind of immortality and, thus, runs into substantial conflict with many popular worldviews. By its emphasis on natural objects and events, it also abjures the existence of anything supernatural.[18]

---

[17]For those who may wish to delve deeper into the various kinds of monisms, I found the analysis offered by Carrier and Mittelstrass (1991) in their defense of their version of dualism to be especially lucid and helpful. I also have previously discussed monist theories in greater detail than presented here in Uttal (1978) and plan to discuss them further in a new book on neuroscientific theories of the mind, now in progress.

[18]It would be wonderful if the world were this consistent and neat. Unfortunately, many of our fellows who live quite comfortably with materialisms in some aspects of their life appeal with minimum difficulty to what appear to be internally inconsistent supernatural concepts in others.

As far as the mind–brain issue is concerned, monists would argue that all thoughts, experiences, phenomena, and forms of consciousness are simply the result of functions carried out by the material brain. Supervenience, emergence, and property dualisms, in general, equivocate on this matter by suggesting that there are stages, levels, or degrees of the association. To the committed monist, mind (otherwise known as soul or consciousness) is a brain process, not unlike the relationship between a wheel and its rotation.

This chapter was introduced by presenting a tabulation of the traditional arguments for dualism originally proposed by Bunge (1980), a deeply committed identity (monist) philosopher. It would be helpful at this point to list his counterarguments; those traditional views that suggest material monisms are more appropriate descriptions of reality than are dualisms. Bunge's tabulation of the traditional criticisms made against dualism may be interpreted as arguments for monisms and include:

1. Dualism is fuzzy.
2. Dualism detaches properties and events from things.
3. Dualism violates conservation of energy.
4. Dualism refuses to acknowledge the evidence for the molecular and cellular roots of mental abilities and disorders.
5. Dualism is consistent with creationism, not with evolutionism.
6. Dualism cannot explain mental disease except as demonic possession or as an escape of the mind from the body.
7. Dualism is at best barren, at worst obstructive.
8. Dualism refuses to answer the six W's of the science of the mind. [What or how, where, when, whence, whither, and why.]
9. Dualism is not a scientific theory but an ideological tenet.
10. Dualism is inconsistent with the ontology of science.
(Bunge, 1980, pp. 16–20)

To organize the following discussions, consider the taxonomy in Table 6.2, a parallel to the Brief Taxonomy of Dualisms presented in Table 6.1.

Immaterial monisms are very much out of date. Their current interest is largely historical. Idealisms of this kind proposed that although there was only one kind of reality, that reality was the mental one rather than the physical one. Proposed in its classic form by Bishop George Berkeley (1685–1753), idealism denied the existence of matter until it was perceived by a human observer and, thus, gave ontological priority to ideas rather than things.

All of the rest of monist theories are materialist. For example, although it is not completely juxtopositionable with materialism, *psychophysical behav-*

TABLE 6.2
A Brief Taxonomy of Materialist Monisms

Immaterialist Monisms—Idealism
Materialist Monisms
  Psychophysical Behaviorism
  Dispositional Monism
  Functionalism
  Emergentism
  Epiphenomenalism
  Psychosomaticism
  Identity Theory
    Token Identity
    Type Identity
    Double Aspect Theory
  Neutral Monism
  Radical (Eliminative) Identity

---

iorism argues that the mind–brain problem cannot be directly studied because of the inaccessibility of the mental processes. Therefore, mental processes may exist, but all that we can do, even in a perfect world, is to study the intrapersonally available and observable behavior of the subjects in our experiments. Typically, this antireductionist approach is bound closely to the idea that the mind is an inaccessible (but real) outcome of brain activity (a monist tenet). It is further argued that because of this inaccessibility it should be ignored in our studies of human behavior. Atypically, the very existence of consciousness is sometimes denied, but this is an anomaly and is surprisingly difficult to identify in the work of any currently active psychologist or philosopher.

Ryle's (1949) *dispositional monism* proposed a monist theory that has many similarities to modern behaviorism. Ryle does not reject the existence of mind any more than did behaviorists such as Skinner. Rather, he argued that mental activity is accessible to us only in terms of observable behavior. At best, Ryle argued that it is only the dispositions of mind (or contingencies as Skinner would have called them) that can be measured. To go any further and attempt to determine the nature of mental processes can only lead us to the search for a "ghost in the machine." Ryle's point of view was also obviously closely related to the operational or positivist view of many of those who preceded him.

Functionalism, as a monist philosophy, is also closely related to behaviorism and takes this idea a step further by describing mental activity as utilitarian, although inaccessibly present. That is, functionalists argue we should study the value that "mind" may have in relating sensory information and behavioral responses. They join with behaviorists in ignoring any attack on the question of how mind is actually produced by brain activity.

Epiphenomenalism, which has been introduced in earlier discussions in this chapter, is difficult to classify. Therefore, as noted earlier, I have included it in both dualist and monist categories. On this theory, although mind is a functional product of the brain, it can have no direct causal link on the brain–body. Our thoughts, therefore, are not capable of producing changes in our body or external behavior. They simply float passively along reflecting the processes going on in the nervous system. Therefore, if the applicable criteria were framed in terms of potential influential interactions, epiphenomenalism would have to be considered to be a dualism. To the contrary, if ones criterion is the origin of the mind and the assumption is accepted that it arises as a function or property of the material structure of the brain, it might better be classified as a monism. Implicit in both versions of epiphenomenalism is the rejection of free will and self-determination. Mind cannot affect matter; therefore our ethical principles, our personal needs, or other similar criteria cannot affect our behavior. It is determined by exogenous stimuli and internal physiological states.

The converse theory, *psychosomaticism* (if one wishes to dignify with such a ponderous title what has become another example of folk psychology) is, arguably, also a material monism; it does not necessarily deny the production of consciousness by brain activity any more than does epiphenomenalism. However, contrary to epiphenomenalism, psychosomatic theory does strongly support the efficacy of "mind over matter." It thus incorporates at least the possibility of free will and free choice, and, in its most extravagant form, the ability of one's convictions, thoughts, or "prayers" to cure one's diseases. This tight causal link between mind and brain expressed by psychosomaticism suggests that it is slightly more materialist than is epiphenomenalism.

Emergentism is another idea that may or may not be considered to be an example of a materialist philosophy. Emergent theorists such as Broad (1925) proposed that mental processes are produced by brain activity whose complexity is so great that we cannot understand this wonderful process. However, contrary to the epiphenomenal position, once produced, this emergent mental activity is capable of influencing the brain states whence it came. The ambiguous nature of emergence regarding its position on the materialism or dualism axis is based on the fact that Broad and others of his philosophical bent seem to suggest that a new form of reality, not accountable to the usual physical laws, must be invoked to explain mind. On the other hand, mind to the emergentists is clearly a brain function. The result is that this point of view can be characterized, like epiphenomenalism, as either a monism or a dualism depending on the proclivities of the particular theorist.

The *identity theories* share the common assumption that brain and mind are not just equivalent to each other but are actually ontologically identical to each other except, perhaps, in the way in which they are measured. Mental experiences are not just the product of brain states; they *are* brain states according to the identity theorists! Feigl (1960) makes the formal case for identity theorists as follows:

> Certain neurophysical [*sic*] terms denote (refer to) the very same events that are also denoted (referred to) by certain phenomenal terms. The identification of the objects of this twofold reference is of course logically contingent, although it constitutes a very fundamental feature of our world as we have come to conceive it in the modern scientific outlook. Using Frege's distinction between *Sinn* ("meaning," "sense," "intention") and *Bedeutung* ("referent," "denotatum," "extension") we may say that the neurophysiological terms and the corresponding phenomenal terms, though widely differing in sense, and hence in the modes of confirmation of statements containing them, do have identical referents. (p. 38)

Other modern philosophers who have been closely associated with identity theories are Place (1956), Smart (1959), Armstrong (1962, 1968), Lewis (1965), Rorty (1965), and Hill (1991). Armstrong, in particular, is considered to be the most radical of the identity theorist by virtue of his early conclusion that it was not just certain experiences, but each and every mental activity is identical to a corresponding brain state. Prior to this strong version, some of his identity theoretical predecessors had argued that only certain elements of consciousness could be identified with brain states.

Needless to say, criticism of identity theory still abounds. A partial list the most prominent critics in recent years would include Kim (1966), Abelson (1970), and Pucetti (1978). It appears, however, that general discussions like their early anti-identity critiques have, in large part, been replaced by a more detailed consideration of the significance of type and token identity theories, respectively.

As shown in the longer discussion of dualisms earlier in this chapter, there is a major dichotomy within the dualist ranks; theories can be considered to be examples of either substance or property dualisms. A similar dichotomy can be discerned in current monist thinking. The two categories that have come into prominence in recent years are referred to as *token materialism* and *type materialism*, respectively.

The former approach, token materialism, argues that each particular mental event has a corresponding neural state. Token identity requires a tight relationship between mind and brain in particular cases but does not demand there be a general relationship between all forms of mental and brain states. Token identity is a statement of particular instances: Mental state A at time T is identical with some brain state B existing at that same time T. By virtue of its tight relationship between specific mental and physical instances, it is often characterized as instantiating the hope of neuro-reductionism should we ever be able to overcome the technical obstacles.

Token materialism, however, does not deny the possibility that there may be multiple realizations: A particular mental state might be explicable or represented (in some ideal world) in terms of several different neural states. In other words, knowledge of a given mental state does not exclusively designate a particular neural state because many neural states can conceivably produce the same mental state. A may be equivalent to B at one time T; however, at some other time T and in some other instance, brain state C may also produce the very same mental state A (or something that is indistinguishable from A). Nevertheless, given tools of sufficient power (ignoring for the moment whether they are ultimately achievable) token materialism does not deny that we should be able to determine which alternative brain state could be accounting for A.

Type identity theory, to the contrary, proposes a much more general and "softer" relationship between mental and brain states. In general, type theorists argue, if there is some "type" of mental state, it is only equivalent to some "type" of mental state. Reductionism would be far more difficult to achieve if type materialism obtained, simply because there would be no specific target brain state to be identified with a particular mental state.

Finally, a few comments are appropriate concerning some of the more esoteric of the monist theories. *Double aspect theory,* another kind of identity theory previously mentioned, suggests that there is but one reality but we have different means of looking at it. Because of this double aspect or viewpoint, what is one reality simply appears to have two different realities. However, this is but an illusion based on the necessity to apply two different sets of measurements to measure two different properties of one underlying reality. That one reality is typically assumed to be a material one (see page 242). Spinoza's argument was that since the measuring instruments are so different, the (in fact) ontologically monist world would prohibit any reduction of mental measurements to material measurements.

Neutral monism also argues that there is a single kind of reality that is seen in different modes (mental and material) by an observer. However, neither one of these modes is fundamental. Instead, this theory proposes that there another kind of reality that accounts for both modes consisting of an ill-defined "stuff" that is neither mental nor physical. A tenet of neutral monism is, since this "stuff" is so elusive, reduction of the mental to neural is unlikely to be achieved. Neutral monism is associated with some surprising names—William James (1842–1910) and Bertrand Russell (1872–1970).

Finally in this tabulation of monist solutions to the mind–brain problem, I would like to contrast two monist theories with quite opposite implications. On the one hand are the *eliminative reductionists*. This point of view

argues that everything mental is so totally neural that all psychological observations, indeed all mental concepts, will ultimately be reduced to neurophysiological concepts, terms, and measurements. The works of Rorty
(1970) and Churchland (1981) are most notable in this regard. What we call
psychology from their viewpoint is nothing other than a set of "folk" ideas
that are utilized because there are a "few" remaining problems to the production of such a pure, and fully explanatory, form of neuroreductionism.

On the other side of the coin, however, is the equally extreme, but antithetical monist approach championed by Davidson (1970). He argued from
very similar materialist premises that there can be "no strict psychophysical laws" (i.e., reductionism from the mental to the neural is not possible).
Here, in a pure form, is presented the idea of materialism without reductionism, a view also proposed by Boyd (1980). I have already indicated how
comfortable I am with this point of view.

The fascinating thing about these two positions—eliminative reductionism and materialism without reductionism—is how they have come to exactly antithetical conclusions based on what are essentially the same data.
This controversy, in particular, speaks to the seemingly intractable problem of the relation between the mind and the brain and the limited power of
both empirical research and logical analysis to solve it.

6.6 INTERIM CONCLUSION

In this chapter I have reviewed the history and present status of modern
philosophical theories of the relation between the mind and the brain—the
modern version of the classic soul–body problem. It is clear that the conundrum revolving around the origins of the mind/spirit/soul are still with us.
Perhaps no other issue in science, history, or theology has so captured the
attention of virtually every individual who has ever lived. It also seems
clear that the evolutionary process that was evident in earlier chapters still
permeates modern scientific and theological discourses. As different as
they may be from earlier attempts to crack this "world knot" (an expression
attributed to Arthur Schopenhauer, 1788–1860), the "new" philosophical
studies of mind have their roots embedded in earlier times as much as any
of the preceding intellectual attacks on this challenging problem. Without
stretching the point too much, 20th-century philosophy of mind studies can
be considered to be the next evolutionary step in this age-old stream of in-

quiry. The techniques, languages, and emphases may have changed, but
the basic problem remains along with all its challenges, difficulties, and obstacles to solution.

An excellent summary of distinctions between philosophical theories,
isms, and opinions and proposed answers to questions relating to brain–

body and mind–consciousness was presented by van Gelder (1998). I found
his summary, which is reproduced in Table 6.3, to be an excellent means of
navigating among the many monist and dualist theories that are mentioned
in this chapter. In constructing this table, van Gelder suggested that there
are two principle dimensions along which the mind–brain problem can be
conceptualized. The first, represented along the vertical axis, is a sampling
of the proposed ways in which the mental and the physical have been related by philosophers. The components on this axis range from the extremes of total ontological identity to the classic dualist parallelism of
Leibniz. This table also makes it clear that not all of the ideas listed here are
mutually exclusive. That is, it is possible to simultaneously accept more
than one of these types of mind–brain relationships in the formulation of
one point of view.

The horizontal axis on van Gelder's table lists summaries of some of the
theoretical positions reviewed in this chapter. These theories are catego-
rized in terms of which of the various relationships (denoted on the vertical
axis) are subsumed within the respective philosophical stance. This chart
brings a good deal of order to the verbal discussions typically encountered
in this field. The most important contribution is that it orders the theories
(ranging from van Gelder's "baseline dualism" to his "baseline physicalism") in terms of a specific set of mental–physical features. The most extreme dualisms can be seen to reject all interactive relations especially including any that can be considered causal; the most extreme material
monisms accepting all kinds of interactions including the identity of mind
and brain. As one moves from the extremities of dualism to those of
physicalism, more and more of the proposed relationships are incorporated into the theories.

There are two important contributions in van Gelder's table. First, it
overcomes the classificatory difficulty of trying to forcibly fit the various
theories in the constraining terms of a simple dichotomy anchored at one
end by material monism and at the other by dualism. The second contribution is that it provides a scale, almost a quantifiable dimension, along which
the various theories can be ordered. The theories are, therefore, laid out on
a continuum representing a much higher resolution spectrum of these theories than is presented elsewhere.

6.6.1 New Trends in a Continuing Evolutionary Process

Two new trends can be discerned in the writings of modern philosophers of
mind that differ in significant ways from their predecessors. The first trend
results from an effort, either intentional or in response to where their logic
may have led their originators, to detheologize the discussion. The "G"

TABLE 6.3
Van Gelder's (1998) Tabulation of the Various Theoretical
Positions Concerning the Mind–Brain Controversy

Relation of Mental to Physical:	Baseline Dualism/Idealism (inc. Parallelism)	Causal Dualism (inc. "Cartesian" Dualism, Epiphenomenalism, Occasionalism)	Weak Supervenience	Non-Reductive Physicalism (inc. Emergentism, Anomalous Monism, Functionalism, Biological Naturalism)	Baseline Physicalism (inc. Australian Materialism, Behaviorism, Neuroscientific Eliminativism)
Identity	No	No	No	Yes	Yes
Reduction	No	No	No	No	Yes
Realization (Constitution)	No	No	Yes	Yes	Yes
Supervenience	No	No	Yes	Yes	Yes
Causal Interaction	No	Yes	Yes	Yes	Yes

word appears less and less frequently in the literature and, when it does, it is not so much an affirmation of the reality of God as it is a literary metaphor useful in describing how something might have happened or as a literary artifice to instantiate, embody, or to personalize certain unknown forces. Discussions of heaven and hell are gone; the immortality of the soul or consciousness is rarely discussed explicitly. In their place, there is an almost antiseptic consideration of relationships, causal forces, and logical outcomes.

The second great trend in modern arguments concerning the mind–brain problem highlighted in this chapter is the increasing effort to use formal logic to prove that mental and material states (as they are now called) do or do not represent two different kinds of reality. Throughout the latter parts of this chapter, we see repeated attempts to prove that which cannot be observed can be studied by hypothesizing axiomatic statements and then coursing through the logical sequence to prove inevitable and valid conclusions.[19] In many cases, I have argued that these logical exercises are seriously flawed, sometimes by the fragility of some of their initial axioms, sometimes by leaps of logic that are unjustified, and sometimes because, on close examination, they turn out to be truisms circling from premises to conclusions that are essentially equivalent.

The strategy of using logic as opposed to empirical evidence is a noble one and is often necessitated in situations in which evidence is not available. As I remarked earlier, however, logic is not infallible and there are many problems in applying it. For example, it is impossible to prove the nonexistence of the logically possible or, even worse, improbable entities that are just barely "conceivable." It is in such cases that the "door" must be opened to prove that the "monster in the closet" is not there. However, in situations in which the entities are purported to be invisible, inaudible, and intangible, even an open door may not satisfy those who assert their existence. Unfortunately, both angels and consciousness fall into the category of the inaccessible and empirically irrefutable. The usual rules of scientific evidence and proof are extremely difficult, if not impossible, to apply to such elusive concepts.

Another important trend in the modern studies of philosophy of mind is the emphasis on an excruciatingly fine definition of the technical vocabulary and equally arcane arguments over logical methodology. A considerable portion of current controversy is concerned with the precise definition of, for example, "token and type identity theories" and the significance of the arcane term *subservience* and their respective implications for mind–brain ontology.

---

[19] It should be pointed out that this is not only a dualist strategy but is also used by modern monist philosophers.

Much of this controversy is pointless and an example of what ethologists previous called "displacement activity"—attacks on irrelevant, but vulnerable, problems when the relevant ones are not accessible or tractable. In other instances, arguments ensue on the basis of Gedanken experiments that can never be executed and on imputed results that can never actually be obtained.

For example, in one bitterly contested battle, the controversy is based on the arguably fallacious assumption that a particular kind of chemical system is necessary for mental states to occur. One side of this argument argues that we must have the sodium-potassium-chloride chemistry known to operate in earthly neurons for consciousness to exist. However, an alternative view is that it is not the chemistry of the neurons that is important in their production of mind, but rather their informational organization. The critical Gedanken experiment in this case assumes that this argument could be resolved if we built a silicon-based brain that exhibited consciousness. However, it does not seem possible that this great analog could be constructed. Even if it could be, there is a powerful argument that we would no more be able to determine if it was conscious than we can answer this question for a mouse or a human. If this is the situation, then any hypothetical arguments pro or con regarding the need for a particular biochemistry as a prerequisite for consciousness are meaningless.

The main barrier faced by identity theorists in empirically proving their argument, however, is an eminently practical one: the combinatorial barrier produced by simple numerousness. Because of the complexities of the brain states and the sheer numbers of neurons involved in the production of mental states, and because of the inaccessibility of those mental states, the key experiment that needs to be done can never, in all likelihood, ever be carried out. Thus, the kind of empirical "proof" needed to support the basic axiom of mind–brain identity is also not likely to be forthcoming. The door, therefore, is opened to alternative (i.e., dualist) hypotheses that do not have the intrinsic simplicity of monist theories. Monism requires only one kind of reality and does not need to invoke invisible supernatural entities (for which there is not a modicum of observational evidence) to provide a complete explanation of that portion of the natural world we call psychological.

Once the door is open even slightly to dualist thinking (because of the intractability of proving the monist position), the personal awareness each of us has of our own minds is so obvious and compelling that it becomes extremely difficult to deny its separate reality. In the absence of an empirical solution to the mind–brain problem, philosophers of mind are left with only a logical, rather than an experimental, strategy to solve this grand problem. As flawless as the logical techniques may be, they depend entirely on the validity of their initial assumptions and axioms and the robustness of their logical procedures. It is in the former context, as we have seen, that the logical approach to the solution of the mind–brain problem fails most completely: Intuitive, but fundamentally incorrect assumptions can often lead to nonsensical conclusions.

Sometimes it seems that everything is controversial and uncertain in the philosophy of mind. Even this newest trend to use formal logical techniques has run into a storm of controversy. Block and Stalnaker (1999), for example, have argued that there can be no conceptual analysis of mental processes in terms of the physical underpinnings. They wrote:

Some concepts are analyzable functionally, or in terms of the concepts of physics. Perhaps even some mental concepts can be given functional or physical analyses. However, consciousness is not one of these analyzable concepts. Further, this nonanalyzability is no accident; any putative functional of physical analysis would leave out the fundamental nature of consciousness. (p. 1)

In an earlier paper, Jackson (1994) makes the opposite case:

... it is the very business of conceptual analysis to address which matters framed in terms of one set of terms and concepts are made true by which matters framed in a different sets of terms and concepts.

What do we do in a situation in which very bright people argue not only both sides of a controversy but also the optimum strategies that might be used to resolve it? One tack is to ask if the problem itself is solvable. McGinn (1989), for example, asked just such a rhetorical question that really has to be deeply considered in light of the many uncertainties and ambiguities of the contending philosophies considered in this chapter. Can we solve the mind–body problem? His answer, unfortunately, is "No and Yes" (p. 366) but the "No" is based on the idea that:

We constitutionally lack the concept-forming capacity to encompass all possible types of conscious state, and this obstructs our path to a general solution to the mind–body problem. (p. 356)

In other words, it is our cognitive inability to solve this problem on which the insolubility is based. McGinn goes on to argue:

... there is nothing inherently eerie or bizarre about this embodiment. (p. 366)

McGinn's rhetorical question, regardless of how it ultimately will be answered, is extremely important in summing up the ideas in this chapter.

There are several important points to be made with regard to it. First, although his argument against the answerability of the mind–brain problem is based on what he presumes to be our cognitive limitations, there may be a much more practical constraint on answering the mind–brain question—the nature of problem itself. Even if we are momentarily challenged by the hypothetical overburdening of our mind's powers, there still remains at least the hope for some mechanical tool (such as a future super-duper computer) that can provide the power necessary to answer the question—to unravel this "world knot." This "hope" is formalized within the context of the eliminative philosophical position that all mental processes can and will ultimately be relegated to neural explanations (Churchland, 1981; Rorty, 1970).

However, there is another way to look at the situation that suggests no future computational tool, however powerful, will ever be able to provide an answer to an alternative formulation of the mind–brain problem: How can macroscopic mind emerge from the action of an array of microscopic neurons? The obstacle in this case is the combinatorial complexity that makes the mind–brain problem into an NP complete problem (i.e., one that is totally intractable to solution within any finite period of time). The "combinatorial explosion" difficulty is the basis of the argument made by Bremermann (1977), among many others, against the solvability of problems in one subfield of artificial intelligence—form recognition. The gist of what he has to say is that problems of this kind are too complex and involve so many interactions and parts that their solution becomes impossible to even the most powerful computer,[20] not just those that are conceivable, but to all possible ones. It is not just a limitation of some aspect of our poor cognitive powers; rather, it is the intrinsic combinatorial complexity of the involved neural networks that will prevent us from ever understanding the details of how mental processes result from brain activity at the level they are most likely to be found—the interactions of huge numbers of neurons.

Regardless of the particular reasons that the problem is either just difficult or actually insoluble, perhaps its incomprehensible nature is such that it drives philosophers and others to what are sometimes such obtuse and murky logical constructions and intuitive leaps. Throughout this chapter, I

---

[20] It is interesting to note that what computers cannot do is often accomplished with great ease by humans. This is a natural or existence proof that the problem can be solved. However, it may be "solved" only in the sense that the task is actually carried out. The implications of this are that we may be able to conceive and grow a problem-solving "computer" but still have the problem remain analytically intractable. The distinction may be between an analog replicate and analytic solvability. That such an organic system may solve a problem is by no means a definitive argument that it can be unraveled and solved by a computer. Readers interested in this point of view should read the article by Casti (1996).

have presented arguments that seem to me, to put it mildly, to be fanciful. Unexecutable Gedanken experiments, postulation of possible (though totally unobservable) alternative universes, "intuitive axioms," wishful thinking, begged questions, and circular reasoning, and many other illogical strategies are repeatedly invoked. Many of the well-structured techniques that both science and logic have developed over the past few centuries to consider evidence seem to be ignored in favor of what is almost another kind of magical thinking.

In seeking an answer to the question of why such a situation should have developed in our modern secular philosophy, we are led back to reconsider some of the same causal forces that impelled the kind of religious thinking that was discussed in earlier chapters. That is, an a priori commitment to religious dualisms based on our old friend, fear of death. However they may be clothed in logical arguments and however devoid of words such as "God," many of the dualist discussions encountered here appear to invoke implausible processes that are very difficult to operationally distinguish from the overtly supernatural entities discussed in previous chapters. In this regard and to an unknown degree, modern philosophy can be seen to be continuous with older religious ideas. It differs in one way: Immortality and God are eschewed. It is alike in another: Dualism remains a topic of deep concern. Modern "physicophilic" psychology, as we see in the next chapter, in large part no longer even considers the monism–dualism issue to be worthy of discussion.

In conclusion, however, it must be appreciated that all of these explanations for the persistence of dualist thinking are secondary. The primary reason that dualism survives is that *we still have no idea how mental phenomena arise out of the microproperties of neuronal interaction and no real hope that such wisdom is on the horizon.* For all of the bluster and "logic" of philosophers on one side or the other of the monism–dualism question, for all of the words that have been spent on the issue, nothing would matter if an empirically sustainable theory for the production of the mind came into being. Unfortunately, as we see, there are substantial obstacles to believing that such a material neuroreductionism is likely or even possible. In such a situation, the fallback strategy is to use secondary criteria (e.g., Occam's Razor or the need to assuage the fear of death) to determine one's personal answer to what is arguably the greatest problem in human history. Unfortunately, these criteria do not necessarily lead us to an answer either and may, for the specific case of mind–brain relations, be wildly misleading.

There are many theoretical expressions and many kinds of belief structures that arise out of this fundamental lack of knowledge. For example, proponents of the concept of strong Artificial Intelligence (AI) assume that if a supercomputer could be constructed with the same design details found in the human brain, then that computer would exhibit the same con-

[handwritten: = Roth's Conc!]

scious properties as the organic system it emulates. Unfortunately, all theories of this genre that have yet been forthcoming are, at best, toy problems that do not come close to simulating the brain's complexity or even some of its relatively simple properties. When they do approximate some human cognitive process, it is usually on the basis of a computational algorithm that few would contend is the same as that used by the organic system.[21]

6.6.2 A Few Final Thoughts

[handwritten: Conc!]

This brief review of current philosophical thinking leaves me, and I hope also my readers, with a substantial feeling of doubt that much progress has been made in dealing with the mind–brain issue by philosophers despite the formal logical procedures that have been applied to it. The current monism–dualism controversy has replaced divine inspiration and biblical exegesis with logical "proofs" that depend on premises that are as unsubstantiated as any from the theological domain. Indeed, after studying this material, I have begun to wonder just how different these new logical philosophies are from their predecessors. The vocabulary is certainly different. However, there is still evidence that down at the very foundation of this new technical philosophical approach lies a network of a priori assumptions that are not too different from the statements of beliefs offered by their more theologically oriented predecessors. Others sense this same degree of confusion and [theoretical] disagreement.

It is particularly valuable when this criticism comes from the inside, from among members of the philosophy of mind community themselves. (I am not a card holding member of this community, but rather just a psychologist who seeks insights into the issues that plague our science and the foundation assumptions that guide it.) The insight of one philosopher (Searle, 1992) is, therefore, of special interest and credibility. Although he and I disagree on the suitability of consciousness as a research topic (he says yes; I argue that consciousness cannot be studied because of its intrinsic inaccessibility and elusive definability) Searle put the problem in a nutshell when he stated:

> In spite of our modern arrogance about how much we know, in spite of the assurance and the universality of our science, where the mind is concerned we

---

[21]All too often, a new computer substitute for some cognitive process is highly touted and then, on testing found to be a dismal failure. One of the clearest examples of this hype is the recent application of a "face recognition" technique for use in identifying people at airports (Palm Beach International) and on city streets (Tampa, Florida). The results of these tests were "flawed" and "dismal." Many studies in robotic systems are also of limited value when autonomous control is utilized. It is only when one considers the actual details of computer applications in more complex tasks than simple clerical work, that the modest progress made in the field of AI can be appreciated.

are characteristically confused and in disagreement. Like the proverbial blind men and the elephant, we grasp onto some alleged feature and pronounce it the essence of the mental. . . . Just as bad, we let our research methods dictate the subject matter, rather than the converse. (p. 247)

Searle is speaking in this context as a philosopher, and I believe that the methodology with which he is uncomfortable is the kind of logical analysis that has characterized so much of the modern work on conceptual analysis discussed in this chapter. It is easy to understand his frustration as one reviews the complex literature. Another similar view of the impotency of philosophy has been expressed by van Gelder (1998):

Concepts and arguments are subject to ever more subtle refinements, expressed in arcane technical vocabularies drowning in neologisms and subscripts. Sharp minds are tied up in baroque dialectics rivaling the achievements of medieval or Talmudic debates. Unfortunately, little by way of deep new understanding results from all this. (p. 80)

He then goes on to conclude:

The prospect of a full science of the mind is as remote as it is appealing. (p. 96)

One must then ask a number of important related questions for scientific psychology. These include: Has psychology fallen victim to some of the same problems that bedevil philosophy? Are many of the ostensibly objective and logical arguments used in the development of psychological theories driven by a cryptic adherence to vestigial kinds of theological (supernatural) beliefs? Must psychology, to at least some degree, also have to be considered to be another step in the evolutionary chain described so far in this book? If so, are there any constraints that could help to alert theoretical psychologists and prevent the most hardnosed versions of scientific psychology from falling victim to this same kind of cryptic logical errors or residual supernatural pressures? These and related questions are the topics of the next chapter.

7

Dualism and Psychology

7.1 THE CRYPTIC ASSUMPTIONS OF MODERN PSYCHOLOGY

The central idea that I stress in this book is both familiar and ignored. Our theories and explanations of ourselves and the world in which we are embedded are, in large part, based on deep-seated assumptions. Most of these assumptions go unrecognized or unspoken as we rush through the mechanical details of our empirical studies. This is not a radical idea; Gleiser (2002) makes a similar argument for cosmology and other scholars (e.g., Hanson, 1958) have argued extensively that all facets of science are subject to this same kind of pressure. The particular argument I present in this chapter is that scientific psychology is likewise impelled in specific directions by long lasting and deeply held beliefs about the nature of the human mind–spirit–soul separate from that of the brain–body.

It does not take too long, once one has listened to the presentations at a meeting of cognitive psychologists to appreciate that all the methods, results, and conclusions of a typical report gloss over what must be powerful, but unexpressed and internalized axioms and assumptions. For example, models and theories abound assuming the analyzability of cognitive functions into modular bits and pieces; rarely are the still unanswered questions of analyzability or accessibility dealt with explicitly. Instead, the axiomatic assumptions instantiated in their acceptance are relegated to another arena. "Oh, let's not deal with that issue, that is a matter of philosophy and we are not concerned with it here," is an oftenheard comment.

The result of these unspoken assumptions, however, on our day-to-day activities is profound for no more complex reason than the fact that they are the major determinants of the psychological *Zeitgeist.* This wonderful old word alludes to the generally accepted corpus of ideas of prominence at a particular time and place. Unfortunately, as we have seen throughout the history of psychology, shifts in the momentary Zeitgeist are more likely to occur as a result of theoretical fatigue than to careful scrutiny of the ideas themselves or to an empirical revolution (Kuhn, 1962) arising from an unexpected discovery. For many decades, the foundation assumptions of behaviorism (reacting against the mentalist ones of structural and functional psychology as well as against introspection and the accessibility of consciousness) defined the Zeitgeist. In more recent times, mentalist assumptions have again reigned supreme as another form of mentalism—cognitive psychology—has held the stage. Nowadays, there is considerably greater acceptance of the idea that the study of the elusive entity called consciousness may be a realistic enterprise.

It is hard to account for the change from behaviorism to cognitivism, other than in terms of newly emerging metaphors (the computer) and a return to more mentalist versions of explanatory theories. As the Zeitgeist changed, so too did the axiomatic structure of psychology, albeit almost imperceptibly. Lurking just below the surface has been the residual attachment to 'mind' as an entity that can be separated from the brain in principle as well as in empirical practice. The powerful and compelling urge to do so, I now argue, is based at the most distant past, on the fear of loss of personal identity—the fear of death itself—and its gradual evolution into a cryptic form of dualism. In other words, although unexpressed, many theological, religious, and philosophical ideas from our collective past have influenced and continue to influence current psychological theory. Specifically, modern mentalisms like cognitive psychology deal with the mind in a way that is all-too-close to the way the idea of separable soul has characterized traditional theology.[7]

Before we dig deeper in the substance of this chapter, I must express one caveat. This chapter is not about the psychology of religion. That is, I am not attempting here to duplicate the extensive writing of a very large number of scholars who have attempted to determine the psychological

Surprisingly, some scholars suggest that by arguing that mind is inaccessible, behaviorists are, themselves, actually invoking a version of dualism. The argument is that, on the one hand, are the observable behaviors; on the other are the "different in kind," unobservable, however real, mental processes. I feel that this is an unacceptable stretch of misunderstanding about the nature of most behaviorist credos and ignores the fact that both the behavior and the mental processes are equally real manifestations of the same fundamental kind, however they may differ in observability and accessibility.

conditions that led to religious beliefs either in general or in particular. To a certain degree, that task has been at least superficially accomplished in the historical chapters that precede this one. This chapter, to the contrary, is concerned with the influence that crypto-religious and dualist ideas of two or more kinds of ontological realities have had on modern scientific psychology. Rather than concentrate on the psychologists who studied religion, I am concerned here with the residual ideas from dualist religion and philosophy that either overtly or implicitly have influenced psychology.

So far in this book I have traced the history of the primitive fear of death as it evolved into highly sophisticated religious doctrines and even into nontheological philosophical thinking. The fear of death, I argue, was the direct result of a universal awareness of one's conscious self and a deep desire on the part of each of us to preserve that consciousness in the face of what is the indisputable transitory and impermanent nature of the physical body. From this primeval fear facilely arose a fundamental dualism that pervades thinking in a diversity of different schools of thought to the present day. By postulating a substantial or even a procedural difference between the objective body and the subjective mind, an "escape hatch" from personal mortality could be provided.

It is not surprising that dualisms are evident in the teachings of all modern religions and that the concept of some kind of a spiritual afterlife following bodily death is ubiquitous among them. This is their raison d'être! Slightly more startling is the observation made in the previous chapter that the traces of dualism could also be seen in many modern nontheological philosophies. Whatever the difference in the level of surprise, both observations reflect a situation in which there is a deep desire to avoid total personal annihilation and the continuing search for immortality of a kind that is not to be found in the material world. Philosophy, not hindered by the strict demands and protocols of scientific investigation, remains especially susceptible to this age-old pressure. Dualisms are to be found scattered and accepted even through its most up-to-date literature.

This chapter turns from the dualisms found in modern philosophy to another contemporary system of thought: scientific psychology and the theories that have emerged from its efforts to explain human behavior, particularly in the 20th century. To recap what I have written about previously (Uttal, 2000), two great theoretical traditions have dominated psychological thought throughout the past century. On the one hand are the various mentalisms including today's dominant psychology—cognitivism. On the other hand are the currently less popular, but still extant, behaviorisms. The key difference between the two great themes, regardless of whatever minor doctrinaire differences may divide their respective subdivisions, is their attitude toward the accessibility of mental functions.[2] Cognitivists believe that mental activity can be accessed and, thus, assayed, and measured. Even more fundamentally, cognitive psychology is based on a foundation assumption that mental processes can be subdivided into component modules. Embedded in this pervasive modularity assumption is the conclusion that mental processes are relatively independent, linear systems that can be isolated and assayed individually.

Most behaviorists, quite to the contrary, believe that mental processes cannot be accessed, measured, and thus, divided, and choose to deal only with observations of the organism's externally observed behavior in what is usually a holistic manner. Behaviorists tend, although nonexclusively, to generally eschew reductive theories that attempt to infer from behavior what the nature of the underlying cognitive processes may be.[3] This is not to say that all brands of either mentalism or behaviorism are the same within their respective boundaries. However, the acceptance or rejection of the accessibility of mind and all that it implies exists as the key distinction between the two great schools of psychological thought.

Cognitive mentalism, thus, takes very seriously its ability to deal with the mind as an investigative target. What a person is thinking, the nature of qualia, the components of a complex mental act leading to an action, and the phenomenological (in the sense of internal experiences), as well as in some cases, the neurophysiological explanations for these phenomena, dominate current cognitive psychology's strategies. Experiments are carried out to determine the "system organization" of mental or cognitive processes: Exquisite logical designs are constructed to execute experimental protocols that are thought to be capable of distinguishing and identifying the component processes of a cognitive process: Formal methodologies and statistico-mathematical techniques are then applied to measure and quantify the results. However, as noted earlier, the fundamental assumptions or issues of analyzability (into component modules)

---

[2]In preview, it is a complete misunderstanding of behaviorism to assert that all members of this school of thought reject the existence of consciousness. A careful study of the axioms of most behaviorisms reveals that they do not reject the existence of mind, consciousness, or mental activity. Rather, they reject their accessibility and take the intrapersonal privacy of mental activity very seriously—an epistemological obstruction to empirical studies of the mind, not an ontological rejection of its reality. (Only a few psychologists, e.g., J. R. Kantor, have in a few special instances denied the existence of mind and then primarily as a scientific entity.)

[3]Tolman's (1932) "teleological behaviorism," although traditionally designated as a form of behaviorism, actually was aimed at the identification of the internal mental states by drawing inferences from behavioral observations. It is more appropriately designated as a mentalism, although one that preferred to use as objective measures of behavior as possible.

and accessibility are rarely even considered it is taken for granted by cognitive mentalists that mental activity is susceptible to experimental *analysis*—in the strongest sense of the word—and that valid measures can be made of these inner structures.

In short, there are two primary axioms of cognitive psychology; the first is the reality of mental functions and the second is their accessibility, analyzability, and measurability. In particular, this means that terms like *consciousness* are taken very seriously, indeed. As Fodor (2000) pointed out, this reified existence of mind or consciousness is associated nowadays with a very specific strategy: the use of computer-like, syntactic explanatory models.

What is consciousness? In chapter 1, I suggested it was a modern near synonym for older terms with the same denotation including soul, mind, self-awareness, or "true ego." Unfortunately, this vaguely defined word—consciousness—is beset with the same lexicographic difficulties that have always bedeviled attempts to define any of those other names for the intrapersonal experiences that are not amenable to direct[4] observation. My previous efforts to define "mind" ended with a failure and an apology; an apology that holds true for "consciousness" as well as whatever other of those words that may be used in its place. I apologize for simply being unable to arrive at a useful definition of what I believe is an inaccessible and indivisible process occurring within the depths of the complex brain.

In spite of the age-old problems of ambiguity and nebulousness faced when one attempts to define mental constructs, some currently active philosophers and psychologists have turned to the study of consciousness as the *sine qua non* of a modern psychology. Books such as those of Dennett (1991), Searle (1992), Crick (1994), and Pinker (1997) have been published in an attempt to revitalize the study of consciousness and to use it as the basis for a new mentalist scientific psychology.[5] Most of these writers quite properly look upon mind as a biological process that results from neural activity; therefore, none of them are explicitly dualists in its traditional form. Nevertheless, there is a trace of process dualism in all of their writing.

---

[4] I don't want to quibble over such adjectives as "direct" or "indirect," or the many terms (e.g., "reflect," "indicate," "suggest") that are all-too-often used as pale surrogates for the term "measure." As we shall see the nature of psychological inquiry forces the most hardnosed cognitivist to qualify the language used in reporting experimental results. Among the wishy-washiest of the phrases used as a substitute for "measure" is the hackneyed "is not inconsistent with." Such a phrasing is virtually meaningless given the fact that any particular behavioral observation may "not be inconsistent" with a huge number of plausible alternative explanations. Here once again arises the one (phenomenon) to many (explanations) problem that seems to have been completely ignored by so many psychological theorists.

[5] This effort to force a new direction in scientific psychology is to be distinguished from the "consciousness enhancing" nonsense of the popular psychological literature that fills so many bookstore shelves these days.

Unfortunately, despite the hopes of many modern students of the mind, the term *consciousness* does not necessarily impute any greater meaning than was denoted by any of the earlier terms. In spite of this obvious fact, there is a groundswell of authors who believe that by reinjecting consciousness into the mainstream of psychology, a profound conceptual revolution will become possible and a scientifically valid mentalism can be developed.

In spite of the present popularity of consciousness as a vehicle for psychological research reflected in these books, it should be noted that most of the authors cited attempted to finesse the "mystery" and dance around the problem of its definition. There is a constant theme of unfathomability, of an unsatisfactory level of confusion in its definition, and of obfuscation whenever the topic is raised. Dennett (1991), for example, referred to the "Mystery of Consciousness" (p. 25). Crick (1994), as another conspicuous example, stated:

Everyone has a rough idea of what is meant by consciousness. It is better to avoid a *precise* definition of consciousness because of the dangers of premature definition. Until the problem is understood much better, any attempt at formal definition is likely to be misleading or overly restrictive or both. (p. 20)

Others try to finesse the problem by asserting the obvious—the fact that the mind is a natural outcome of neural complexity—all the while eschewing any effort to develop a strategy by which we might operationalize such a concept. Searle (1992), for example, asserted that:

Consciousness, in short, is a biological feature of human and certain animal brains. It is caused by neurobiological processes and is as much a part of the natural biological order as any other biological features such as photosynthesis, digestion, or mitosis. (p. 90)[6]

"Good enough"—one might say and easily agree with this assertion of a fundamental neuroreductionist (in principle) ontology. However, this definition of consciousness nee mind remains as inadequate as any other in serving the needs of a "scientific" psychology. Later, Searle (1992) went into greater detail and sought to achieve some deeper understanding of what is consciousness in the following way:

All of the processes we think of as especially mental—whether perception, learning, inference, decision making, problem solving, the emotions, etc.—are in one way or another crucially related to consciousness. (p. 227)

---

[6]See also Searle's quote on page 254 where he deals with the confusion surrounding what he sees as the disorganized state of the cognitive sciences.

In fact, however, this approach by inductive inclusion also has the effect of avoiding precise definition, and more seriously, avoids the declaration of a strategy suitable for scientific investigation of the mind, conscious or unconscious.

Pinker (1997) put it even more succinctly and bluntly in his response to a proposed list of questions that deal with the nature of consciousness. Asked how he would answer such queries, he stated:

> Beats the heck out of me! I have some prejudices, but no idea of how to look for a defensible answer. And neither does anyone else. The computational theory of mind offers no insight; neither does any finding in neuroscience, once you clear up the confusion of sentience with access and self-knowledge. (p. 147)

The question arising in such a chaotic environment is: Does such an ill-defined entity as consciousness or mind provide an adequate foundation for the scientific study of this particular aspect of human nature? Scholars, such as Bloch (1995) and Nagel (1974) argued that, whatever consciousness is, it is extremely difficult to define, access, or deal with it in the way that psychologists regularly attempt. Thus, they imply that including it in the mind–brain problem may make the problem even less tractable to solution. However, they also suggest that leaving it out may make the problem "meaningless."

Despite the enormous amount of thought and writing paid to the problem of its nature, not only has there never been a satisfactory definition of consciousness, but in point of fact, we also know absolutely nothing about its origins or nature. The only encounter any of us has with consciousness is our own private personal awareness. In that context, it is perceived as a unified entity and we have no insights into its structure or its origins—only the result. Although the accessibility of mind may be the focus of the behaviorist–mentalist debate, we do not have even an objective (i.e., interpersonal) means of detecting or measuring it. For that matter, nor do we have the barest glimmerings of a hypothesis concerning how such an amazing macroscopic entity as conscious self-awareness could emerge from the action of a myriad of microscopic neurons. Don't let anyone fool you that this kind of knowledge is available or that we are on the verge of understanding or explanation because of the application of some wonderful new machine. Anyone who is arguing to the contrary is simply confusing hypotheses, metaphors, and analogies (of varying levels of significance and validity) as well as the results of irrelevant "displacement" activity with exact and deep knowledge.

Not only do we not know the details, but also we remain ignorant about even the most basic facts of the transition from brain to conscious mind. All that a modern cognitive neuroscience can offer is the very high and generally accepted (among neuroscientists and psychologists alike) likelihood that mind is a brain function arising from an enormously complex neuronal matrix. To go further than that is to insult the word "theory" and degrade the idea of even a partial explanation to "wild speculation."

A further discouraging caveat is that the neurophysiological system that gives rise to consciousness or mind may itself not be amenable to any kind of theoretical or analytic explanation, not because of any fundamental mystery, but rather because of simple practical problems of complexity and numerousness. That such is the case is more fully developed in Uttal (1998).

The most serious barrier to the study of consciousness is that it is private and discernible only to the individual experiencing it. No one other than ourselves has or can have direct experience of our own personal consciousness. Mental processes are not transparent to psychophysical research. Thus, even if some unlikely future science were able to recreate a network of a complexity comparable to our own brains, how would we be able to tell if it was truly conscious or just simulating human behavior by the actions of a complex automaton?

Contrary to popular mythology, there is no "Turing" test that could possibly distinguish between a human and a refined synthetic or "artificial" intelligence. The criterion traditionally used in such a test is "indistinguishable behavior" (between the automaton and the human). However, identical external responses can be obtained without any equivalence of internal mechanism. Even the best conceivable AI system, the one most closely approximating human *behavior*, may be operating on principles vastly different than those of the organic brain and still produce indistinguishable behavior. Whether a brain (or pseudo-brain) is enjoying some kind of putative consciousness can be known only to itself. There is no way to externally test self-awareness or, as it may otherwise be known, sentience. There is no better evidence than the extreme difficulty we have in coping with the presence or absence of the consciousness of our pets; why is there any reason to expect that it would be any easier to determine consciousness on the part of a super computer?

Philosophers deal with this constraint on our ability to peer into the consciousness of other entities as the problem of "other minds." That is, How do I know for certain that another entity is conscious? Because of the absence of any direct interpersonal communication of mental states, the only way to approach this problem has been to argue by analogy. Analogical reasoning, however, is fraught with inadequacies. Unfortunately, psychology's efforts to go from observed behavior to inner experiences can often be considered just such a form of analogical reasoning.

A typical account would go as follows: If "I" have an experience (e.g., pain) that leads me to express it (respond) in some way, then any other person who responds in the same way is assumed to be suffering the same (or equivalent) experience. Obviously there are deep flaws in such logic, a flaw that I might note in passing, is not shared by behaviorism with the mentalist psychologies. Malcolm (1971) pointed out that:

> It is evident that those philosophers who think it necessary to reason from analogy to the existence of other minds are committed to the Cartesian-Lockean assumption of a conceptual gap between the mental and the physical. (p. 25)

Malcolm is thus equating analogical reasoning with a dualist assumption. I believe that Malcolm's point is in agreement with the one I am making in this book; namely, given that analogies are so widely used, dualism (or some vestiges of it) is deeply embedded in the thinking of many modern theorists of mental function. Indeed, a case may be made that the very formulation of the mind–brain problem that goes beyond the structure–function dichotomy is itself tantamount to the acceptance of a cryptic form of dualism. (A fuller, although somewhat dated, discussion of the problem of knowing other minds can be found in Shorter, 1967.)

Some aspects of the debate between behaviorism and mentalism are very long standing. For example, given the behaviorist's view of the intrapersonal and private nature of the mind, what credence should a psychologist give to the introspective report of a subject who is being asked to do more than just make a simple discrimination? Here arises the issue of *incorrigibility*, on one side of which are those who argue that an individual's reports of his own thoughts are not subject to amendment or correction. On the other side, are those who believe that introspective reports are even more fallible than other "more objective reports" because of the many opportunities for deception both in terms of what one believes about one's own thoughts and what one would like to have another person believe one believes.

Intent to deceive is not the only problem. It is also likely that unintentional distortions occur between a thought and a response. This kind of distortion may include failures of memory, simplifying "assumptions," and other kinds of cognitive massaging of mental activity on the part of the introspector that we collectively refer to as "cognitive penetration." Eyewitness testimony and post hoc theories justifying one's behavior are practical examples of such distortions.

Either the acceptance or rejection of the assumption of introspective incorrigibility creates major problems for psychology. Accepting it means that introspective data of all kinds cannot be changed or denied, and, therefore, however fantastic, self-serving, or unbelievable, it must be accepted as raw data. Rejecting incorrigibility (and, thus, accepting the possibility of self-delusion or intentional deception) for all practical purposes, rules out a host of psychologies that depend on the accessibility of consciousness and meaningful reporting by the patient, client, or subject. For a host of empirical reasons (most notably exemplified by Nisbett & Wilson's, 1977, very important paper) we now appreciate that the interpretation of their own mental processes by subjects is a deeply flawed strategy and does not always (to be conservative) provide a window into the real reasons that a person does what he does.

Furthermore, since it is rare to collect subjective reports immediately, and memory, it is agreed by all concerned, is corrigible to the extreme, first-person reports are further flawed by <u>the inevitable decay of the immediate experience. Thus, corrigibility walks hand in hand with inaccessibility and,</u> again with the exception of the simplest and immediate discriminative processes, <u>invalidates much of the data of cognitive psychology</u>. This simple concatenation of barriers to understanding suggests that whatever mind or consciousness is, it is terribly difficult to both define and to accurately measure it.[7]

To base a science on such a fuzzy foundation as an inaccessible, corrigible, and ill-defined entity as consciousness leads to quasi-scientific answers to some of the greatest questions of human nature. To understand this argument better we have to look at the history of consciousness as it has influenced modern psychology.

7.2 PSYCHOLOGISTS OF CONSCIOUSNESS

The history of psychology is a convoluted one. Attempts to draw a flow chart of the ebb and flow of ideas or to precisely designate the properties of the many schools that have come and gone are always less than elucidating. If one picks one dimension that characterizes psychological thinking on which to concentrate, inevitably conceptual paths cross and denotational inconsistencies arise like sea serpents to confuse and complicate, if not frighten, the intrepid scholar. Nevertheless, some order can be maintained in the following discussion if we concentrate on a single conceptual strand. The strand I choose to follow here is <u>the psychological history of the idea of the intrapersonally sentient mind—consciousness.</u> The past concentration

---

[7]The alternative, of course, is to observe behavior on carefully controlled situations and then to attempt to infer from it what are the likely internal mechanisms that might account for it. However, here the mentalist psychologist is confronted with the fact that there are many possible and equally plausible explanations or inferences that may be drawn from a single behavioral observation. There is no completely satisfactory way that the "correct" one can be distinguished from a host of plausible alternatives without invoking propositions that are even more suspect than the accessibility and incorrigibility assumptions.

on and the recent reawakening of interest in this kind of self-awareness, however flawed, makes it a useful organizing principle; the classic interest in and emphasis on consciousness throughout recent and traditional psychological history provides a convenient theme on which to base this discussion of the influence of dualist ideas in modern psychology. The point being that modern psychological thinking, just as modern philosophical thought, has yet to fully emerge from a long tradition of concern with the theory of dual nature of the human mind and brain. Although modern scientific psychology typically tries to ignore these ancient roots, I argue they still influence and constrain its activities and theories.

7.2.1   William James

There is no better place to begin than with one of the fathers of modern scientific psychology—William James. James (1842–1910) was the son of Henry James Sr., an idiosyncratic theologian, and the brother of Henry James the author. From the beginning William James' life was centered on intellectual topics both from the viewpoints of theology, philosophy, and psychology. Although James spent a good deal of his life setting the scene for modern scientific psychology, he ultimately reentered the arena of religion (James, 1902/1935) and then, somewhat unfortunately for his scientific reputation, descended further into a troubled advocacy of the reality of psychic phenomena.

Much of James' youth was spent in the environment established by his father who had been deeply influenced by the mystical theologian Emanuel Swedenborg (1688–1772). Swedenborg attempted to combine the scientific orientation of Lockean empiricism with a profound commitment to theological principles, including what seems very much like the classic Cartesian substance dualism of mind and body. Swedenborg called his philosophy Theosophy and incorporated into it many mystical ideas (including a rather occult interpretation of Egyptian hieroglyphics) along with more conventional Christian theology and, somewhat incongruously, the natural sciences of geology and biology.

The salient issue of Swedenborg's influence on the James family was the impact it may have had on the young William during his formative years. Whether or not he was directly influenced by Theosophic ideas remains an open question. Nevertheless, either in accepting or rejecting Swedenborg's ideas, there seems little question that the emphasis placed on certain topics, including theology, mind, and science, was to have a profound influence on James' later life. The quest that Swedenborg had set out on—to unify theology, spirit, and science—also, according to one view, became James' lifelong quest, even if he diverged from the Theosophic mysticism. It is hard to imagine how this youthful experience could not have set the stage for his later accomplishments as an intellectual and, ultimately, as a psychologist. The subject matters of Theosophy and psychology are all too similar even if the respective solutions and strategies differ greatly!

In writing his classic and monumental psychological treatise, *The Principles of Psychology* (James, 1890), he is reputed to have set the stage for most of modern psychology. The "Principles" is thought by many to be the dividing line in psychology between the study of mind as a philosophical diversion and what is presented as a modern objective science. His impact has been enormous, sometimes waning under the influence of contrary traditions such as behaviorism, but then regaining theoretical potency as the more mentalist traditions of present day psychology have been resurrected.

James has been classified as a functionalist by historians of psychology. However, his breadth was much broader than that and it is difficult to classify him within this or any other single category or school. His "Principles" begins with 100 pages of brain anatomy and motor skills before he diverges off into the much more difficult challenge of trying to spell out what consciousness means. The importance and seminal nature of James' work is such that he is often given credit for being among the first to argue that psychology is a natural science. This may be disputed by others who would recall that such German luminaries as F. C. Donders (1818–1889), E. H. Weber (1795–1878), G. T. Fechner (1801–1887), and W. Wundt (1832–1920) had all coexisted or preceded him. Some of these predecessors (Fechner, in particular) carried out their work to achieve quasi-religious or spiritualistic goals that we now appreciate were wildly discrepant from the objective scientific ones James pursued.[8] Nevertheless, what Fechner and these other proto-psychologists were doing was indistinguishable from what was to be done in scientific laboratories albeit possibly for quite different motivating reasons. Regardless of the historical details and controversies over priority, it is on James that the mantle of "The First Scientific Psychologist" has stuck. The only qualifier that may have to be added is "American" for it was here that his influence was so great and subsequently so appreciated.

Perhaps it was the times and the new ideas that were being contemporaneously generated that made James' impact especially significant. Charles Darwin's (1859, 1871) explanations of the origin of species and human evolution were becoming widely accepted; Ernst Mach (1885/1959) had just completed his great work on the sensations; Herman Helmholtz had published his books on optics (1866/1894) and hearing (1863/1962); and the seminal work on animal behavior had just been published by Romanes (1883). Not

---

[8]Others (e.g., Kantor, 1963, p. 364; 1978, p. 335) would also add even some of other giants of psychology's history (including such luminaries as Helmholtz and Ebbinghaus) to this list of those whose goals were spiritualist rather than scientific.

to be underestimated is the Zeitgeist of James' time—the emerging American spirit of pragmatism. Indeed, his functionalism, should we label it as such, was aimed at rescuing psychology from what he considered to be the socially irrelevant and sterile form—structuralism—practiced by his contemporary E. B. Titchener (1867–1927) and the latter's teachers in Germany. The introspective study of the "bits and pieces" of sensory experience that were supposed to combine to form mental activities was not a satisfactory solution to the question of the nature of mind for James.

Although James is regularly included among the dualists, his "dualism" went through several different stages over the course of his career. Early in his scientific years, the idea of a completely separate "soul" was repugnant to him. His feelings on this matter *at that time* could not have been more specific as demonstrated on the very first page of the *Principles*:

> [Soul] is the orthodox "spiritualistic" theory of scholasticism and of common sense. (p. 1)

As we read through his work, a precise definition of mind turned out to be as elusive to him as it remains to our generation. Some inklings of his attitude can be found scattered throughout the *Principles*. The mind, to the pragmatic James, was not simply a passive entity. It was an active determinant of human behavior; indeed, influenced as he was by Darwinism, he believed that the mind had specifically evolved as a problem solver, as the director of the individual's life. His emphasis was, therefore, on the functions performed by the conscious mind.

However, there was a crucial difference between his mentalism and modern cognitivism. James did not believe that the mind was divisible or, in modern terms, modular. Rather, to him it was a holistic stream of "consciousness" that acted to continuously modulate the interactions between stimuli and responses. He also argued strongly against the molecules of structuralism stating that:

> [Starting with sensations] is abandoning the empirical method of investigation. No one has ever had a simple sensation by itself. Consciousness, from our natal day, is of a teeming multiplicity of objects and relations, and what we call simple sensations are the results of discriminative attention, pushed often to a very high degree. (*Principles*, p. 224)

No Wundtian or Titchenerean elements here! Rather the functional or process-oriented aspects of the mind dominated his interpretation.

Another important point about James' theory of mind (and many other students of mind, behaviorists included) is that he did not deny that mental processes exist. He subsequently made a statement that essentially reflects the core of mentalist psychological thinking:

The first fact for us, as psychologists, is that thinking of some sort goes on. (p. 224)

He then proceeded to characterize what he believed were the accessible properties of that thinking:

1. Every thought tends to be part of a personal consciousness.
2. Within each personal consciousness thought is always changing.
3. Within each personal consciousness thought is sensibly continuous.
4. It always appears to deal with objects independent of itself.
5. It is interested in some parts of these objects to the exclusion of others, and welcomes or rejects—chooses from among them, in a word—all the while. (p. 225)

It is the examination of these properties of thought that James argues is the essence of the science of psychology. The very first line in the *Principles* is the oft quoted:

Psychology is the Science of Mental Life, both of its phenomena and their conditions. (p. 1)

How, then, did he propose that we must go about studying "mental life" in the context of these properties? To answer this question, James joined with the structuralists in championing introspection as the "first and foremost and always" (p. 187) method of choice. Armed with such a tool, however, as we have already seen, the psychologist is inevitably confronted with the problem of the corrigibility of thoughts and the purity and validity of any reports of them. James' attitude toward these problems was not that introspection was infallible, but rather that it is "difficult and fallible" (p. 191). In this regard, he argued, it is no different than any other kind of measurement and, therefore, introspection is essential if we are to have any insights into the nature of what he considered to be the prime target—the thoughts occurring during mental activity. Clearly, James made a huge implicit commitment to the accessibility of mental activity to the experimental tools of the psychologist. This became the crux of the major schism in the psychology that was to follow functionalism: The "war" between mentalism and behaviorism was declared over this issue more than any other.

James, thus, pushed psychology from a structural to a functional strategy in which the mind was dealt with in terms of a holistic stream rather than a mass of sensory particles. In doing so, however, he continued to accept the accessibility of thought and the meaningfulness of consciousness as a target of scientific inquiry. On the other hand, he was well aware of the residual problems and did express an appreciation of the limits of that accessibility and the ease with which introspective reports may be distorted. Most interesting was his declaration of the "psychologist's fallacy"—the error that the observing psychologist may tend to make in studying the mental activity of the observed individual. The psychologist's fallacy comes in two varieties according to James:

1. The confusion of his [the psychologist's] own standpoint with that of the mental fact about which he is making his report.

2. The assumption that the mental state studied must be conscious of itself as the psychologist is conscious of it.

Here, in spite of his concern with mental, we see James' appreciation of the anti-accessibility argument, not in a "spiritualistic" sense but rather from the point of view of a very practical empirical science. The first form of the psychologist's fallacy is a precursor of the modern idea that identical behaviors may not be based on identical mental states; the second is an equally prescient suggestion that consciousness may not be present even when analogous behavior is observed. The first, therefore, may be considered an early expression of the one-to-many (behavior to explanations) problem challenging philosophers and psychologists even today. The second is a precursor of the problems that are confronted by AI scholars as they attempt to assay the purported consciousness of intelligent automata, animals, or other humans than ourselves.

Another important point in James' psychological theory was his assumption that mind was not epiphenomenal. Rather, he saw it as effective in modulating behavior and determining the course of events. Although it may have been produced by brain activity (and there is little argument that he viewed mind as a function of the nervous system at least in the days of writing the *Principles*), it was also able to feed back influentially onto brain activity to change the nature of the response. (James' personal views, however, became far more complex in his later writing on religion and subsequently his ill-advised foray into spiritualism.)

This brings us back to James' views on dualism, which seemed to be constantly in a state of flux. Influenced as he was by Darwin and others of his time, James argued strongly that the mind was dependent on the conditions of the brain. However, that was not all. In his later book (James, 1902/ 1935) entitled *The Varieties of Religious Experience*, he presented himself as a deeply religious man with specific attitudes about the role of mind. For example, he tried to reconcile science and religion, and expressed what we can only consider to be what was by then a firmly dualist point of view when he said:

The Self [*sic*] manifests through the organism; but there is always some part of the self unmanifested; . . . (p. 511)

Then, referring to the problem of "over-belief," by which I assume he means his attitudes toward a set of concepts and ideas that transcend science, James went on:

I believe that the pragmatic way of taking religion to be the deeper way. It gives it body as well as soul, it makes it claim, as everything real must claim, some characteristic realm of fact as its very own. What the more characteristically divine facts are, apart from the actual inflow of energy in the faith-state and prayer-state, I know not. But the over-belief on which I am ready to make my personal venture is that they exist. (p. 519)

And

I believe that a candid consideration of piecemeal supernaturalism and a complete discussion of its metaphysical bearings will show it to be the hypothesis by which the largest number of legitimate requirements are met. (p. 523)[9]

Clearly, James was by the later years of his career a religious (i.e., dualist) person, perhaps without dogmatism and even eschewing rituals, but still one who accepted the idea of a distinction between the natural and the supernatural and their respective realities. The "Varieties" adopted what is essentially a pragmatic stance on the subject, both extolling the values of religion in increasing the quality of life and also arguing that it could be brought, in part at least, under the scope of scientific examination. His ever-changing philosophy was characterized in the following line from his 1902 book:

. . . the visible world is part of a more spiritual universe from which it draws its chief significance. (p. 485)

Clearly, James developed what is indisputatively a mentalist philosophy of the states of mind, one that is increasingly dualist as the years went by. Curiously, he argues strongly that this philosophy be designated as a monistic view of mind. However, his understanding of the meaning of "monism" is very difficult to make compatible with his pronouncements in his work on religion and, even more incongruous with his spiritualistic stud-

---

[9]In the later years of his career, James' pursuit of studies of psychic phenomena led to his selection as president of the Society for Psychical Research.

ies of his later years. Some students of Jamesian psychology (e.g., Taylor & Wozniak, 1996) argue that James' monism was only a "formalism" designed to maintain his scientific credentials. They argued that his single kind of reality, which James referred to as pure experience, was actually a mélange of many different kinds of experiences that collectively make up what he called reality. Indeed, as we read deeper into his works, it becomes increasingly clear that, despite his monistic pretensions, James, in his emphasis on "pure experience," was actually a dualist in a way that was consistent with the deepest meanings of the word. It was not, however, a Cartesian theory of substance dualism in which mind and matter or body and soul were distinguished. Nor was it the then popular dualism of consciousness and content, the widely accepted version of dualism at the time. Taylor and Wozniak (1996) described this then popular dualism as follows:

> By the 19th century, however, the dualism of body and soul had been transformed into one of knower and known or consciousness and content. The essence of this dualism lay in a reification of consciousness and a separation of consciousness from its content. (p. xiii)

Taylor and Wozniak (1996) pointed out that James was reacting to this prevalent form of dualism by proposing a kind of empiricism. It seems to me that James' effort to tag "pure experience" as a monism is, to the contrary, actually a version of idealism in which mental activity took priority over the material world. So much for the ambiguity of the written word!

Throughout his career James continued to equivocate on the nature of consciousness. In his classic paper, "Does 'Consciousness' Exist?" (James, 1904), he answered his rhetorical question in the negative, yet his substitute for it—pure experience—is hardly distinguishable from the modern use of the words "consciousness" or "mind." On the other hand, James was not a fan of the concept of the unconscious. In the *Principles* James asks the rhetorical questions: Can states of mind be unconscious? (p. 162) and Do unconscious mental states exist? (p. 164). He then spends a dozen pages refuting arguments for their existence. The crux of his argument was that there could not be two different kinds of mental activity, one accessible to introspection and one inaccessible.

James also was well aware of the role that personal identity (i.e., fear of death) played in religious thinking. In his book on religion (James, 1902/1935) he stated that:

> The pivot round which the religious life, as we have traced it, is the interest of the individual in his private personal destiny. (p. 491)

In conclusion, there is little question that William James had enormous influence on modern psychology. His contributions, sometimes internally inconsistent, still reverberate through the language we currently use as scientific psychologists. Because of this influence it is essential we understand that the "mental life," "mind," "consciousness," "pure experience," or whatever he called it at various times in his career, was the essential target of psychology from his point of view. Psychology was no longer the servant of philosophy, theology, or even of neuroanatomy or physiology, but a science in its own right. It is here that his contribution becomes unequivocal. Whether the science was to be behaviorist or mentalist, psychologists now undertook the enormous task of defining their science as a distinct program of research and theory.

James' early religious beliefs interacted with his scientific ones in a way that set the stage for the emergence of American functionalism. This was for his time a unique approach greatly distinguished from the austere Germanic structuralism with its search for mental "atoms" and the "chemical" rules by which they were combined. The bottom line of Jamesian psychology, nevertheless, is that it was a mentalism aimed at exploring what was going on in the mind—whatever we wish to call it. In this regard, he explicitly accepted the accessibility of mental processes and set the stage for a revival of mentalism in American psychology in our times.

A final evaluative comment: Although James is considered to be the outstanding psychologist of the past century by many, his writing is often confused and sections are inconsistent with each other. Furthermore, it is extremely difficult to pin him down on a specific issue or to determine his personal interpretation of some of the key ideas by searching through his many books and papers. For example, in researching his work in support of this section, I have encountered totally different interpretations of his views of both the words "consciousness" and "unconscious." Perhaps this equivocation is a fault of the subject matter of psychology itself. Perhaps it is a result of the times in which he lived or the dynamics of the changes that occurred in his thinking over his life span. Perhaps it is just a result of the evolution of language from his time to our own. Much of the interest in his work in the past century by historians has been aimed at trying to unravel some of these ambiguities in thinking, rather than building upon his work as a conceptual foundation for a modern psychology. To a considerable degree, it was for this reason—the ambiguity of James' thinking—that the door to the next wave of psychological theory—behaviorism—opened.

The topic of behaviorism and the role it played in directing our study of human nature is dealt with later in this chapter. However, it is now necessary to briefly digress to consider another enormous influence on current day psychology—an influence that came from a physician who must be considered, at best, to be a clinical, as opposed to scientific, psychologist.

274

CHAPTER 7

7.2.2 Sigmund Freud and the Unconscious

Another great influence on American psychology was the work of Sigmund Freud (1856–1939). However, correct or incorrect; however, persistent or forgotten, he cannot be overlooked in any discussion of the roots of modern psychology.

In some ways, it is hard to understand his influence on the science. Freud was neither philosopher nor established laboratory scientist (although he did publish a number of papers on neuroanatomy early in his career). Nevertheless, his work on psychotherapeutic methods ("psychoanalysis" in his lexicon) came to be what is probably the best known and culturally influential corpus of work in any field of psychology, and along with the work of Newton, Darwin, and Einstein is considered to be among one of the most notable milestones in the history of the human search for understanding. Although still extremely controversial and much diminished in acceptance these days, his ideas about psychotherapy still stimulate one of the mainstreams of psychological thought around the world.[10]

It is not Freud's effort to define a new approach to the treatment of mental illness that brought him fame, however. It was his popularization of a largely unexplained and previously rejected (by James) aspect of mental activity—the *unconscious*, a subliminal level of mental activity that presumably went on below the "pure experience" of James or the accessible components of thought of modern cognitive mentalists.

The issues of whether the unconscious is real or fictional and influential or epiphenomenal are certainly not closed. Many philosophers and proto-psychologists had also considered the role of the unconscious. Leibniz, Herbart, Schopenhauer and, most relevant to the present discussion, Helmholtz' concept of unconscious inference, had predated Freud's work. However, the unconscious became the centerpiece of Freud's approach to psychology. Distinguishing between the role of the unconscious and the conscious and proposing a putative explanation of how the two levels of mentation interacted was the essence of Freud's enormous influence on psychology of all kinds. Indeed, he went so far as constructing a taxonomy of the parts of the mind as he saw it, an idea that perhaps reflected his early training as a physician and anatomist. The four parts of the Freudian model

---

[10]Indeed, Freud's psychotherapy has come to be the archetype of psychology in the popular mind. Both his methods and his theories are now considered to be somewhat archaic, even by many modern psychotherapists. Certainly, they are no longer as influential as in the first half of the 20th century. Nevertheless, his continued high visibility has obscured the fact among the general public that, in addition to psychoanalysis, there is another main current of activity in psychology—the scientific psychology of the empirical laboratory. Scientific psychology is only indirectly connected to curing neuroses and psychoses. It is dignified by its primary goal of seeking understanding.

of mind included the unconscious Libido (the energy source for mental activity), the Id (the storage location of libidinous energy), the Superego (the constraining force operating on the ego to defer gratification), and the Ego (the conscious decision maker that seeks to obtain gratification).

Freud was, from some points of view, engaged in a debate with the psychologists (arguably, but probably, including William James) who denied the existence of the unconscious. The motivating force behind Freud's pursuit of this very important idea was his search for a theory of subconscious causes of abnormal behavior. For our purposes, it was important because it succored a stream of psychological thought that enhanced the idea of the accessibility of mental activity beyond that championed by any preceding or subsequent psychology. In other words, Freud, although not actively involved in the development of what I have designated the scientific side of psychology, created an atmosphere of mental accessibility, introspective efficacy, and cognitive componentry, all important parts of the modern mentalism that is now called cognitive psychology.

At this point, it is interesting to point out that both James and Freud, each in their own way, was influenced by their particular religious backgrounds. James was the product of a somewhat unusual but basically Christian environment and went on to write and study religion contemporaneously with his psychology and philosophy. (His progression to mysticism and other "psychic" topics should also not be overlooked.) James' emphasis on a personal religious experience, as opposed to a doctrinaire form, both fed into and drew from his psychological theories. Many of the ideas expressed in the "Varieties" are still actively discussed today.

Freud, on the other was a Jewish atheist who rejected the dogma and theology of Judaism but at the same time dwelled on some aspects of its cultural and historical substance. Like James, Freud went on to write about religion (e.g., Freud, 1918/1952, 1939) in books in which he frequently argued that religion was just an illusion arising from vague feelings of subconscious activity or from persisting echoes of infantile experiences. Indeed, Freud suggested in several places that the "fear of loss of love" was the underlying cause of religious feeling. It is hard to distinguish this phrase from the previously encountered fear of death, since both would have the same operational effect—personal oblivion—and, thus, both may well refer to the same primeval origins of religious thought. Other psychoanalysts (e.g., Rank, 1941) have pursued the fear of death idea directly in a prodigious literature that can be only briefly mentioned here.

It seems possible that, without realizing it, both James and Freud were attempting to make their psychological theories coherent with their religious attitudes. Freud was doing so by providing an abstract reconstruction of his lost theology in the form of deeply embedded psychological modules that mimicked anatomical structures. James created a science of consciousness that left room for the dualism of his Christian upbringing yet formulated in a way that was not beyond what he thought were the methods of scientific inquiry. Whether or not either of these two psychological giants was explicitly aware of the impact of their most fundamental assumptions and beliefs on their theories and methods, we cannot know. The volume of the interpretations and inferences drawn about what and why they were thinking and the lack of consensus on these matters is another piece of evidence of how inaccessible mental activity may be, even in the face of the prodigious written legacy both men left behind.

7.2.3 Roger W. Sperry

Another distinguished scientist from a cognate field who wrote about the importance of a mentalist–cognitivist approach to psychology was the Zoologist Roger W. Sperry (1913–1994). Sperry developed his version of a psychology of the mind mainly as a reaction to what he considered the incomplete (i.e., consciousness free) behaviorism that had dominated psychology until the 1960s. His new "mentalist" point of view received a high visibility because of Sperry's scientific credentials, most notably sharing the Nobel Prize in 1981.

Sperry argued (see, e.g., Sperry, 1992, 1993a, 1993b) for a return to a cognitive–mentalist psychology in which consciousness once again played the role that it had been denied by behaviorism. Consciousness, according to him, was a natural emergent property of the action of the brain. Most significantly for him, it was not just an epiphenomenon that exerted no causal force on behavior. Rather, consciousness (including unconscious mental activity) was able to influence brain activities equally as well as the converse was true. This two-way causal relationship between brain activity and cognitive activity, Sperry believed, was required to replace what he interpreted was a one-way materialist and reductionist, brain centered theory. For him, consciousness, as one form of cognitive activity, was as capable of determining behavior as were the underlying brain states. In other words, Sperry (1993a) was adding the concept of "downward determinism" to the upward determinism implied by a neuroreductive interpretation of consciousness. Again, we see an example of the rejection of a passive epiphenomenal role for the mind. In his words:

> The new position is mentalistic, holding that behavior is mentally and subjectively driven. (p. 879)

and

Subjective human values, no longer written off as ineffectual epiphenomena nor reduced to microphenomena, become the most critically powerful force shaping today's civilized world. (p. 879)

Sperry's ideas were repeatedly criticized (see his own list of his critics on page 259 of Sperry, 1992) as being implicitly dualistic. He vigorously argued against this criticism maintaining that his point of view was intended to be monistic. He believed and wrote that his approach to a theory of the efficacy of mind represented a middle ground between the old dualisms and the newer reductive or "identity" versions of monism. The core of his explanation was that although consciousness was an emergent product of brain activity, it was capable of feeding back onto the physical brain to control and regulate behavior. Both consciousness and brain were aspects, according to Sperry, of the same kind of a single reality. Unfortunately, simply by proposing that there was a two-way interaction between two forms of a single monistic entity, Sperry comes indistinguishably close to championing a dualism in which consciousness plays a predominant rather than subservient role. Assuming an interaction between the two entities is a much different idea than suggesting that one is mechanism and one is process—a truly monistic idea.

How can we explain this trend toward a dualist cognitive mentalism on the part of a distinguished cognitive neuroscientist such as Sperry? Neuroscience, it may be argued, almost by virtue of its pursuit of the mechanistic equivalents of mental activity must be, at its most basic roots, identified as a monism. Any deviation from the fundamental principle of ontological equivalence of mind (process) and brain (mechanism) raises fundamental questions about the rationale of the science. A hint of the roots of his thinking can be found in an earlier article (Sperry, 1965). Here Sperry contended that then current "experimental objective psychology" (by which he is referring to the then popular behaviorism) was excluding some of the most important human values from consideration. His own words conveyed his ideas as well as any when he said that this kind of psychology (i.e., behaviorism):

... would dispense not only with the conscious mind but also with most of the other spiritual components of human nature, including the immortal soul. Before science, man used to think he was a spiritually free agent possessing free will. Science tells us free will is just an illusion and gives us, instead, causal determinism. Where there used to be purpose and meaning in human behavior, science now shows us a complex biophysical machine ... (p. 73)

Nowhere is there a clearer statement of the impact one's deeply held religious beliefs can have on one's psychological theories. However hidden, I believe that such thinking is far more prevalent, though much less explicitly expressed, in psychology than is usually appreciated.

Sperry's motives and basic assumptions also became clear when he went on to say:

> When the humanist is led to favor the implications of modern materialism over the older idealistic values in these and related matters, I suspect that he has been taken, that science has sold society and itself a somewhat questionable bill of goods. (p. 74)

Here, we see additional evidence of the foundation assumptions that were guiding Sperry's early thinking on such matters. It becomes increasingly clear that his attempts late in his career to develop a mentalist theory of mind and brain and to embrace the causal efficacy of an emergent consciousness arose from his personal humanistic and religious assumptions and needs.

The confusion of monism and dualism exhibited in Sperry's written legacy is not due to any lack of clarity in his writing; his language is clearer than most who have had the temerity to tackle such issues. Rather, it is a reflection of the internal inconsistency of his logic as he made an effort to combine the tenets of what is hardly distinguishable from a classic theological dualism with modern science. Sperry's attempts to accomplish this difficult if not impossible task exemplified what has become a constant theme of modern mentalisms. It is to his credit that he, at least, was brave enough to tangle publicly with this issue rather than to submerge it in obscurity or obfuscation, the usual approach.

7.2.4 Bernard J. Baars

Among the most articulate of currently active scholars of consciousness is Bernard J. Baars. Baars' writing differs greatly from the enormous amount of flapdoodle produced by many other psychologists and philosophers who have chosen to consider this very difficult problem. His clarity of presentation permits a degree of critical analysis that is often not possible with the vaguely phrased work of other cognitivists.

In a particularly cogent analysis, Baars (2003) explores the nature of consciousness in an interesting comparison of human and animal consciousness. He argues, contra behaviorism, that:

> The evidence is now massive that behavioristic skeptics were wrong. The functional importance of consciousness in humans, as assessed by objective evidence that has accelerated in the last two decades, is beyond serious dispute. (p. 3)

To support this argument, the "Thesis" of his article, Baars discusses several items on a list of findings that he believes supports both the existence and the functional role played by consciousness.

1. Accurate Reports: Baars (1998) argues that one piece of evidence of the existence of consciousness is an abundance of "accurate, verifiable reports."

2. The Commentary Key: Baars alludes to experiments by Cowey and Stoerig (1995) in which macaques with brain lesions cannot discriminate between a stimulus in a surgically induced lacuna and no stimulus in an intact region. He interprets this to mean that the conscious qualia of an experience are no longer present (i.e., the monkey is not aware of the stimulus). Consciousness, which had been present, regarding this particular stimulus event has been lost following a lesion of a particular brain area.

3. Behavioral Evidence for Animal Consciousness: Distractibility, deception, catching other animals unaware, obvious signs of sleep, and drowsiness all, according to Baars reflect a kind of "conscious" effort on the part of animals to deceive or differential behavior in the conscious and unconscious states.

4. Brain Electrical Signals Correlated With Consciousness: EEG and EVBP signals are very different when humans are asleep or awake.

5. Brain Anatomy Correlated With Consciousness: Specific parts of the brain, typically in the brain stem, are associated with sleep and wakefulness.

6. Brain Chemistry Correlated With Consciousness: Particular transmitter substances seem to be able to control consciousness. In particular, anesthetics seem to work on a pathway between the thalamus and the cortex.

(Abstracted from Baars, 2003)

Specific rejoinders to some of Baars' arguments are possible. Concerning his first argument, it is difficult to understand what "verifiable" means in terms of inner cognitive or mental processes. Here, once again, arises the problem of corrigibility of introspective reports. As discussed earlier, the "noise" confounding the meaning of an uttered statement places it beyond verifiability. If Baars is referring to the verifiability of behavioral responses, he makes the argument for behaviorism without necessary recourse to the construct of consciousness. If not, then verifiability becomes a chimera, a will-o'-the-wisp, that is hardly likely to be captured by any conceivable empirical method. In both of these comments, Baars invokes consciousness as a possible explanation of behavior ignoring the possibility of automatic mechanisms that could equally well account for it.

The deception argument had earlier been made by Cheney and Seyfarth (1990) but has been vigorously and, I believe, correctly challenged by Baum (1994). Baum argued that there are two conditions that must be fulfilled to define a behavior as "deception" or "lying." The first condition is that there must be some reinforcement for the inaccurate behavior. The second is the inconsistency of that behavior. What is done one day must be inconsistent with what is done another day. However, even if both of these conditions are satisfied, the danger in extrapolating from them to consciousness arises from the unknown origins of the deceptive behavior. There can, however, be no direct answer to this question of origins according to Baum. Unfortunately, in seeking such an explanation, we tend to make serious conceptual errors. Baum (1994) put it this way:

> The temptation to mentalism arises just from the absence of this information.... When we are ignorant of the past history of reinforcement, it is no help to make up stories about ghostly inner origins.... Further research might reveal that such progressions [of reinforcements] occur. This would explain the monkey's action without any reference to its mental life and without giving any special significance to its "lie." (p. 96)

To evaluate Baars' arguments more generally, it is very important to be completely clear about exactly which issues are being raised in discussions of consciousness, such as the one he raises. Six closely interrelated queries—which I designate as the "consciousness" questions—can be distinguished from each other.

The first is the actual existence of consciousness. Is an entity sentient, that is, is it aware of itself and its environment? There are two issues here: Am I conscious? Are there other conscious minds? I have already touched on these problems elsewhere, in this and earlier chapters of this book. The conclusion I reached was a positive one; there were only rare instances in which the existential fact of consciousness was rejected by even the most extreme behaviorist interpretations. We all have first-hand evidence of our own experiential phenomena; this is a powerful and compelling existence proof of the reality of consciousness. The very act of asking the question about one's personal sentience further buttresses the argument that consciousness in some form is as real as any other natural phenomenon or process. It would immediately raise logical questions if the proffered answer to this ontological question were negative. Such a negative answer would immediately lead to logical paradoxes not too dissimilar from those raised when one is asked to interpret the meaning of the statement, "I am lying." "I am not conscious" is equally paradoxical in its significance and import.

If we accept the reality of our own consciousness, then it is very difficult to reject the idea that other humans are also equally aware of their own mentation. The reasoning in this case, is, however, by analogy and reasoning by analogy is, admittedly, fragile. A denial of the fact of "other minds" and the assertion that "I" am the only conscious entity would assert an egocentrism and the concept of a supernatural universe that is so extreme it cannot be accepted without disrupting the entire scientific enterprise of psychology as well as the social fabric of human existence. For this reason, if for no other, it is almost axiomatic that consciousness exists and is a real process of not only my brain but also of the brains of other members of my species. Furthermore, if this is axiom is accepted, it raises the question of the consciousness of other species, a question answered in the affirmative by Baars, but one that still remains controversial simply because the analogies are more strained across species than between humans.

Finally, although there is considerable misunderstanding about what behaviorists have been saying, it is a point of fact that few behaviorists deny or have denied the existence of personal human consciousness. What has traditionally been asserted by this intrepid troop of positivists is that consciousness is private, cannot be explored scientifically and, therefore, we should concentrate on what is indisputatively interpersonally observable.

This second "consciousness" question is: Is consciousness accessible to the external observer? That is, are there any robust introspective or experimental techniques for assaying consciousness? The answer to this question is to behaviorists as unequivocally negative as the answer to the first "consciousness" question (the reality of the conscious mind) was affirmative. Consciousness to followers of this school of psychological thought is an unobservable, inaccessible, intrapersonal, and essentially private experience that cannot be assayed directly or indirectly. Everything else about behaviorism follows from this conclusion of inaccessibility.

Why should mind be inaccessible? The answer to this rhetorical question lies in consideration of a third "consciousness" question: Does interpersonally observable behavior track consciousness closely enough so that it can be used as a indicator of these intrapersonal events? I dealt with this problem in an earlier book (Uttal, 2000) and concluded that mental events such as consciousness are not sufficiently mirrored by behavior to make the private, intrapersonal states accessible to even the most well regulated and controlled method of scientific examination. Intrapersonal consciousness is "in principle" inaccessible. Both verbal and motor behavior can be dissociated from underlying experiences through intent or self-misunderstanding in a way that argues strongly against any kind of behavior as a valid measure of consciousness. At best, what we can do is study the transformations that occur between a stimulus and a response and attribute those changes to some inaccessible central processing.[11]

---

[11]In fact, much of modern scientific psychology seems to be going in this direction without explicitly acknowledging it. Reports of findings, including those from "cognitive laboratories" are increasingly devoid of fanciful reductive theories. It is much more likely to find descriptive models than reductively explanatory ones. Perhaps behaviorism has had a stronger impact than generally appreciated!

A close corollary of this third question is the fourth "consciousness" question: Can we distinguish between a conscious human, on the one hand, and an automaton or even an animal functioning on the basis of hard-wired instincts, on the other? To phrase the same question in quite a different terminology: Is there a "Turing test" that can be used to distinguish between a conscious entity and a suitably high-powered computer? Again, the answer is most likely to be a negative if one accepts the tenet that behavior is neutral with regard to underlying mechanisms. A conscious human, a powerful computer, and an instinctive animal cannot be distinguished (within the limits of their own respective response repertoires) with regard to their inner mental mechanisms or degree of sentient consciousness.

The fifth "consciousness" question asks: Does consciousness have an effect on behavior? That is, is it functionally important? This is a variant of the free-will question that has been answered, on the one hand, by those who support the idea that we have freedom of choice and that the brain function called consciousness can modulate and control the brain processes leading to observable behavior. On the other hand, there are those who argue that consciousness is just an epiphenomenon that has no causal influence on behavior; it just reflects what the brain is doing. In fact, this question is probably also unanswerable because indistinguishable behavior could be produced either by an influential cognitive act or by an automatic response. The difficulty is that brain activity may be reflected onto epiphenomenal self-awareness whether or not it (i.e., self-awareness) is causally influential. The basic problem is that behavior does not discriminate between many plausible alternative system organizations. (See Shallice, 1988, for a particularly eloquent and well balanced account of this problem.)

To put it simply, there is no way to determine what is influential and what is simply concurrent and passively generated when both are perfectly correlated. The intractability of this question suggests that debates over free will[12] and mental causation are likely to be with us for quite a long time. Perhaps, if the humanistic and social consequence of such a debate were not so important, this issue would not be quite so contentious.

Finally, the sixth "consciousness" question asks: Do humans and other animals share the same or similar consciousness even if the magnitude or the quality of the sentience may change as one descends the phylogenetic tree? Although there is an additional major handicap to the facile accep-

---

[12]The similarity between the concepts of free will and Skinner's contingencies of reinforcement has been noted by a number of authors. Morality and ethical behavior are possible for behavioral atheists and the "God fearing" alike. To the former, the schedules of reinforcement experienced during a lifetime dictate optimum behavior. To the religious person, these rules are divinely inspired. Either one of these "explanations" can produce identical behavior. There is no reason that either could not provide a foundation for an ethical society.

tance of animal consciousness—the absence of language skills—this is not really an issue. Animals have other behavioral means of communication (e.g., the use of keyboards by chimpanzees and the acquisition of complex retrieval behavior by dolphins) that are probably adequate substitutes for language. Indeed, if by some magic animals could speak, it would no more resolve the consciousness issue than does speech accomplish this for humans. The logical link between introspective reports and our consciousness provided by language is no stronger in fundamental principle than that between animal behavior and what is going on in their brains—conscious or not. The same perplexities remain whether the response pattern is fallible and corrigible introspective language or pigeon pecks on a lever. I can do nothing more than others when I speculate that there is no reason lower animals are likely to have some awareness comparable, if not as rich, as our own. On the other hand, it would be impossible to prove such a hypothesis no matter how clever the training protocols. Evidence for this conclusion is forthcoming in the continuing controversy surrounding animal consciousness despite the substantial corpus of research into the topic.

Given the context of the half dozen "consciousness" questions posed here (which are not likely to exhaust the set), it is worthwhile to ask which of them has Baars actually answered? Baars' retreat from behaviorism to a kind of Jamesian approach to dealing with consciousness (see Baars, 2003, p. 2) is not justified in my opinion simply because he has not actually linked consciousness with any of the factors he raised in his six-point list of evidence. The accuracy and verifiability of reports of consciousness are contraindicated by a significant body of experimental evidence, most notably Nisbett and Wilson (1977). Their classic article and other research (discussed in Uttal, 2000) raise substantial questions about the accuracy of introspective reports. Beyond that, all of the other five candidates for correlates of consciousness are not what they appear. I argue that they are not measures of consciousness at all! Rather, each can be considered to be a correlation of some kind of behavior (e.g., sleep, wakefulness, distractibility, automatic problem solving, and so on) with measurements in some other domain of measurable variation (e.g., neurochemistry, electrical brain activity, and so on). As such, their link to consciousness is as tenuous as any other hypothesis or inference drawn by any other student of the mind.

The general counterargument to Baars' defense of consciousness, therefore, is that all of these behavioral responses he designates are not the same thing as consciousness. It requires other assumptions and inferences to permit them to serve as valid indicators that bridge to consciousness. The electrical, anatomical, and chemical correlates of behaviors to which he alludes could or could not be indicators of the underlying mechanisms of consciousness. They simply represent necessary conditions for "wakefulness" much as a switch between a power source and a light bulb must necessarily be closed for photons to be boiled off the filament. It would take a substantial stretch of any putative explanation to describe the light bulb as conscious, yet the basic logics of the two situations are not dissimilar. Indeed, even introspectively reported consciousness is not a guarantee of sentience for anyone other then the introspectors themselves. It would be easy enough, even with today's limited computational power, to program a consciousness-free automaton to report that it is conscious. The problem is that we do not have any way to verify the properties or nature of consciousness, only its pale reflections in behavior—a measurement domain that is, as I have repeatedly argued, neutral with regard to internal states, processes, and mechanisms.

Baars (2001) may be entirely correct when he argued "There are no known differences in fundamental brain mechanisms of sensory consciousness between human and other mammals" (p. 1). The lack of differences between brain anatomy and physiology, he suggests, imply that there may be only minimal quantitative difference in human and animal consciousness. However, such a conclusion finesses the real questions about the existence and nature of consciousness that are unequivocally exhibited neither in the behavior nor in any measure of brain activity of animal and human alike.

This brings us to the final matter about the nature of consciousness. A seventh "consciousness" metaquestion can be posed that asks: Are the first six questions answerable? Some (or all) of the six preceding "consciousness" questions, indeed, may not be answerable. What is clear, at the minimum, is that a priori assumptions are going to play an enormous role in the development of our theories of consciousness and any proposed answers to these questions. Unfortunately, I do not feel that any of them (with the possible exception of the existential one) have come close to a final answer. The simple fact that all potential answers are "assumption dependent" raises severe obstructions to their resolvability. Certainly the presence of contemporary alternative theories and unending debates suggests we are not yet close to the resolution of any of them. In such a situation, theory can go off in several different directions (e.g., cognitive and behaviorist) without the possibility of a solid resolution concerning which represents some ultimate truth. There is no "smoking gun" available here nor in many other areas of human dispute.

It seems to me that, in such a situation, the safe and rational course of action is to acknowledge inaccessibility and not to proceed too far in the direction of fanciful hypothetical entities epitomized by the construct "consciousness." Unlike Baars who argues that there is strong "objective evidence for consciousness," I feel that there is no irrefutable evidence to distinguish between a conscious entity and an automaton with the single exception of our own personal self-awareness. Any purported neural or chemical evidence for consciousness is severely damaged by the questionable bridge between behavior and consciousness. Furthermore, the same difficulties arise for both humans and animals.

To reiterate, an important point, none of this arcane criticism of the nature of consciousness should be interpreted as rejecting the practical existence of conscious experience. The individual surgeon, dentist, or acupuncturist (among many others who must deal with human behavior as being real) is obligated to respond to a patient's discomfort under the assumption that there is a private experience of pain occurring no matter how tenuous may be the link between the behavior and the putative conscious experience nor how effective the malingering.

The core of the criticism I make here is that an objective science cannot cope with inaccessible, private, intrapersonal experiences even though they may be very important in practical social interactions. The inability to distinguish between sentience and automatic behavior is no excuse for not dealing with the practical matters of everyday life. In such a situation, it is both easy and desirable to invent plausible properties for the inaccessible that cannot be justified by scientific standards. At the moment, poets may have much more to say about consciousness than does scientific psychology.

The caveat expressed in the preceding paragraphs is that mind or consciousness, as real as it may be and as necessary a part of informal language, is not likely to be accessed, measured, analyzed, or studied in the same way as are the neural actions of the brain or behavioral motor responses. Midgley and Morris (2002) remind us of two comments made by J. R. Kantor (1959) concerning the distinction between events (e.g., mental events) and constructs (e.g., attributed properties of mental events):

> [Events refer to] anything that happens which may or may not become known or studied. (p. 258)

and

> [Constructs include] words of description, records of measurements or manipulations, mathematical or symbological [sic] equations, or formulae in all their various forms.... In general, the term "construct" may be applied to acts as well as [to] products of action. But constructs in any form or style are not to be confounded with the events or stimulus objects in connection with which they are engendered. (p. 259)

Herein lies the same warning made by MacCorquodale and Meehl (1948) when they suggested that many psychological "entities" dealt with as objects were actually nothing more than "hypothetical constructs." All of these scholars are asking us not to confuse the inaccessible mind with hypothetical reifications.

7.3   THE REVOLT AGAINST CONSCIOUSNESS: BEHAVIORISM

In the previous section of this chapter, I concentrated on a few of the classic and contemporary scholars who championed a mentalist view of human nature, one in which consciousness played a central role. Although there is substantial variation in their views and motives, they all share the conviction that the mind can be examined by appropriate scientific methods; in other words, that the mental processes of the brain (as well as the neuronal ones) are accessible to our research armamentaria. With few exceptions, the entire current crop of cognitive psychologists shares this same general perspective even as they differ in detail.

Some contemporary mentalists approach mind from the viewpoint of a computer metaphor. They seek to break down mental activity into modular subfunctions and to isolate and then measure the properties of each module. Others have a less mechanical approach, approaching the problem of mind–consciousness in a more holistic fashion. Regardless of the tactical difference, all who now believe it is possible to study consciousness or mental configurations, base their work on the assumption that mind is real, accessible, measurable, and quantifiable in the same way as any other natural event.

Within this framework is the germ of another cryptic and implicit, but widely accepted assumption: Mind is a structure, an object made of many parts, each of which can be studied independently using the Cartesian *Méthode*. Even more deeply embedded is the primeval idea that this structure is of a different nature than the brain from which it emerged. Therein lies the current vestige of the dualism that arose long ago from the primitive fear of death.

A different foundation assumption, however, guides the psychological theories of the other main school of psychological thought—behaviorism. Although generally[13] accepting the reality of mind as a process of the brain, mind cum consciousness is not considered to be accessible and thus not measurable or even quantifiable in the sense assumed by the mentalists.[14] Since the 19th century there existed a revisionist (contra mentalism) undercurrent of what has come to be called positivist or objectivist thinking about science including the science of the mind. Among the proponents of

---

[13]This statement is not universally true. As we shall see some of the great behaviorists (e.g., Jacob Kantor) equivocated on this matter. If a mental construct referred to "events," that was ok; if, on the other hand, it referred to some fictional power or entity, their reality was very questionable. (See also page 285.)

[14]The measurability and quantifiability of mental events is a topic I considered earlier in some detail (Uttal, 2003). My readers are directed there for an analysis of the ways in which these properties may or may not be applicable to studies of mental events.

this line of thought were Auguste Comte, the original positivist, and Richard Avenarius, the empirocriticist, both of whom expressed ideas that antedated if not influenced the later development of modern behaviorism initially formulated by John B. Watson. It is this antithetical position taken with regard to the mentalism that otherwise dominated American psychology prior to the 1920s and subsequent to the 1960s to which I now turn.

7.3.1 Auguste Comte's Positivism[15]

The term *positivism* seems first to have been used by Auguste Comte (1798–1857) in the early part of the 19th century. Comte was particularly concerned about the evolution of explanatory thought. The progression, he asserted, originally started with the earliest theological or religious theories of existence. (Comte's personal religious feelings can be succinctly characterized by the single adjective he used to describe theologies—fictitious—as well as by his self-professed atheism.) At the most primitive stage, he argued (Comte, 1858) behavior was assumed to be driven by entities complete with minds much like our own, though much more powerful. Tree-sprites, demons, angels, Gods, and many other supernatural but personalized entities fill out the dramatis personae of this initial approach to explaining human nature and its interactions with its environment.

This first "fictitious" stage of explanation was followed by a "metaphysical" (his use of the term) or abstract approach to explanation in which inner psychological forces of a less personal kind were assumed to drive behavior. These forces (e.g., psychological drives such as curiosity, hunger, and lust) had to be inferred from what the organism was doing (i.e., from its behavior).

Finally, in the last and ideal stage of explanation according to Comte—the scientific or positivist stage—science sought to explain without inferring the existence of any of these mysterious internal mental forces and entities. Rather, the goal of this ultimate stage of explanation was merely to describe the relations among the observable antecedents and resultants. No longer, Comte suggested, was there any need for what he believed was a futile search for "first causes." Nor were scientists required to futilely seek complete reductive explanations of events that could only be indirectly observed.

The conceptual, if not the specific historical, links between Comte's philosophy of science and a behaviorism declaring itself incapable of evaluating inner consciousness or any other kind of mental workings are obvious.

---

[15]The material on Comte, Avenarius, and Watson in this section have been updated and adapted from my earlier book on Behaviorism (Uttal, 2000). It is central to the development of the ideas presented here and, thus, I feel it is important to include it in this present work to make it self-contained.

Nevertheless, it is interesting to note that although his impact on behaviorist thinking should have been enormous, in point of historical fact, Comte felt that it was impossible to have a science of psychology. Perhaps it was because most "psychologies" (or at least the philosophies of mind then prevalent) were introspective, invoked immeasurable hypothetical entities, and clearly violated his notions of what the highest stage of science should be like. However, there is no question that Comte's philosophy was a major antecedent of modern behaviorist thinking if not a lineal ancestor. What we do not know is whether or not Watson or any of his successors was directly influenced by Comte's positivist philosophy.

7.3.2 Richard Avenarius' Empirocriticism

Another important personage in the succession of ideas that preceded, if not influenced, behaviorism was the 19th-century philosopher Richard Avenarius (1843–1896). Avenarius was one of the first to specifically challenge the validity and value of the introspective method. He argued that only the most basic direct perceptions, unmodified either by the subject's or the scientist's interpretations, were useful in any attempt to understand human thought. In this regard, it seems that he may have anticipated Brindley's (1960) objection to "Class B" observations. To the followers of Avenarius' "empirocriticism," only the most direct discriminative indicators of perception (Brindley's "Class A" observations) were acceptable as data. He asserted that subjective interpretations of one's thought processes would be, at best, misleading and, at worst, false.

Although he was certainly an early positivist or, if you will, proto-behaviorist, Avenarius seems to have been willing to accept verbal reports of direct perceptions, limited only by the constraint that any elaboration of these basic reports was not appropriate to be used as scientific data. As such, he challenged the popularity and utility of the introspective technique, a method that was to play such an important part in the later parts of 19th century psychology.

7.3.3 Henry Maudsley

Introspection, thus, has long been the bête noir of anti-consciousness theorists. Avenarius may have been one of the earliest of those who argued against such a procedure for accessing cognitive states, but he was certainly not the last. In the several sections that follow, repeated evidence is given of how important this issue has been and how salient it remains.

Among the most cogent and still relevant arguments against introspection was the list tabulated by Henry Maudsley (1835–1918), a British physician well known for his attempt to have mental illness considered as a disease. Maudsley (1867) suggested that introspection was deficient because:

1. By focusing upon itself, by its rendering the introspective state static, introspection falsifies its own subject matter. As explicitly stated by Kant and Comte, one cannot introspect the act of introspection.
2. There is little agreement among introspectionists.
3. Where agreement does occur, it can be attributed to the fact that introspectionists must be meticulously trained, and thereby have a bias built into their observations.
4. A body of knowledge built on introspection cannot be inductive; no discovery is possible from those who are trained specifically on what to observe.
5. Due to the extent of the pathology of mind, self-report is hardly to be trusted.
6. Introspective knowledge cannot have the generality we expect of science; it must be restricted to the class of sophisticated, trained adult subjects.
7. Much of behavior (habit and performance) occurs without conscious correlates.
8. Mind and consciousness are not coextensive.
9. Introspection and consciousness cannot give an adequate explanation of consciousness ("the static state of the mind").
10. The arousal of a conscious image is not itself introspectible.
11. The brain records unconsciously; its response is a function of organic states that are not introspectible.
12. Emphasis upon introspection minimizes attention given to physiological processes without which there would be no mental states.

(This secondary rendition of Maudsley's list is quoted from Turner, 1965.)

Given that this critique is almost a century and half old, it is a remarkable testament to both the insight that Maudsley had into this most profound of psychological controversies and to the fact that there are powerful intellectual forces that have continued to propel scientific psychology toward mentalism in spite of such criticisms. Whatever counterarguments (based on alternative inferential strategies) there may be to the inaccessibility of cognition, the insights of the proto-behaviorists such as Avenarius and Maudsley should have had a much greater impact than they ultimately were to have on modern psychological theorizing.

7.3.4 John B. Watson

All of these ideas percolated below the surface of psychological thinking until another of the great psychologists who were to reshape modern scientific thinking appeared on the scene—John B. Watson (1878–1958). Watson probably had many motives and goals that stimulated his development of his behaviorist psychology, but whatever they were, he was from all points of view the first to articulate the shape of modern nonmentalist behaviorism. His childhood had been spent in rural schools in South Carolina, hardly an environment that would have been expected to produce the antitheological tenets that explicitly characterized Watson's subsequent writing and, implicitly, the future development of behaviorism.

In the first chapter of his first book (Watson, 1914) succinctly characterized his behaviorist philosophy in the following ways:

> Psychology as the behaviorist views it is a purely objective experimental branch of natural science. Its theoretical goal is the prediction and control of behavior. Introspection forms no essential part of its methods, nor is the scientific value of its data dependent on the readiness with which they lend themselves to interpretation in terms of consciousness. (p. 1)

and

> The time seems to have come when psychology must discard all reference to consciousness; when it need no longer delude itself into thinking that it is making mental states the object of observation. (p. 7)

and

> It is possible to write a science of psychology, to define it as Pillsbury does (as the "science of behavior") and never go back on the definition: never to use the terms consciousness, mental states, mind, content, will, imagery, and the like. . . . It can be done in terms of the stimulus and response, in terms of habit formation, habit integration, and the like. (p. 9)

Quotations like these leave little doubt that Watson had massive disagreements with the mentalist psychologies that had dominated the 19th century. The differences between James' emphasis on consciousness and Watson's behaviorism are based on different assumptions about accessibility of mental activity that are both profound and still unresolved.

In the introductory chapter of his seminal book (Watson, 1914), he went on to attack three other erroneous strategies that he perceived to be constraining and misleading the then prevailing mentalist psychologies. The first was reasoning by analogy; the second was the use of the concept of the image (i.e., a "centrally aroused sensation")—something that Watson considered to be the "most serious obstacle in the way of a free passage from structuralism to behaviorism" (p. 16); and the third was the concept of "affection." By *affection*, Watson was referring to feelings and emotions in general. He believed that in spite of some efforts to merge the concepts of sensation and feeling, any attempt to do so would be futile.

The first of Watson's three "erroneous strategies" is a methodological issue, but the other two (imagery and affect) are rejections of some of the most prized aspects of human existence. It is not surprising that from the beginning his ideas were considered anathema to many other interpretations of intellectual life. If ever a phrase was overused, it was the expression "throwing the baby out with the bathwater" (applied to Watson's early behaviorism) by a chorus of mentalists that continues to this day.

Nevertheless, behaviorism attracted the attention of a number of psychologists and dominated psychological science for almost 40 years. One reason for its attractiveness was that it was relatively free of questionable inferences and mysterious and unobservable entities. Once Watson's initial premises and assumptions were set, the logical chain to the ultimate technical nature of behaviorism was straightforward. It was not just introspection that was the target of Watson's behaviorism, it was the fundamental acceptance of the idea that intrapersonal mind could be measured and accessed that he rejected. Observations limited to observable behavior led to conclusions that were much simpler, cleaner, neater, and less ambiguous than the intrinsically controversial ones produced by inferences from that behavior. Indeed, Watson's behaviorism swept the scene of ideas that were very, very close to the kind of supernatural thinking characteristic of theology rather than a truly scientific psychology. Speaking of his predecessors' assumptions, Watson (1924) went on to say:

As a result of this major assumption that there is such a thing as consciousness and that we can analyze it by introspection, we find as many analyses as there are individual psychologists. There is no way of experimentally attacking and solving psychological problems and standardizing methods. (p. 4)

Here, once again, a prescient statement of the one-to-many (i.e., single observation-to-many explanations) problem made explicit by the work of such automata theorists as Moore (1956) and such neuropsychologists as Shallice (1988).

There is no question that Watson's original form of behaviorism was extreme for its time in relegating consciousness to the realm of the inaccessible. He argued that behaviorists must use a scientific vocabulary that does not include even such quasi-subjective terms as "sensation, perception, image, desire, purpose, thinking, and emotion . . ." (Watson, 1924, p. 4). In doing so, he sought to remove much of the subject matter that is, from the point of view of many, essential for the understanding of human experience and the appreciation of the intangible pleasures and moral requirements for the "good" life. The difficulty faced by any who challenge the behaviorist approach in this way is that these aspects of human experience may well be, as much as all of us would like it to be otherwise, inaccessible to a truly objective scientific scrutiny. As I noted earlier, other criteria for establishing important social values are available that do not require that we fully understand the nature and workings of the mind or impute to it some kind a supernatural duality.

In formulating his version of an objective, positivist, nonmentalist, behaviorist science, Watson thus rejected the observability or accessibility of private mental experiences and the measurability of consciousness. However, contrary to much popular opinion about "mindless" behaviorism, this did not imply a parallel rejection of the reality of mental experiences themselves. Like all other humans, he had first-hand evidence of the existence of at least one mind—his own. Neither, did Watson reject the basic psychobiological premise that mind was a function of the brain. To Watson, as to many other material monists and nonreductive psychologists, mind was a direct manifestation of the physiological apparatus, as real as both the measurable aspects of behavior and the physical brain itself. It was just not directly accessible to measurement and thus could not be an object of a scientific inquiry into the human condition.

As one rereads the eloquent statement of the behaviorist position presented in his first book (Watson, 1914) (which was really more a text of comparative psychology than either a polemic or a logical analysis supporting his philosophy of a behaviorist psychology), one might reasonably infer that the genesis of his ideas was a purely technical reaction to the methods and limitations of structuralism and functionalism. The conventional view is that Watson had directed his attention mainly at the introspective techniques and mentalist speculations of those structuralist and functionalist traditions that were dominant when he began the 1914 work. However, a careful reading of his later works suggests this may not be the entire story.

It now seems clear there were other motives driving his work of a much more personal nature. Virtually the first comment in Watson's (1924) book (where he was speaking more freely and in a less pedagogic manner than in the 1914 text) is one in which he refers to the "religious background of current introspective psychology" (p. 3). He went on to assert that "If the fear element were dropped out of any religion, that religion could not long survive" (p. 4). In the very next paragraph he vehemently argued against the concept of the "soul" and indicated that its new incarnation in the form of a concept of consciousness is nothing more than a resurrection of classical dualist thinking. Finally, in the latter pages of this introductory chapter, Watson made clear his point of view, referring to the fact that religion is in the process of "being replaced among the educated by experimental ethics" (p. 18).

Watson's psychology was, therefore, much like many other psychologists who preceded him, motivated at least in part by more than abstract scientific principles. His was not simply a technical rebellion against the scientific status quo but another step in the centuries old debate between dualist (theological) and monist (materialist) philosophies. Cloaked in its scientific terminology, it was also an ontological statement in the long tradition of physicalist and positivist thinking that attempted to bring psychology into the realm of scientific analysis and physico-chemical materialism. To do so, he argued that the supernatural (i.e., "metaphysical" in his lexicon) and unobservable mental elements had to be removed from the discussion. The study of consciousness (the central subject matter of introspective structuralists) was to Watson nothing other than the newest manifestation of the "improvable" and "unapproachable" soul of earlier theologies.[16]

If this analysis of his writing is correct, Watson, whatever he was otherwise as a scientist, was also a philosopher dealing with the age-old dualism–monism issue. His "methodological behaviorism" is really an academically respectable materialist monism, a neo-critical alternative to the traditional theological points of view that had dominated psychology up to his time. No wonder that he was confronted with such enormous critical hostility in the 1910s and 1920s in the United States when his books and other writings became well known to the public as well as to the academic community. Watson was attacking some of the most fundamental beliefs of at least some of his colleagues and certainly most of the members of the nonacademic society in which he lived. Even the appearance of atheism had then and has now few friends in a crypto-theocracy! Its actuality induced a kind of criticism that was highly unusual even for the contentions science of psychology.

7.3.5   Jacob R. Kantor

Jacob R. Kantor (1888–1984) has a very curious role in the history of psychological thinking. Despite a prolific career and extreme longevity (he was still

---

[16]It is important, once again, to keep in mind the distinction that must be drawn between the plausible *reality of consciousness* and the impossibility of the *study of consciousness*.

publishing at the age of 90), his impact on current psychology has been relatively modest compared to the other giants of behaviorism. Although a frail
measure of influence, the Citation Index lists only 14 different articles that
cite his work in 2001. For comparison, B. F. Skinner, another distinguished
founding behaviorist, whose work at the conceptual level was arguably less
detailed and philosophically deep, albeit much more influential, was cited in
more than 100 articles in the same period.[17] Other less precise comparison
criteria are the discrepancy between the number of times each behaviorist
is discussed in contemporary classes or in history of psychology texts.

This relative obscurity should not be interpreted to mean that Kantor
has been completely forgotten; rather, his followers represent a dedicated,
but relatively small, group. A workshop here (e.g., Smith, 1996), a retrospec-
tive review there (e.g., Smith, Mountjoy, & Ruben, 1983), a web site (http://
web.utk.edu/~wverplan/kantor/kantor.html) maintained by a devoted follower and distinguished psychologist in his own right—William Verplanck,[18]
and some articles (e.g., Delprato, 1987; Morris, 1984; Morris, Higgins, &
Bickel, 1982; Verplanck, 1996) scattered about in the last few decades are
the vestiges of his greatly underappreciated contribution.

My colleague Peter Killeen has suggested that the reason for this discrepancy between the influence of Kantor and Skinner was due to the fact
that Skinner was essentially an experimentalist whereas Kantor was primarily a speculative philosopher. Such an insight has the ring of truth but also
smacks of reluctance on the part of the main body of today's psychologists
to consider deeply the foundation concepts of their science. Certainly, laboratory activity is much more highly regarded today in scientific psychology
than is the kind of philosophical analysis and speculation at which Kantor
excelled. Unfortunately, most of our colleagues have chosen to charge
ahead with a kind of single-minded and hyperempirical "physicophilia" of
the kind that Koch (1992) ridiculed so severely.

Jacob R. Kantor's personal history is also of interest in understanding
the development of his scientific ideas. He was the son of a rabbi who died
when Jacob was only 11 years old forcing him to leave school at the time.
As Mountjoy and Cone (in press) noted in what is probably the only extensive biography of Kantor's life, he never graduated from high school, but
was admitted to the University of Chicago in 1911 at the relatively old age of
age of 23. It took him only 3 years to receive his baccalaureate degree. Just

---

[17]Another equally poor, but superficially objective, measurement of influence can be gleaned
by simply asking our Internet search engine for counts of the references to the two men. This
measure produces 44,901 responses for the entry "B. F. Skinner" and 12,800 for the entry "J. R.
Kantor."

[18]Sadly, Bill Verplanck passed away in 2002 after contributing so much to psychology. I am
personally grateful to him for the warm support he gave me during the earliest of this series of
books.

3 years later he received his doctorate degree, also from Chicago. Most of the rest of his long career was spent at Indiana University.

From the beginning, Kantor was something of an iconoclastic critic, first challenging intelligence testing and then, the capstone of his career, mentalist psychology in general. The root sources of what turned out to be a lifetime of iconoclasm and criticism are alluded to in Mountjoy and Cone's biography. They quote friends and colleagues of many years who say that Kantor told them he was disillusioned by inconsistencies in the behavior of public servants in the scandal ridden Chicago of his youth and members of his father's congregation. This early disillusionment with authority figures seems to have had a profound effect on Kantor's subsequent psychological philosophy.

Kantor's most important theoretical contribution was to propose a school of psychological thought that he designated as interbehaviorism (Kantor, 1924, 1926, 1971). Interbehaviorism, like all other forms of behaviorism,[19] was designed by him as an objective approach to understanding psychological functions in which the interpersonal observations of the organism's behavior were the primary data and the creation of unobservable hypothetical mental constructs such as consciousness and thought were minimized, if not completely ignored.[20] Like other behaviorists he rejected the study of hypothetical mental processes but, almost uniquely, also went on to reject a purely materialist monism (i.e., neuroreductionist) form of psychological thinking. In the words of Kanfer and Karoly (1972):

> Kantor . . . argued eloquently against the use in psychology of metaphysical abstractions, which find extreme representations in the "bodyless [sic] mind" of the psychists [sic] and the "mindless body" of the mechanists. (p. 399)

Thus, interbehaviorism was concerned not with mental constructs or physiological mechanisms, but rather with observables such as stimuli and responses and their interactions with the organism and the environment.

Kantor's view of the psychological world considered the organism as an interacting mediator between the objects of the environment. In particular, the organism was considered to be an adaptive entity whose behavior was continually being modified by the interactions it had with that environment. So strong was this interaction that Kantor (1978) argued there was no mean-

---

[19]It is interesting to note that Kantor separated himself from other forms of behaviorism. He argued that conventional behaviorism did not completely reject mentalist terms and entities. Nevertheless, in the context of a dichotomy of mentalism and behaviorism, he clearly falls in the latter camp. The difference between other behaviorists and Kantor lie only in the details, not in the general principles.

[20]Bryan Midgley, in a personal communication (2003), suggested that Kantor ignored mental constructs because he felt there was nothing to ignore. As usual, it is hard to find a specific expression of Kantor's beliefs. What is clear is that the internal "unobservables" did not play a role in Kantor's behaviorism.

ingful boundary between the organism and the environment. Psychology, as he defined it, was (or, rather, should be) a science that studied the:

> ... interbehavior of organisms with other organisms, or inorganic things [i.e., the environment] with an accumulation of repertoires of behavior. (p. 331)

This view can be particularized even further. Kantorian interbehaviorism has been described (Midgley & Morris, in press) as not only being concerned with the interactions between a stimulus and a response, but rather as an interaction of six different factors within the "interbehavioral field." These factors included:

1. The organism
2. The response function
3. The stimulus object
4. The stimulus function
5. Setting factors (biological or environmental factors)
6. The medium of contact (sensory conditions) as well as past stimulus–responses interactions.

Psychology, therefore, had to be explained not in simple terms of the raw stimulus and the response but also in terms of the values and roles the response might have in changing the course of the organism's existence.

Kantor was an early proponent of the idea that the study of mental processes by cognitive psychologists was deeply and profoundly influenced by residual religious concepts and beliefs. There can be no more succinct summary of his thoughts on the matter than the abstract of what can only be identified as one of the least well remembered, but most insightful articles (Kantor, 1978) of modern psychology. He said:

> Because the current resurgence of mentalist interpretations of cognitive events runs counter to scientific norms, it prompts a thorough analysis of the source and nature of Cognitivism. As to the source, Cognitive psychology is definitively a continuation of the spiritistic [sic] way of thinking developed by the Church Fathers as early as the 2nd century B.C. The evidence of this continuity is well symbolized by the antiscientific writings of St. Augustine.
> What Cognitivism basically signifies is that such activities as perceiving and reasoning comprise some sort of transcendental internal entity or process, not amenable to observation.[21] Clearly events are being verbally trans-

---

[21]Kantor's expression in this quotation that cognitivists believed that these mental processes are "not amenable to observation" is a curious inconsistency. This is such a behaviorist ideal and so contrary to most mentalist assumptions, that one wonders whether this might have been a typographical error, a slip of the pen, a particularly unharmonious phrasing.

muted into mystical psychic constructs. How such errors can be accounted for is by (a) the power of traditional beliefs and (b) the misunderstanding of Behavioristic doctrine. In conclusion, the article also raises the question of whether mentalism can ever be extruded from psychology, with suggestions concerning the scientific treatment of cognitive events. (p. 329)

My personal agreement with so many of Kantor's ideas, as he expressed them in this article, quite probably colors my high admiration for this "forgotten" work. Nevertheless, the side of the debate that he was among the first to champion is rarely raised these days. At the very least, arguments such as the one both Kantor and I make lie at the core of the behaviorism–cognitive mentalism debate that should be raging these days. Unfortunately, it is not. The Citation Index lists only six citations to this extraordinary paper since 1955, three of which were patently histories of Kantor's interbehaviorism. Only one (Sperry, 1980) seems to have concerned itself with the issues raised by Kantor and then by rejection rather than acceptance.

Kantor argued that cognitive psychology arose in part as a reaction of what was thought to be the excluded areas of psychology such as perception and thinking. However, as this abstract of Kantor's 1978 article suggests, there was another force at work—a deep seated need on the part of mentalist psychologists to reinject what he referred to as "transcendentalism" into scientific psychology.[22] By transcendentalism, Kantor pejoratively referred to a kind of psychology that emphasized the primacy of the unknowable, even spiritual, aspects of reality over the empirical and accessible aspects. It was, according to him, the ancient concept of the transcendental "soul" that evolved into the modern concept of a substance or object-like mind complete with specific faculties championed by cognitive psychologists. In suggesting this subtle transformation from soul to faculties, Kantor's views antedate the current discussion on the modularity of mind. Clearly he considers mental faculties to be the indivisible properties of a mental world that are not "amenable to observation" and all but synonymous with the religious concept of the soul.

Like Watson and Skinner, Kantor was arguing that dualist, transcendental ideas abounding in religious history were making their way into scientific psychology, and that this was not a healthy development. His history of scientific psychology (Kantor, 1963) makes it clear that he also felt this influ-

---

[22]In an earlier work I (Uttal, 2000, p. 136) I highlighted some of the other social and humanistic arguments that were raised against behaviorism including its ignoring consciousness, its dehumanizing reduction of humans to automata, as well as that it is both antidemocratic and antireligious. That such issues should be involved in the scientific analysis of the pros and cons of the various approaches to scientific psychology continue to perplex me. However noble such views may be, they seem totally irrelevant to the scientific issue at hand.

ence was profound, had been going on for centuries, and stood in the way of a scientific approach to this critically important approach to understanding of the human condition.

Another of Kantor's ideas that resonates with my own was his conclusion that interbehavioral "events" were being incorrectly equated with mental "properties," "faculties," or other substantial and even tangible attributes of "consciousness."[23] (I earlier referred to this erroneous fallacy as the confusion of processes with objects. See page 36.) He preceded current thinking in criticizing cognitive psychology for internalizing and reifying the behavior in much the same sense as MacCorquodale and Meehl (1948) postulated the hypothesizing of constructs on the basis of behavioral observations.

Finally, Kantor (1978) asks the rhetorical question: Can mentalism be eliminated? (p. 337). Kantor argued that powerful personal, social, and cultural pressures would always tend to force psychology toward mentalism. His proposed strategy to counteract this enormous pressure was the traditional behavioral one—"to cleave securely to pristine events" (p. 338) (i.e., to observe the behavior of the organism without allusion to the unobservable internal states). To do otherwise, according to Kantor (1963), is to create a situation in which:

> ... the acts of the organism and the influences of the environing factors are transformed into hidden powers localized in a psychic entity called "mind" or in the brain which is presumed to be the substitute or surrogate of the "mind." (p. 10)

Therefore, his answers to the great questions of psychology do *not* include the neuroreductionist approach in which mind becomes either an epiphenomenal function of the brain or the brain itself (p. 338).

In conclusion, Kantor saw a powerful influence of religion in modern psychology with the "mind" replacing the "soul" in what had to be considered synonyms of the ineffable conscious experience. Presciently agreeing with the inaccessibility assumption, he declared for an objective behaviorism. His contemporary, B. F. Skinner, shared many of these same principles and it is to this other distinguished antimentalist to whom we now turn. As we shall see, Skinner agreed that enormous pressure on psychology to become a mentalism was coming from preexisting dualist ideas.

---

[23]It is possible in this context to see that Kantor, like many of the other behaviorists, was uncomfortable with the fractionation, modularization, or faculty-ization of cognitive processes. He shared with Skinner, although not with Watson, the idea that an analysis of cognition into parts was not an obtainable goal.

7.3.6   B. F. Skinner

Much has been said of and written about the most visible of the modern behaviorists—B. F. Skinner (1904–1990). Indeed it has been suggested that
among psychologists, only Freud has been cited more often than Skinner.
Skinner carried the banner of behaviorism after the departure of the pio-
neer John B. Watson from the academic scene and his views and interpretation of this brand of psychology embodied the meaning of the term for
many decades of the 20th century.

Skinner's early life seems to have been particularly uneventful. His early
ambitions were to be a writer and his undergraduate degree was in English.
From his earliest days, he seems to have been an atheist and it is possible
to see in this stance the same predilection to nonmentalist psychologies
that drove others such as Watson and Kantor. In the latter years of his life,
Skinner became more and more open about his own atheism, an openness
that provides illumination into some of the foundation assumptions that
most likely influenced his version of scientific psychology.

Throughout his career, like many other behaviorists, Skinner rejected
the idea that mental activities could be broken up into faculties or components. He believed that whatever was going on either inside the head or in
behavior was a unified, even holistic process. As he said (Skinner, 1963):

[We cannot] escape from primitive features by breaking the little man into
pieces and dealing with his wishes, cognitions, motives, and so on, bit by bit.
The objection is not that these things are mental but that they offer no real
explanation and stand in the way of a more effective analysis. (p. 951)

Skinner was very much aware of the influence that dualist ideas of a separable soul left over from primitive times and primitive beliefs had on theory in psychology. He stated very firmly (Skinner, 1963) that:

Mentalist or psychic explanations of human behavior almost certainly originated in primitive animisms. When a man dreamed of being at a distant place in
spite of incontrovertible evidence that he had stayed in his bed, it was easy to
conclude that some part of him had actually left his body.... The theory of an
invisible, detachable self eventually proved useful for other purposes. (p. 951)

In another important paper (Skinner, 1987), he was very specific about the
forces he believed were underlying the rise of what he saw as a new
mentalism. These forces were, according to him, forcing psychology out of
the scientific and into the domain of unverifiable supernaturalism. His criticism was directed at what he considered to be "three formidable obstacles"

(p. 782)–namely, humanistic psychology, psychotherapy, and cognitive psychology.

Skinner (1987) argued that one of the reasons such obstacles existed was that humanistic psychologies were challenged by both behaviorism and evolutionary theory at their very conceptual roots. At the core of this challenge was the impact that these two modern scientific endeavors (behaviorism and evolutionism) had on the dominant belief in ". . . a creative, mind or plan, or for purpose and goal direction" (p. 783). He went on to suggest that the "disenthronement of a creator seems to some to threaten personal freedom" (p. 783). Thus, one of his main challenges to cognitive mentalism was that it is based on a foundation of religious and humanistic beliefs that themselves have no place in science. It was the primitive fear emerging from a perceived threat to some deeply held hope of an afterlife that Skinner suggested is the foundation of many of the mentalist approaches to psychology—at the expense of the truly objective alternative—behaviorism.

Skinner was, like many other behaviorists, uncomfortable with the mentalist psychologies that gave substance to indirect inferences of what he believed was an inaccessible mind. Many of the constructs of psychology were to him mere metaphors, rather than realities, that could not realistically be inferred from behavioral observations. In the place of such constructs, Skinner chose to put forth well-controlled experimental methodologies, specifically including his invention—operant conditioning—as the methodology of choice. This procedure was based on the idea that the organism encountered numerous stimulus situations as it moved about in whatever environment of which it was a part, responding in whatever way served to fulfill its needs at the moment. Certain stimuli exerted powerful "reinforcing" effects on particular behaviors, generally the behavior that was just being concurrently executed. That behavior or "operant" was strengthened (i.e., its "contingency" of response was increased), as a result of the coincidence of the momentary behavior and the reinforcing stimulus. Depending upon the selection of stimuli, behavior could be modified in the laboratory or, for that matter, in the world outside the laboratory.

In short, behavior was guided by experience and learning, not by an internal decision maker. Skinner was an extreme empiricist in this regard; he argued along with Watson that a person's personality was not defined at birth but, rather, was amenable to "shaping" into anything that the shaper desired. In this regard, Skinner was asserting the idea that humans are monumentally pliable and that their behavior, to a very large extent, could be controlled.

Skinner extended this scientific view into the practicalities of the social environment with disastrous effect. His extreme social empiricism became the source of much of the criticism that was raised against his scientific behaviorism. One wonders how different psychology would have been if both Watson and Skinner had eschewed their abundant social commentary and not threatened the intangible, but highly revered, humanistic values of popular life?

Skinner remained true to his ideas about the relationship of religion and cognitive psychology until the end. On August 10, 1990, only a few days before his death on August 18, he gave a brief keynote address[24] (Skinner, 1990a, 1990b) to the American Psychological Association in which he uttered one of his most famous lines:

> So far as I'm concerned, cognitive science is the creationism of psychology. It is an effort to reinstate that inner initiating-or-originating-creative self or mind that, in a scientific analysis, simply does not exist. (Skinner, 1990a)

Skinner (1990a) then went on to equate the cognitive mentalist search for the mind with the search for a supernatural creator:

> If I say that psychologists in searching for this inner self or mind had wasted their time, you may feel that I am being arrogant. If I say that philosophers who over the centuries have tried to discover themselves in that sense, wasted their time, you may feel that I'm being arrogant. But I recall your attention to the fact that equally or even more brilliant men and women, over a much longer period of time, have been trying to establish the existence of a different creator.[25]

Clearly, Skinner was drawing a parallel between the searches for an unobservable supernatural entity (God) and for what he felt were equally unobservable, however natural, mental constructs. His argument was that the search for the hypothetical construct represented by an "inner-originating-initiating self" (i.e., the mind) was a far poorer scientific strategy than one that was founded on the idea that behavior resulted from result-dependent

---

[24]It was extremely difficult to find the text of Skinner's (1990) actual address to the American Psychological Association. It finally was discovered in the archives of the Los Angeles Times (Skinner, 1990a). A heavily edited and somewhat more moderated version of the article he was supposed to present that evening was published in the American Psychologist (Skinner, 1990b). Skinner is said to have made the final editorial revisions the night he died. The exact wording differs in the two documents. Whether one agrees with what he had to say or not, both documents represent a very important summary statement of his views.

[25]Of course, Skinner's self admitted "arrogance" was exhibited in another way. He alluded to the similarity and comparable importance of the Darwinian concept of evolution and his ideas about contingencies of reinforcement: Contingency modulated behavior was supposed to meet challenges in situations that were too short term or too "unstable" (Skinner, 1990a, p. 1) to work through natural selection.

contingencies of reinforcement. Although, to my knowledge, he never explicitly expressed the idea that vestigial dualist ideas, deeply embedded in our religious and philosophical history, were driving the cognitivist search for the mind, it seems clear he would have been very comfortable with such an extrapolation of his views.

Although, like many other scientists and scholars, there is considerable variation in what Skinner believed at different times in his career about the reality of the mind, it seems that as the end approached he was perfectly willing to argue that the mind "in a scientific analysis, simply does not exist" (Skinner, 1990). We will probably never know whether he meant that mind did not exist in an absolute sense or that its inaccessibility simply meant that it did not exist scientifically. Of course, even that dichotomy is tinged with a certain ambiguity.

7.3.6 William M. Baum

Other critics of mentalism have followed in the intellectual footsteps of Comte, Avenarius, Watson, and Skinner. Although it is impossible to cite all of the current behaviorists who labor in the shadow of today's overpowering cognitive mentalism, some have been specific enough to deserve brief attention at this point. For example, William M. Baum (1994) raised the classic behaviorist objection to mentalism. He argued, "Mentalism is the practice of inventing mental fictions to try to explain behavior" (p. 32). Baum suggested that these "fictions" actually explain nothing for two main reasons—"Autonomy" and "Superfluity."

For Baum, autonomy is an extension of the homunculus idea; it implies that there is some kind of a decision maker inside the head that is ultimately responsible for behavior. In this way, Baum was equating the hypothetical construct of the mind to this slightly more tangible, but equally inaccessible "little decision maker." He then argued that by trying to understand how this inner decision maker works, attention is deflected from the true science of interpersonally observable behavior and, therefore, "mental causes obstruct inquiry" (p. 32).

Superfluity, according to Baum, is another characteristic of mentalism in that it postulates entities (e.g., mind and consciousness) in order to explain behavior in a way that is uneconomical. In other words, Baum argues that mentalism violates Occam's razor—a criterion of scientific credulity that champions frugality of underlying assumptions. These new constructs also raise the false problem of how one can explain the relationship between needs and drives (exemplar mental constructs) and behavior, again diverting attention from the primary scientific goal of psychology—to observe and describe behavior alone.

7.3.7 Jay C. Moore

Another currently active behaviorist of note is Jay C. Moore. In looking for something to balance Baars' lucid defense of consciousness and today's cognitive mentalism, I encountered an equally eloquent statement of the basic nature of today's behaviorism in the form of Moore's (2002) Internet tutorial. Moore has been an effective proponent of the behaviorist position for many years and his tutorial clarified many of the misunderstandings associated with the several different kinds of scientific theory that have been commingled under the rubric behaviorism. Moore (2002) proposed a useful taxonomy of behaviorism that includes the following types:

1. Metaphysical behaviorism argues that nothing was real unless it was publicly observable. Thus, behaviorists of this ilk rejected all mental constructs including consciousness. It is likely that this extreme view is not held by any significant number of behaviorists, who are all presumably sentient human beings and, thus, all have first-hand evidence of their own consciousness. (However, there has been some suggestion that Skinner came close to this point of view in his later years.)

2. Logical behaviorism is a variant that argues the existence of mental concepts must be verified by behavior, thus finessing the problem of the reality of mental entities.

3. Philosophical behaviorism argues that mental terms are "nothing more than dispositions to engage in publicly observable behavior." Neither logical nor philosophical behaviorism resolve the question of the existence of "mental" things, they simply say it is not interpersonally observable and, therefore, outside the realm of psychological science.

4. Classical S–R behaviorism sought to link stimuli and responses directly.

5. Mediational S–O–R behaviorism took another step away from that purist S–R version by acknowledging the role of the organism in mediating the transformations from stimuli and responses. Such an approach was content to deal with theories of the internal observer or its properties to the extent they could be inferred from the discrepancies between the stimuli and the responses.

6. Methodological behaviorism is another view that mental terms may be used as hypotheses if they can be operationally defined. (Moore considers this form of behaviorism actually to be a mentalism in disguise.)

7. Radical behaviorism asserts that only behavioral observations are valid grist for the scientific mill. Mental terminology and mentalist hypothetical constructs are, in Moore's words, "fictions."

Again, words do not do justice to the problem; as we see in Moore's taxonomy of behaviorisms, there is considerable controversy even among behaviorists. Debates rage concerning the basic assumptions of whether or not mental activity is or not "publicly observable" as well as does the act of rejecting the observability of mental processes reject its ontological existence. Further complicating the issue is that none of these behaviorists deny the fact that something was happening inside the head to transform stimuli into relevant and adaptive responses. That the nervous system (and it processes) exerted influences on behavior is not the issue; what is the issue, is whether these internal mental events are real, but not observable, or do not exist at all. This, of course, is the crux of the controversy over the reality and nature of consciousness.

Behaviorists believe it is vitally important not to permit any theories of mental states to be reified into pseudo-tangible constructs that will inevitably be dealt with as entities with properties of their own. It is this error that mentalists regularly make—assuming that some property or aspect of behavior is identical to some object or entity. In other words, psychology must always guard against descriptive theoretical concepts being misunderstood as tangible explanations composed of objects and structures. In Moore's (2002) words:

> . . . an approach that validates itself through appeals to theoretical concepts remains suspect because the theoretical concepts are presumed to refer to phenomenon from a dimension that differs from the behavioral dimension. (Part 1, Section 3, p. 2)

Moore takes off from this point to make what I consider an excellent summary of the relationship between human intellectual history and psychology:

> Radical behaviorists argue that a critical examination of mentalism and methodological behaviorism reveals that mentalism began thousands of years ago, when individuals misinterpreted such phenomena as dreams and perception. Mentalism was then institutionalized as Western culture developed. . . . Today, mentalism is strongly entrenched in various societal and cultural institutions that are cherished for extraneous and irrelevant reasons. Our religious and judicial practices are two examples of such institutions (Part 1, Section 5, p. 2)

Which, to make the obvious blatant, is the message of this present book. Not only are our "societal and cultural institutions" deeply affected, but so, too, are other avenues of investigation about the nature of the human mind, most prominent among them being scientific psychology.

7.4   A SUMMARY

This chapter presents the core psychological thesis of this book and an additional body of evidence supporting my argument (Uttal, 1998, 2000) that there is a strong need for a revitalization of a materialist, positivist, and behaviorist psychology as an alternative to what is essentially a dualist mentalism—cognitive psychology. The cognitive dualism that pervades so much of modern psychology is instantiated in the search for a form of mind that has the properties of an object—an object that is characterized by a divisible modularity, interpersonal accessibility, and quantitative measurability.

The dualism that pervades modern cognitive psychology has the deepest of human roots. The history presented in previous chapters suggests it has been influencing human thought for a time period that may be literally measured in thousands of centuries. It is a dualism that arose out of primitive fears (of death or tribal exclusion) or misunderstandings (of dreams and hallucinations) and evolved through several stages of religious thought (i.e., animism, polytheism, and monotheism) to influence modern philosophy and ultimately psychology. Dualist assumptions about the existence of a supernatural side of our world operating according to rules that do not obtain on the physical side are not just widespread but are ubiquitous. It is estimated that well over 95% of the world's populations have some religious or philosophical commitment to extraphysical processes or supernatural entities as well as a belief in their personal immortality.

This chapter has shown that both the existence and rejection of dualism have played a role in our science. Psychology is a science whose purported range of subject matters, more than any other, overlaps with that of other approaches to understanding the human condition. It is not surprising, therefore, that the topics and concepts of religion, philosophy, and psychology should overlap. It is also obvious that archeology, anthropology, and paleontology play important roles in our appreciation of how current views of human nature evolved.

In this chapter, a considerable amount of attention has been paid, wherever possible, to the religious beliefs and philosophical stances of the various psychologists. Although it is no longer fashionable to parade one's personal views toward religion, enough of the founding fathers of modern psychology did make their views explicit for a picture, however fuzzy it may have been initially, to begin to clarify. Watson, Kantor, and Skinner all professed their view that religion was contaminating scientific psychology. "Mind" or, in its currently popular instantiation, "consciousness," each of these scholars argued, was nothing more or less than a manifestation in modern terminology of the "soul." A search for such unobservables, each argued, was unlikely to lead to an objective science of behavior.

James, Eccles, Sperry, on the other hand, presented their ideas in a way that made it clear their theological assumptions were strongly interacting with their scientific ones. (An idiosyncratic case among the founding giants—Sigmund Freud—seems to have combined his mentalist and atheistic views.) Among the currently active group of psychologists on one side or the other of the mentalism–behaviorism debate, few have declared themselves, so there is no evidence with which to determine their basic theological views.

It would be nice if the situation were simple and a conclusive answer could be given to the question of the relationship between the history of dualist views and scientific theories. However, it would be straining more than just a bit to try to draw from this insufficient sample, a final answer to the questions: Do atheists become behaviorists? Alternatively—Do theists become mentalists?

Nor does one have to limit consideration of the influences on scientific psychology specifically to religion. The influence of values on cognitive psychology has also been noted by Sampson (1981). He suggested that cognitive psychology is strongly influenced by two long-standing "reductions."

> The first is a *subjectivist* reduction, which grants primacy to the structures and processes of the knowing subject. The second involves an *individualist* reduction, which grants primacy to the thinking and knowing of the individual knower, for example, Descartes' heritage of the "I think." (p. 730)

And:

> The knower's psychological states, the ideas in his or her head, are held to be more important, more knowable, and more certain than any underlying material interests, social practices or objective properties of the stimulus situation. . . . The combination of subjectivism and individualism converges to yield a picture of a reality that gains in its coherence by virtue of the orderliness and universality of the building blocks of the individual mind. (p. 731)

Subjectivism and *individualism* are compelling forces and, although devoid of any theological terminology, bear a close resemblance to the yearning for a persevering soul. Cartwright (1979) presented a similar argument for social psychology in which he asserted that the "social system" of social psychology exerts strong influences on its research systems.

Many other metaphors or points of view have guided and constrained thinking in this particularly vulnerable science. The core of modern cognitivism, the idea that some computational-like syntax is the mode of mental activity, has played a central role in this newest mentalism. However, as many philosophers of psychology have pointed out, the computer metaphor "does not capture enough about the human mind." The performance analogies offered by students of artificial intelligence are today almost entirely based on the capabilities and limitations of computer technology and offer little to the serious student of psychology beyond the toy existence proofs that only barely supplement the most compelling proof of all that sentience exists—our own intrapersonal self-awareness.

Similarly the neuroscientific metaphor of mind as a brain function, although indisputable as an ontological statement, is so clouded by epistemological unknowns as to be virtually useless for psychology. We still don't have even the glimmering of an idea about how the many neurons of the brain can produce mentation after a couple of centuries of neuroscientific research. Furthermore, this avenue to understanding may forever be blocked by simple computational complexity.[26]

What does seem clear given the history and overlap of subject matters is that there are profound influences of some of the older dualist ideas on modern psychological thinking. Rarely, however, is this vestigial dualism made explicit. Instead of looking upon mental functions (including consciousness) as being functions of a complex neural substrate, they are often dealt with as quasi-concrete objects with components that have material properties of their own. The concept of the modularity of mental functions is the most prominent example of such confusion. The classic cognitive flow chart model of the mind characterizes a part-like mechanical view of the nature of cognition as opposed to its overall functional or process nature. The essential unitary (phenomenologically speaking) nature of mental processes is, thus, obscured by the main thrust of modern cognitive psychology.

That traditional dualist views can and do influence psychology is not a new proposal; it has a long history in psychology and, from some points of view may represent the best explanation for the persistence of mentalist psychologies, however unexpressed and cryptic its influence may be. Indeed, the idea that one's assumptions can influence one's conclusions is hardly limited to psychology. Evidence for such a hypothesis is evident throughout the history of science in general. The many examples of misperceptions of not only the meaning of data, but also of the data themselves are ubiquitous throughout scientific history.

In conclusion, let me restate what I see is the essential problem faced by modern psychology. Behaviorists argue that mind cum consciousness is, for all practical scientific purposes, incapable of being defined and is inaccessible to objective scientific measurement. Mentalists take the antithetical position. Although we psychologists do not spend a lot time arguing this issue, it remains both unresolved and critical in defining the future of our science. Nevertheless, in the absence of a "killer" argument for either side

---

[26] I am currently at work on a book dealing with this topic.

of the debate, we tend to allow extraneous issues to dictate our behavior. This book has reviewed the history of one of these issues—dualism—and has culminated in a consideration of its impact on psychological theory. My personal view is that we should seek to develop a nonreductive, non-inferential, descriptive, naturalistic approach to a scientific psychology that concentrates on interpersonally observable events in place of the naïve and overly optimistic hope that somehow the intrapersonal, private mind will become interpersonally accessible.

8

Summary and Conclusions

Cognitive psychology arose as the response to a confluence of ideas maturing in the early 1950s and 1960s. Several important ideas contributed to this resurrection of mentalism. Some, such as the classic dualism that is the main topic of this book, continued to influence psychological thinking. Other newly maturing concepts and technologies added to the impetus to revitalize mentalism. For example, the role of the computer as a metaphor for mind must not be underestimated. In the glow of this magnificent technological development, scientists and engineers were able to look at the inner information-processing activity of a machine that bore many operational and information-processing similarities to the mind. Computers possessed sensory, motor, and, most interestingly, central-processing agents that mimicked cognitive activity as they processed well-defined units of activity. The fact that it was possible to actually design and construct these CPUs (Central Processing Units) and to understand the operation of the entire system raised hopes that centuries old problems about the role of internal mental mechanisms and processes might also become amenable to similar explanations.

Another important scientific development that stimulated cognitive neuroscience was the realization of the ability to study the activity of single neurons. Although the neuron theory had been well established by then, it was not until the 1950s that techniques were developed for observing the activity of single neurons. Once again, cognitive psychologists were excited by the implications of examining the activity of the actual units of which the brain was constructed. Since it was generally agreed that mental activity arose from the interaction of large numbers of these neural units, it seemed reasonable to expect that psychology was on the edge of an enormous breakthrough in our understanding of how neurons might produce mind. It took several decades for this hope to fall victim to the realization that the number of neurons involved in even the simplest thought was so large and the interconnection pattern so irregular that simple combinatorics might forever prohibit such a reduction of the mental to the cellular neurophysiological. The theoretical assignment of cognitive processes to single neurons or the development of toy "connectionist networks" did not alleviate the profound and fundamental difficulty produced by simple complexity and numerousness. For all scientific purposes, in spite of what we have learned about them, it is still the case that how neurons produce mentation remains as much a mystery nowadays at it did centuries ago.

There were other influences, social and scientific, that also provided a fertile ground and ultimately led to the resurrection of cognitive mentalism after a half-century of behaviorist dominance. This book explores one of those that is infrequently considered in histories of scientific psychology— dualism; a worldview that has motivated and concerned humans from what we now believe to be the very dawn of human cognitive activity. This book is both a historical review of a particular idea and an example of the impact that a sometimes persistent and irrelevant belief can have on current scientific attitudes and theories.

The general argument presented here is that the Zeitgeist established by powerful social influences is capable of directing science in directions that may be misleading, if not downright incorrect. The particular thesis of this work is that the dominant dualist intellectual climate of our times has pushed scientific psychology back into the arms of the mentalists after a period of a conceptually more correct behaviorism.

Dualism, in a nutshell, is the conviction that there are at least two levels of ontological reality. This view of nature has come in many versions over the millennia, Dualisms range from primeval spirit–body dichotomies to sophisticated and arcane mind–brain distinctions made by today's technical philosophers and cognitive neuroscientists. Whatever the respective form it took at one or another period of human cognitive activity, the strong belief that there may be distinguishable kinds of reality has played a central role in human affairs including, as I argue here, scientific psychology. From its earliest manifestation as a response to the observation of death and bodily decay, through its essential role in religions of increasingly sophisticated kinds, to an arguably nontheological technical philosophy, to modern cognitive neuroscience, dualist ideas have exerted a powerful influence on how humans construct their environments and live their lives. Not only has its influence been strong, but also it is indisputable that if one were to simply count noses, the dualists would vastly outnumber holders of the opposing view—material monism—the belief that only one kind of ontological reality exists. The single form of reality to a monist is the material one; a corollary concept is that all other events and phenomena arise from processes and actions of the material substrate. Included among these "other" events and phenomena are the observable aspects of behavior and, to whatever limited extent it may be possible, the inferred properties of mind.

For reasons that will always be debated, proto-dualistic thinking now seems, on the basis of the best paleoanthropological evidence, to have arisen along with the first signs of human cognitive activity, arguably about 100,000 BP, but certainly by 40,000 BP. I have argued here that proto-dualisms initially arose as a response to the emerging awareness of and the resulting fear of death. By hypothesizing a distinct kind of reality for mental processes different than that of the material world, an escape hatch opened through which individuals could avoid the horror of the termination of their personal consciousness.

The possibility of the persistence of the mind-cum-soul-cum-consciousness after death was buttressed by the introspective self-examination of workings of the mind; dreams, selective perception, mental disturbances, and hallucinations all added credibility to the idea that self-awareness could have a separate and continuing kind of existence that was not possible for the body. The mind could come and go from the physical constraints of the body; it could transcend the natural world; most important of all, it could persist after bodily death.

Once that basic dualist principle of a mental or spiritual reality separate from the physical one was invented, what followed was a logical and reasonable evolution of religious ideas of the transcendent supernatural. The paleoanthropological and archeological evidence of such beliefs can be traced out in the material remains and ultimately in the written record of earlier societies. On this theory, the most primitive dualism of "my body and my mind" initially evolved into animisms in which consciousness was attributed to inanimate objects of all kinds. From those early multispirit, proto-religious stages emerged the first personalized polytheisms in which attempts were made to explain the human condition and its origins by means of myth and folklore and by the invocation of supernatural and superpowerful beings. Of the earliest polytheisms we know very little, because they left few records of their ideas and beliefs. With the coming of writing, however, a door was opened to the thoughts of the priests and the rituals and doctrines of past theologies. Of particular interest was the nature of their creation myths, all of which invoked dualist concepts.

Polytheisms have generally, but not exclusively, evolved into the modern monotheistic religions. However, even the most ardent claimants of monotheisms usually have auxiliary demons, angels, and jinn of one kind or another to support and supplement their primary God. The many different religions that have remained active into modern times vary enormously in their rituals and core beliefs. Nevertheless, they all share one common feature—the belief that there is some kind of continuity of the spiritual essence of a person following bodily death. Therefore, soul–body dualism is the central and universal core doctrine of all modern religions. Appended to this central core are the rituals and details of the supernatural world including remarkably pervasive descriptions of the nature and locus of the afterlife. Although it may offend many to make the point, there is not a shred of empirical evidence to support this substantial and ubiquitous enterprise.

Thus, the universal promise of immortality unifies all previous and all current religions. It is the one tenet of religion that is taught by every sect, discipline, and denomination. Not even the central idea of an omnipotent and personified God is found in all religions. I argue here that the main reason for the success and continuity of religion in our own modern scientific eras is this promise it presents of an escape from the termination of personal consciousness. This is a powerful promise, indeed!

The idea of some kind of personal immortality permeates both the thinking of individuals as well as most of the intellectual constructs of human society in deep and often unexpressed ways. It is not necessary for individuals to spend a significant proportion of their thinking time concerned with this issue to have a strong commitment to it; dualistic concepts are so much a part of all facets of human culture that they are easily absorbed, *en passant* so to speak, as the individual passes through the social environment.

Other modes of studying mind beyond religion have evolved over the centuries. Philosophy offered speculation and logic as tools for studying mentation as a substitute for the raw acceptance of religious dogma. Nevertheless, much of philosophy is still engaged with such topics as the possibility of "other worlds" and other quasi-religious and supernatural ideas. This is not surprising since throughout a substantial portion of human history, philosophy and religion were virtually the same, especially in the huge historical gap between the classical Greek and modern philosophical eras. During this period, which lasted from the late pre-Christian years until the 16th century, philosophy was mainly practiced in the service of religion. Logic was applied to justify and authenticate teachings of the temple, church, mosque, and synagogue. However, since the time of Bacon and Descartes, nontheological philosophies emerged in which arguments were increasingly aimed at the ontological nature of the natural world rather than the theological existence or nonexistence of God. However, philosophy could not, any more than any other domain of human activity, escape the pressure toward dualism that had become such a ubiquitous part of all kinds of human learning. The possibility of nonmaterial, dualistic ontologies still reverberates through the teachings of even the most recent philosophers, particularly when they deal with the meaning of such new ideas as "supervenience."

The newest approach to the study of mind is scientific psychology, or as it is known these days—cognitive neuroscience. Dualists and material monists, joined now by psychologists and other neuroscientists, debate what is now called the mind–brain problem in the halls of academia. Much of this debate remains inconclusive and shows no visible sign of resolution. New terminology, invented in the hopes that a neologism must clarify something about the nature of reality, itself become reified and the object of further debate over what in the final analysis must ultimately be considered to be lexicographic nonissues.

A great schism still divides scientific psychology. On the one hand are the mentalists; on the other the behaviorists. The former direct their attention at the description and analysis of the *mind* or, in its most recently resurrected manifestation—*consciousness*. The latter, although generally not rejecting the existence of intrapersonal sentience, believe that such processes and actions are inaccessible and any attempt to study them, directly or indirectly, would be wasted effort. The best we can do, according to behaviorism is to measure and describe the *interpersonally* observable (or potentially observable) patterns of response we collectively refer to as behavior.

Behaviorists are convinced that the effort to study *intrapersonal* and private cognitive processes is beset by a host of difficulties, some of which are due to the existence of intractable "in principle" barriers and some due to practical considerations such as complexity and combinatorial numerousness. Nevertheless, "consciousness studies" and other kinds of mentalist cognitive psychology in which attempts are made to both analyze and reduce mental activity to isolable modules and components remain the dominant themes of most modern experimental psychological research. The question focused on in the rest of this summary chapter is: Why should this be the case?

The following list tabulates a few of the reasons that mentalism continues to play such a powerful role in modern psychology, especially in the form of its most recent version—cognitive neuroscience.

1. Persistent and prevailing dualist views.
2. The general intractability of the problem posed by the intrapersonal privacy of mind.
3. The enormous nonlinear and interactive complexity of the neuronal interactions that produce the mind.
4. Limited human cognitive abilities leading to the necessity to create hypothetical constructs.
5. The demands of our curiosity that we seek answers to the mysteries of life and the universe regardless of their intrinsic answerability.

6. The inescapable fact that basic assumptions drive every human endeavor and, so too, do they drive psychological theory.

(I) Persistent and Prevailing Dualist Views

It would have been instructive to find that cognitivists generally came from religious backgrounds and behaviorists either came from nonreligious backgrounds or had adopted a less religious point of view. Unfortunately, once beyond the founding fathers of modern psychology, there is little source material that can lead to any such conclusion concerning the religious attitudes of either current cognitivists or behaviorists. Among the early behaviorists such as Watson, Tolman, Kantor, and Skinner, however, there was a repeated allusion that their personal monist atheisms played an important role in the development of their scientific theories. Similarly, from William James onward, there is the suggestion that one's religious beliefs subtly propelled a psychologist toward the study of mental constructs such as the mind and consciousness.

One does not have to delve too deeply into the modern philosophy of science literature to observe the persistence of implicit dualist ideas. As distinguished a scholar as Kurt Gödel, famous for his proof of the essential indeterminacy of the consistency of mathematical systems, spoke out against a raw monistic materialism in a way that is fundamentally flawed:

> Simple mechanisms can't yield the brain. I think the basic elements of the universe are simple. Life force is a primitive element of the universe and it obeys certain laws of action. These laws are not simple and not mechanical. (Cited in Dennett, 1995, p. 444)

Allusion to a "life force" by Gödel smacks not so much of a simple dualism as it does of an even earlier form of animism or of Bergson's (1929) élan vital; the latter being another extraphysical and supernatural substitute for a strict materialism and itself an explicitly religious idea. The traces of the personal religious beliefs of many other scholars on their subsequent theories are similarly discernible.

Gödel's comment also embodies a rather curious misunderstanding of evolutionary processes by many who feel the need to impose a goal or purpose (i.e., teleological imprint) on the mind. That is the view that the human mind is so improbable that it would have required some creative and intentional direction for its ultimate emergence. The problem with such an idea is that the human mind (or any other evolutionary outcome) is not improbable; rather, it exists *with a probability of 1*! That is, no matter how complex and uncertain was each step of the process that led from some primeval biochemical reaction to us and notwithstanding the fact that, a priori, our particular form of being was the improbable outcome of that process, our *ex post facto* existence is the highly probable outcome of that uncertainty. It is what we might well call an *existence proof*. That which is, is highly probable; in fact; it is certain. Whatever random and selective processes that may have intervened between the first molecules and us played out any uncertainty of the improbabilities. What we have now is the certain end product, however unanticipated or unpredictable it may have been at the outset. Gödel was just flat wrong when he said that simple processes could not have produced the brain. Our existence is the falsification of his assumption. The classic illogic expressed by this great logician was based on what we can only surmise was a lingering dualism in his thinking.

That such dualisms should exist even in the thought processes of the "hardest" of scientists should not surprise any of us. Dualism is a powerfully influential part of our culture because it is the core assumption of all religions. Furthermore, dualist ideologies and assumptions thoroughly permeate even the most secular aspects of our society. Combined with the natural desire to avoid personal mortality, this powerful and compelling influence provokes powerful tendencies toward thinking of the mind as an analyzable *object* rather than a unitary *process*. However cryptic and subliminal such influences may be, they provide a fertile ground for any philosophy or psychology that is prone to suggest that the mind is more than a complex, but natural, function of a mess of neurons [a la Crick!]

(2) The General Intractability of the Problem Posed by the Intrapersonal Privacy of Mind

The mind poses a challenge to its interpretation and understanding that, although not unique among scientific topics, does impede the generation of scientific answers concerning its origin and nature. That difficulty is to be found in its intrapersonal nature and inaccessibility to direct examination despite widespread acceptance of the idea that mental processes can be assayed by appropriate techniques. (See Uttal, 2000, for a discussion of the arguments against accessibility and the limits on measuring intrapersonal mental states.)

Because of the fact that only we are privy to our own self-awarenesses, it is not possible to directly measure or verify that any kind of behavioral report is an accurate reading of the cognitive process at work. All theories that make the transition from behavior observations to internal structure do so on the basis of what are at best indirect inferences. Inference can only sample the plausible, but as argued here, externally observable behavior is neutral concerning intrapersonal private events. Inferences from such external observations to internal processes or mechanisms are clouded by a substantial number of factors. One of the foremost is the one-to-many problem: the fact that any single external, behavioral observation may be explained by what is virtually an infinite number of alternative internal mechanisms. Another is the profound, but unknown, degree to which intentional or unintentional cognitive processes penetrate the transformations from thoughts to behavior to modulate, modify, or obscure the nature of the underlying processes.

In short, there is no golden road to exploration of the inner processes and activities we call "mind" available to psychology. In other simpler sciences, mathematics often provides a powerful tool for at least describing the domain of the plausible. In psychology, basic questions about the quantifiability of mental dimensions and events raise further barriers to our ability to construct sufficiently constrained reductionist explanations. (See Uttal, 2003, for a discussion of the problems raised when one wishes to measure psychological processes.)

(3)   The Enormous Complexity of Brain

Beyond the arguably debatable problem of inaccessible mental processes lies a much more concrete issue for which there should be much less controversy. The human brain, indisputatively the material organ that executes the processes we call mind, is complex to a degree that is almost beyond definition and certainly beyond intuitive appreciation. One measure of its enormous complexity is that each of its 10^{10} (or, according to some, 10^{13}) neurons is irregularly connected to an estimated 10^3 other neurons. Numbers like these suggest a number of combinations and permutations that are so large as to be beyond any hope of analysis or representation. Nevertheless, this is the level at which the action involved in producing mentation most likely occurs. Even at higher levels, such as the unknown number of interacting centers, nuclei, and nodes in the brain, there is great uncertainty whether or not even the most fundamental hierarchical arrangement of the cerebral centers could ever be established. (See Uttal, 1998, for a more extensive discussion of the problems of numerousness and complexity and Hilgetag, O'Neil, & Young, 1996, 2000, for the specifics of this argument.)

(4)   Limited Human Cognitive Capabilities

In spite of the wonderful powers of our minds to solve problems of generalization and categorization, the human brain's capacity to solve other kinds of problems is limited. Some of the limits are imposed by the complexity of the situation and some by our own inherent limited powers. The problems faced by humans in many aspects of our lives sometime appear to have no simple explanation. Mysteries abound not only in the interpretation of the meaning of the deeper aspects of our existence but also in the simple responses that must be made to recurring events in daily life. To early humans, the natural environments offered up imponderables enough. Floods, winds, volcanoes, drought, famines, and innumerable other calamities all seemed to require explanations from cognitively active entities like us. The skies, the pleasures, and pains of life and death, as well as the times of abundance or "good fortune" also demanded explanations.

The prototypical response to such mysterious events was to personalize them. It was an easy cognitive step to the idea that there existed events that were not random but, rather, were the results of conscious decisions on the part of other sentient entities (than ourselves). These supernatural entities coexisted with us and were powerful enough to account for both the catastrophes and the delights. Thus arose the early animisms, a major step in the evolutionary sequence of dualist ideas that have been described in this book.

The important point is that human limitations led to the postulation of unobservable and supernatural entities to "explain" what was, at those prescientific times, mysterious. Where events were of uncertain origin, the additional assistance of supernatural and superpowerful forces and beings could bring a substantial amount of solace, if not justification, to the human questioner.

I maintain that the same process holds for modern day psychological theory. We are confronted with enormous challenges. Our profession attacks questions of such monumental complexity that, like our primitive predecessors, we are pressured to invent plausible entities to explain what is currently inexplicable. The invention of hypothetical constructs and the interpretation of what they might mean by psychologists bears a strong similarity to the dualist construction of supernatural entities existing outside the observable natural world.

(5) Human Curiosity

In the previous paragraphs, I touched on another powerful force for the development of fanciful ideas about the mind. There is the natural proclivity on the part of humans to seek answers to the many questions that arise in their daily lives. There is perhaps no more positive driving force to the improvement of the human condition than this basic curiosity. Developments in science, medicine, and engineering applications are constantly raising our standard of living, mainly because of the curiosity of our fellow humans. However, even more important than these practical accomplishments is the prevailing need to achieve understanding of our origins, our nature, and our future prospects. Unfortunately, in the presence of what are the intractable problems of human nature, our curiosity frequently overdrives us to posit superficially simple and unverifiable answers to some of the great issues. The invention of a universe made up of two different kinds of realities, each operating according to different sets of laws is an understandable, but inherently incorrect response to this basic curiosity. To the degree it feeds back onto our psychological theories, such a dualism misleads and misdirects this important scientific enterprise.

(6)   Research Based on Implicit Basic Assumptions Is the *Modus Operandi* of All Sciences; So, Why Not for Psychology?

The fact that fundamental dualist concepts and assumptions can influence psychological science should not be surprising. The power of underlying and covert assumptions to influence behavior is ubiquitous in virtually every other aspect of human activity. Government policies are driven by prejudices and assumptions almost to the exclusion of scientific findings. Given the complexity of our social, economic, and political systems, it is likely that ideas well down the logical tree will exert influences on policies and proposals. Nowhere is this clearer than in the current political debates about how best to solve the lingering economic crisis. "Conservatives" argue that this can best be accomplished by direct support of business and the wealthy who pay taxes; "liberals" support the contrary idea: A solution will only emerge as a result of actions that directly provide support to workers lower down on the economic ladder.

Which policy is more likely to solve the economic problems we face is still uncertain; what is certain is that these alternative proposed policies are strongly influenced by deeply held beliefs and assumptions that are rarely made explicit. In such a situation, propaganda and euphemisms reign supreme. Although these techniques may be effective tools to convince the public of one policy or the other, the underlying sociopolitical assumptions that led to the respective policies are usually hidden deep below the surface discussion.

Initial assumptions also color the outcome of the social sciences. Whether one is convinced that equalitarianism or that a laissez-faire social Darwinism is more likely to produce the greater good can have profound consequences on the resultant economic theory. The continuing debate over which of these assumptions is correct suggests there has as yet been no resolution forthcoming.

The physical sciences are no less sensitive to their underlying assumptions than are politics or the social and psychological sciences. Foundation axioms or starting points are found in even the purest forms of mathematics and are as necessary there as in any other scientific approach. It should not be overlooked that even the "simplest" of sciences, for example cosmology, faces the same problems as does psychology. Formal mathematical models are often indeterminate and can lead to controversies about underlying mechanisms that are resolved by different individuals according to their own fundamental assumptions. The recent debate between "dark matter" theorists and those who propose that Newton's laws do not exactly work at very large distances is an example of the open-ended nature of mathematical theories even in this pristine field of science. Models can describe, but cannot, in principle, exactly define the nature of the underlying forces.

In such a context, one might fairly ask why should psychology not be permitted to also develop from its own fundamental assumptions? The answer, of course, is that it does and will continue to do so. However, mentalist approaches have some special flaws and constraints that should alert *Caveat* us to how especially sensitive they are to their basic assumptions and how much easier it is to go wildly astray here than in physics, for example. Because of the special elusiveness of the subject matter, some of psychology's foundation assumptions have a tendency to be much closer to dualist myths than objective interpretations of data. A major extra difficulty for psychology is, therefore, that it is too close and too relevant to human ambitions and fears.

There is another problem facing psychology that makes it unique. Arising out of the inaccessibility of mind and the complexity of mechanism and process that I have just discussed is a substantial fragility of the empirical findings from its laboratories. Because of the narrowness and small scale of most of the experiments conducted by psychologists there is a strong tendency for individual empirical findings to not last very long before they are contraindicated by another set of data. Models and theories of human cognitive rarely last a generation. It is quite a challenge to be asked to identify a particular psychological theory that has persisted for more than a few years. Our history is littered with explanations and ideas that have simply been discarded rather than disproven in any empirical sense. Although it may not be generally appreciated, even the empirical results of well-designed and narrowly conceived experiments often are rejected soon after their publication. (See Uttal, 1988 and 2003 for an extended discussion of the fragile data problem.)

Even more fundamentally, we have not yet adequately defined the components of cognition. What definitions we do have come and go with whatever new metaphor attracts momentary attention. As far as the study of the properties of even the most basic of psychological terms, there are very few broad meta-reviews of the data from comparable experiments at laboratories where interests overlap considerably.

The susceptibility of studies of behavior and the mind to external influences and to artifacts and other misconceptions is considerably deeper than that of many of the other sciences. Additional reasons why this should be the case include:

- A confusion between endogenous and exogenous causal forces
- The misunderstanding of the power of inevitable natural laws and superpowerful mathematics
- Misunderstandings about the quantifiability and measurability of psychological dimensions
- The uncertainty introduced by the extraordinary variability of human behavior (From Uttal, 2003)

For all the reasons discussed in this book, it seems appropriate to raise a note of caution for psychological science. The caveat is that we must be especially aware of the cryptic and implicit assumptions on which experimental designs and theory are based. As one considers the state of psychological research these days, there are hopeful signs suggesting that today's dominant mentalism may have run its course and that we are becoming more aware concerning the axiomatic premises underlying scientific psychology. The literature of the patently psychological (as opposed to the neuroscientific) journals seem to display much less gratuitous reductive theorizing and hypothetical constructing than was evident even a few years ago. Behavioral data is more likely to be presented in a much more pristine fashion without attempts to develop complex theoretical explanations or to suggest fanciful underlying mechanisms. Instead, current models tend to be acknowledgedly descriptive rather than reductive; that is to say only—"This is what we have observed and this is what people do." Furthermore, remote and far-fetched physiological explanation is also harder to find in the nonreductive psychological literature. The great exception to this apparent generalization, of course, is the enormous amount of activity in the field of PET and fMRI imaging, but that is another story told in Uttal (2001).

Unfortunately, criticism such as that presented in this book has to be inherently negative in tone. Iconoclastic critics rarely have the privilege of presenting a positive alternative. I hope it is obvious at this point that there is a positive alternative to what must be considered to be, at it most fundamental intellectual roots, a dualist cognitive mentalism. This alternative exists in the form of a modified and renewed version of an objective, positivist behaviorism. In my previous books I have tried to remind my readers of what the properties of this scientifically sounder form of psychology should be. I can think of no better way to conclude this book than to do so again by tabulating the features of what I believe should be the framework of a new behaviorism. This new behaviorism should be characterized by the following properties:

1. Psychophysical: It must utilize the well-controlled methods of psychophysical research.

2. Anchored Stimuli: Stimuli must be anchored to independent physical measures.

3. Simple Responses: Responses must be limited to simple (Class A) discriminations (e.g., "same" or "different") to minimize the cognitive penetration effects that distort functional relationships.

4. Operational: It must define its concepts in terms of procedures, not in terms of unverifiable, ad hoc hypothetical constructs.

5. Mathematically descriptive: Its formal theories must be acknowledged to be only behaviorally descriptive and to be neutral with regard to underlying mechanisms.

6. Neuronally Nonreductive: It must abandon any hope of reducing psychological phenomena to the details of neural nets because of their computational intractability.

7. Experimental: It must continue to maintain the empirical tussle with nature that has characterized the best psychology in the past.

8. Molar: It must look at behavior in terms of the overall, unitary, integrated process it is and avoid invoking a false modularity.

9. Empiricist and Nativist: It must accept the compromise that both experience and evolved mechanisms motivate and drive behavior.

10. Empiricist and Rationalist: It must accept the compromise that behavior accrues from both stimulus determined (automatic) and logical (inferential) causal sequences.

11. Anti-Pragmatic: Psychology must accept its primary role as a theoretical science and base its goals on the quest for knowledge of the nature of our nature rather than on the immediate needs of society or the utility that some of its findings may seem to have. *Useful* theories do not necessarily have the same validity as *true* theories.

In conclusion, the point of this book is that a residual dualism is cryptically embedded in cognitive mentalism—the currently dominant form of scientific psychology. I believe that the epistemological problems such an approach entails can be overcome by adhering to a revitalized behavioral psychology that eschews any effort to make accessible the inherently inaccessible.

References

Abelson, R. (1970). A refutation of mind-body identity. *Philosophical Studies, 18,* 85–90.

Achté, K. (1980). Death and ancient Finnish culture. In R. A. Kalish (Ed.), *Death and dying: Views from many cultures.* Farmingdale, NY: Baywood.

Adovasio, J. M., Gunn, J., Donahue, J., & Stuckenrath, R. (1978). Meadowcroft rockshelter: An overview. *American Antiquity, 43,* 632–651.

Adovasio, J. M., Gunn, J. D., Donahue, J., Stuckenrath, R., Guilday, J. E., & Volman, K. (1980). Yes Virginia, it really is that old: A reply to Haynes and Mead. *American Antiquity, 45,* 588–595.

Albright, W. F. (1937). A biblical fragment from the Maccabean age: The Nash papyrus. *Journal of Biblical Literature, 56,* 145–176.

Allport, G. W. (1950). *The individual and his religion: A psychological interpretation.* New York: Macmillan.

Anonymous. (1974). *Excavation reports of neolithic tombs at Dawenkou.* Beijing: Wenwu Press.

Arensburg, B., Bar-Yosef, O., Chech, M., Goldberg, P., Laville, H., Rak, Y., Tchernov, E., Tiller, A. M., & Vandermeersch, B. (1985). Un sepulture neanderthaienne dans la grotte de Kerbara (Israel). *Comptes Rendus de l'Académie des Sciences, 300,* 227–230.

Armstrong, D. M. (1962). *Bodily sensations.* London: Routledge & Kegan Paul.

Armstrong, D. (1968). *A materialist theory of mind.* London: Routledge & Kegan Paul.

Atkinson, R. (1956). *Stonehenge.* London: Hamilton.

Ayers, S. A. (1998). *Shang bronzes: A window in the ancient Chinese culture (1523 B.C.–1028 B. C.).* Available online at: http://www.yale.edu/ynhti/curriculum/1998/3/98.03.01.x.html

Baars, B. J. (2003). There are no known differences in fundamental brain mechanisms of sensory consciousness between humans and other mammals. Available online at: http://www.hum.au.dk/semiotics/docs/epub/arc/baars/bbaars3/mammals.pdf

Bader, O. N. (1978). *Sungir: Verkhnepaleoliticcheskaia Stoianka.* Moscow: Nauka.

Baum, W. M. (1994). *Understanding behaviorism.* New York: HarperCollins.

Beek, M. A. (1962). *Atlas of Mesopotamia: A survey of the history and civilization of Mesopotamia from the stone age to the fall of Babylon* (D. R. Welsh, Trans.). New York: Nelson.

Beit-Hallahmi, B. (2001). Explaining religious utterances by taking seriously super-natural (and naturalist) claims. In H. Hon & S. S. Rakover (Eds.), *Explanation: Theoretical approaches and applications.* Dordrecht: Kluwer Academic Publishers.

Bell, J. A. (1994). Interpretation and testability in theories about prehistoric thinking. In C. Renfrew & E. Z. B. Zubrow (Eds.), *The ancient mind: Elements of cognitive archeology.* Cambridge, England: Cambridge University Press.

Bergson, H. (1929). *Matter and memory* (N. M. Paul & W. S. Palmer, Trans.). New York: Macmillan.

Bichat, X. (1827). *Physiological researches on life and death* (F. Gold, Trans.). Boston: Richardson & Lord.

Binford, S. R., & Binford, L. R. (Eds.). (1968). *New perspectives in archeology.* Chicago: Aldine.

Binford, L. R. (1987). Data, relativism and archeological science. *Man, 22,* 391–404.

Block, N. (1995). On a confusion about a function of consciousness. *Behavioral and Brain Sciences, 18,* 227–247.

Block, N., & Stalnaker, R. (1999). Conceptual analysis, dualism, and the explanatory gap. *Philosophical Review, 108,* 1–46.

Boas, F. (1938). *General anthropology.* Madison, WI: United States Armed Forces Institute.

Boeree, C. G. (2002). *Buddhist cosmology.* Available online at: http://www.ship.edu/~cgboeree/buddhacosmo.html

Bonifay, E. (1962). *Un ensemble rituel mousterien a la grotte de Regourdou (Montignac, Dordogne).* Paper presented at the Proceedings of the Sixth International Congress of Prehistoric and Protohistoric Sciences, Rome.

Bouyssonie, A., Bouyssonie, J., & Bardon, L. (1908). Decouverte d'un squelette mousterien a la Boffia de la Chapelle-aux-Saints (Correze). *Anthropologie, Paris, 19,* 513–518.

Bouyssonie, A., Bouyssonie, J., & Bardon, L. (1913). La station mousterienne de la "Bouffia" Bonneval, a la Chapelle-aux-Saints. *Anthropologie, Paris, 24,* 609–634.

Boyd, R. (1980). Materialism without reductionism: What physicalism does not entail. In N. Block (Ed.), *Readings in philosophy and psychology, Vol. 1* (pp. 67–106). Cambridge, MA: Harvard University Press.

Brauer, G. (2001). The KNM-ER 3884 hominid and the emergence of modern anatomy in Africa. In P. V. Tobias, M. A. Rath, J. Moggi-Cecchi, & G. A. Doyle (Eds.), *Humanity from African naissance to coming millennia.* Florence, Italy: Firenza University Press.

Bremermann, H. J. (1977). Complexity and transcomputability. In R. Duncan & M. Weston-Smith (Eds.), *The encyclopedia of ignorance.* New York: Pocket Books.

Brindley, G. S. (1960). *Physiology of the retina and the visual pathways.* London: Edward Arnold.

Broad, C. D. (1925). *The mind and its place in nature.* London: Routledge & Kegan Paul.

Broca, P. (1868). Sur les cranes et ossements des Eyzies. *Bulletin de la Societe d'Anthropologie de Paris, 3,* 335–349.

Bruins, J., van der Plicht, J., & Mazar, A. (2003). Carbon 14 dates from Tel Rehov: Iron-age chronology, pharaohs, and Hebrew kings. *Science, 300,* 315–318.

Budge, E. A. W. (1895). *The book of the dead.* London: Longmans.

Bunge, M. (1980). *The mind-body problem: A psychobiological approach.* Oxford, England: Pergamon Press.

Butzer, K. W., Beamont, P. B., & Vogel, J. C. (1978). Lithostratigraphy of Border cave, KwaZulu, South Africa: A middle stone age sequence beginning 195,000 BP. *Journal of Archeological Science, 5,* 317–341.

Cahill, T. (1996). *How the Irish saved civilization: The untold story of Ireland's heroic role from the fall of Rome to the rise of medieval Europe.* New York: Anchor Books.

Campbell, J. (1974). *The mythic image.* Princeton, NJ: Princeton University Press.

Capitan, L., & Peyrony, D. (1909). Deux squelettes humains au milieu de foyers de l'epoque mousterienne. *Revue de l'Ecole d'Anthropologie, 19,* 402–409.

Carrier, M., & Mittelstrass, J. (1991). *Mind, brain, behavior: The mind-body problem and the philosophy of psychology.* Berlin: Walter de Greater.

Carter, H. (1954). *The tomb of Tutankhamen.* New York: Dutton.

Cartwright, D. (1979). Contemporary social psychology in historical perspective. *Social Psychology Quarterly, 42,* 82–93.

Casti, J. L. (1996). Confronting science's logical limits. *Scientific American* (October), 102–105.

Cauvin, J. (2000). *The birth of the Gods and the origins of agriculture* (T. Watkins, Trans.). Cambridge, England: Cambridge University Press.

Ceccarelli, L. (2001). *Shaping science with rhetoric: The cases of Dobzhansky, Schrödinger, and Wilson.* Chicago: University of Chicago Press.

Chadwick, J. (1959). *The decipherment of linear B.* Cambridge, England: Cambridge University Press.

Chalmers, D. J. (1996). *The conscious mind: In search of a fundamental theory.* New York: Oxford University Press.

Chalmers, D. J. (Ed.). (2002). *Philosophy of mind: Classical and contemporary readings.* New York: Oxford University Press.

Chang, K. C. (1986). *The archaeology of ancient China.* New Haven: Yale University Press.

Chase, P., & Dibble, H. (1987). Middle paleolithic symbolism: A review of current evidence and interpretations. *Journal of Anthropological Archeology, 6,* 263–296.

Cheney, D. L., & Seyfarth, R. (1990). *How monkeys see the world: Inside the mind of another species.* Chicago: University of Chicago Press.

Churchland, P. M. (1981). Eliminative materialism and the propositional attritudes. *Journal of Philosophy, 78,* 67–90.

Churchland, P. S. (1986). *Neurophilosophy.* Cambridge, MA: MIT Press.

Coe, M. D. (1999). *The Maya* (6th ed.). London: Thames & Hudson.

Comte, A. (1858). *Positive philosophy* (H. Martineau, Trans.). New York: C. Blanchard.

Cook, S. A. (1903). A pre-Massoretic biblical papyrus. *Proceedings of the Society of Biblical Archeology, 25,* 34–56.

Cotterell, A. (1981). *The first emperor of China: The greatest archeological find of our time.* New York: Holt, Rinehart & Winston.

Cowey, A., & Stoerig, P. (1995). Blindsight in monkeys. *Nature, 373,* 247–249.

Crick, F. (1981). *Life itself: Its origin and nature.* New York: Simon & Schuster.

Crick, F. (1994). *The astonishing hypothesis: The scientific search for the soul.* New York: Simon & Schuster.

Darnell, J. C., & Darnell, D. (1997). New inscriptions of the late first intermediate period from the Theban western desert and the beginnings of the northern expansion of the eleventh dynasty. *Journal of Near Eastern Studies, 56,* 241–258.

Darnell, J. C., & Darnell, D. (2002). *Theban desert road survey in the Egyptian western desert.* Chicago: The Oriental Institute of the University of Chicago.

Darwin, C. (1859). *On the origin of species by means of natural selection.* London: Murray.

Darwin, C. (1871). *The descent of man and selection in relation to sex.* London: Murray.

Davidson, D. (1970). Mental events. In L. Foster & J. W. Swanson (Eds.), *Experience and theory.* Amherst: University of Massachusetts Press.

Davies, W. V. (1987). *Egyptian hieroglyphics.* London: British Museum Publications.

Deacon, H. J. (1979). Excavations at Boomplaas cave—A sequence through the upper pleistocene and holocene in South Africa. *World Archeology, 10,* 241–257.

Delprato, D. J. (1987). J. R. Kantor's contributions to scientific psychology. *The Interbehaviorist, 15,* 18–20, 41–42.

Dennett, D. C. (1991). *Consciousness explained.* Boston: Little Brown.

Dennett, D. C. (1995). *Darwin's dangerous idea: Evolution and the meanings of life.* New York: Simon & Schuster.

Dennett, D. C. (2001). *Review of Renfrew & Zubrow, Eds., The ancient mind.* Available online at: http://ase/tufts.edu/cogstud/papers/ancmind.htm

Dewey, J. (1886). *Psychology.* New York: Harper.

Dom, H. (1999). *Myth of one Hindu religion exploded.* Jabalpur, India: Sudrastan Books.

Donald, M. (1991). *Origins of the modern mind: Three stages in the evolution of culture and cognition.* Cambridge, MA: Harvard University Press.

Dreyer, G. (1998). *Umm el Qaab I: Das predynastiche Konigsgrab U-j und seine fruhen Schrift-zeugnisse.* Mainz: Verlag Philipp von Zabern.

Dreyer, G. (1999). Abydos: Umm el-Qa'ab. In K. A. Bard (Ed.), *Encyclopedia of the archeology of ancient Egypt* (pp. 109–114). London: Routledge.

Dreyer, G., von Driesch, A., Engel, E.-M., Hartmann, R., Hartung, U., Hikade, T., Muller, V., & Petres, J. (2000). Umm el-Qaab. Nachuntersuchungen im fruhzeitlichen Konigsfriedhof. *Vorbericht.MDAIK, 56,* 43–129.

Eccles, J. C. (Ed.). (1966). *Brain and conscious experience.* New York: Springer Verlag.

Eccles, J. C. (1970). *Facing reality.* Berlin: Springer Verlag.

Eccles, J. C. (1973). *The understanding of the brain.* New York: McGraw Hill.

Einstein, A. (1941). Paper presented at the conference on *Science, Philosophy, and Religion in Their Relation to the Democratic Way of Life,* New York.

Eliade, M. (1978). *A history of religious ideas: Vol. 1. From the stone age to the Eleusinian mysteries* (W. R. Trask, Trans.). Chicago: University of Chicago.

Estling, R. (2002). The logic that dare not speak its name. *Skeptical Inquirer, 26,* 58–59.

Evans, A. (1964). *The palace of Minos; a comparative account of the successive stages of the early Cretan civilization as illustrated by the discoveries at Knossos.* New York: Biblo and Tannen.

Faulkner, R. O. (1994). *The Egyptian book of the dead.* San Francisco: Chronicle.

Feigl, H. (1958). The mental and the physical. In H. Feigl, M. Scriven, & G. Maxwell (Eds.), *The Minnesota studies in the philosophy of science: Vol. II. Concepts, theories, and the mind-body problem* (pp. 370–497). Minneapolis: University of Minnesota Press.

Feigl, H. (1960). Mind-body is not a pseudoproblem. In S. Hook (Ed.), *Dimensions of mind: A symposium.* New York: New York University.

Finkelstein, I., & Silberman, N. A. (2001). *The bible unearthed: Archeology's new vision of ancient Israel and the origin of its sacred texts.* New York: Simon & Schuster.

Fodor, J. (1983). *The modularity of mind: An essay on faculty psychology.* Cambridge, MA: MIT Press.

Fodor, J. (2000). *The mind doesn't work that way.* Cambridge, MA: MIT Press.

Follensbee, B. (1999). *Olmec heads: A product of the Americas.* Available online at: http://copan.bioz.unibas.ch/meso/olmec.html

Foster, J. (1991). *The immaterial self: A defense of the Cartesian dualist conception of the mind.* New York: Routledge.

Frazer, J. G. (1911). *The golden bough: A study in magic and religion.* London: Macmillan.

Freke, T., & Gandy, P. (1999). *The Jesus mysteries.* London: HarperCollins.

Freud, S. (1918/1952). *Totem and taboo: Some points of agreement between the mental lives of savages and neurotics* (J. Strachey, Trans.). New York: Norton.

Freud, S. (1939). *Moses and monotheism* (K. Jones, Trans.). New York: Vintage.

Gardiner, A. H. (1935). *The Egyptian coffin texts.* Chicago: University of Chicago Press.

Gargett, R. H. (1989). Grave shortcomings; the evidence for Neanderthal burial. *Current Anthropology, 30,* 157–190.

Gargett, R. H. (1999). Middle paleolithic burial is not a dead issue: The view from Qafzeh, Saint-Cesaire, Kebara, Amud, and Dederiyeh. *Journal of Human Evolution, 37,* 27–90.

Garstang, J., & Garstang, J. B. E. (1940). *The story of Jericho.* London: Hodder & Stoughton.

Gaur, A. (1984). *A history of writing.* London: British Library.

Gilman, N. (1997). *The death of death: Resurrection and immortality in Jewish thought.* Woodstock, VT: Jewish Lights.

Gleiser, M. (2002). *The prophet and the astronomer: A scientific journey to the end of time.* New York: Norton.

Gordon-Childe, V. (1945). *What happened in history.* London: Penquin.

Gould, J. A. (Ed.). (1971). *Classic philosophical questions.* Columbus, OH: Charles E. Merrill.

Greenberg, G. (2001, August 13). As good as dead. *The New Yorker.*

Gremyatsky, M. A., & Nestourkh, M. F. (1949). *Teshik-Tash paleolithic man.* Moscow: Moscow University Press.

Hall, N. (1999). *Science and religion: Conflict or conciliation. Commentary on the Skeptical Inquirer Special Issue on Science and Religion, July/August* 1999. (http://www.godless.org/sci/skeptinq/summary.html).

Hanson, N. R. (1958). *Patterns of discovery.* Cambridge, England: Cambridge University Press.

Harris, R. (1986). *The origin of writing.* London: Duckworth.

Hart, W. D. (1988). *The engines of the soul.* Cambridge, England: Cambridge University Press.

Hawass, Z. A. (2000). *The valley of the golden mummies.* New York: Harry N. Abrams.

Hayden, B. (1993). The cultural capacities of Neanderthals: A review and re-evaluation. *Journal of Human Evolution, 24,* 113–146.

Haynes, C. V. (1980). Paleoindian charcoal from meadocroft rockshelter: Is contamination a problem. *American Antiquity, 45,* 582–587.

Helmholtz, H. v. (1863/1962). *On the sensations of tone as a physiological basis for the theory of music* (A. J. Ellis, Trans.). New York: Dover.

Helmholtz, H. v. (1866/1894). *Helmholtz's treatise on physiological optics* (J. P. C. Southall, Trans.). New York: Dover.

Henshilwood, C. S., d'Errico, F., Yates, R., Jacobs, Z., Tribolo, C., Duller, G. A. T., Mercier, N., Sealy, J. C., Valladas, H., Watts, I., & Wintle, A. G. (2002). *Emergence of modern human behavior: Middle stone age engravings from South Africa.* Available online at: www.scienceexpress.org/10 January 2002/

Hilgetag, C. C., O'Neil, M. A., & Young, M. P. (1996). Indeterminate organization of the visual system. *Science, 271,* 776–777.

Hilgetag, C. C., O'Neil, M. A., & Young, M. P. (2000). Hierarchical organization of macaque and cat cortical sensory mechanisms explored with a novel network processor. *Philosophical Transactions of the Royal Society of London, B., 355,* 71–89.

Hill, C. S. (1991). *Sensations: A defense of type materialism.* Cambridge, England: Cambridge University Press.

Himelfarb, E. J. (2000). First alphabet found in Egypt. *Archaeology, 53.*

Hoerth, A. J. (1998). *Archaeology and the Old Testament.* Grand Rapids, MI: Baker Books.

Holtorf, C. (2002). *Megaliths in Mecklenburg-Vorpommern.* Available online at: http://citd.scar.utoronto.ca/CITDPress/Holtorf/1.1.html

Horgan, T. (1993). Nonreductive materialism and the explanatory autonomy of psychology. In S. J. Wagner & R. Warner (Eds.), *Naturalism: A critical appraisal* (pp. 295–320). Notre Dame, IN: University of Indiana Press.

Hourani, A. (1991). *A history of the Arab peoples.* Cambridge, MA: Harvard University Press.

Jackson, F. (1994). Finding the mind in the natural world. In R. Casati, B. Smith, & G. White (Eds.), *Philosophy and the cognitive sciences.* Vienna, Austria: Holder-Pichler-Tempsky.

Jacobsen, T. W. (1981). Franchthi cave and the beginning of settled life in Greece. *Hesperia, 50,* 303–319.

James, W. (1890). *The principles of psychology.* New York: Henry Holt.

James, W. (1902/1935). *The varieties of religious experience: A study in human nature.* London: Longmans, Green.

James, W. (1904). Does "consciousness" exist? *Journal of Philosophy, Psychology, and Scientific Methods, 1,* 477–491.

Jha, N., & Rajaram, N. S. (1996). *The deciphered Indus script.* New Delhi: Aditya Prakashan.

Josephus. (1999). *The new complete works of Josephus* (W. Whiston, Trans.). Grand Rapids, MI: Kregal.

Justeson, J. S., & Kaufman, T. (1993). A decipherment of Epi-Olmec hieroglyphic writing. *Science, 259,* 1703–1711.

Kanfer, F. H., & Karoly, P. (1972). Self-control: A behavioristic excursion into the lion's den. *Behavior Therapy, 3,* 398–416.

Kantor, J. R. (1924). *Principles of psychology: Vol. 1.* Chicago: Principia Press.

Kantor, J. R. (1926). *Principles of psychology: Vol. 2.* Chicago: Principia Press.

Kantor, J. R. (1959). *Interbehavioral psychology: An example of scientific systems construction.* Chicago: Principia Press.

Kantor, J. R. (1963). *The scientific evolution of psychology: Vol. 1.* Chicago: Principia Press.

Kantor, J. R. (1971). *The aim and progress of psychology and other sciences.* Chicago: Principia Press.

Kantor, J. R. (1978). Cognition as events and as psychic constructions. *The Psychological Record, 28,* 239–342.

Katsiavriades, K., & Qureshi, T. (2001). *Writing.* Available online at: http://www.krysstal.com/writing.html

Keatinge, R. W. (1988). *Peruvian prehistory: An overview of pre-Inca and Inca society.* Cambridge, England: Cambridge University Press.

Kenoyer, J. M. (1998). *Ancient cities of the Indus valley civilization.* New York: Oxford University Press.

Kenyon, K. M. (1957). *Digging up Jericho.* London: Benn.

Kety, S. S. (1960). A biologist examines the mind and behavior. *Science, 132,* 1867–1869.

Killen, J. T. (1984). The textile industries at Pylos and Knossos. In T. G. Palaima & C. W. Shelmerdine (Eds.), *Pylos comes alive* (pp. 49–63). New York: Fordham University.

Killen, J. T. (1985). The Linear B tablets and the Mycenaean economy. In A. M. Davies & Y. Duhoux (Eds.), *Linear B: A 1984 survey.* Louvain-la-Neuve: Cabay.

Killen, J. T. (1993). Records of sheep and goats at Mycenaean Knossos and Pylos. *Bulletin on Sumerian Agriculture, 7,* 209–218.

Kim, J. (1966). On the psycho-physical identity theory. *American Philosophical Quarterly, 3,* 227–235.

Kim, J. (1993). *Supervenience and mind: Selected philosophical essays.* Cambridge, England: Cambridge University Press.

King, W. P. (Ed.). (1930). *Behaviorism: A battle line.* Nashville, TN: Cokesbury Press.

Klee, R. (1997). *Introduction to the philosophy of science: Cutting nature at its seams.* New York: Oxford University Press.

Klima, B. (1995). *Dolni Vestonice II, Ein Mammutjägerrastplatz und Seine Bestattungen.* Leige: University of Leige.

Koch, S. (1992). Psychology's Bridgman vs. Bridgman's Bridgman. *Theory and Psychology, 2,* 261–290.

Koshland, D. E., Jr. (2002). The seven pillars of life. *Science, 295,* 2215–2216.

Kozlowski, J. K. (1996). Cultural context of the last Neanderthals and early modern humans in central-eastern Europe. In O. Bar-Yosef, L. L. Cavalli-Sforzo, R. J. March, & M. Piperno (Eds.), *The lower and middle paleolithic (Colloquia of the xiii International Congress of Prehistoric and Protohistoric Sciences* (No. 5, pp. 205–218). Forli, Italy: ABACO Edizioni.

Kripke, S. A. (1980). *Naming and necessity.* Cambridge, MA: Harvard University Press.

Kuhn, T. (1962). *The structure of scientific revolutions.* Chicago: University of Chicago Press.

Lahr, M. M., & Foley, R. (1994). Multiple dispersions and modern human origins. *Evolutionary Anthropology, 3,* 48–60.

Landa, D. de (1937). *Yucatan before and after the conquest.* Baltimore: The Maya Society.

Larson, E. J., & Witham, L. (1998). Leading scientists still reject God. *Nature, 394,* 313.

Lartet, L. (1868). Une seputure des troglodytes du Perigord (cranes des Eyzies). *Bulletin de la Societe d'Anthropologie de Paris, 3,* 335–349.

Leveque, F., & Vandermeersch, B. (1981). Le neandertalien de Saint Cesaire. *Recherche, 12,* 242–244.

Levine, J. (1983). Materialism and qualia: The explanatory gap. *Pacific Philosophical Quarterly, 64,* 354–361.

Levy, G. R. (1946). *The Gate of Horn: A study of the religious conceptions of the stone age, and their influence upon European thought.* New York: Book Collectors Society.

Lewis, D. (1965). An argument for the identity theory. *Journal of Philosophy, 63,* 17–25.

Li, X., Harbottle, G., Zhang, J., & Wang, C. (2003). The earliest writing? Sign use in the seventh millennium BC at Jiahu, Henan Province, China. *Antiquity, 77,* 31–44.

Lindly, J. M., & Clark, G. A. (1990). Symbolism and modern human origins. *Current Anthropology, 31,* 233–261.

Lippman, T. W. (1995). *Understanding Islam: An introduction to the Muslim world.* New York: Meridian.

Littleton, C. S. (2002). *Shinto: Origins, rituals, spirits, sacred places.* New York: Oxford University Press.

Liu, L., & Chen, X. (2003). *Early state formation in China.* London: Duckworth.

Loftin, J. D. (2000). *The big picture: A short world history of religions.* London: McFarland.

Lovejoy, A. O. (1930). *The revolt against dualism: An inquiry concerning the existence of ideas.* Chicago: Open Court.

MacCorquodale, K., & Meehl, P. E. (1948). On a distinction between hypothetical constructs and intervening variables. *Psychological Review, 55,* 95–107.

Mach, E. (1885/1959). *The analysis of sensations and the relation of the physical to the psychical* (C. M. Williams, Trans.). New York: Dover.

Malan, D. B., & Wells, L. H. (1943). A further report on the Wonderwerk cave, Kuruma. *South African Journal of Science, 40,* 258–270.

Malcolm, N. (1971). *Problems of mind: Descartes to Wittgenstein.* New York: Harper & Row.

Malville, J. M., Wendorf, F., Mazar, A. A., & Schild, R. (1998). Megaliths and neolithic astronomy in southern Egypt. *Nature, 392,* 488–491.

Marcus, J., & Flannery, K. V. (1994). Ancient Zapotec ritual and religion: An application of the direct historical approach. In C. Renfrew & E. Z. B. Zubrow (Eds.), *The ancient mind: Elements of cognitive archeology* (pp. 55–74). Cambridge, England: Cambridge University Press.

Margulis, L., & Sagan, D. (1995). *What is life?* New York: Simon & Schuster.

Mark, J. (1930). Behaviorism and religion. In W. P. King (Ed.), *Behaviorism: A battle line.* Nashville, TN: Cokesbury Press.

Marx, M. H., & Hillix, W. A. (1963). *Systems and theories in psychology.* New York: McGraw-Hill.

Masson, C. (1842). *Narrative of various journeys in Balochistan, Afghanistan, and the Punjab.* London: Richard Bentley.

Maudsley, H. (1867). *The physiology and pathology of the mind.* New York: Appleton.

McCown, T., & Keith, A. (1939). *The stone age of Mt. Carmel, Vol 2: The fossil human remains from the Levalloiso-Mousterian.* London: Clarendon Press.

McDougall, W. (1911). *Body and mind: A history and a defense of animism.* London: Methuen.

McGinn, C. (1989). Can we solve the mind-body problem? *Mind, 98,* 349–366.

McKim, J., Wendorf, F., Mazhar, A., & Schild, R. (1998). Megaliths and neolithic astronomy in southern Egypt. *Nature, 392,* 488–492.

Mellaart, J. (1967). *Catal Huyuk: A neolithic town in Anatolia.* New York: McGraw Hill.

Melzack, R., & Wall, P. D. (1965). Pain mechanisms: A new theory. *Science, 150,* 971–979.

Mendenhall, G. E. (1962). The Hebrew conquest of Palestine. *Biblical Archeologist, 25,* 66–87.

Midgley, B. D., & Morris, E. K. (in press). Subjectivity and behaviorism: Skinner, Kantor, and Stephenson. *Operant Subjectivity, 25.*

Miller, J. G. (1978). *Living systems.* New York: McGraw Hill.

Minsky, M. (1963). Steps toward artificial intelligence. In E. A. Feigenbaum & J. Feldman (Eds.), *Computers and thought* (chap. 7). New York: McGraw Hill.

Mithen, S. (1994). From domain specific to generalized intelligence: A cognitive interpretation of the middle/upper palaeolithic transition. In C. Renfrew & E. Z. B. Zubrow (Eds.), *The ancient mind: Elements of cognitive archeology* (pp. 29–39). Cambridge, England: Cambridge University Press.

Mohanty, R. K., & Walimbe, S. R. (2002). *The Vidarbha megaliths: A demographic approach.* Available online at: http://www.picatype.com/dig/dc/dc0aa04.htm

Momen, M. (1999). *A short introduction to the Baha'i faith.* Oxford, England: Oneworld Publications.

Moore, E. F. (1956). Gedanken-experiments on sequential machines. In C. E. Shannon & J. McCarthy (Eds.), *Automata studies* (pp. 129–153). Princeton, NJ: Princeton University Press.

Moore, J. C. (1981). On mentalism, methodological behaviorism, and radical behaviorism. *Behaviorism, 9,* 55–77.

Moore, J. C. (2002). *Behaviorism tutorial.* Available online at: http://psych.athabascau.ca/html/Behaviorism

Morin, R. (2000). *Do Americans believe in God?* Available online at: http://www.washingtonpost.com/wp-srv/politics/wat/archive

Morris, E. K. (1984). Interbehavioral psychology and radical behaviorism: Some similarities and differences. *The Behavior Analyst, 7,* 197–204.

Morris, E. K., Higgins, S. T., & Bickel, W. K. (1982). The influence of Kantor's interbehavioral psychology on behavior analysis. *The Behavior Analyst, 5,* 158–173.

Mountjoy, P. T., & Cone, D. M. (in press). A biographical sketch of Jacob Robert Kantor. In B. D. Midgley & E. K. Morris (Eds.), *Modern perspectives on J. R. Kantor and interbehaviorism.* Westport, CT: Greenwood Press.

Nagel, T. (1974). What is it like to be a bat? *Philosophical Reviews, 83,* 435–450.

Nisbett, R. E., & Wilson, T. D. (1977). Telling more than we know: Verbal reports on mental processes. *Psychological Review, 84,* 231–259.

O'Connor, J. J., & Robertson, E. F. (2001). *Mathematics of the Inca.* Available online at: http://www-gap.dcs.st-and.ac.uk/~history/HistTopics/Inca_mathematics

O'Leary-Hawthorne, J., & McDonough, J. K. (1998). Numbers, minds, and bodies: A fresh look at mind-body dualism. *Philosophical Perspectives (Language, Mind, and Ontology), 12,* 349–371.

Ornstein, J. H. (1972). *The mind and the brain: A multi-aspect interpretation.* The Hague: Martinus Nijhoff.

Parpola, A. (2000). Of Rajaram's "Horses," decipherment, and civilization issues. *Frontline, 17.*

Perrot, J. (1966). Le gisement Natoufien de Mallaha (Eynan), Israel. *L'Anthropologie, 70,* 437–483.

Perry, J. (2001). *Knowledge, possibility, and consciousness.* Cambridge, MA: MIT Press.

Peyrony, D. (1930). Le Moustier: ses gisements, ses industries, ses couches geologiques. *Rev. Anthropologie, 40,* 48–76.

Pidwirny, M. (2000). *Definition of life.* Available online at: http://www.geog.ouc.bc.ca/conted/onlinecourses/geog_111/7a.html

Pinker, S. (1997). *How the mind works.* New York: W. W. Norton.

Place, U. T. (1956). Is consciousness a brain process? *British Journal of Psychology, 47,* 44–50.

Poe, E. A. (1850). The premature burial. *The works of the late Edgar Allen Poe* (Vol. 1, pp. 325–338). New York: J. S. Redfield.

Polten, E. P. (1973). *Critique of the psycho-physical identity theory.* The Hague: Mouton.

Pope, M. E. D., Pope, K. O., & von Nagy, C. (2002). Olmec origins of Mesoamerican writing. *Science, 298,* 1984–1987.

Popper, K. R. (1959). *The logic of scientific discovery.* New York: Basic Books.

Porter, B. N. (Ed.). (2000). *One God or many?* Chebeaque Island, ME: Casco Bay Assyriological Institute.

Possehl, G. (1996). *The Indus age: The writing system.* Philadelphia: University of Pennsylvania.

Prescott, W. H. (1936). *The complete and unexpurgated history of the conquest of Mexico and history of the conquest of Peru.* New York: Random House.

Pruner-Bey, F. (1868). Description sommaire de restes humains decouverts les grottes de Cro-Magnon, pres de la station de Eyzies, arrondissment de Sarlat (Dordogne) en Avril 1868. *Annee des Sciences naturelles Zoologie, 10,* 144–155.

Pucetti, R. (1978). The refutation of materialism. *Canadian Journal of Philosophy, 8,* 157–162.

Putnam, H. (1988). *Representation and reality.* Cambridge, MA: MIT Press.

Rank, O. (1909/1990). *The myth of the birth of the hero.* Princeton, NJ: Princeton University Press.

Rank, O. (1941). *Beyond psychology.* Philadelphia: E. Hauser.

Rawl, H. F. (1930). What does behaviorism mean for religion? In W. P. King (Ed.), *Behaviorism: A battle line.* Nashville, TN: Cokesbury Press.

Redford, D. B. (1987). The monotheism of the heretic pharaoh. *Biblical Archeology Review, 13,* 16–32.

Riel-Salvatore, J., & Clark, G. A. (2001). Grave markers: Middle and early upper paleolithic burials and the use of chronotypology in contemporary paleolithic research. *Current Anthropology, 42,* 449–479.

Riviere, E. (1887). *De l'Antiquitie de l'Homme dans les Alpes-Maritimes.* Paris: J. B. Baillière et fils.

Robinson, A. (1995). *The story of writing.* London: Thames & Hudson.

Robinson, D. N. (Ed.). (1998). *The mind.* New York: Oxford University Press.

Romanes, G. J. (1883). *Animal intelligence.* New York: Appleton.

Rorty, R. (1965). Mind-body identity, privacy, and categories. *Review of Metaphysics, 19,* 24–54.

Rorty, R. (1970). In defense of eliminative materialism. *Review of Metaphysics, 24,* 112–121.

Rorty, R. (2001). Studied ambiguity. *Science, 293,* 2399–2400.

Rosen, R. (1991). *Life itself: A comprehensive inquiry in the nature, origin, and fabrication of life.* New York: Columbia University Press.

Ryle, G. (1949). *The concept of mind.* London: Hutchinson's University Library.

Sadakata, A., & Sekimori, G. T. (1997). *Buddhist cosmology: Philosophy and origins.* Tokyo: Kosei.

Salmon, M. H. (2001). Explanation in archeology. In G. Hon & S. S. Rakover (Eds.), *Explanation: Theoretical approaches and applications* (pp. 231–248). Dordrecht: Kluwer.

Sampson, E. E. (1981). Cognitive psychology as ideology. *American Psychologist, 36,* 730–743.

Schmandt-Besserat, D. (1996). *How writing came about.* Austin: University of Texas Press.

Schrödinger, E. (1944). *What is life? The physical aspects of the living cell.* Cambridge, England: Cambridge University Press.

Schuldt, E. (1972). Die mecklenburgischen Megalithgraber. Untersuchungen zu ihrer Architektur un Funktion. *Beitrage zur Ur- and Fruhgeschicte dr Bezirke, Schwerin un Neubrandenburg, Vol. 6.* Berlin: Deutscher Verlag der Wissenschaften.

Searle, J. R. (1992). *The rediscovery of the mind.* Cambridge, MA: MIT Press.

Seidel, A. (1987). Chinese concepts (of the afterlife). In M. Eliade (Ed.), *The encyclopedia of religion* (pp. 183–188). New York: Macmillan.

Shallice, T. (1988). *From neuropsychology to mental structure.* Cambridge, England: Cambridge University Press.

Shorter, J. M. (1967). Other minds. In P. Edwards (Ed.), *The encyclopedia of philosophy* (Vol. 6, pp. 7–13). New York: Macmillan.

Singer, R., & Wymer, J. (1982). *The middle stone age at Klasies River mouth in South Africa.* Chicago: University of Chicago Press.

Skinner, B. F. (1963). Behaviorism at fifty. *Science, 140,* 951–958.

Skinner, B. F. (1987). Whatever happened to psychology as a science of behavior? *American Psychologist, 42,* 780–786.

Skinner, B. F. (1990a, August). *Keynote address.* Paper presented at the American Psychological Association annual meeting, Boston, MA. Reported in the *Los Angeles Times,* August 26, 1990.

Skinner, B. F. (1990b). Can psychology be a science of the mind? *American Psychologist, 45,* 1206–1210.

Smart, J. J. C. (1959). Sensations and brain processes. *Philosophical Studies, 68,* 141–156.

Smart, J. J. C. (1971). Identity, designation, essentialism, and physicalism. *Synthese, 22,* 346–359.

Smith, N. W. (1996, June). *Interbehavioral field psychology.* Paper presented at the J. R. Kantor's Interbehavioral Psychology: Beyond Mechanism and Mentalism, Earlham College, Richmond, IN.

Smith, N. W., Mountjoy, P. T., & Ruben, D. H. (Eds.). (1983). *Reassessment in psychology*. Landham, MD: University Press of America.

Solecki, R. S. (1975). Shanidar IV, a neanderthal flower burial in northern Iraq. *Science, 190*, 880–881.

Sommer, J. D. (1999). The Shanidar IV "Flower Burial": A reevaluation of neanderthal burial ritual. *Cambridge Archeological Journal, 9*, 127–129.

Sperry, R. W. (1965). Mind, brain, and humanist values. In J. R. Platt (Ed.), *New views on the nature of man*. Chicago: University of Chicago Press.

Sperry, R. W. (1980). Mind-brain interaction: Mentalism, yes; dualism, no. *Neuroscience, 5*, 195–206.

Sperry, R. W. (1992). Turnabout on consciousness: A mentalist view. *The Journal of Mind and Behavior, 13*, 259–280.

Sperry, R. W. (1993a). The impact and promise of the cognitive revolution. *American Psychologist, 48*, 878–885.

Sperry, R. W. (1993b). The cognitive revolution: A new paradigm for causation. *International Journal of Psychiatry, 3*, 3–9.

Stokstad, E. (2002). Oldest new world writing suggests Olmec innovation. *Science, 298*, 1872–1874.

Stringer, C. (2000). Coasting out of Africa. *Nature, 405*, 24–27.

Szombathy, J. (1909). Die Aurignacienschichten in Loes von Willendorf. *Korrespondenzblatt der Deutschen Gesellschaft fur Anthropologie, Etnologie, und Urgeschicte, XL*, 85–88.

Tattersall, I. (1997). *Becoming human: Evolution and human uniqueness*. Orlando, FL: Harcourt, Brace.

Taylor, E. I., & Wozniak, R. H. (1996). Pure experience, the response to William James: An introduction. In E. I. Taylor & R. H. Wozniak (Eds.), *Pure experience: The response to William James* (pp. ix–xxxii). Bristol: Thoemmes Press.

Theertha, D. (1992). *History of Hindu imperialism*. Madras, India.

Thomas, J. (1991). *Rethinking the neolithic*. Cambridge, England: Cambridge University Press.

Thorne, A., Grun, R., G., M., Spooner, N. A., Simpson, J. J., McCulloch, M., Taylor, L., & Curnoe, D. (1999). Australia's oldest human remains: Age of the Lake Mungo 3 skeleton. *Journal of Human Evolution, 36*, 591–612.

Thorpe, R. L. (1991). Erlitou and the search for the Xia. *Early China, 16*, 1–38.

Thouless, R. H., & Wiesner, B. P. (1948). The Psi processes in normal and "paranormal" psychology. *Journal of Parapsychology, 12*, 192–212.

Titchener, E. B. (1899). *An outline of psychology*. New York: Macmillan.

Tolman, E. C. (1932). *Purposive behavior in animals and man*. New York: Macmillan.

Toynbee, J. M. C. (1971). *Death and burial in the Roman world*. Ithaca, NY: Cornell University Press.

Tye, M. (1999). Phenomenal consciousness: The explanatory gap as cognitive illusion. *Mind, 108*, 705–725.

Uttal, W. R. (1973). *The psychobiology of sensory coding*. New York: Harper & Row.

Uttal, W. R. (1978). *The psychobiology of mind*. Hillsdale, NJ: Lawrence Erlbaum Associates.

Uttal, W. R. (1988). *On seeing forms*. Hillsdale, NJ: Lawrence Erlbaum Associates.

Uttal, W. R. (1998). *Toward a new behaviorism: The case against perceptual reductionism*. Mahwah, NJ: Lawrence Erlbaum Associates.

Uttal, W. R. (2000). *The war between mentalism and behaviorism: On the accessibility of mental processes*. Mahwah, NJ: Lawrence Erlbaum Associates.

Uttal, W. R. (2001). *The new phrenology: The limits of localizing cognitive processes in the brain*. Cambridge, MA: MIT Press.

Uttal, W. R. (2002). *A behaviorist looks at form recognition*. Mahwah, NJ: Lawrence Erlbaum Associates.

Uttal, W. R. (2003). *Psychomythics: Sources of artifact and misconceptions in scientific psychology.* Mahwah, NJ: Lawrence Erlbaum Associates.

van Gelder, T. J. (1998). Monism, dualism, pluralism. *Mind and Language, 13,* 76–97.

Vandermeersch, B. (1969). Les nouveaux squelettes Mousteriens decourverts a Qafzeh (Israel). *Comptes Rendus de l'Académie des Sciences Paris D, 268,* 2562–2565.

Vandermeersch, B. (1996). Nouvelles decouvertes de restes humanins dans les couches Levalloiso-mousteriennes du gisement de Qafzeh (Israel). *Comptes Rendus de l'Académie des Sciences Paris D, 262,* 1434–1436.

Vekua, A., Lordkipanidze, D., Rightmire, G. P., Agusti, J., Ferring, R., Maisuradze, G., Mouskhelishvili, A., Nioradze, M., Ponce de Leon, M., Tappen, M., Tvalchrelidze, M., & Zollikofer, C. (2002). A new skull of early Homo from Dmanisi, Georgia. *Science, 297,* 85–89.

Verplanck, W. S. (1996). From 1924 to 1996, and into the future: Operation-analytic behaviorism. *Journal of Behavior Analysis, Monograph Issue, 22,* 19–60.

Vogel, J. C. (2001). Radiometric dates for the middle stone age in Africa. In P. V. Tobias, M. A. Rath, J. Moggi-Cecchi, & G. A. Doyle (Eds.), *Humanity from African naissance to coming millennia* (pp. 261–268). Florence, Italy: Firenze University Press.

von Oppenheim, M. (1933). *Tel Halaf: A new culture in oldest Mesopotamia* (G. Wheeler, Trans.). New York: G. P. Putnam's Sons.

Wallace, A. F. C. (1966). *Religion: An anthropological view.* New York: Random House.

Watson, J. B. (1914). *Behavior: An introduction to comparative psychology.* New York: Henry Holt.

Watson, J. B. (1924). *Psychology from the point of view of a behaviorist.* Philadelphia: Lippincott.

Watson, P., Leblanc, S., & Redman, C. (1971). *Explanation in archeology.* New York: Columbia University Press.

Wendorf, F., Schild, R., & Zedeno, N. (1996). A late neolithic megalithic complex in the eastern Sahara: A preliminary report. In L. Krzyzaniak, K. Kroeper, & M. Kobusiewicz (Eds.), *Interregional contacts in the later prehistory of northeastern Africa* (Vol. 5, pp. 125–132). Poznan: Poznan Archaeological Museum.

Wendorf, F., Schild, R., & Associates (Eds.). (2001). *Holocene settlement of the Egyptian Sahara, Vol. 1.* New York: Kluwer Academic/Plenum.

Wheeler, R. E. M. (1996). *Civilizations of the Indus valley and beyond.* New York: McGraw Hill.

Winters, C. A. (1977). The influence of Mande scripts on American ancient writing systems. *Bulletin de l'Institut Fondamental Afrique Noire, 39 (Series B),* 81–97.

Winters, C. A. (1979). Manding writing in the New World—Part 1. *Journal of African Civilization, 1,* 81–97.

Winters, C. A. (1989). A grammar of Dravido-Harappan writing. *Journal of Tamil Studies, 35,* 53–71.

Winters, C. A. (1990). The Dravidian language and the Harappan script. *Archiv Orientalni, 58,* 301–309.

Witcombe, C. (2002). *Prehistoric art.* Available online at: http://witcombe.sbc.edu/ARTH prehistoric.html#neolithic

Witzel, M., & Farmer, S. (2000). Horseplay in Harappa. *Frontline, 17.*

Wundt, W. (1894). *Human and animal psychology.* New York: Macmillan.

Yablo, S. (1993). Is conceivability a guide to possibility? *Philosophy and Phenomenological Research, 53,* 1–42.

Author Index

333

335

Subject Index